The Morton W. Bloomfield Lectures
1989–2005

Medieval Institute Publications is a program of
The Medieval Institute, College of Arts and Sciences
and Western Michigan University

The Morton W. Bloomfield Lectures
1989–2005

Edited by

Daniel Donoghue, James Simpson,
and Nicholas Watson

MEDIEVAL INSTITUTE PUBLICATIONS
Western Michigan University
Kalamazoo

The editors thank Sol Kim Bentley, Rachel Bergmann, and Marta Figlerowicz for their valuable help at various stages of the project.

Publication of this work is made possible by the Morton W. Bloomfield Lecture Fund, supported in his memory by contributions from his family, friends, colleagues, and students.

© 2010 by the Board of Trustees of Western Michigan University

Manufactured in the United States of America

This book is printed on acid-free paper.

Library of Congress Cataloging-in-Publication Data

The Morton W. Bloomfield lectures, 1989-2005 / edited by Daniel Donoghue, James Simpson, and Nicholas Watson.
     p. cm.
  Includes bibliographical references.
  ISBN 978-1-58044-146-9 (clothbound : acid-free paper) – ISBN 978-1-58044-147-6 (paperbound : acid-free paper)
  1. Bloomfield, Morton W. (Morton Wilfred), 1913-1987. 2. Critics–United States –Biography. 3. Scholars–United States–Biography. 4. Medievalists–United States –Biography. 5. Literature–History and criticism–Theory, etc. 6. Criticism–United States–History–20th century. I. Donoghue, Daniel, 1956- II. Simpson, James, 1954- III. Watson, Nicholas.
  PR55.B59M67 2009
  801'.95–dc22
                              2009032450

1 2 3 4 5 C P 5 4 3 2 1

Contents

Introduction
Larry Benson ... ix

Morton Wilfred Bloomfield (May 19, 1913–April 14, 1987)
Fred C. Robinson ... xi

Poets and the Poetics of Sin [1989]
†*George Kane* ... 1

Langland and Allegory [1991]
Jill Mann ... 20

Monastic Preaching in the Age of Chaucer [1993]
Siegfried Wenzel ... 42

"Love and Do What You Will": The Medieval History of an Augustinian Precept [1996]
Giles Constable ... 65

Piers Plowman, the Monsters, and the Critics: Some Embarrassments of Literary History [1998]
Anne Middleton ... 94

"The Place of the Apocalyptic View of History in the Later Middle Ages" and the Legacy of Morton Bloomfield [1999]
Kathryn Kerby-Fulton ... 116

Jewish Sages and German Schoolmen [1999]
Bernard McGinn ... 141

Imagining and Imaging the End: Universal and Individual Eschatology in Two Carthusian Illustrated Manuscripts [1999]
Richard K. Emmerson ... 163

William Langland, William Blake, and the Poetry of Hope [2001]
Derek Pearsall ... 201

What Was the *Maiden in the Moor* Made For? [2004]
    Richard Firth Green   220

Marketing Oðinn's Mead in a Strange Land [2005]
    Roberta Frank   246

Bibliography of Morton W. Bloomfield's Publications
for the Years 1981–1993   271

Notes on Contributors   273

Morton W. Bloomfield [photographic portrait, ca. 1986]. Courtesy of Harvard University Archives [UAV 605.295.20 Bloomfield, Morton Box 1].

Introduction

Larry D. Benson

Shortly after Morton Bloomfield died in 1987, a number of his academic friends and colleagues sought a way to honor and preserve his memory. It was suggested (by whom I do not remember) that the most fitting memorial would be a biennial lecture—a lecture of more than ordinary interest and more than ordinary prominence, signified by the fact that each would be published for individual circulation and then would be collected, as they are now, to appear in print for a wider audience.

The organizers used as their model the Israel Gollancz lectures sponsored by the British Academy. But the Gollancz lectures are generally restricted to Middle English literary subjects. The idea for the Bloomfield Lectures was much broader in scope, for it was to reflect to some extent Morton Bloomfield's own wide and varied interests—in literature, in the history of philosophy, in language studies, in Judaic studies. The contents of the present volume show to what extent the lectures reflect this range; doubtless those lectures to come will reflect even more of the areas of study that Morton pursued. Not that the contributors restrict themselves to subjects and ideas that Morton held: some of them may even disagree with some of his ideas. Morton would have been delighted. He relished the pleasures of scholarly disputation, and he enjoyed almost as much listening to others lecture as he did delivering his own.

Members of Morton Bloomfield's own family were among the first to help raise the not inconsiderable funds necessary to endow this lectureship. Caroline, his wife, Micah and Samuel, his sons, and Hannah, his daughter, were joined in this effort by a number of Morton's immediate and distant relatives. The family's enthusiastic participation was instrumental in raising the necessary funds.

Equally impressive was the outpouring of support from Morton's friends in the broader Boston community and from his colleagues both at Harvard and throughout the larger academic world. Their financial generosity is but one indication of the universal esteem for Morton's own warmth and generosity as a teacher, friend, and colleague. Without such an outpouring of support, the lectures in this volume would never have been given, and we would all be the poorer.

As the committee looks back on twenty years of a successful lecture series, we think Morton would be pleased to find in the pages of this volume so many of his old friends and former students, who make up the bulk of the contributors, and, given his interest in younger scholars, we think that he would be happy that future lectures will be produced by those who know him only in print. That future generations of young scholars should draw inspiration from his scholarship would especially please Morton Bloomfield:

> For out of olde feldes, as men seith,
> Cometh al this newe corn fro yeer to yere;
> Out of olde bokes, in good feyth,
> Cometh al this newe science that men lere.
>
> (Chaucer, *Parliament of Fowls*, lines 22–25)

Morton Wilfred Bloomfield
(May 19, 1913—April 14, 1987)

Fred C. Robinson

Morton W. Bloomfield, whose broad learning and personal popularity were unrivaled among his fellow medievalists, died of cancer on April 14, 1987, at Mount Auburn Hospital, Cambridge, Massachusetts. He was seventy-three. Because of his scholarly range, his active engagement in the profession both nationally and internationally, and his eager fostering of young scholars, his career has had an impact not only on medieval studies but on humanistic scholarship as a whole in the latter part of the twentieth century.

Bloomfield's lifelong conviction that scholarship is above all an international enterprise may have stemmed in part from the fact that he was himself an international person—a Canadian who, after post-graduate study abroad, returned to North America and adopted (in 1943) United States citizenship. Born in Montreal on May 19, 1913, he took his A.B. and M.A. degrees at McGill University in 1934 and 1935. In 1935 and 1936 he studied at University College, University of London, an experience which impressed him deeply. He spoke gratefully of the help and instruction he had received from eminent English scholars like R. W. Chambers and of the high quality of literary scholarship in England then. From London he traveled to the University of Wisconsin, where he took a Ph.D. in English in 1938. He then accepted an appointment as instructor at Wisconsin before moving on to the University of Akron, where he became an assistant professor in 1941. From 1942 to 1945 he served in the U.S. Army, receiving the Bronze Star before he was discharged. In 1946 he left Akron for fifteen productive years at Ohio State University, becoming full professor there in 1956. He, his wife Caroline, and their three children enjoyed their Ohio experience and seemed for a time to be confirmed Midwesterners. But he was called to Harvard in 1961, and from 1968 to 1972 he was chairman of the Harvard English Department. These were difficult years for university administrators, but Bloomfield held his department together by his courtesy, his openness to new ideas, and his patient reasoning with dissident students and colleagues. In 1972 his university named him Arthur Kingsley Porter Professor of English. He retired from Harvard in 1983 but continued teaching intermittently as a Distinguished Visiting Professor of Humanities at Stanford University until his full retirement in 1986.

Bloomfield once characterized his own scholarly work as showing "a concern with philology in its most exact significance as well as a feeling or perhaps a groping for the underlying structure of literary, linguistic, and historical experience" (*Essays and Explorations: Studies in Ideas, Language, and Literature* [Cambridge: Harvard University Press, 1970], p. viii). The ambitious scope of his interests is attested in his publications from the very outset of his career. Before the appearance of his first book in 1952, he had already published substantial essays on Chaucer, Prudentius, Canadian English, Boccaccio, *Beowulf, Piers Plowman*, and linguistic method. In 1952 appeared *The Seven Deadly Sins: An Introduction to the History of a Religious Concept, with Special Reference to Medieval English Literature* (East Lansing: Michigan State College Press, 1952; repr., with slight revisions, 1967). An amazingly comprehensive digest of learning from various fields, this book also bristles with acute suggestions for future research, suggestions which subsequent scholars have eagerly heeded. It traces the deadly sins from their classical pagan and Jewish origins through an elaborate florescence in the Middle Ages to a gradual decrement in the Renaissance. The book is dedicated to R. W. Chambers of the University of London, George W. Latham of McGill University, and William Ellery Leonard of the University of Wisconsin, all of whom had been Bloomfield's teachers.

The range and variety of Bloomfield's intellectual pursuits continued to grow. His linguistic interests culminated in *A Linguistic Introduction to the History of English*, which he wrote with Leonard Newmark (New York: Knopf, 1963). An application to English language history of recent developments in theoretical linguistics, this volume was popular for many years (it was reprinted in Westport, CT, in 1979) and has been translated into Japanese. *Piers Plowman as a Fourteenth-Century Apocalypse* (New Brunswick: Rutgers University Press, 1962) is a bold new interpretation of a long and complex Middle English poem, an interpretation based on a solid foundation of learning, but one which also points out imaginative parallels between the apocalyptic outlook of medieval man and the thermonuclear anxieties of America in the 1960s. Another major interest of Bloomfield's found initial expression in a monograph on "Joachim of Flora, A Critical Survey of His Canon, Teaching, Sources, Biography, and Influence," *Traditio* 13 (1957): 249–311. This and later studies by Bloomfield on the same figure have inaugurated a small industry of Joachist scholarship over the past two decades. Bloomfield devoted several studies to exploring the mechanics of narrative, and he became interested in the influence of linguistic science on literary theory. Allegory was a lifelong interest, and he took spirited issue with the Princeton school of allegorical interpretation.

One of Bloomfield's greatest legacies to scholarship is the index of *Incipits of Latin Works on the Virtues and Vices, 1100–1500, Including a Section of Incipits of Works on the Pater Noster* (Cambridge: Medieval Academy of America, 1979), at which he labored for many years, eventually completing it in collaboration with B. G. Guyot, O.P., Donald R. Howard, and Thyra B. Kabealo. Toward the end of his teaching career he became absorbed in wisdom literature, a subject which extended into several of the traditions he knew so well, such as the classical, the Biblical, and the medieval vernaculars. Larry D. Benson and Siegfried Wenzel appropriately edited a festschrift for him with this theme—*The Wisdom of Poetry: Essays in Early English Literature in Honor of Morton W. Bloomfield* (Kalamazoo: Medieval Institute Publications, Western Michigan University, 1982)—and appropriately apologized for the fact that a book on one subject "does not adequately reflect [Bloomfield's] contributions to the broader fields of medieval thought and literature, literary theory, and linguistics." No one book could. George H. Brown's bibliography of Bloomfield's writings, which concludes the festschrift, lists 203 separate publications through 1981.

Bloomfield's vast learning was always at the disposal of any student or colleague who cared to question him, and many did, for he shared what he knew with grace. "He was actually very humble about his formidable learning," recalls his colleague Larry Benson, "and he never bullied anyone with it." His system for controlling and retrieving knowledge was an impressive and ever-growing bibliographical file of three-by-five notecards covered on both sides from top to bottom with the information gathered over a lifetime. He sometimes lamented that his greatest professional regret was that he had not started out in his career using larger cards. The bibliographical file was an expression of an important side of his scholarly nature. "I like to do two kinds of scholarship," he would say, "one is exhaustive syntheses of all that is known about some subject; the other is presenting a new way of thinking about some subject." The bibliographical file resulted from the former impulse, and it served him and those who sought his help exceedingly well, three-by-five cards notwithstanding.

The variety of scholarly organizations in which Morton Bloomfield participated is another witness to the diversity of his intellectual interests. Besides being a member of the American Philosophical Society, he was a Fellow and former President (1973–74) of the Medieval Academy of America, and a Fellow and former Vice President (1972–76) of the American Academy of Arts and Sciences, a Corresponding Fellow of the British Academy and the Medieval Society of Southern Africa, and a member of the executive committees of the Dante Society of America, the Modern Language Association of America, and the International Association of University Professors of English. He was a member of the Renaissance Society of America, of the American Dialect Society, of the Canadian Linguistic Association, of the Linguistic Society of America, of the Modern Humanities Research Association, and of the Societé Internationale pour l'étude de la Philosophie Médiévale. Most important, he was Chairman of the Planning Committee for the National Humanities Center (1973–76) and gave time unstintingly to help set up the North Carolina Center. Every scholar who spends a term at the Research Triangle Park owes thanks to Morton Bloomfield for the scholarly opportunities which that splendid Center now provides.

As an eminent authority in many fields Bloomfield was often called on to assess and evaluate scholars, their books, and their projects, and he always responded promptly, if not always with strict judgment. His tolerance and eagerness to entertain new ideas sometimes led him to err on the side of generosity in his recommendations of scholars for promotion or of projects for funding. But this indulgence was characteristic only of his confidential assessments. In published reviews, where his evaluations were exposed to general view and could be challenged, he was professional, forthright, and at times even severe.

Morton Bloomfield's achievements in scholarship and his exemplary professional conduct are the hallmarks of his career, but they alone do not explain the deep affection in which he was held by all who knew him. It was his innate generosity combined with a sweetness of character bordering on innocence that endeared him to his colleagues. Characteristic of the man was the elaborate apology he used to offer his friends for his habitual remissness in not acknowledging the offprints they sent him. "I appreciate them and read them, but you established scholars don't need to hear from me. The only offprints that I feel I must respond to are those that young scholars send me, because they need the feedback. Helping young scholars is the only way I can pay back those who helped me to get started. Our mentors are like our parents: what we owe them can never be repaid, and so we must give to our children what our parents gave to us." In mourning a master of men whom he also called father, Tacitus spoke words which we might fittingly address to our own departed master of humane letters: "admiratione te potius quam temporalibus laudibus, et, si natura suppeditet, similitudine decoremus" (*Agricola* 46).

NOTES

Originally published as "Morton Wilfred Bloomfield: Biographical Memoir." *American Philosophical Society Year Book 1987* (Philadelphia: American Philosophical Society, 1988), 116–21. Reprinted with permission.

Poets and the Poetics of Sin [1989]

† George Kane

Morton Bloomfield, whom we commemorate today, was influential in his time in many fields of scholarship: the range and depth of his erudition appear from a bibliography of more than 200 items, a number of them very substantial. He and I first met at University College London where, as long ago as 1949, he had the room next to mine in Foster Court. I began to learn from him directly. But after his encyclopedic work on the Seven Deadly Sins came out in 1952 he often seemed to be standing beside me while I tried to come to terms with medieval literature,[1] and when his *Piers Plowman as a Fourteenth Century Apocalypse* was published ten years later it gave me what I still recall as my first real insight into the shape and character of that unusual poem.[2]

If the insights I base my suggestions on today are valid, this is largely a product of his writings. My topic is the relation of hamartiology—the minute scrutiny of human misbehavior, the pathology of the moral life in the Christian terms of sin, along with the fourteenth century's apocalyptic sense of impending moral and spiritual catastrophe—to the composition of vernacular poetry by Langland and Chaucer. I propose that those two factors, related but essentially of radical difference, interacted to intensify each other. The awareness of sin, as a cause of crisis, turned the observant eye to its presumed sources in human conduct, and what that eye saw deepened the sense of crisis, generating a kind of energy of concern that afforded the two exceptional poets a class of topic to match their capabilities and their involvement in language as a medium of creativity.

I hope, incidentally, to sketch a case for the historical approach in the face of the present vogue for "rewriting" medieval literature in clinical, sociopolitical, sometimes called "cultural" terms. There is still much to be clarified, and many a misconception needs to be corrected, in our understanding of the medieval past. Maybe I can contribute a little to that today. But I judge that the novel approaches, whether or not they actually confer new insights, actually substitute, as far as poetry goes, an inferior order of perception: they induce a kind of refraction, as if someone were to set out to write a new law of general optics based wholly on observations and measurements made through water. At best sociopolitical study can only abstract the past, as do an archaeologist's measurements, notes, and diagrams about a rich site: its original *quality* is recovered only in general terms. The quality of experience of a time past, which is what these poets signally recorded as their own experience, is preserved in the language that they themselves used to identify, define, and describe it. The emotional charge carried by that language is an essential qualifying part of the experience. Not the technical language of modern psychology of religion, nor even the Latin of contemporary *libri poenitentionales*, but the often inelegant vernacular of the wise confessor or of the lay-folks' devotional books is the idiom of the lonely soul's need to be saved, of its possessor's sense of imperfection, of having been in opposition to God (the dictionary definition of sin), of guilt, of the restoration of favor by forgiveness and grace.

As for the term *poetics*, which I use for want of a better word, by this I mean not such theoretical notions as either poet might have had about the half-instinctive, half-pragmatic, largely subconscious and sublogical operation of writing poetry, but the individual poet's praxis—his manner of proceeding as artist, having regard to the nature of his subject, the degree of his concern for it, and his sense of status, but also to his sense of being a component of what he is registering, that is to the observing poet's perception of himself as part of a creation he is observing from within.

The historical approach rests on appreciating the differences of that creation, as an existential orientation, from almost any modern conception. For many young and some not so young the orientation is wholly alien. It was based on a postulate of man divinely created but through divine forbearance satanically betrayed. At creation an image of divinity was imprinted (Langland uses that word) in man. But by his fall the image was defaced, flawed, tarnished; with the Fall man became subject to sickness hereditarily, genetically transmitting it to all sons and daughters of Adam. This manifested itself in persistent inclination to withstand God's will, that is, to sin. To sin was to incur God's wrath. Sacramental reconciliation with God was possible upon certain specific conditions. But those who died in divine disfavor, that is, in a state of sin, were damned, consigned to torment not for all time but for inconceivable eternity. Doctrine proclaimed that each man received sufficient grace, that is to say, an extension of divine benevolence, to avoid damnation; but there was an unsuppressible counterdoctrine of election, not indeed canonically sanctioned, but going back at least to Augustine of Hippo: the salvation or damnation of the individual soul was, because preknown to God, predestined. Thus not even a wholly righteous life ensured salvation, escape from everlasting torment.

Because of Adam's sin man alone in the natural world behaved unreasonably, notwithstanding his possession of a "resonabil soule," drawn by its created nature to God, who is perfect reason. According to a standard fourteenth-century description, if that soul, fulfilling the reason which is its principle, turned to God, it was "byschyned, amendid and imade parfite," or made radiant, healed and perfected; the divine image was restored. But the soul, although immortal, was susceptible to damage. Through original sin the body to which it was bonded at creation was subject to "likynge of fleische" and to "loue of worldly catel," that is, to the animal appetites and the acquisitive instinct. And to the extent that the reasonable soul submerged itself in the body to which it was bound, so much it was darkened, corrupted, damaged, and thus failed in the control of its behavior. Then it experienced "ymaginacioun of fantasie," that is delusive error, or failure of rationality.

That account, from Bartholomew the Englishman's *De Proprietatibus Rerum* in Trevisa's translation,[3] notwithstanding some bizarre physiology on which it was founded, can be transposed into medieval moral terms to make sense. Reason, rational thinking as a divine, that is, an absolutely admirable principle, should ideally control appetite. When such control fails through "ymaginacioun of fantasie," namely confusion between true and false good, there is a concomitant failure of principle and the personality is damaged. Thus sins of desire and sins of thought between them turn the reasonable soul from God to surrender to appetite. Even pride, in that sense, is a physical sin, a "flesshes likynge."

The inherent anomaly of that situation, creature in a stance of unreasonable opposition to creator, was a main impulse to the minute classification of sin which developed into the medieval science of hamartiology. A sort of natural critical curiosity and the practical need for regulation of confessional and penitential practices led to the identification and definition of ramifications and cross-patterns so intricate as to have an intellectual interest of their own, which, moreover, brought the whole range of contemporary human activity into focus. The main heads of the classification were, of course, the deadly sins.

The actual topic, sin, was part of every schoolboy's religious instruction and was clearly expounded in the medieval layman's catechism.[4] Shrewd insights into the extent of injury by sin—its wider moral implication beyond the moral quality of the immediate offense—described adultery, for instance, as a form of theft;[5] gluttony and sloth both offended against the commandment of charity.[6] An emblematic iconography of sin developed in which, again for instance, gluttony was, not surprisingly, a pig; anger a wild boar or lion; pride a woman, or, indeed a lion; lechery a goat.[7] Simple enough: but in the right imagination such figures could generate striking extensions into language. Allegorical personifications of the sins accumulated, typifying physiognomies and mannerisms, all ultimately based on observed instances, and correspondingly inducing observation. The cultural effect of such developments was powerful. By the fourteenth century the seven deadly—that is, the damnable or capital—sins, as conceptual matrices for the assessment of behavior, were deeply imprinted. So indeed they remained long after 1400, as Morton Bloomfield showed, commonplaces in Spenser, and later, of course, in Shakespeare and Ben Jonson and Donne.[8] Much later, one finds the "hero" of Moliere's *L'Avare* still practicing a moneylender's trick that was in the repertory of Covetousness in *Piers Plowman*.[9] It is really only since the emergence of modern psychology that behavior has come to be assessed in other conceptual and linguistic terms than those of sin. Some of us still describe a man as "good and true" rather than as a "well-adjusted personality."

Almost all the significant fourteenth-century literature not in the tradition of Provence, or of the first part of the *Roman de la Rose*, or of the French romances is seriously concerned about human behavior, about the private or public consequences of sin for the individual or through him the community or the realm or the Church. The deeper insights, the more sensitive and compassionate treatments, are of the individual caught up in the misery of the human condition, but the public concern actually bulks larger before Chaucer in a peculiarly medieval literary and social phenomenon called "estates satire."[10] This developed through extension of the moral conception of personality to the typical conduct of official, professional, and other key members of the social order, which was itself seen as a divinely appointed structure of three estates—clergy, knightly class, and commons. Within each of these there were gradations or degrees, to some one of which, and so to its special duties or responsibilities, each man was born or appointed.

Estates satire, more precisely moral reprobation than satire, appears already in the twelfth century as formulated criticisms of classes of persons with office or responsibility or some important social function, from pope to day laborer. The early instances are in Latin. By 1300 there was an extensive vernacular body of such criticisms, mainly in French, stereotypes of immoral or selfish or irresponsible behavior that afflicted others beyond the sinner, and further, impaired the social order.[11] Underlying this satire was the concept of the besetting sin of a particular office or occupation, the deadly sin to which those holding or practicing it were especially tempted and prone. Here, then, was another, more specialized set of concepts for organizing personally observed experience, and a further prompting to assessment of personality in moral terms.

Two more circumstances intensified the situation. One was theodical teaching and preaching explaining and so justifying the bad state of the world as God's visitation upon men for their evil ways.[12] The other was the sense of apocalyptic imminence, of the soon-to-come ending of the second age in the relation of God and man, as the historical pattern of the created world was then perceived. This is the state of mind by which Morton Bloomfield explained a main structural feature of *Piers Plowman*.[13]

The dominance of the hamartiological and eschatological modes of thought in fourteenth-century literature is unquestionable. A main instance of their effect is their direction of narrative form. Every schoolboy had it drummed into his head that any story, any succession of events with a perceptible beginning and end, was inherently a moral demonstration: by that early teaching he became the more alert to the relation between character and outcome in a story, thus to the closer analysis of character and, because of the moral context, of character analyzed in terms of sin.

That combination lent itself to extravagances like the *Confessio Amantis* of John Gower, Chaucer's contemporary.[14] Gower's poem, organized upon the ritual of an oral confession of sin by a person with the poet's name to the priest of the goddess Venus and further on that Confessor's examination of his penitent according to the schema of the Christian deadly sins, has simultaneously the character of an extended, often moving renunciation of unrequited love, a frame for a huge range of stories from the classical past, medieval romance, and what we call folklore—often exquisitely told, but all illustrating the applicability of the successive sins to the lover's condition as a devotee of *fine amour*, and beyond that, a multiplicity of underlying moral directions to practical virtue. But this poem is a tour de force.

More commonly the sinfulness of an action is simply and directly turned to poetic effect. For instance: dancing on consecrated ground was forbidden as sacrilegious. A fourteenth-century English moralist cites an exemplum of a group of young folk who sinned by that act, and describes with relish the punishment cursed upon them by the parish priest: to dance in that place, day and night without cease, for a year.[15] But the Galician *trovador* Martin Codax makes the same sacrilege into a *cantiga d'amigo* where a love-struck girl sings of herself and the man who will not notice her, "Eno sagrad ẽ Vigo baylaua corpo uelido" (there she was, dancing lissom and lovely in a hallowed place).[16] The naughty courtship in the satirical Provençal romance *Flamenca* runs its course impiously in a church, the lover disguised as a cleric.[17] Peire Cardenal, who mainly wrote devout lyrics, also wrote a sirventes to deliver to his Creator on the day of judgment, accusing him of injustice to his creation.[18] Aucassin wants no part of heaven, for it is full of dull and dreary people, unless Nicolette can be with him.[19] A sonnet of Cecco Angiolieri fantasizes about the outrages Cecco would commit if he were God or pope or emperor or Life itself.[20] An exquisite miniature of poetic blasphemy is a lyric in English of about 1400 attributed to the French prince Charles of Orleans: a penitent tells his confessor that he has stolen a kiss. His sin of theft cannot be forgiven until he has restored his ill-gotten gain; but it turns out that his confessor is the woman in the case.[21] In countless such poetic situations the circumstance of sin contributes to tension and effect. Sin has its advantages for the poet.

But in such instances, whether elaborate and on the scale of Gower's *Confessio*, miniature as in the confession lyric and the *cantiga*, or simply incidental functions of narrative, the reference is of a different order than that in the writing of Langland and Chaucer. The poetry of these two, like Dante's a little earlier, addresses sin not as a means of displaying ingenuity, evoking poignancy, or committing naughty outrage but in a radical extension of poetic sensibility, implying major creative experience. The unmistakable difference is a critical challenge. One predicates that each possessed to an extreme degree that as yet not, and possibly never-to-be, satisfactorily explained supralogical aptitude for which productive immersion in language constitutes artistic fulfillment, and along with it the capacity for empathy and compassion, both in generative linguistic circumstances. This last condition mattered in the Middle Ages as the vernaculars developed, and was not always present. But certainly their writing proclaims a remarkable coincidence between one class of historical event, the state of the immediate world in their time, and another, the exceptional quality of their individual acts of language.

It seems to me that Roland Barthes, more often iconoclastic than respectful, in the course of dismissing the vatic concept of poetry identified the problem in *Ecrivains et Ecrivants*. His *écrivain*, that is, poet (whether in verse or prose), "is a man who completely absorbs the 'why' of existence (*le pourquoi du monde*) in a 'how shall I write' (*un comment écrire*)?" And the miracle (Barthes' word), if one may use the term, he adds, is that this self-loving (*narcissique*) activity, as far as secular literature goes (his qualification), never ceases to prompt a spirit of enquiry. The poet, enclosing himself in the *comment écrire*, in the fulfillment of the sense of how he must write, ends up rediscovering the open question par excellence: "pourquoi le monde? Quel est le sens des choses?"[22]

To our two poets the notion of absorbing the "why" of existence in the "how to write" is apt enough. Both seem pretty clearly to have been compulsive writers, subconsciously acknowledging "I am because I write." In that sense their obsessive activity was necessarily *narcissique*, self-centered, self-gratifying. But both were, directly or indirectly, religious poets, and in their world the questions "pourquoi le monde?" and "quel est le sens des choses?" had doctrinal answers. And indeed that circumstance, an essential difference between them and the nineteenth- or twentieth-century poets whom Barthes had in mind, may have been the point of fusion which released the creative energy—the semantic and insight-yielding capability of their intelligences. For there is no question that the doctrinal answers to the questions "pourquoi" and "quel est le sens" were constraints upon both.

As to their rediscovering these questions, how is one to describe the process and result without sectarian color or modern condescension? The questions, essentially to do with sin, were inherent in their world and had been often asked: it may be best said that the two poets realized them in themselves with a particular intensity corresponding to a condition of their immediate time, namely the intensity of their experience of language. And this may even relate to the apparently prosaic, but actually formative educational circumstance that at school they had learned their Latin in French with illustrations from both French and English. There is plenty of evidence of parallel conceptual and semantic growth in the English of their time, for instance in the recorded fourteenth-century development of meanings for words like *conscience, fair, reason,* and *truth*, all implying value and all in the end doctrinally acceptable, but refined by these two poets above all, beyond the intellectual range of a "thou shalt" religion. In their minds concerned with *comment écrire*, whether extra- or ultralogically, the profusion of language to do with sin and the many aspects of the morality it implied, the ultimate practical expression of an existential arrangement based on doctrinal assumptions about *pourquoi le monde* and *quel est le sens des choses*, would inexorably and persistently raise those questions.

This expression was the consummation of a relation between poetry and sin, which could begin with the poet's concern, supposing he disengaged himself from the activity of composition and reflected on the morality of his obsession with it—for there was by no means any consensus of approval of the art of poetry. Apologists might argue that all poetry, however sinful its content or attitudes, was justified by the moral truths allegorically hidden in it,[23] or more particularly that because poetry was about behavior it was essentially moral: "moralis quia de moribus tractat"; the conveniently punning Latin lent itself to that proposition.[24] But moralists had an unmodern notion of the relation between form and content in poetry. To them beautiful language, a fine style, in no way justified a reprehensible subject. The point was made with great authority: I cite from *Speculum Christiani*, a fourteenth-century English treatise.[25] Here is Augustine: "Quociens plus me delectat cantus quam res que cantatur, tociens me graviter pecasse confiteor"; then Gregory: "Cum in cantu blanda vox queritur, sobria vita deseritur"; then Bernard: "cum cantat cantor mulcet populum vocibus, dominum irritat pravis moribus." All are summed up in two condemnations by Jerome. First, a flat dismissal of the value of style and logical organization: "Omnis pompa structuraque et argumenta dialectica rediguntur ad nihilum (Moralia super Isayam)," then a burst of pulpit thunder, itself rhetorically ingenious, "Demonum cibus est carmina poetarum, sapiencie vanitas, rhetoricorum pompa verborum."[26] The passage is, incidentally, glossed "De cantu superbo."[27]

All these critics except Gregory, who cherished plainness and correctness in prose (thus a model for administrators like himself), were deeply responsive to poetry, of course classical pagan poetry and therefore immoral at the outset. Augustine had poetic aspirations and wrote like a poet more often than not; Jerome, taught by Donatus and the best rhetoricians in Rome, conferred good Latinity upon the Bible; Bernard continues to be admired for his ability to please, at the same time, the mind and the ear. It is hard not to see a relation between such backgrounds and their moralist's vehemence. The authority of the condemnations, which lose nothing except their smooth Latinity in the English version, was evidently formidable, and the dissemination of *Speculum Christiani* was wide. The survival of sixty-six manuscripts in England implies an initial currency of many hundreds.[28]

Both English poets are likely to have encountered it, and obviously must have come to terms with such reprobations. Of Langland I would judge that he was totally committed to his poem before he realized how self-centered was his involvement in poetry.[29] As for Chaucer, his initial engagements with poetry were trials of strength of a sort to exclude niceties about its moral warrant.

By contrast, Langland's professed object in the first version of *Piers*, his earliest identified work, was professedly moral. The involvement of the poem with sin, and in particular the capital sins and their schema, is immediate. The first main movement of *Piers* is organized on the besetting capital sin of covetousness, personified in the power of money to corrupt administration and the course of justice.[30] The interest, which raises this treatment above estates satire about government officials and the various kinds of lawyers, lies in an ingenious personification—the corrupting force is a woman with an ambiguous name than can mean both just reward and bribery[31]—and in evident topical reference to Edward III's court and rule some time before 1371.[32] In the second movement a sermon by the personified Moral Instinct turns the folk in the field to repentance. Six of the seven sins (Anger is not here yet) come forward to confess. Each recites what in the abstract would be a more or less complete list of offenses coming under its head in the confession manuals.[33] The self-relation is a homiletic convention: here is an instance of *Gula*, Gluttony,

> I loue mi wombe aboue al þing
> him most to plese is my likyng
> y haue no reste nyȝt nor day
> til he be seruid al to his pay.[34]

Following that elementary convention Langland weaves the lists into textures of intensely realistic detail in a succession of heroically grotesque figures. In the second version he adds the sin of anger to complete his show, and develops the other figures.[35] Much later in that version the sins appear again to represent the spiritual plight of his Everyman, Hawkyn, a man of good intention who nevertheless, in a spate of self-revelation, shows himself guilty of each of the seven sins. The finely graphic detail brings him very close: Langland demands our sympathy for Hawkyn in his ultimate contrition; "Allas!" he says, "that I did not die directly I was christened" (when his soul would have gone straight to heaven); "It is so hard to live as a sinful man. We can never escape sin."[36] In the last version, for larger reasons, Langland substitutes another character for Hawkyn, but Langland fits the self-revelations, in his most painstaking revision, into the great confession of the people in the field.[37] The care he takes here, as well as the power of effect of this movement from the first version on, bespeak his involvement with penitence.

Chaucer's earlier work gives no indication how he came by the hamartiological expertise and command of moralist's language evident in his mature writing. His Parson's Tale, combining a sin schema and a set of *remedia*—that is, protective spiritual or penitential exercises against the several sins—has not been convincingly dated.[38] His magnificent story of desperate infatuation, *Troilus and Criseyde*, can be read in the terms I described from Trevisa's Bartholomew: the reasonable soul of Troilus, more and more deeply immersed in "likynge of fleische," or libido, suffers progressive loss of understanding ending in despair.[39] In the process the elegant language and behavior-rituals of *fine amour* project the "ymaginacioun of fantasie."

Chaucer's subsequent writings, the Canterbury Prologue and many of the tales, contain personages brilliantly designed upon susceptibility to one or another of the capital sins, personalities subject to a dominant impulse. I have in mind especially the rogues and scoundrels and charlatans among the pilgrims, who can appear as studies of the effect of such a condition on personality.

To go by a predominance of topics in the *Canterbury Tales*, Chaucer identified two capital sins as especially damaging, namely covetousness and lechery. The former is presented as a besetting sin, damaging in the dishonesty it induces, whether behind the façade of the Merchant and Man of Law, or the plausibility of the charlatan Physician, or the joviality of the criminal Summoner: it is variously absurd or horrifying, but always, unmistakably, unadmirable. As for the second sin, what we would call sexuality, whether masculine or feminine, Chaucer represents heroic instances of both: notably the sporting seducers Jason, Theseus, the Prologue Friar, and the Wife of Bath. In the narrative contexts this sin appears reprehensible less in the physical act itself than for the harm it does, whether by selfish adventurism or as a means of financial advantage, but almost always as a cause of unhappiness; and even, under the extenuating circumstances of an intolerable marriage in the case of several lovely women, by the deceit it occasions and how this devalues them.

As to the formulation of sins and delinquencies associated with a particular office or station in life, estates satire, the work of these two poets is both shaped by and transcends it. Both accept the concept of divinely appointed estate and degree: not the "system" but those who operate it need to be reformed.

In *Piers Plowman* estates satire is pervasive rather than structurally dominant. Detail of familiar estates criticism abounds, but only as one of many threads in the texture. Langland breaks down the stereotypes and incorporates particular estates satire criticisms in the consideration of larger issues. So, for instance, satire of lawyers in both the ecclesiastical and the king's courts acquires a new dimension through outrageous personification allegory (I recall Morton Bloomfield's seminal essay about that trope),[40] and in the Great Confession particulars of estates criticism appear reassigned as offenses of the individual confessing Sins. Thus personified Anger promotes the notorious hostility between friars and secular clergy and breeds slander and strife in a convent of nuns. Covetousness tells how he contrives the banker's sin of getting around the canonical prohibition of usury; Sloth, among other estate offenses, confesses to the illiteracy of an incompetent parish priest who does not know the service of the mass and cannot give religious instruction or expound the psalms.[41]

By contrast, so many of Chaucer's Canterbury pilgrims look like particularizations of estates satire figures as to suggest that he used the system as a criterion for selecting them. If he did so, the apparently casual miscellany, called by the Narrator "a group of various people thrown together by chance,"[42] must be morally diagrammatic. Especially the clerical pilgrims—Monk, Friar, and pathetic Prioress—answer to estates criticism; so does even the Parson, for all his saintliness, for he is, attribute by attribute, the very obverse of the estates satire parson, a compound of corresponding virtues.

Even while some of Chaucer's pilgrims recall the stereotype, certain of them are represented, in appearance and action, with such particularity as to have suggested that Chaucer might here have been drawing from life.[43] There are actually points where Chaucer seems to encourage the notion of topicality—once by the Narrator's emphatic denial that he knows the name of a particular pilgrim, a gratuitous assertion if there was no name in the air, another time where he makes his Pardoner describe how to suggest identity without specifying it.

> Though I telle nat his propre name
> Men shal wel knowe that it is the same
> By signes and by other circumstances.[44]
> [Even though I may not actually name him he is bound
> to be recognized from indicative circumstantial details.]

It hardly matters: what is notable is the artistic serviceability of the stereotype and the poet's vitalization of it. Either Chaucer was stimulated by perception of its accuracy, or he set out to design from it a fictional personage real enough to invite identification with a historical person.

Other literary extensions of the "poetics of sin" are notable. The first is, of course, establishment of the "proper study," mankind, as also the proper subject of literary art. A second is the development of a practical decorum of style in secular writing to match that already established in sermon rhetoric, namely, a sensitivity to the appropriate language register of an immediate context, rather than a prescription of high, middle, and low styles. Langland, who knew sermon rhetoric, took it for granted. Both poets exhibit the sensitivity, highly developed. Related to this, in Chaucer's case as a frequently secular writer, is his subtle use of an underlying idiom of religious and moral reference: thus the sort of gown worn by the engaging Prologue Squire is actually condemned as sinful in the Parson's Tale;[45] the Franklin's hospitality shows him not only sinning in gluttony but also failing in charity—for what he lavishes on his guests, and will recover, so to speak, in hospitality returned, should have been given to the destitute, for whom Christ will repay;[46] the otherwise admirable Clerk seems to lack a sense of pastoral mission at a time when the parishes of England cannot be staffed with even barely literate priests of good life.[47] We miss these references easily, where Chaucer's contemporaries would not. The idiom is also very often used in those of Chaucer's writings that by any fourteenth-century definition were sinful, such as his fabliaux.

I suppose the most fundamental extension in the poetics of sin to have been the absolute intensification of interest in human behavior, *Kreaturlichkeit*, or what people are like and why they are that way, a direction away from the mythical and the fabulous.[48] This was bound to come some day: it came violently with the eschatological anxiety of the fourteenth century, the unavoidably ultimate question of why man is not reasonable, whether asked in Christian terms or those of moral philosophy.

More than anything that question sharpened observation in the artist and, concomitantly, in the artist as writer, development of techniques of representing personality, narrative personages more sophisticated than in previous vernacular literature, conte, or romance. With the development of such techniques there was development of correlatives of representation. For instance, hamartiology in its homiletic expression had used physical ugliness as an index of immorality where, of course, this was appropriate. The inner defacement of the *imago dei* externally revealed: Langland brought this use to a peak in the Great Confession. Chaucer followed on in the Canterbury Prologue portraits of Monk and Summoner and Pardoner. But Chaucer also saw the matching further dimension. His Friar's career of immorality is enabled by charm and plausibility. The ugliness that he exhibits is of another order, for in his soul the lineament of the *imago dei* that is defaced is the one that reflects God's infinite truth. This projection is recurrent in both the Prologue and tales.

The grotesque portrait is an art form inherent in hamartiology. I find its literary perfection in the final version of the Great Confession in *Piers Plowman*. Here that portrait is still morally terrible: the issue is still absolute, damnation—by the sixteenth century, for instance in Rabelais, it seems to me to have degenerated into buffoonery. The individual portraits in *Piers C* are variously shaped. Glutton's, the only one of its kind, is based on an episode of gross overindulgence, dreadful to conceive but conceivable. All the others are superbly accurate in detail, but in each of these this detail is of such various reference that in sum it could hardly be imputed to any single person. The effect of grotesque comes from the consistently wrong, consistently sinful choice, the unreasonable failure of reason. Every wrong choice is credibly relatable to experience, but the sum of offense by each personified sin would be humanly impossible in any one person, simply because of the difficulty of relating the individually plausible sins to a plausible individual's sins. This deliberately distorted representation is itself an element of the grotesque.

Among Chaucer's pilgrims, and he had certainly read *Piers Plowman*, there are notable grotesques, foremost the Prioress whose every attribute is unsuitable to a woman in religion, however venial in itself—and it must be noticed that she is oversize; be sure, says the Narrator, "nat undergrowe," not stunted, but in plain language unusually large.[49] But Chaucer's grotesques are humanly possible, real enough to evoke Bradleian response.[50] Further, Chaucer developed the hamartiological schema which Langland had made into a gallery by devising reportage: the structural principle of the Canterbury Prologue is "I will tell you what I saw and heard." Even more particularly, long before Robert Browning, Chaucer identified the formal serviceability of the dramatic monologue in an accidental contrivance of Jean de Meung's, and perfected it, as a totally plausible discourse of self-revelation with narrative extensions, in his Wife of Bath's prologue to her tale.[51] The initial model, by then remote, was, of course, the elementary self-revelation of a capital sin.

Both Langland and Chaucer use the sins for comic effect. Some of this is light, not uncomfortable. Hawkyn's vanity, his desire to be thought well of, is an instance. In Chaucer's Prologue we relish, with the Narrator, how easily the Manciple, the catering manager of a small college of lawyers, a man without education, could cheat his thirty and more learned employers.[52] And there is the Prologue Reeve, an illiterate peasant, but so astute and with such a memory that by dishonest management of his lord's estates he has money put by, a lovely house of his own, and cash left to lend the lord and be thanked for it.[53] Lawyers, after all, and spendthrift aristocrats are fair game. But mainly the comedy of sin in Langland and Chaucer is black, unhappy. I see it in the decline and fall of Langland's Glutton, though, to be sure, as a paradigm of saving grace, he rises and repents in the end.[54] Black comedy informs the fearful onslaught of Antichrist, whose hosts are commanded by Pride, in the last movement of *Piers Plowman*.[55] In the *Canterbury Tales* its most sustained manifestation is, of course, the Pardoner's Prologue and Tale. Although very frequent in this work, it is mostly incidental and immediately contextual, a recurrent, almost despairing reminder that admirable values, especially truth and integrity, are vulnerable to damaging disregard and apparent devaluation.[56]

It would take a book to do justice to what I see as the other integral development of the poetics of sin, namely Chaucer's realization, in both senses of that word, of narrative logic. In what for want of a better term I call his dramatic narratives, he demonstrates extensively his understanding that the excellence of a narrative structure consists in the necessity of relation between, on the one hand, the plausibility of the personages involved in an action, and on the other the events leading to its outcome.

In that understanding I see the operation of two factors: (1) the moralist's conventional presumption that a story, that is a set of events with discernible shape, is in itself inherently meaningful; (2) the heightened perception of the relation between character and conduct developed in hamartiological analysis. So it seems appropriate that the most superb demonstration of Chaucer's understanding of narrative structure is a sinful story of sin, his Miller's Tale.

The relation between sin and poetry comprises our poets themselves. I spoke earlier of their observing a situation from within as components. They were, and certainly knew themselves to be, contributors to the "multa malitia hominum" that, according to Genesis, made God regret his creation of man.[57] Neither poet escaped the sense of fear and guilt which their Christianity imposed and promoted.

Both unmistakably identified the anomalies inherent in the doctrines of original sin and damnation, faith and works, election and free will. Each poet expressed a point of view about them. In *Piers Plowman* Christ proclaims, in his raid on hell between crucifixion and resurrection, that he has the power to exercise a mercy that overrides his infinite righteousness, and that in the fullness of time he will return and have all men's souls out of hell.[58] Chaucer in the *Parliament of Fowls* reports how the righteous pagan Scipio Africanus proclaimed the ultimate admission of all men's souls to eternal bliss.[59] But both eventuations of deep-seated hope are experienced in dreams.

Of the two poets Langland the more openly registers awareness that his poetry is a self-indulgence. Whereas Piers Plowman turned from a wholly righteous active life to one of prayer and penitential exercises, the Dreamer with the poet's name ignores a suggestion that he should do the same and goes on with his writing.[60] As for Chaucer, maybe he thought of his devout works, which taking the lost ones into account were numerous,[61] as penitential exercises. But he gave up writing. "I used to have literary ambitions," he says in a verse letter to his friend Scogan, "but everything that men write is bound to come to nothing in the end."[62] Does one hear in this an echo of Jerome's "rediguntur ad nihilum"?[63]

Even if the poetic act was not sinful in essence, it was frivolous, a vanity, unless made an act of piety in the Psalmist's sense, "cantabiles mihi erant justificationes tuae."[64] The poetic act was, moreover, doubly dangerous, for the sense of achievement it conferred was a form of pride. And the poetry of sin could easily constitute failure in charity. A quotation Langland used against the friars could apply to our poets: "Vos qui peccata hominum comeditis, nisi pro eis lacrimas et oraciones effuderitis, ea que in deliciis comeditis, in tormentis evometis."[65] For in the fulfillment of their art these two were making capital of human frailty. And both knew the Pauline answer to the question, what is achievement without charity? "Synne seweþ vs euere" ("We can never escape sin") was Hawkyn's lament.[66] This was true for the poets too.

Notes

1. Morton W. Bloomfield, *The Seven Deadly Sins: An Introduction to a Religious Concept with Special Reference to Middle English Literature* (East Lansing: Michigan State College Press, 1952).

2. Morton W. Bloomfield, *Piers Plowman as a Fourteenth-Century Apocalypse* (New Brunswick, NJ: Rutgers Univ. Press, 1961).

3. *On the Properties of Things: John Trevisa's Translation of Bartholomaeus Anglicus De Proprietatibus Rerum*, vol. 1, ed. M. C. Seymour (Oxford: Clarendon Press, 1975), 101.

4. *The Lay Folks' Catechism*, ed. T. F. Simmons and H. E. Nolloth, Early English Text Society Original Series 118 (London: K. Paul, Trench, Trübner & Co., 1901), esp. 86–97.

5. Cf. Chaucer, Parson's Tale, 876ff. Chaucer quotations are from *The Riverside Chaucer*, ed. Larry D. Benson, 3rd ed. (Boston: Houghton Mifflin, 1987).

6. Chaucer's Franklin would instance this of gluttony: he is described as notably hospitable, "An housholdere and that a greet was he; Seint Julian he was in his contree" (CT Prol., 339, 340). This, however, was anything but charity. "When you give parties," runs the teaching of Christ in *Piers Plowman*, "invite not your friends but the distressed and the crippled and the destitute; for your friends will exert themselves to repay your hospitality, whereas I, Christ, will pay for the poor." (B.XI.190–96. *Piers* quotations are from *Piers Plowman: The B Version*, ed. G. Kane and E. T. Donaldson [London: Athlone Press, 1975], unless otherwise indicated.) As for sloth, it generated the neglect by which what the pauper might have eaten was allowed to spoil. (*Piers Plowman*, B.V.435–38).

7. Bloomfield, *Seven Deadly Sins*, 245–49, gives a tabulation.

8. Ibid., chap. 7.

9. *Piers Plowman*, B.V.244, 245, 252, 253; Moliere, *L'Avare*, Act II, scene i.

10. See Ruth Mohl, *The Three Estates in Medieval and Renaissance Literature* (New York: Columbia University Press, 1933); J. A. Yunck, *The Lineage of Lady Meed: The Development of Medieval Venality Satire* (Notre Dame, IN: Notre Dame University Press, 1963); Jill Mann, *Chaucer and Medieval Estates Satire* (Cambridge: Cambridge University Press, 1973).

11. Mann, *Medieval Estates Satire*, 297–312, gives a list of estates satire writings in the various languages.

12. This commonplace of medieval preaching is neatly illustrated in *Piers Plowman*, B.V.13–20.

13. An extended demonstration of the importance of Bloomfield's insight is afforded by Bernard McGinn's *Visions of the End: Apocalyptic Traditions in the Middle Ages* (New York: Columbia University Press, 1979).

14. John Gower, *Confessio Amantis*, ed. G. C. Macaulay, Early English Text Society Extra Series 81, 82 (London: K. Paul, Trench, Trübner & Co., 1900–1901).

15. Robert Manning of Brunne, *Handlyng Synne*, ed. Frederick J. Furnivall, 2 vols., Early English Text Society, 119, 123 (Millwood, NY: Kraus Reprint, 1978), lines 8987–9242.

16. *Textos Portugueses Medievais*, ed. António Correa de Oliveira and Luís Saavedra Machado (Coimbra: Coimbra Editora, 1968), 102.

17. *Le Roman de Flamenca*, ed. Ulrich Gschwind, vol. 1, Romanica Helvetica 86a (Berne: Francke, 1976), lines 3374, 3375, 3579ff, 3947ff. There is a translation of a sort by Merton Jerome Hubert in *The Romance of Flamenca: A Provençal Poem of the Thirteenth Century*, ed. Marion E. Porter (Princeton, NJ: Princeton University Press, 1962). The line numbering differs very slightly from Gschwind's.

18. *Poésies Complètes du Troubadour Peire Cardenal* (1180–1278), ed. René Lavaud (Tolouse: Privat, 1967), 222: "un sirventes novel vueill comensar."

19. *Aucassin et Nicolette: Chantefable du XIIIe Siècle*, ed. Mario Roques, 2nd ed. (Paris: Champion, 1936), p. 6, lines 24ff.

20. Gifford P. Owen, *Cecco Angiolieri: A Study*, North Carolina Studies in the Romance Languages and Literatures 215 (Chapel Hill: University of North Carolina Department of Romance Languages, 1979), 93.

21. *The English Poems of Charles of Orleans*, ed. Robert Steele, Early English Text Society, original series, 215 (London: Oxford University Press, 1941), 133.

22. "L' écrivain est un homme qui absorbe radicalement le *pourqoui* du monde dans un *comment écrire*. Et le miracle, si l'on peut dire, c'est que cette activité narcissique ne cesse de provoquer, au long d'une littérature séculaire, une interrogation au monde: en s'enfermant dans le comment écrire l'écrivain finit par retrouver la question ouverte par excellence: pourquoi le monde? Quel est le sens des choses?" ("The true writer [sc. poet?] is a man who completely absorbs the 'why' of existence in a 'how shall I write?' And the miracle, if one may use the term, is that this self-gratifying activity, as far as secular literature goes, never fails to prompt a general spirit of enquiry. Enclosing himself in the *comment écrire*, the fulfilment of his sense of how to write, the writer ends up by rediscovering the open question of all open questions: what is the meaning of existence?") Roland Barthes, *Essais Critiques* (Paris: Éditiones du Seuil, 1964), 148, 149.

23. This proposition occurs often in book 14 of Boccaccio's *De Genealogia Deorum Gentilium*.

24. See Judson B. Allen, *The Ethical Poetic of the Later Middle Ages* (Toronto: University of Toronto Press, 1982), chap. 1.

25. *Speculum Christiani: A Middle English Religious Treatise of the 14th Century*, ed. Gustaf Holmstedt (Millwood, NY: Kraus Reprint, 1971).

26. Ibid., 228–31.

27. Ibid., 229.

28. Ibid., xvi–xviii.

29. I find no indication of concern about this in the first (A) version of *Piers Plowman*. In the second (B) version the legitimacy of moral criticism, specifically criticism of venal friars, is raised and answered affirmatively in XI.86–106: the Dreamer-Narrator is assured that there is no reason why he should refrain from versifying about what is common knowledge. Then, presently, at the very center of the poem in XII.16–28, his poetic activity is dismissed as frivolous: "You concern yourself with verses when you could be saying your Psalter and praying for those who support you; in any case there are plenty of books about your topic." For more extended consideration see my *Chaucer and Langland: Critical and Historical Approaches* (London: Athlone Press, 1989), 129–32.

30. Passus II–IV are almost exclusively about this topic.

31. She is Lady Meed. For discussions see A. G. Mitchell, *Lady Meed and the Art of Piers Plowman* (London: H. K. Lewis, 1956); and Yunck, *Lineage of Lady Meed*, n. 10 above.

32. *Piers Plowman: The A Version*, ed. George Kane (London: Athlone Press, 1960), IV.31, 32. This passage implies that the Black Prince, who was grievously ill by 1371, was still active and in good health at the time of its composition.

33. A.V.45–232.

34. *Speculum Christiani*, p. 69. "I cherish my belly beyond all things. I delight in giving it the greatest possible gratification. I do not rest at any time until it is fully satisfied."

35. B.V.62–460. The treatment here is seen to be more than twice as long as that in A; the new entry, Anger, occupies only the fifty-odd lines 135–87.

36. B.XIII.273–407; B.XIV.1–60, 323–35.

37. C.VI.2–VII.68.

38. The arguments are sketched in Benson, *Riverside Chaucer*, 956–57. Other considerations apart, from its size this compilation (as it appears) must have demanded leisure and sustained labor, which argues against an early date. To make it is the kind of heavy but condign penance one would, as Chaucer's confessor, have imposed on him when, in later life, compunction for his naughty works brought him to regret their composition.

39. See my *Geoffrey Chaucer* (Oxford: Oxford University Press, 1984), 79, 85.

40. Morton Bloomfield, "A Grammatical Approach to Personification Allegory," *Modern Philology* 60 (1962–63): 242–60.

41. B.V.137–65, 237–353, 415–21.

42. CT Prol., lines 24–26.

43. This was proposed long ago by J. M. Manly in *Some New Light on Chaucer* (New York: M. Holt, 1926).

44. CT Prol., line 284; Pardoner's Prologue, lines 417–19.

45. The cost of elaborate embroidery is criticized at Pars. T. 416, the waste of cloth in the long, wide sleeves at 419, and the shortness of the garment (because indecent) at 421–24.

46. See n. 6 above.

47. "Of studie took he moost cure and moost heede" (his concern and his attention were principally for his studies). He is in sharp contrast to the pilgrimage Parson, "also a lerned man, a clerk," who also would "gladly teche, but who taught Cristes loore," not Aristotle ("non enim regnat spiritus Christi ubi dominatur spiritus Aristotelis").

48. The Nun's Priest's dismissal of the book of *Launcelot de Lake* as something "That wommen holde in ful greet reverence" (VII.3212–14) comes to mind.

49. CT Prol., 155.

50. A large part of Chaucer "criticism" discusses them as if they were real people; Chaucer would have relished that success, but it is a commentary on the critics.

51. Charles Muscatine, *Chaucer and the French Tradition* (Berkeley: University of California Press, 1956), 204, 205.

52. CT Prol., 573–86.

53. CT Prol., 597–612.

54. B.V.296–362.

55. B.XX.51–198. This passage is in a style that vibrates with the power and energy of evil; but one means of this effect is that the ease with which evil prevails over good and the calamitous nature of the situation are represented in essentially comic rhetorical figures and language.

56. I wrote about this in "The Liberating Truth: The Concept of Integrity in Chaucer's Writings" in *Chaucer and Langland*, chap. 4 (London: Athlone Press, 1989), 46–62.

57. Genesis 6:5, 6.

58. B.XVIII.386, "I may do mercy þoru3 my rightwisnesse and alle my wordes trewe" (I have the power to confer mercy overriding my strict justice and still to remain true to my word); XVIII.371, 372, "Þanne shal I come as a kyng . . . and haue out of helle alle mennes soules" (Then I shall come in royal splendor and release all men's souls from hell).

59. Chaucer, *Parliament of Fowls*, 78–84.

60. N. 29 above. Piers states his dedication to a life of preparation for death in VII.124, 125.

61. In the Prologue to *The Legend of Good Women* Chaucer's Dreamer lays claim to a translation of Innocent's *De Contemptu Mundi* and a homily attributed to Origen, *De Maria Magdalena*, which have not survived.

62. "Al shal passe that men prose or ryme," *Envoy to Scogan*, line 41.

63. See n. 26 and p. 10 above.

64. My student Michael Kuczynski drew the appropriateness of this verse from Psalm 118 to my attention; it is even more apt to religious poetry in the true sense in the modern translation, "Carmina facta sunt mihi statuta tua."

65. B.XIII.45a. I do not know that this quotation has been identified.

66. B.XIV.36. This passage, in which Hawkyn is shown reduced to the fine border between hope and despair and must throw himself abjectly upon God's mercy, instances a state of mind arising out of the sense of sin that cannot be ignored without clouding out understanding of the English fourteenth century and its literature.

LANGLAND AND ALLEGORY [1991]

JILL MANN

I am delighted to have been asked to give this lecture in memory of Morton Bloomfield. I never—alas—knew him personally, but several of the things he wrote have such special importance to me that they almost do duty for a personal relationship. "My" Morton Bloomfield is not so much the author of *The Seven Deadly Sins* or *Piers Plowman as a Fourteenth-Century Apocalypse*, important as these books undoubtedly are to all medievalists; rather, he is especially the author of "Episodic Motivation and Marvels in Epic and Romance," "The Miller's Tale—An UnBoethian Interpretation," and the article which is the starting-point of my discussion today, "A Grammatical Approach to Personification Allegory."[1] At the time this article appeared in 1963, allegory was still very generally despised, seen as merely a poor relation of symbolism. But from about the same date, a whole series of studies by Rosemond Tuve, Pamela Gradon, David Aers, and others have cumulatively transformed this view, reestablishing allegory's claims to literary complexity, and demonstrating that the distinction between allegory and symbolism is an arbitrary and artificial one.[2] Some of this work has drawn attention to the linguistic implications of allegorical writing: Maureen Quilligan, for example, has argued that all allegory is ultimately about language and has drawn on a wide range of texts, including *Piers Plowman*, to illustrate this claim.[3] But it was Bloomfield's article (building on some insights of Donald Davie)[4] which led the way in this direction, and it still offers avenues for exploration, as I hope to show.

Personification allegory, Bloomfield says, is "the process of animating inanimate objects or abstract notions" (246).[5] This animation of inanimate entities is signaled by various grammatical clues, such as the use of personal pronouns, or of verbs which imply the activity of an animate being (247). The sentence "Truth has shaken off her chains" is an illustration of both features. The interest of personification allegory lies not in the noun—the named abstraction—but in what the named abstraction is presented as doing, what is said about it (250). To put it in grammatical terms, the interest is not in the subject of the sentence but in the predicate (258). And this predicate is a metaphoric predicate (254); truth metaphorically shakes off metaphorical chains. It is this use of metaphor that links personification allegory with the kind of allegory which does not deal in abstractions, but attaches a metaphoric predicate to a metaphoric subject (258)—as, for example, one might describe a political crisis in terms of a storm blowing up and driving the ship of state off course.

To compare the two types of allegory in this way might make it seem that personification allegory is more restricted than other allegory—that it is less imaginatively rich, because its use of metaphor is not so thoroughgoing.[6] But in compensation, it gives personification allegory a possibility that an entirely metaphoric allegory lacks, a possibility which is implied in Bloomfield's account of the grammatical shift in the nature of the noun which is entailed by its personification:

> When we make inanimate nouns animate, we are making deictic (or pointer) nouns out of nondeictic nouns. In other words, unless the animation is individualized, it is not a true animation. (249)

What we are doing when we turn an inanimate noun ("truth") into an animate noun ("Lady Truth") is "making proper nouns out of our source nouns."[7] Truth is something that exists as a quality perceptible in innumerable individual manifestations, but "Lady Truth" exists only as an individual, identifiable by her name just as much as the characters in any other kind of narrative would be (249). Yet of course the link with the (nondeictic) abstract noun is not completely severed; it survives at the semantic level, where it gives point and meaning to all that might be said about Lady Truth. And this, in my view, gives the personification an ambivalent quality which an imaginative writer—such as Langland—can use for complex effects, by playing off against each other the two roles of the noun, its role as generalizing abstraction, and its role as the name of an individual.[8]

My first example of this ambivalence is the miniature history of Lyer at the end of Passus II of the B-Text. It is not quite a perfect example, since "Lyer" is not an abstract noun; Langland has already moved the word one stage along towards personalization. But semantically "Lyer" has a generalizing application which runs counter to its use as a proper name, and it therefore retains the ambivalence I have described. It is also important that Langland does not represent Lyer as telling lies, which would be to make the narrative exemplary rather than allegorical. He is not so much a typical liar as lying in general, and the action associated with him is thoroughly metaphorical. Lyer is a member of Lady Meed's wedding procession; when word comes that the king has ordered the arrest of all those participating, the company breaks up in confusion, and Lyer flees with the rest.

> Lightliche Lyere leep awey thenne,
> Lurkynge thorugh lanes, tolugged of manye.
> He was nowher welcome for his manye tales,
> Over al yhouted and yhote trusse,
> Til pardoners hadde pite, and pulled hym into house.
> They wesshen hym and wiped hym and wounden hym in cloutes,
> And senten hym [on Sondayes with seles] to chirches,
> And gaf pardoun for pens poundemele aboute.
> Thanne lourede leches, and lettres thei sente
> That he sholde wonye with hem watres to loke.
> Spycers speken to hym to spien hire ware,
> For he kouthe on hir craft and knew many gommes.
> Ac mynstrales and messagers mette with hym ones,
> And [with]helden hym half a yeer and ellevene dayes.
> Freres with fair speche fetten hym thennes,
> And for knowynge of comeres coped hym as a frere;
> Ac he hath leve to lepen out as ofte as hym liketh,
> And is welcome whan he wile, and woneth with hem ofte.
> (II.216–33)[9]

The temptation with a passage like this is simply to decode it, to see it as merely a fanciful way of saying that pardoners, doctors, spicers, minstrels, and friars all practice lying. But what *more* does this passage say? What can Langland add to such a plain statement by casting it in allegorical form—by turning lying into a person called Lyer and giving him a role in a narrative? If we close our eyes to the content of the name and see Lyer simply as an individual, what will strike us most is that the course of events seems entirely admirable: Lyer is transformed from a social outcast into a desirable houseguest. And it is an act of charity that initiates this process; the pardoners have pity on this wretched vagrant, take him in, clean him up, and send him to church. But the allegorical meaning of this action—that pardoners introduce lying into churches—is, of course, anything but admirable; narrative surface and underlying meaning are diametrically opposed to each other. And the contrast does not just provide an ironic spice to the passage; it also tells us something about lying. That is, both in its content and in its mode, this passage shows us *lying being made respectable.* In its content, because that is literally what the story of Lyer's rehabilitation represents, and in its mode, because it is itself disguising the unpleasant fact that pardoners, friars, and the rest lie, by the use of a linguistic sophistication that smooths away its shocking quality. The "fair speche" with which the friars cloak their lying also characterizes this passage. And this suave linguistic disguise also suggests, I think, the state of mind of those doing the lying; it suggests that they manage to represent their own actions in a respectable light *even to themselves*. The easy sociability and genial tolerance which characterizes Lyer's relations with the friars exemplifies the general mental comfortableness which allows them to avoid confronting the unpleasant fact that they are lying.

This passage, then, asks for a double reading; we read it one way by taking Lyer as a proper name, and at the same time read it another by taking Lyer as the name of an abstraction, lying. And it is in playing off the one reading against the other that we release the full meaning of the passage. In the following Passus the same grammatically equivocal role is given to Lady Meed: she leads a dual existence, as an abstraction and as a person.[10] As an abstraction, she represents unjust profit, bribery, cash payments rather than the reciprocal fulfillment of obligations—in short, money, pure and simple, which has the power to unbalance the just social relationships established by the life of honest labor and the practice of Christian duty. As an abstraction, that is, Meed is cold, unattractive, corrupting. As a person, however, Lady Meed has both feminine helplessness and feminine charm, which can elicit sympathy and a willingness to forgive her faults. We can see Langland bringing forward this personal aspect of Meed in the few lines with which he concludes the passage about Lyer:

> Alle fledden for fere and flowen into hernes;
> Save Mede the mayde na mo dorste abide.
> Ac trewely to telle, she trembled for fere,
> And ek wepte and wrong whan she was attached.
> (II.234–37)

Responding to Meed as a person, we feel sympathy for her distress and an interest in her fate. And we are still responding this way in the following Passus. The king orders Meed to be kindly treated, and declares his intention of forgiving her guilt if she agrees to marry the husband he chooses for her. Everything seems to be sorting itself out very satisfactorily: Meed is generally welcomed at Westminster; lawyers and clerks promise to help her, and she promises them appropriate rewards in return. A friar turns up and offers to hear her confession, which is handled with the usual mendicant urbanity, dispensing with such uncomfortable things as contrition and moral sermons. The friar then invites Meed to pay for a stained-glass window which is being made for his convent; if she does, her soul is sure to go to heaven. Meed happily agrees to this mutually beneficial arrangement:

> "Wiste I that," quod the womman, "I wolde noght spare
> For to be youre frend, frere, and faile yow nevere
> While ye love lordes that lecherie haunten
> And lakketh noght ladies that loven wel the same.
> It is a freletee of flessh—ye fynden it in bokes—
> And a cours of kynde, wherof we comen alle. . . .
>
> Have mercy," quod Mede, "of men that it haunteth
> And I shal covere youre kirk, youre cloistre do maken,
> Wowes do whiten and wyndowes glazen,
> Do peynten and portraye [who paied] for the makynge,
> That every segge shal see I am suster of youre house."
>
> (III.51–63)

We all know the proverbial saying that "money talks," but so vivid is our sense of Meed as a person that it is with something of a shock that we realize that this is money talking. The activities which, on the narrative surface of the allegory, are performed by a person turn out, when we concentrate on its meaning, to be the impersonal operations of money. Part of Langland's point here is the way that natural human relationships are counterfeited by the operations of money: Meed becomes the friars' "sister" not by the power of nature but by the power of cash. It is precisely as we watch a three-dimensional human being shrink to the flatness of an abstraction—as we cease to read "Meed" as a proper name and read it as a general term—that we can measure the loss in the substitution of cash relationships for real ones. Bloomfield quotes Samuel Johnson's disapproving comment on allegory that it "shock[s] the mind by ascribing effects to non-entity" (253); such a shock is precisely what Langland here aims to create.

The double meaning of this passage also has interesting implications for Lady Meed's plea on behalf of lechery. If we take "Meed" as a proper name, and see her as simply a representative rich lady trying to buy an easy absolution for her sins, then the lechery is clearly literal. But if we see Meed as an abstraction, then her weakness for lechery becomes metaphorical: it represents the promiscuousness of money. This way of looking at it comes to the fore in the immediately following scene when Meed is brought before the king. The king is still treating her as a person, courteously offering to forgive her guilt and proposing to marry her off to his knight Conscience. Meed, with the easy neutrality of money, has no objections, and we are ready to fall into approval of the king's judicious course of action. But Conscience upsets this comfortable accord by vigorously rejecting the proposal. His rejection turns Meed back into an abstraction, which cannot be "forgiven" as a person can, and with which there can be no compromise. Conscience gives a long list of the corrupt practices of Meed, perverting justice and enfeebling the clergy. He also accuses her of lechery:

> Is noght a better baude, by Hym that me made,
> Bitwene hevene and helle, in erthe though men soghte!
> For she is tikel of hire tail, talewis of tonge,
> As commune as the cartwey to [knaves and to alle]—
> To monkes, to mynstrales, to meseles in hegges.
> (III.129–33)

This time the lechery is clearly metaphorical, a representation of the promiscuity of money. But if we set it beside Meed's earlier plea for lechery as "a cours of kynde," as something natural, certain troubling questions about the role of money arise. Human promiscuity is "natural"; is pecuniary promiscuity likewise "natural," something to be controlled and channeled as sexuality is controlled and channeled within the institution of marriage? Or is this an instance of money simply counterfeiting nature, as we have seen it do in making Meed a "sister" of the friars? To put the question even more simply: is money part of the natural order or not? This very question is posed by the dreamer's words to Holy Church in Passus I:

> Ac the moneie of this molde that men so faste holdeth—
> Telleth me to whom that tresour appendeth. (44–45)

Where does money fit in the panoramic vision of the world that the dreamer sees in front of him? Does it belong to Treuthe, or to Wrong? Is it part of the natural scheme of things, or a perversion disrupting that scheme?

Langland's attempts to answer these questions are not part of my present subject; I am concerned only to show how the ambivalent grammatical status of Lady Meed (and not just the ambivalent meanings of the word "meed") is the source of the larger ambivalence about how she should be dealt with. The linguistic ambivalence reflects an ambivalence in life, where an abstract principle will always be merged into the texture of lived reality. Whereas other allegorists work on "Platonizing" principles, penetrating the veil of physical experience to reach the transcendental reality behind it, Langland shows us abstractions as inextricably embedded in concrete individuals. So his Seven Deadly Sins are not represented as the timeless "essence" of Gluttony, Avarice, Sloth, and so on, but are the sum of a myriad of individual instances of gluttonous or slothful or avaricious behavior. Avarice has no existence apart from the avaricious. Sin exists only in the sinner—which makes it hard to see how God can forgive the sinner and damn the sin. So it is that Langland's allegorical fiction never leaves the world of concrete reality behind but subsumes it, in the awareness that its role is more important than to be merely a source of metaphor. He uses the ambivalent grammatical status of his personifications to establish a bridge between his allegorical fiction and the realities of fourteenth-century society, in a way that has important implications for his poem and for his view of the world.

Meed's declaration of her willingness to help pay for the friary's building works launches Langland into a direct address to real-life fourteenth-century lords exhorting them not to do such things.

> Ac God to alle good folk swich gravynge defendeth—
> To writen in wyndowes of hir wel dedes—
> An aventure pride be peynted there, and pomp of the worlde;
> For God knoweth thi conscience and thi kynde wille,
> Thi cost and thi coveitise and who the catel oughte.
> Forthi I lere yow, lordes, leveth swiche werkes—
> To writen in wyndowes of youre wel dedes
> Or to greden after Goddes men whan ye [gyve] doles,
> On aventure ye have youre hire here and youre hevene alse.
> *Nesciat sinistra quid faciat dextra*:
> Lat noght thi left half, late ne rathe,
> Wite what thow werchest with thi right syde—
> For thus [the Gospel bit] goode men doon hir almesse.
> (III.64–75)

Meed's role as an individual puts her on the same footing as the well-to-do members of Langland's society; the metaphorical narrative is temporarily suspended and we are returned to a direct contemplation of the realities of everyday life. This movement in and out of allegory—or perhaps it would be better to say in and out of metaphor—is characteristic of Langland, so characteristic that we hardly register it most of the time. It is apparent, for example, in the opening vision of the poem, which shows us the tower of Treuthe and the "dongeon" of Wrong on either side of the Field Full of

Folk. The strongholds of Treuthe and Wrong are metaphorical buildings, but the Field Full of Folk is simply fourteenth-century England, seen in a single synoptic vision. The king who deals with Lady Meed is given a realistic context in both geography and history: he resides not in a timeless world of abstractions but at Westminster, in a court peopled with perfectly ordinary lawyers and clerks, and he is credited with Edward III's campaigns in Normandy (III.189–208). Of course allegory is not definitively barred from referring to historical events, people, or places: Prudentius's *Psychomachia*, the earliest example of personification allegory, includes figures of biblical history in the battle between seven vices and seven virtues in such a way as to give a temporal dimension to the supra-temporal conflict.[11] What we have in Langland, however, is something of a quite different order: a constant oscillation between the metaphorical world and the real world, which has a radical effect on the nature of his allegory.[12]

A good example of what I have in mind is the pilgrimage to Treuthe which turns imperceptibly into the plowing of Piers's half-acre. Under the influence of Repentance's preaching, "a thousand of men" set out to look for Treuthe, but have trouble in finding the way. Piers Plowman makes his first appearance in the poem and offers to guide them. But first, he says, he has a half acre that must be plowed and sown. The women offer to sew and spin while they are waiting; the knight is assigned the task of hunting vermin and punishing "wastours and . . . wikked men" (VI.28). And then, in a strange speech from Piers, the pilgrimage and the plowing become one:

> "And I shal apparaille me," quod Perkyn, "in pilgrymes wise
> And wende with yow I wile til we fynde Truthe."
>   [He] caste on [hise] clothes, yclouted and hole,
> [Hise] cokeres and [hise] coffes for cold of [hise] nailes,
> And [heng his] hoper at [his] hals in stede of a scryppe:
> "A busshel of bred corn brynge me therinne,
> For I wol sowe it myself, and sithenes wol I wende
> To pilgrymage as palmeres doon, pardon for to have.
> And whoso helpeth me to erie or sowen here er I wende,
> Shal have leve, by Oure Lorde, to lese here in hervest
> And make hym murie thermyd, maugree whoso bigrucche it."
> (VI.57–67)

Like a pilgrim leaving home, Piers makes his will, recording the payment of his debts, his obligations to his family and the Church; with what is left, he says,

"I wol worshipe therwith Truthe by my lyve,
And ben His pilgrym atte plow for povere mennes sake.
My plowpote shal be my pikstaf, and picche atwo the rotes,
And helpe my cultour to kerve and clense the furwes."
                                    (VI.101–4)

Piers says he will *first* do his plowing and *then* go on pilgrimage; but in fact everyone starts plowing and the pilgrimage never takes place. The meaning of this passage—that the life of honest labor is a road to Treuthe—is clear enough; what I want to emphasize is the unusual nature of the allegorical method here, which has its own meaning. Going on a pilgrimage is a metaphor for seeking Treuthe; a spiritual advancement is represented in terms of a concrete activity. Most allegories would be content to stick to this initial narrative metaphor; Deguileville's *Pilgrimage of the Life of Man*, for example, or Bunyan's *Pilgrim's Progress* adhere consistently to the dominant fiction of the journey. But Langland does not. Having represented the search for Treuthe as a pilgrimage, he then represents the pilgrimage as a plowing—and he does so in such a way as to suggest that it is not metaphorical plowing but *real* plowing that is involved. The search for Treuthe is enacted in the labor of everyday life. This is not the same as saying that the plowing is the *meaning* of the pilgrimage; rather, it is the search for Treuthe which is the meaning that unites plowing and pilgrimage. The effect of creating this "club sandwich" by piling plowing and pilgrimage one on top of the other is to make reality into a metaphor. Piers's hopper becomes a metaphorical scrip (the pilgrim's wallet); his plow-pusher becomes a metaphorical pilgrim's staff; his plowing becomes a metaphorical pilgrimage. The spiritual meaning is embodied, not in a fiction which exists only as a literary device, but in an everyday reality to which it has a real relevance.

When Prudentius's *Psychomachia* shows us Faith choking the life out of Worship of the Old Gods (30–35), or Sobriety smashing Luxury's face to a pulp with a rock (417–26), or Good Works mercilessly strangling Avarice (589–95), he is not saying anything about the spiritual dimensions of thuggery;[13] the actions remain metaphorical, and indeed their literal inappropriateness to virtue is what prompts the reader to see in them an allegorical meaning. When Deguileville has his dreamer begin his journey to the heavenly Jerusalem by wading through a river, he is representing the spiritual cleansing of baptism (479–92);[14] he is not talking about the character-forming effects of an early morning dip. When he shows us the figure of Penance holding a broom in her teeth, he is using a vivid metaphor to represent the cleansing role of the tongue in confession (2029–34, 2187–278); he is not saying something about the spiritual benefits of housework. But when Langland represents the search for Treuthe as plowing, he is saying something about the spiritual dimensions of real-life plowing. The metaphor dissolves back into reality. Or rather, it becomes harder to say which is which. For it may be that we are to see pilgrimage as a metaphorical plowing, as well as vice versa; that is, going on pilgrimage is represented as spiritually productive labor worthy to be set beside labor of a physically productive kind. When in Passus III Conscience looks forward to the time when Meed's power will be no more, "leaute" will rule, and Conscience and "kynde love" will "make of lawe a laborer" (III.300), is the laboring real or metaphorical? Does he mean that lawyers will have to work on the land because there will be no more need for their services (as might be suggested by the fact that Conscience goes on to talk about turning swords into plowshares)? Or does he mean that the law will be functioning properly for the first time, instead of being driven by the oiled wheels of corruption (as might be suggested by the fact that Conscience goes on to talk about the proper dispensing of justice in a single court presided over by "Trewetonge")? I think we should have to say that he means both; his allegory translates itself into multiple meanings.

One of the reasons why Langland can move so easily between metaphor and reality is that there is a much greater congruity between the "tenor" and the "vehicle" of the allegorical metaphor than is usual or necessary in allegorical writing. When Piers plows with an oxteam composed of the four evangelists and sows the seeds of the four cardinal virtues in man's soul (XIX.277), we are hardly surprised when this metaphorical labor culminates in Conscience's invitation to the people to come and partake of an Easter feast, represented by the Eucharist—*real* bread which is really consumed (XIX.387–89). The metaphor of plowing merges into the real plowing which is the everyday work of the Christian community. Another example might be the description of Charity in Passus XV:

>Of rentes ne of richesse rekketh he nevere,
>For a frend that fynt hym, failed hym nevere at nede:
>*Fiat-voluntas-tua* fynt hym everemoore.
>And if he soupeth, eet but a sop of *Spera in Deo*.
>He kan portreye wel the *Paternoster* and peynte it with *Aves*,
>And outherwhile is his wone to wende on pilgrymages
>Ther poore men and prisons liggeth, hir pardon to have;

> Though he bere hem no breed, he bereth hem swetter liflode,
> Loveth hem as Oure Lorde bit and loketh how thei fare.
>   And whan he is wery of that werk than wole he som tyme
> Labouren in a lavendrye wel the lengthe of a mile,
> And yerne into youthe, and yepeliche seche
> Pride, with al the appurtenaunce, and pakken hem togideres,
> And bouken hem at his brest and beten hem clene,
> And leggen on longe with *Laboravi in gemitu meo,*
> And with warm water at hise eighen wasshen hem after,
> Thanne he syngeth whan he doth so, and som tyme seith wepynge,
> *Cor contritum et humiliatum, Deus, non despicies.* (177–94)

This passage begins with a picture of Charity being metaphorically "fed" by doing God's will (dramatizing Christ's words in John 4:34, "My meat is to do the will of him that sent me"); then it moves on to Charity's visits to poor men and prisoners, where the metaphor lies not in the nature of the actions themselves but simply in the notion that it is Charity that performs them. Finally we revert to a metaphorical action, Charity's work in a laundry, washing out the stains of pride with the tears of contrition. But the disparity between the "real" actions of visiting the poor and the metaphorical labor in the laundry does not trouble us, I think, because the latter shares the quality of holiness that surrounds all honest toil in this poem. So far from seeing Charity's laundry work as purely metaphorical, we derive the impression that washing clothes could really have a penitential dimension. Likewise, an allegorical metaphor such as the description of the Tree of Charity in Passus XVI is not merely an expository device of the type familiar in so many allegorical treatises; the fact that it is all of a piece with the agricultural realities that pervade the poem makes it more than a literary trope. Charity and the growth of an everyday tree become parallel mysteries, neither of which takes precedence over the other.

The effect of this mixed mode of allegory is to make it impossible to distinguish, as one so easily could in many other medieval allegories, between a material world which constitutes the vehicle of the allegorical metaphor, and the spiritual world which constitutes its meaning. Instead, Langland makes us constantly aware of the way in which life is lived at the intersection of the material and the non-material, the concrete and the abstract. His allegory does not "layer" concrete and abstract, fictional action and meaning, but shows them as different facets of the same multi-angled reality. The word "law" can refer us both to an abstract concept and to a set of concrete individuals; "clergye" and "knyghthode" have the same Janus-like ability to face towards timeless abstraction and social reality at one and the same time. When, in the prologue, Langland says of the king "Knyghthod hym ladde" (112), does he mean that he is preceded by a group of knights, or that he is guided by the spirit of chivalry? Again, I think the answer is both. It is this duality of reference that gives Langland's allegory a far richer texture than most other medieval examples of the genre, which so often seem to reduce experience to a mere shadow of itself; Langland's allegory, in contrast, uses the multiple potentialities of language to make us constantly aware of the multiple dimensions of experience.

We are back, then, to language—or rather, to the recognition that we have never really left it, for it is in our everyday linguistic practices that we can see the merger of these multiple dimensions of experience. Bloomfield talks about the generalized "metaphoric habit" of using animate verbs in connection with inanimate nouns ("the storm is howling outside"); such primitive metaphors should be distinguished, he says, from full-blown personification (247). Richard Glasser similarly distinguishes what he calls the *abstractum agens* in such phrases as "fear gripped me," "grief overcame me," "folly led me astray" from allegory proper; it is not until such abstractions become the actors in an autonomously developing narrative that we can speak of allegory.[15] But the strength of Langland's allegory is precisely that he realizes the allegorical potential of these simple linguistic formulae. His writing is full of *abstracta agentia* which can at any moment turn into large-scale personifications, stepping forward to take a role in the allegorical drama.[16] This is why, although it would be possible to draw up a list of allegorical figures in the *Faerie Queene* or the *Pilgrim's Progress*, it would be quite impossible to do so for *Piers Plowman*. It is the editors of the poem who have the unenviable task of bestowing on the *abstractum agens* the capital letter which baptizes it as a full personification,[17] and the difficulties involved in deciding the precise moment of such a baptism can be seen if we compare two editorial versions of the "coronation scene" in the B-text version of the Prologue. Skeat withholds capital letters entirely:

> Thanne come ther a kyng · kny3thod hym ladde,
> Mi3t of the comunes · made hym to regne,
> And thanne cam kynde wytte · and clerkes he made,
> For to conseille the kyng · and the comune saue.
> The kyng and kny3thode · and clergye bothe
> Casten that the comune · shulde hem-self fynde.
> The comune contreued · of kynde witte craftes,
> And for profit of alle the poeple · plowmen ordeygned,

> To tile and trauaile · as trewe lyf asketh.
> The kynge and the comune · and kynde witte the thridde
> Shope lawe and lewte · eche man to knowe his owne. (112–22)[18]

The effect of this is to make "kny3thod" and "clergye" virtually synonymous with "knihtes" and "clerkes," which puts them on the same existential plane as the king and the commons, but leaves "kynde witte" rather out on a limb as the only agent in this process which is not a social group. This gives no problem in line 118, where "kynde witte" is a simple attribute of one of these social groups, but lines 114 and 121 are a different matter, for they represent "kynde witte" as an independent entity acting on the same footing as clerks, king, or commons. Schmidt's version of this passage goes to the opposite extreme, sprinkling it with capital letters throughout:

> Thanne kam ther a Kyng: Knyghthod hym ladde;
> Might of the communes made hym to regne.
> And thanne cam Kynde Wit and clerkes he made,
> For to counseillen the Kyng and the Commune save.
> The Kyng and Knyghthod and Clergie bothe
> Casten that the Commune sholde hem [communes] fynde.
> The Commune contreved of Kynde Wit craftes,
> And for profit of al the peple plowmen ordeyned
> To tilie and to travaille as trewe lif asketh.
> The Kyng and the Commune and Kynde Wit the thridde
> Shopen lawe and leaute—ech lif to knowe his owene. (112–22)

The capital letter for the king presumably does not imply a personification but simply reflects a spelling convention for titles; nevertheless it helps to blur over the very disparate kinds of entity which are here represented as working in concert. It is hard to see the justification in giving a capital letter to "the Commune" (115), which seems to make it something different from "the communes" in the phrase "Might of the communes" (113). Kynde Wit receives the capital letters he seems to demand in lines 114 and 121, but he also gets them in line 118, where it is extremely difficult to see how a personified figure can be the means by which the Commune invents crafts. Finally, we may note that "lawe and leaute" are left with lowercase letters in the last line, but if they were capitalized there would be an even more striking extension to the drama, with the King and his associates playing a Pygmalion-like role (as Kynde Wit does in 114). Presumably because "leaute" has a lowercase l here, Schmidt also gives it a lowercase l a few lines later, when the "lunatik" wishes that God may grant that the King rule his land "so leaute thee lovye" (126), implying "so that just men may love you," but it could equally well be turned into a fully-fledged personification with a capital letter, in which case it would mean "so that Justice loves you." And indeed Derek Pearsall opts for this reading in his edition of the C-Text (in the rest of the passage he has a much smoother ride, since differences in the text remove the more obvious discrepancies between the various actors in the scene).[19] The point I am making is not that one editor's choice is better than another, but that the necessity for choice which results from modern spelling habits falsifies the ambivalence which is fundamental to Langland's writing by tipping the balance on one side or the other. And no sooner has an editor tipped the balance in one direction than he finds himself tipping it in the other. Having perhaps given "clergye" and "kynde wit" more than their due as personifications in the coronation scene, Schmidt later seems to deny their much stronger claims to personification in Passus XII:

> Forthi I counseille thee for Cristes sake, clergie that thow lovye,
> For kynde wit is of his kyn and neighe cosynes bothe
> To Oure Lord, leve me—forthi love hem, I rede.
> For bothe [as mirours ben] to amenden oure defautes,
> And lederes for lewed men and for lettred bothe. (92–96)

The reason the capital letters are withheld here, despite the personalization of "clergie" and "kynde wit" in the use of words like "kyn," "cosyns," "lederes," is presumably that this little allegorical vignette emerges out of a long and serious discussion of the different roles of clergy (learning), "kynde wit," and grace in ensuring salvation, in which they are most of the time used as ordinary abstract nouns. But it is precisely the persistent emergence of miniature allegories out of this ordinary use of abstract nouns which I want to highlight as one of the most interesting features of Langland's allegorical method.

The consciousness that an *abstractum agens* may at any moment turn into a personification proper, with a developed role in the allegorical action, gives us the sense that language is instinct with life. The power latent in the role of the abstraction in the sentence is for Langland, I think, an index of the latent power it has in life; it is in language that its role can be grasped. So it is language itself that becomes the stuff of Langland's imagined world, the reality out of which it is made. One feature of his poem which illustrates this well is his idiosyncratic use of entire syntactic units as names of people, places, or things. There are Latin examples in the passage on Charity already quoted: Charity's friend is called "*Fiat-voluntas-tua*"; Charity eats "*Spera in Deo.*" When Piers is telling the pilgrims the way to Treuthe, the geographical landmarks on the route have enormously long names, such as

>Swere-noght-but-if-it-be-for-nede-
>And-nameliche-on-ydel-the-name-of-God-almyghty,

or

>Coveite-noght-mennes-catel-ne-hire-wyves-
>Ne-noon-of-hire-servaunts-that-noyen-hem-myghte
>(V.570–71, 573–74).

When they are functioning as names, the semantic content of these sentences is reduced to a mere label, serving to identify the referent—the cottage or brook or whatever it may be; the sentence plays the role of a noun in the larger sentence of the narrative. But when they are considered as syntactic units in their own right, the full semantic content is restored and we enter a kind of miniature linguistic world, like one Russian doll hidden inside another. In this inner linguistic world, the meaning of the sentence is not dependent on an external object but exists as an autonomous whole, internal to itself; the power of language is something more than its power to name objects in the outer world. Rather, it is the outer world (here, the fictional landscape) which becomes subservient to these sentences, its function being simply to articulate their relationship to each other.

There is a particularly interesting example of the dual role of these very long names in an odd passage of the C-Text which we might take to represent Langland nodding. The members of Piers's family are given names which are complete sentences; when we come to the name of Piers's son, the name runs off the rails, as it were, launching itself forwards under its own steam.

>His Sone hihte Soffre-thy-soueryenes-haue-her-wille-
>Deme-hem-nat-for-yf-thow-doest-thow-shalt-hit-dere-abygge.
>"Consayle nat so the comune the kyng to desplese,
>Ne hem that han lawes to loke lacke hem nat, Y hote the.
>Lat god yworthe with al, as holy wryt techeth:
>>*Super cathedram Moysi sedent. &c*

> Maystres, as the mayres ben, and grete menne, senatours,
> What thei comaunde as by the kyng countreplede hit neuere;
> Al that they hoten, Y hote; heiliche thow soffre hem
> And aftur here warnynge and wordynge worche thou theraftur.
> *Omnia que dicunt facite et seruate.*
> Ac aftur here doynge ne do thow nat, my dere sone," quod Peres.
> (C.VIII.82–91)

A sentence that starts off as the name of Piers's son ends up as an exhortation addressed by Piers *to* his son. At what point does the name turn into the exhortation? Again, it is the editor's decision. The change *could* come a line earlier than Derek Pearsall places it. Or it could come as late as the end of line 86, just before the first Latin quotation. What is important is the shift from nominal function to independent syntactic unit, a shift which not only gives two referents to a single linguistic entity but also two different ways of referring. And also two functions within the allegory: within the allegorical fiction, the names have a metaphorical role, identifying metaphorical places or personages. But considered in their own right, they are naked of metaphor, simply straightforward didactic exhortations which refer themselves directly to real life. Metaphor again leads straight back into reality.

It is in a much-discussed passage that Langland added to the C-Text that we can see that the linguistic games played in his poem are not there by accident but result from his deep imaginative engagement with the nature of language.[20] In the confrontation between Conscience and Lady Meed, Conscience compares right relations in society to right relations in grammar, when nouns and adjectives accord properly with each other and with their antecedents, in gender ("kynde"), case, and number (C.III.344–62). The unregulated relations created by the indiscriminate operations of Meed flout these rules and create confusion, just as grammatical confusion would follow from the failure to restrict a noun or adjective to the appropriate case or number (363–73). The grammatical analogy represents not only the relations between men but also the relation between man and God: God, says Langland, is "the ground of al, a graciouse antecedent," to whom man must accord. God is the substantive, man takes the place of the forms grammatically dependent on this antecedent. But this relationship, like all grammatical relationships, turns out to be reversible: when Langland repeats this idea a little later, it is gradually turned around so that finally it is man who takes the role of substantive and God who is the adjective that qualifies him.

> Ac adiectyf and sustantyf is as Y er tolde,
> That is vnite acordaunde in case, in gendre and in noumbre,
> And is to mene in oure mouthe more ne mynne
> But that alle maner men, wymmen and childrene
> Sholde confourme hem to o kynde on holy kyrke to bileue
> And coueyte the case when thei couthe vnderstande
> To syke for here synnes and soffre harde penaunces
> For that lordes loue that for oure loue deyede
> And coueytede oure kynde and be kald in oure name,
> > *Deus homo,*
> And nyme hym into oure noumbre now and eueremore.
> > *Qui in caritate manet in deo manet et deus in eo.*
> Thus is man and mankynde in maner of sustantyf
> As *hic et hec homo* askyng an adiectyf
> Of thre trewe termisones, *trinitas unus deus*;
> > *Nominatiuo, pater et filius et spiritus sanctus.* (C.III.394–405)

In the Incarnation, it is man who is the substance represented by the noun and God the accident represented by the adjective, with its three endings representing the three Persons of the Trinity. The quality of divinity is grounded in man's substance. And it is the philosophical understanding of grammar that shows how humanity and divinity can be distinct and yet one. If we talk of a "sweet song," we are not talking of two separate things but of one thing, considered under two aspects. The accidental quality denoted by an adjective cannot exist apart from the substance in which it adheres; the sweetness of a song has no existence apart from the song. But it can be turned into a substantive in language; "sweet" becomes "sweetness" (and "of a song" qualifies it). This is precisely what personification allegory does, as the teacher in Conrad of Hirsau's *Dialogus super auctores* patiently explains to his student.[21] Allegory turns accidents into substances in order to show that they are no less real than substances; the transformative properties of language enable us to perceive the realities of the world. And they also make us aware that any grammatical formulation is only a *provisional* formulation, which can be reshaped by seeing reality in a different way. God may play the role of substance; man may play the role of substance; the reality is the union of man and God. And it may be that if we saw the world as God does, those things we see as accidents—truth, "leaute," meed—would appear as substances, those things we take to be metaphors would be reality, and what for us is reality become a metaphor. (Do we use a metaphor when we call God a king, or is it God who embodies the reality of kingship, and the earthly king who is a kind of physical metaphor for God?)

The provisional nature of the naming enacted in language is made clear in a passage where Langland makes poetry out of Isidore's *Etymologies*: Anima describes his many functions to the dreamer, each function resulting in a different name:

> "The whiles I quykke the cors," quod he, "called am I Anima;
> And whan I wilne and wolde, *Animus* ich hatte;
> And for that I kan and knowe, called am I *Mens*, 'Thoughte';
> And whan I make mone to God, *Memoria* is my name;
> And whan I deme domes and do as truthe techeth,
> Thanne is *Racio* my righte name, 'Reson' on Englissh;
> And whan I feele that folk telleth, my firste name is Sensus—
> And that is wit and wisdom, the welle of alle craftes;
> And whan I chalange or chalange noght, chepe or refuse,
> Thanne am I Conscience ycalled, Goddes clerk and his notarie;
> And whan I love leelly Oure Lord and alle othere,
> Thanne is 'Lele Love' my name, and in Latyn *Amor*;
> And whan I flee fro the flessh and forsake the careyne,
> Thanne am I spirit spechelees—and *Spiritus* thanne ich hatte."
>
> (XV.23–36)

There is no one-to-one relationship of name and thing here. So far from representing a multiplicity of things, the many nouns converge on an underlying unity, which is verbal not nominal. The noun is dissolved into the verb; it is simply the freeze-frame in which verbal activity is artificially stilled.

Dissolving the noun into the verb is one way in which Langland solves the problem which occupies him throughout *Piers Plowman*, the problem of reconciling Justice and Mercy. The problem is already introduced in the contradictory advice given to the king in the Prologue by the angel (who exhorts him to be merciful) and the "goliardeis" (who tells him he ceases to be a king if he ceases to administer justice, and supports this by appealing to the linguistic laws which tie the word *rex* to the word *regere*). In Passus I, Holy Church tells the dreamer he can save his soul by Treuthe, which she defines in terms of strict justice—it means kings and knights hunting down criminals, God punishing Lucifer for his pride. But when the dreamer enquires further about Treuthe, Holy Church puzzlingly redefines it as something that teaches love, exemplified in the God who forgave those who put him to death (as opposed to the God who punished Lucifer). Without love, she says, Treuthe is useless. Now it is not Treuthe that administers the law, but love:

> Right so is love a ledere and the lawe shapeth:
> Upon man for his mysdedes the mercyment he taxeth.   (I.161–62)

How is it that law and love can so easily combine? The passage offers several linguistic answers to this question. One of them is in the wordplay which counters the goliard's appeal to the logic of language by finding the word "mercy" within the word "merciment." Another is in the matching of active and passive in the two biblical quotations cited by Holy Church:

> *Eadem mensura qua mensi fueritis remecietur vobis.* . . .
>
> *Date, et dabitur vobis*—for I deele yow alle.
> And that is the lok of love that leteth out my grace,
> To conforten the carefulle acombred with synne.
>   (I.178a, 201–3)

The first of these active/passive combinations might be coincidental; the metaphor of the lock which is used of the second makes it more likely that Langland is conscious of the way active and passive "lock" into a perfect whole with the balance that characterizes justice. And the mysterious power of the active to generate the passive is the key to the mysterious power of Treuthe to generate Love. Treuthe is present in the balanced form of the sentence; Love is the meaning generated from that form. Lastly, there is the little phrase of which Langland is so fond, "loven leelly":

> For though ye be trewe of youre tonge and treweliche wynne,
> And as chaste as a child that in chirche wepeth,
> But if ye loven leelly and lene the povere,
> Of swich good as God yow sent goodliche parteth,
> Ye ne have na moore merite in masse ne in houres
> Than Malkyne of hire maydenhede, that no man desireth.
>   (I.179–84)

Even as Treuthe and Love are contrasted with each other and Treuthe is relegated to second place, it is absorbed into the action of Love. Seen as nouns, "Love" and "Lewte" are isolated things, each with their own identity, resisting merger on a semantic level. Dissolved back into their role as qualities, they unite easily and fluidly, as Love becomes a verb and is modified by the adverb "leelly." "Lewte" is a dimension of loving; their semantic separation fragments a fundamental unity.

Language is for Langland not merely a mirror of reality, it is a mirror of *more* than reality. It not only names the objects that make up our physical life, it also names the invisible qualities which animate the physical world and constitute its hidden dynamics. And it does more than name: its generative capacities, its transformational powers are the index of the world's multiplicity, multiplicity of dimensions, relationships, potentialities. Medieval philosophy was as familiar as present-day philosophy with the notion that language structures our experience.[22] But whereas nowadays this notion can create unease, implying that we are imprisoned in language, barred by it from contact with reality, Langland responded to the idea with excitement and enthusiasm. For him the structure of language is not a distortion but the sign of an extra dimension of meaning. Grammar is, says Langland, the "grounde of al" (C.XVII.108); it is, as we have seen, an expression he also uses of God. In exploring the powers of language, he must have felt he was getting close to God.

Notes

This essay is reprinted by permission of the author.

1. The first and third of these articles are reprinted in Morton Bloomfield, *Essays and Explorations: Studies in Ideas, Language and Literature* (Cambridge, MA: Harvard University Press, 1970), 97–128 and 243–60; the second was published in *Medieval Literature and Folklore Studies: Essays in Honor of Francis Lee Utley*, ed. Jerome Mandel and Bruce A. Rosenberg (New Brunswick, NJ: Rutgers University Press, 1970), 205–11.

2. Rosemond Tuve, *Allegorical Imagery: Some Mediaeval Books and their Posterity* (Princeton, NJ: Princeton University Press, 1966); Pamela Gradon, *Form and Style in Early English Literature* (London: Methuen, 1971), chaps. 1 and 6; David Aers, *Piers Plowman and Christian Allegory* (London: E. Arnold, 1975). Two important contributions which predate Bloomfield's article, and of which it makes use, are: Robert Worth Frank, Jr., "The Art of Reading Medieval Personification-Allegory," ELH 20 (1953): 237–50; and Hans Robert Jauss, "Form und Auffassung der Allegorie in der Tradition der *Psychomachia*," *Medium Aevum Vivum: Festschrift für Walther Bulst*, ed. Hans Robert Jauss and Dieter Schaller (Heidelberg: C. Winter, 1960), 179–206.

3. Maureen Quilligan, *The Language of Allegory: Defining the Genre* (Ithaca: Cornell University Press, 1979).

4. Donald Davie had emphasized the importance of the verb in personification in his *Purity of Diction in English Verse*, rev. ed. (London: Routledge, 1969), 38–39; see Bloomfield, *Essays and Explorations*, 251, n. 12.

5. Page numbers given in the text refer to the reprint of Bloomfield's article in his *Essays and Explorations*.

6. Cf. the comment of Frank: "in symbol-allegory the reader translates characters (and significant details) *and* relationships and actions. In personification-allegory, he translates *only* relationships and actions" ("Reading Medieval Personification-Allegory," 245).

7. Lavinia Griffiths adopts this definition of personification as the basis of her study, *Personification in Piers Plowman* (Cambridge: D. S. Brewer, 1985); see p. 5.

8. Cf. the similar comments of Lavinia Griffiths, *Personification*, 10.

9. Quotations of the B-text of Piers Plowman are taken, unless otherwise stated, from the edition by A. V. C. Schmidt, *The Vision of Piers Plowman: A Critical Edition of the B-Text*, 2nd ed. (London: Everyman, 1995).

10. Lavinia Griffiths's discussion of Lady Meed (*Personification*, 26–40) starts from the same point but follows different lines from my discussion.

11. See Jauss, "Form und Auffassung der Allegorie," 188–89, and Macklin Smith, *Prudentius' Psychomachia: A Reexamination* (Princeton: Princeton University Press, 1976), chap. 1.

12. Compare Griffiths's comment on the way that Langland's metaphors tend to merge with the "real" features of his fictional world (*Personification*, 97).

13. The *Psychomachia* is edited and translated by H. J. Thomson in vol. 1 of the Loeb Classical Library *Prudentius* (Cambridge, MA: Harvard University Press, 1949).

14. Guillaume de Deguileville, *Le Pèlerinage de vie humaine*, ed. J. J. Stürzinger, Roxburghe Club 124 (London, 1893).

15. Richard Glasser, "Abstractum agens und Allegorie im älteren Französisch," *Zeitschrift für romanische Philologie* 69 (1953): 43–122, esp. 57–8.

16. Marc-René Jung notes a similar (though less vividly realized) "flottement général entre *l'abstractum agens*, la personnification et l'adjectif nominal" in the Miserere of the Reclus de Moilliens (*Etudes sur le poème allégorique en France au moyen âge* (Bern: Franke, 1971), 265). Griffiths uses Inge Crosman's term "brief conceits" for these short-term transformations of *abstracta agentia* into personifications (*Personification*, 12).

17. Compare the comments of Siegfried Heinimann on the similar problems faced by the editors of Chrétien de Troyes: "Die Verschiedenartigkeit der als handelnde Wesen aufgefassten Abstrakta, der rasche Wechsel vom allegorischen zum eigentlichen Sprachgebrauch und die vielen Zwischenstufen zwischen der Personifikation und einer kaum mehr als übertragen empfundenen Verwendung des Nomens stellen den Herausgeber mittelalterlicher Texte vor ein schwieriges

Problem: Welche Abstrakta sollen mit Majuskel geschrieben werden? Der Philologe muss sich für eine der beiden Schriebweisen entscheiden. Mit der Schrift lassen sich nicht alle Grade der Bildhaftigkeit kennzeichnen. So ergeben sich zwangsläufig Inkonsequenzen innerhalb eines Werkes und Unterschiede zwischen den verschiedenen Ausgaben eines Textes" (*Das Abstraktum in der französischen Literatursprache des Mittelalters*, Romanica Helvetica 73 [Bern: Francke, 1963], 117).

18. *The Vision of William Concerning Piers the Plowman in Three Parallel Texts*, ed. Walter W. Skeat, 2 vols. (Oxford: Oxford University Press: 1886; repr. with added bibliography, 1954).

19. *William Langland: Piers Plowman; A New Annotated Edition of the C-Text*, ed. Derek Pearsall (Exeter: Exeter University Press, 2008), prol. 147–50.

20. If this engagement took on more original manifestations in Langland, it was nevertheless something he shared with the Middle Ages in general; see John A. Alford, "The Grammatical Metaphor: A Survey of its Use in the Middle Ages," Speculum 57 (1982): 728–60.

21. The discussion concerns Prudentius's *Psychomachia*; see *Accessus ad Auctores*, ed. R. B. C. Huygens (Leiden: E. J. Brill, 1970), 99–100:

> (D[iscipulus]) Non tam miror ipsam significativae literae subtilitatem quam fidem vel pudiciciam et ceteras virtutes vitiorum choro rebellantes, cum magis hoc fideli et pudico vel patienti accidat quam eorum qualitatibus, quae nec videntur nec pugnare posse probantur: videri possunt loca vel personae vel quarumcumque corporalium vel contrectabilium rerum substantiae, qualitates earum, sicut a te didici, videri non possunt. (M[agister]) Recte sentis: album lignum, rubrum, nigrum vel cuiuscumque coloris videri quidem possunt substantiae, albedo, rubedo, nigredo, <nec> videri nec tangi possunt, quia subiectorum suorum qualitates vel accidentia sunt; sic de fide quamvis substantia sed invisibili, sic de pudicicia, sic de patientia et ceteris suo ordine viciis obpositis intellige. (D) Qualiter igitur me vis intelligere duellum singulare viciorum vel virtutum sine personali materia? (M) Tropice, id est per figuram metonomiam haec accipienda sunt, ubi ponitur continens pro eo quod continetur, id est fides pro fideli, ydolatria pro ydolatra et sic de ceteris, ut virtuosus per virtutem, per vicia viciosus ostendatur.

Similarly, Dante, in commenting on his own poetry, tells his readers not to be surprised if he has represented Love as a substance when it is in reality an accident (*Vita Nuova* XXV).

22. Cf. Maureen Quilligan's comment: "the whirligig of time has brought in some strange resemblances, and . . . we are in a peculiar position to understand the medieval concern for the way language structures the world: we can now sense its affinities for our own concerns" (*Language of Allegory*, 279).

Monastic Preaching in the Age of Chaucer [1993]

Siegfried Wenzel

As the Middle Ages drew to an end—in England, the late fourteenth and fifteenth centuries—the great monastic orders certainly cannot be said to have vibrated any longer with an energetic intellectual and spiritual life. The age of saintly founders and reformers of orders and of houses that not only fostered the spiritual life but also led to the highest achievements in the liturgy, architecture, learning, literature, and the making of manuscripts had long since gone. What in earlier centuries had been achieved by Benedictine and Cistercian monks was now paralleled or even superseded by the hearts, heads, and mouths of members of newer orders, primarily Dominican and Franciscan friars. Such decline and sterility seems to characterize the monks' activity as preachers as well. In consequence, preaching by members of the older monastic orders and before monastic audiences during the last medieval centuries has never attracted much interest among historians or literary scholars. To be sure, the large-scale overviews of medieval preaching in general—Schneyer's for Germany, Longère's for France, and Owst's for England[1]—give us the names of some monk preachers who were active in the fourteenth and fifteenth centuries. But at the same time, these historical accounts draw a picture in which monks had occupied the stage during earlier ages, their preaching attaining a climax with St. Bernard of Clairvaux in the twelfth century, but from about 1200 on yielded the task of preaching the Good News to the new orders, the friars, whose work from then on dominates our modern attention. The reason for the historical shift from monks to friars is not hard to see: by definition, monks withdrew from the world and lived lives that were devoted to the performance of the liturgy and to the pursuit of an ideal of holiness that was to be attained within the walls of the cloister; on the other hand, the new orders that came into being shortly after 1200 made it their business to go out and preach God's word to the masses—St. Dominic and his fellow preachers to heretics and wavering Christians in southern France, St. Francis and his companions to the masses in the Italian countryside as well as the newly flourishing urban centers, who were then not being reached by the established parish clergy or the older religious orders. Hence it is that in the view of modern accounts, once Dominicans and Franciscans began their tremendously energetic work of preaching, the older monastic orders lose nearly all significance in the history of preaching during the later medieval centuries. In Gerald Owst's words: "By the time . . . that the age of Fitzralph and of Wycliffe has begun, all the great names in the history of monastic eloquence have disappeared, and the pulpit here seems to share in the general decline of cloister fame and cloister influence. . . . Vital, potent interest in preaching . . . appears to be dead. This fact may possibly be reflected in the actual dearth of fresh monastic sermon literature for the periods under our examination."[2]

While there may be some truth to the general tenor of this assertion, its details are by no means accurate and call for revision, because the later fourteenth century witnessed a definite resurgence of interest in preaching among Benedictines and other monastic orders, and fresh monastic sermon literature produced near the end of the fourteenth and the early fifteenth centuries does in fact exist. The renewed interest in preaching left its traces at various levels, from monastic legislation to actual sermon collections. In 1336, Pope Benedict XII, himself a devout Benedictine monk, issued a bull that revitalized earlier monastic customs and formulated precise laws about two aspects of Benedictine life in England that were closely related to preaching: the provincial chapter and higher studies of monks at the university, to which I shall return in a moment.[3] Signs of this renewed interest can likewise be found in relevant activities of individual monks that are known to us by name. For example, John Sheppey of Rochester priory (ca. 1300–60) left two manuscripts filled with sermons given by preachers, including Franciscans, which he collected while he was studying at Oxford.[4] Another monk, Thomas Brinton from Norwich, collected the sermons he had preached while he was bishop of Rochester between 1373 and 1389.[5] Rochester priory itself owned a copy of the great collection of preaching materials made by the Dominican John Bromyard, which is so well known to and frequently quoted by students of Chaucer and Langland.[6] And still another monk, Ranulph Higden from Chester (d. 1363 or 1365), even wrote a handbook for preachers.[7]

There are, in addition, monastic records that tell us of particular occasions at which monastic sermons were given. The most detailed information we have concerns the provincial chapter. The already mentioned bull by Pope Benedict XII, *Summi magistri*, ordered that the heads of Benedictine houses in both ecclesiastical provinces of England, that is, Canterbury and York, should no longer meet separately as they had done for some time but come together in one place every three years to discuss and legislate on matters pertaining to the order in England. That was indeed done, from 1338 on, in the geographical center of England, Northampton. A good number of records have preserved detailed accounts of the agendas of these chapters as well as the ceremonies that accompanied them. Thus, as the chapter opened, all the abbots and priors and other clergy who had traveled to Northampton would, at the sign of a bell, assemble to hear a mass of the Holy Spirit. When mass was over, the bell would ring again, and the attendants then proceeded to the chapter house, where they put on their monastic habits and listened to a sermon, which was preached in Latin, "as it was fitting." When that was over, all secular clergy had to leave, and the business of the Benedictine provincial chapter began in earnest. Two days later, the chapter would close with another procession, mass, and sermon, but this one was to be given "to the people in the vulgar tongue," that is, presumably, in English. Just before these closing ceremonies, the chapter had already selected preachers who were to give these two sermons at the next provincial chapter three years later.[8] Our records have preserved the names of several preachers who were assigned to these occasions as well as the biblical texts for their sermons and occasionally even the amount of whatever remuneration they received for their labors.[9]

Similar formalities were used for chapter meetings in individual houses, especially when the community gathered for such momentous events as the election of a new abbot[10] or, in the case of Canterbury, the archbishop.[11] Some preaching may also have occurred at the daily or weekly chapter meetings in each Benedictine monastery, at which matters concerning the welfare of the community and the morals of its individual members were discussed, though such preaching has left no unequivocal traces in the manuscripts I have drawn on. Another occasion at which a sermon was given before the monastic community was the visitation, when a member of the same or a different order or any high-ranking prelate came from outside to see if all was well within a monastic house.[12] Thus, in 1378 the large monastery of St. Albans was visited by two monks from Ramsey, one of whom started the check-up with a sermon.[13] Again, some forty years later the same monastery was visited by the prior of Bardeney, who preached a sermon on the thema "A wellspring rose from the earth." It is pleasant to hear that "in this visitation they found nothing except that all things were worthy of praise."[14] Among several surviving visitation sermons, one explicitly states that preaching on this occasion was indeed "customary in our order."[15]

And there were other special occasions thus distinguished with a sermon, ranging from the profession of two monks at St. Albans in 1430[16] to the funeral ceremonies for Duchess Blanche of Lancaster, whose sermon, delivered by the bishop of Cloyne, Ireland, has, as far as I know, to the regret of Chaucerians not been preserved.[17]

But Benedictines gave sermons outside the monastery as well. In the beginning years of the fifteenth century, several monks from Canterbury are on record as having preached at various synodal meetings in London, an honor they shared with the bishop of Carlisle as well as the Franciscan provincial for England.[18] Yet another occasion must not only be mentioned but highlighted, because of the relatively large number of extant sermons connected with it. This is the preaching of academic sermons at the university, presumably Oxford. By the end of the fourteenth century, Oxford had three study houses for Benedictine monks: one only recently founded by and for monks from Canterbury; another for monks from Durham priory, which by then was about a century old; and the third—Gloucester College on the grounds of what today is Worcester College—for students that came mostly from southern England and also in operation for about a century. These foundations owed their existence to various orders coming all the way from Rome. Though Pope Benedict and his predecessors did not actually found a college, dreading, as it were, to leave an illiterate ministry to the Church, they were certainly much concerned with educating the clergy including young monks. A number of mandates thus stipulated that each Benedictine house was to send a determined proportion of its younger members to the university, where they should live in a common house of studies, and that their abbots were to make sufficient funds available so that these young men could devote themselves to the study of theology and, to a lesser degree, canon and civil law (1336).[19] Such papal orders were not only eagerly taken up by the English provincial chapter but in fact extended. In particular, the bull *Summi magistri* had only spoken of theology and law as disciplines for which monks should be sent to the university.[20] In the resolutions issued by provincial chapters in England, however, we find an added, strong emphasis on preaching as another subject to study at the university. For example, the chapter of 1338 declares:

> In order that our faith, which through the ages has spread its fronds from sea to sea, may be fittingly illumined by the bright rays of virtues, it has been firmly enjoined through the aforementioned presidents [of the chapter] by apostolic authority that each prelate is to ordain and install

those from his convent whom he knows to be able and prepared for the office of preaching, to preach God's word both in private and in public, with wisdom and discretion, so that the candle that has once been lighted may not be hid under the bushel but, placed on a candlestick, may shine forth to all who are in the house of God.[21]

And a later chapter, probably of 1363, makes it clear that some monks were sent to Oxford, not to read philosophy or theology but specifically to learn how to preach. The prelates meeting at this chapter, after recommending that students of philosophy and theology should engage in regular disputations, then turned their attention to "those who are sent to the university for the single purpose of learning how they may fittingly preach God's word to others," and ordered that they, "according to the disposition made by their prior and the more advanced students preach frequently both in Latin and in English, in our common study house in Oxford or elsewhere, as their prior and the more advanced students may decree. In this way they will be able to preach more boldly and readily when it is necessary to recall them to their monastery."[22] And indeed, other records tell us not only of students returning to their monasteries for major feast days and preaching there to their spiritual family,[23] but also of established Benedictine university professors being recalled to look after the business of preaching at home.[24]

In this wide array of occasions for preaching, one place and time one would have expected to find, however, is missing, and that is the normal parish church on a Sunday morning. The reason for this absence is that Benedictine monks were normally not in charge of parishes and did not engage in the cure of souls. Although many monasteries held parish churches as their property and sources of income, the required pastoral duties were usually carried out by non-monastic vicars appointed for that purpose.[25] On the other hand, we must remember that many of those magnificent buildings which make the Middle Ages so delightfully visible to present-day visitors to England: Westminster Abbey, Canterbury Cathedral, the cathedrals at York, Worcester, Winchester, Durham, Rochester, and many others, were formerly parts of monastic institutions. These are large churches which must have been filled with layfolk for the Sunday and other services. It stands to reason that in them monks not only said mass and heard confession but also preached on occasion. Quite recently Dr. Joan Greatrex has studied the extant documentary evidence from Worcester and pointed out that in 1290 the pope granted the monks there license "to preach in public before the people in Worcester and in other churches belonging to them or of their patronage." A number of unpublished records from the fourteenth and early fifteenth century further indicate that indeed Worcester monks were charged with preaching in public, were paid for it, and were called home from Oxford for just that purpose.[26] Similarly, Thomas Brinton was asked to come home from Oxford to preach in the monastic cathedral of Norwich;[27] and after he became bishop of Rochester, he preached not only in his own cathedral in the city but at several churches in the countryside as well.[28]

The records on which I have so far relied, therefore, show quite clearly that in the fourteenth and fifteenth centuries Benedictines were actively interested in the office of preaching and in fact practiced it on a variety of occasions. This much has been known for some time. What has remained obscure to date is precisely what was said on those occasions, and in what form it was spoken; in other words, what has been missing in this picture are actual sermons made and preached by English Benedictines. The sermons by Bishop Thomas Brinton, which were edited nearly forty years ago, are not as helpful in this respect as one could hope, since they were given to all sorts of audiences and hence can, in their totality, not be considered characteristic of a specifically monastic milieu. In contrast, my own work on bilingual sermons from the age of Chaucer has led me to a number of precisely such sermons, which have so far not received the attention they deserve as documents of monastic preaching. I must stress that this material has come to my notice coincidentally, in the wake of trawling the seas of manuscripts in search of macaronic pieces of whatever provenance. Undoubtedly there are other manuscripts in existence that contain further fruits of Benedictine preaching in the period from about 1380 to about 1430; but I am confident that the material I will in the following draw on gives us a good and sufficiently trustworthy picture of what English Benedictines spoke from the pulpit during this period.

But first a few words must be said about how we know that a given sermon is monastic. Medieval manuscripts, alas, never contain neat title pages that might say something like, "Monastic Sermons by Dom So-and-So, published at St. Mary's Abbey, York, in 1399." Even worse, manuscripts of sermons more often than not gather a wide variety of pieces that were given before all sorts of audiences, monastic and otherwise, and were very probably not written by a single author. Thus, the best we can do is to examine each sermon separately, look for incidental notes in the margins, and often be content with inferences drawn from the texts themselves. The surest kind of evidence for monastic provenance would be a title or a marginal remark that tells us the name of a monk who wrote or preached the piece. Thus we learn that John Paunteley gave a sermon at the funeral of Walter Frouceter, abbot of Gloucester, on May 3, 1412;[29] or that Master John Fordham, who is known to us from other sources as a monk from Worcester priory, preached a sermon at the general chapter;[30] or that Hugh Legat, a monk from St. Albans, made a sermon for Passion Sunday.[31] Somewhat less satisfactory are rubrics that tell us that a sermon was preached in a definitely monastic environment but that withhold the name of its preacher. For instance, we hear that one piece was delivered "at Northampton in the general chapter of the black monks," and another similarly "in convocation or the general chapter."[32] But even such brief marginal labels are, unfortunately, extremely rare, and the search for monastic sermons must often be satisfied with clues that occur within the texts of the sermons themselves. Here our best indication comes from direct references to the order and its founder. Such remarks as "our venerable father Benedict"[33] or "the lawgiver of monks, the most holy father Benedict"[34] or "we religious who entered the religious life and strive to be imitators of blessed Benedict"[35] or "let us not be followers of Epicurus but . . . rather imitate, as per our rule, the footsteps of our patron, who in fact and name was Benedictus"[36] clearly establish the religious affiliation of the preacher and his audience. Yet another possible indicator is the form of address used at the beginning of a sermon. Sermons beginning with "Reverendi domini" or "Venerandi patres et domini" indicate that their audiences were clerical, though these need not have been monastic communities. To be sure of the latter, one must look for further support from the text itself, support that may include certain stylistic features that also occur in undoubtedly monastic pieces. For example, the already mentioned Master John Fordham of Worcester cultivated a style and rhetoric of his own and even used a peculiar form of address in the sermon which bears his name. When we find the same features elsewhere, we can reasonably add further pieces to his output.

With the use of these various indicators one can establish a fairly sizeable and certain corpus of Benedictine sermons made and preached in the period with which I am concerned. In the following, I will limit myself to those sermons that address a Benedictine audience explicitly. There are, in the manuscripts I have examined, about thirty-five that do so clearly.[37] Four of them were given at provincial chapters, four or five at visitations, and two to a university audience, most likely at Oxford. In addition, beyond one funeral sermon we have six or seven pieces for various Sundays or feast days of the church year, and at least a dozen for saints' feasts. The latter are for

St. Alban, St. Benedict, and the Blessed Virgin, who received a surprising total of seven sermons.

As one might expect, sermons in honor of a saint are basically eulogistic oratory, and indeed much in this entire body of texts follows the conventions of medieval pulpit rhetoric in both form and content. Like medieval preaching in general, monastic sermons largely exhort their audiences to do penance and strive for the good life by praising virtues and condemning vices. Rather than belaboring these commonplaces, I will focus on three more particular concerns that strike me as characteristic and significant. These relate to the monastic ideal, the state of the nation, and the intellectual life.

The monastic ideal is, in our sermons, not unexpectedly presented as having a special and privileged status in God's kingdom on earth:

> The heavenly husbandman—order and measure of the entire sublunary world as well as the eternal mansion . . . planted a chosen vineyard in a rich soil, namely our holy monastic order . . . The plants of this monastic vineyard have given such strength to the garden of the church on earth that before all other orders it grows strong in its vines, blossoms in its sprigs, and constantly brings forth fruit in its grapes; it gets often tied fast with the bonds of obedience, cleaned out with diligence through giving up one's property, dug up deeply through mortification of one's flesh, and enlarged through health-giving statutes and counsels.[38]

Thus the monastic life is said to have been established as a special school, a *gymnasium* superior to the Platonic Academy in Athens, because in it divine Wisdom herself has made her dwelling place to teach man virtue and to help him on his way to heaven.[39] Its founder in the West, St. Benedict, was a second Abraham because he left his kin and homeland to follow God's call and promises and was rewarded with a large offspring.[40] His disciples have vowed themselves to walk the narrow path; they are set to worship the divine name before all other men, and their lifestyle is exemplary for the whole church. Monks must be models to all Christians by the holiness of their life and their works of contemplation. "You who are more firm and experienced in Christian spiritual warfare," says one preacher, "must feed your brethren, namely by teaching and example . . . , now in devout prayer, now in waking, now in chastising your bodies by fasting, and in practicing other works of a similar nature."[41]

The cornerstones of this lifestyle and the foundation of monastic discipline are the traditional vows of obedience, poverty, chastity, and stability of place. In a life shaped by the rule of St. Benedict, these vows translate into such specific practices as submitting oneself to the will and guidance of one's superior, fasting and praying, abstaining from meat, guarding one's senses, and keeping silence. If this rule is truly observed, it will foster humility, charity, and love, and lead to the peace of a community that lives in complete harmony. "Let us therefore give our hearts to God through silence and holy meditation with respect to our intellect; through love and compassion with respect to our will; and through obedience, chastity and the renunciation of our possessions with regard to our actions, so that clad in this threefold armor of our monastic life, by following the footsteps of our father Benedict we may keep ourselves the more securely unstained of the world."[42]

The harmonious community thus aimed for, so Master John Ford tells the abbots and priors gathered at the provincial chapter, is like a living organism. It must not be "a tumultuous crowd but a group of people at peace forming one mystical body" in which "the minds of all individuals should be bound to each other inseparably with the bond of charity and the glue of love, so that, like members in one and the same body, they suffer or rejoice with each other over" whatever bad or good fortune might befall a single member of their community.[43] In this living organism, different members have different functions. The majority of monks would devote themselves to prayer and contemplation, while a few others would serve as officers of the monastery and look after the necessary physical, economic, and financial details to ensure the conditions for a life of contemplation. Finally the abbot or prior would rule and guide the whole house with wisdom, strength, and clemency.[44] It is interesting to note that in this analysis of different functions within the same organism, the active life of monastic officers is often discussed in almost apologetic tones: they are absolutely necessary to the fulfillment of the religious vocation of all the monks and must not be looked down upon as, so to speak, second-class citizens. In the words of another sermon, which uses a simpler twofold pattern, "the city of our religious life is, as it were, governed and protected by two kinds of troops. Our officials and administrators of temporal goods procure and provide what is necessary for the life of the brothers and defend the rights of our order against the outside. At the same time, our cloistered monks give themselves to continuous prayer, to meditations on scripture, and to the performance of the divine services. Thus Mary is at her leisure and Martha is busily at work."[45]

But sermons by nature deal not only with ideals and virtues, they also look at vices and failings. Hence a number of those directed to Benedictine audiences speak, however generally, of the moral shortcomings and the decadence which the entire order has fallen into. Things nowadays are no longer what they once were. "Where under the roof of the cloister, I pray," one preacher exclaims, "do we find a Jerome who through his prolonged zeal for virtue and his diligent reading tries to come to the light of true learning and a knowledge of letters? Nor can hardly anyone be found who with Bernard savors the sweetness of devotion," and so forth.[46] Not only do the main goals of the monastic life remain unattained, but the very activities and practices typical of cloistered life as it is regulated by St. Benedict's Rule are being neglected:

> To our monks of today the sweetness of holy reading does not appeal, the eagerness of devout prayer has faded, and devotion to contemplative holiness has become tedious. Where, I ask, does the ready obedience of our holy fathers still rule? Where are that perfect charity and genuine humility that once flourished in the cloistered school for an honest life, that is, the paradise of monks? If I must speak the truth, obedience is dead, humility is banished, charity has vanished away, and that honorable reverence that younger monks ought to give to the advanced years of their seniors has, through boyish levity, been turned into derision. Now the limits of modesty are being overstepped, the discipline of fasting is broken, and the tongues of quiet monks who should attend to holy readings and keep a devout silence, are loosened for frivolous and idle tales in the treasury of the cloister. And so they often seem to practice the school of virtues, not in exercises of pious contemplation, but rather in strife and contention.[47]

Such behavior of course goes directly against the foundation of the monastic life, the Rule:

> Our rule suggests and commands that at opportune times we observe silence; but certain monks go directly against this when they take no care to guard against scurrilous words and foul speech in the choir or the dormitory. Our rule commands us to observe a religious and disciplined lifestyle; but some monks go directly against this when they take too much delight in fanciful, precious, and superfluous clothing. Our rule tells us what is sufficient for our livelihood and admonishes us to be modest and sparing in what we eat and drink; but some monks go directly against this when

they think they may eat as often and whenever and in whatever places they desire and engage in drunken revelry and singing until midnight. Our rule forbids us to leave the cloister without permission from the abbot or prior; but some monks go directly against this when, contrary to canon law, they go hunting in fields and woods with loud shouting and keep hunting dogs in the monastic enclosure. . . . We monks are held to celebrate Mass twice or three times a week; but some monks go directly against this constitution when they claim they are unfit or indisposed to celebrate because of their administrative duties. . . . And when such monks are reproved for their abuses in chapter, they try to defend their sins against their superiors, to appeal the penalties they receive according to the rule, and to murmur and rebel against the commands and counsels of their superiors.[48]

To these infractions of monastic regulations and practices I will add two further failings that might be of special interest for historians of literature. First, the vice of slander and envy, which not only reappears in several laments of this kind but is frequently singled out for more detailed elaboration: "If a monk studies or devotes his time to contemplation, they call him a hypocrite; if he practices patience, they call him timid; if he strives after simpleness, they call him a fool; if he is intent upon justice, they call him impatient; if he is devout, they call him an oddball; if he is solicitous about his preaching, they say he is after praise; and if he is well liked by the people, they call him a flatterer."[49] So it is no wonder when, in contrast, a funeral sermon eulogizes the deceased abbot of Gloucester at some length for "this commendable quality, that he would not willingly hear any evil about anyone, nor believe any stories, and if he heard any, he would interpret them in the best way. . . . It was extremely difficult to make him think ill of a friend. And even if someone told him something bad about his friend, he would answer as Socrates did with regard to his disciple: 'So you say,' as if he were saying, you have said so, whether it is true or not."[50]

The other peculiar feature is the lament at the decadence in monastic book production:

> In former times both older and younger brothers used to write books with their own hands. Many wrote a large number of codices in the free time they could snatch between the canonical hours of prayer, and they devoted times that were set aside for their bodily rest to the making of books. As a result of their labors, sacred treasuries shine in many monastic houses to our day, filled with divers books, to give salutary knowledge to those who

wish to study it and a pleasant light on their way to others.... But alas, books are yielding to Bacchus, compilation gives way to compotation,

and so on.[51]

Complaints at current vices, at the falling off from a higher state that had been reached in the past, also form part of the second major concern that appears throughout these monastic sermons, namely the lamentable condition of contemporary society. It is especially a group of very remarkable pieces in Oxford, Bodleian Library, MS Bodley 649 that return again and again to this topic, sermons that have deservedly drawn the attention of such church historians as Professor Roy Haines.[52] Using several different images, such as the ship of state or the vineyard, the preacher speaks of the glory and high reputation England enjoyed in the past, both at home and abroad. "All Christian nations," he says in once case,

> once feared and honored the English because of their strength, their good government, and the good life they led. While our ship was thus steered with the rudder of virtue, we traveled on a sea of wealth and prosperity. Fortune was our friend, our honor increased. But as soon as virtue declined and vices began to rule, Fortune changed her face and our honor started to wane. Our ship was so feeble, our enemies set so little store by us, that the little fishing boats of Wales were about to oversail us. Through pride and sin we traveled from wealth to woe. There was much woe and tribulation in this country; many mishaps rose up among us on account of sin; storms of conflict and dissent blew up hard. Our ship was so hurled and tossed about among tempests and straits that is was in great peril and often in danger of drowning.

He then lists a number of specific political upheavals that occurred in the reigns of Richard II and Henry IV, but eventually goes on to praise Henry V, "this wise mariner, this most worthy warrior," for leading the ship of state out of those troubled waters into the new glory achieved at Agincourt.[53]

The same group of sermons links another theme to that of military decadence, namely the coming of heresy, which has undermined faith and traditional religious practices. It is the Lollards, normally referred to by that name, who have sown tares in the English wheat and who are leading simple folks astray with their erroneous teachings about the Eucharist, the spiritual power of pope and parish priests, the effectiveness and required use of the sacraments, and the legitimacy of giving tithes and of following such traditional practices as praying to saints, worshipping images, and going on pilgrimages.

This anti-Lollard stance and the pride in England's military achievement are very characteristic of the sermons in MS Bodley 649; but they appear also elsewhere in Benedictine preaching. In one of the Middle English sermons contained in a manuscript of Worcester Cathedral and edited by Grisdale, for example, the preacher, after mentioning the Lollards by name, exclaims: "You see well what battles and war we have among us, may God for his great mercy stop them in good time! What pestilence also, what scarcity of goods, for there is hardly anyone, whether poor or rich, who does not complain about his goods. Yea, and many other countries look at us with hatred and scorn and hold us to be the worst people, the most false under the sun. And this, trust you well, is because of our wickedness and our bad morals and these cursed errors and heresies that are upheld in our midst."[54]

I now turn to the third major concern of Benedictine preaching, the intellectual life. A number of sermons express without equivocation the view that learning is an integral and necessary part of the monastic existence. We have already heard one preacher lament that manuscripts are no longer copied, and another look in vain for the likes of St. Jerome and his great learning. The ideal is nicely formulated in a sermon that likens the monastery to a vineyard and concludes that, like the lily which is pale in its roots, green in its leaves, and redolent, monks should "grow pale in the fruitful recitation of holy scripture, . . . put forth green leaves in writing books, and . . . spread a sweet odor in acquiring knowledge."[55]

Such learning included the technical study of philosophy and theology as it was undertaken at the university. One of the monastic sermon collections I am dealing with has preserved several formal eulogies of these disciplines in what must have been opening lectures in academic courses on Peter Lombard and the Bible. These pieces link graduate study at the university intimately to the monastic and contemplative life. And they expect that monk students bring a greater seriousness and holier life to the university than their fellow students: "The more we progress in learning, the more we are obligated to grow in good morals and increase in virtues, and to display this increase publicly. For the monk student must appear more mature in his behavior than others, less given to laughter, more pure in his speech, more humble in his bearing, more meek in appearance, more devout in his dress, so that whoever looks at him will grant that he sees a son of Saint Benedict, an angel of the Lord as it were, indeed the very rule of life."[56]

Concern with the intellectual life shows itself further quite concretely in the style of these sermons. Their general structure is unvaryingly that of the so-called scholastic sermon, with its peculiar logical and rhetorical rigor that underlies their tight logical and verbal structure and a careful, often labored development. These sermons are not products of the moment, of an ad hoc inspiration, but instead smell of the lamp and midnight oil. They are learned, in the sense of gathering a wealth of carefully chosen and apt biblical and other quotations, and they are sophisticated, often to the point of being tortuous, in carrying out the structural rules set forth in contemporary arts of preaching. The result must often have been appealing to refined intellects, though one suspects that it also may have left some hearts rather cold and, perhaps, some faces blank and yawning. There is a little vignette of some relevance in a contemporary monastic chronicle which I cannot help finding rather amusing in this respect. In 1374 King Edward III called together a council at Westminster. There the king and the archbishop of Canterbury sit in the middle, with the higher prelates of the realm next to the archbishop, and the lords of the kingdom next to the king. In front of them are four masters of theology on a bench: the provincial of the Franciscans, the Benedictine monk Uhtred from Durham priory, the Franciscan friar John Mardesley, and an Austin friar. The pope had written to king Edward claiming that he, the pope, was the general overlord over all temporal possessions of the church in England, and Edward now wants to know what his higher churchmen think of that. So the archbishop says, yes, we can't deny that the pope has such overlordship. The Franciscan provincial begs to be excused until he has recited the hymn "Veni Creator Spiritus" or at least said a Mass of the Holy Spirit. Then our monk Uhtred gets up and "answers in the form of a sermon, taking as his beginning the verse 'Lo, here are two swords,' by which he intends to show that Peter has both temporal and spiritual lordship." But when he sits down. Friar Mardesley rises to his feet, quotes the scriptural words "Put your sword into its sheath," and shows that those swords do not signify temporal power. "Which he did by quoting Scripture and the gospels, with authoritative words of the fathers as well as the example of monks who left their possessions behind, and with decretals from Canon Law." The discussion goes on for quite a bit longer, in which the archbishop mumbles, "We had good advice in England without the friars," and in turn gets himself called "ass" by his king.[57] But what matters in this little drama for our purposes is the apparent difference in the style in which Benedictine monk and Franciscan friar—both incidentally university men and professors—address the issue and clash: one producing a sermon on a text that was an old chestnut in discussions of this issue, the other evidently furnishing a more rational argumentation based on a much wider array of texts and proofs. Friar Mardesley simply throws the book, not only at the papist position but also at Dom Uhtred of Boldon.

I should, in all fairness, add that the British historian William Pantin has called this account "a picturesque but probably unreliable passage," possibly "fictitious and in the nature of a pamphlet."[58] But whatever its historical accuracy may be, the impression of stodginess, rhetorical inefficiency, and even political irrelevance which the account conveys of Master Uhtred is of course precisely what lies at the root of the modern view of the decline of monastic preaching with which I began this lecture. And yet, I have to say that this impression does not do justice to the reflections of an intellectual and literary life that I find in the monastic preaching of around 1400. For one thing, these sermons quote, not only the Bible, church fathers, and pagan writers as any good medieval sermon does, but also medieval poets of more recent vintage. Especially Alanus of Lille appears in several Benedictine sermons, with quotations from both his *Anticlaudianus* and the *De planctu Naturae*.[59] Another medieval poem, likewise of the twelfth century, that finds its way into monastic preaching is the *Architrenius* by John of Hanville.[60] In addition, these sermons show a knowledge of classical literature which, by medieval standards, must be called respectable. This appears not only in the fact that monastic preachers borrowed stories from Ovid which here come from farther afield than the normal run-of-the-mill material, but also in the very style these Benedictine writers cultivate. They do not hesitate to refer to the Almighty as *rector Olimpi*[61] or speak of Homer's Golden Chain.[62] Nor do they refrain from weaving classical allusions intimately into monastic discourse, as in the following sentence, where the allusion to the labyrinth of the Minotaur appears suddenly without a previous reference to the classical myth: "You therefore, reverend brethren, . . . with the thread of our reasonable Rule as your guide walk out of the labyrinth of such abuses."[63] Nor do they abstain from producing some scintillating rhetorical firework, often at points where, of all places, they protest their own humility: "If I had acquired the keys of worldly knowledge with Paul and had learned all kinds of languages so that I could, with the honey-sweet voice of Mercury, pass beyond the flowery verbal eloquence of Cicero's throat, I would still be found to be insufficient, dumb and ignorant when it comes to speak the praise of our keeper [the Blessed Virgin]."[64] The speaker of these lines identifies himself as a junior member of his community, and one could therefore see in the quoted lines the rhetorical exuberance of an undergraduate fresh home from, say, Oxford or Harvard. Yet more mature heads took an equal delight in starting a sermon off with similar fireworks or addressing the assembled heads of religious houses as *patres conscripti*, as if they were Roman senators,[65] and putting in an ironic aside that some of them might have come to the provincial chapter in order to taste what he labels "Falernian cups" rather than attend to the order's business.[66]

This is rather different from the revival of interest in classical myth and fable which engaged earlier fourteenth-century friars and which Beryl Smalley has called attention to.[67] Like those friars, monastic preachers also draw on Ovid and moralize with gusto, but as my quotations will have shown, their classical learning penetrates more deeply into the very texture of their style than is the case with the preaching friars. Such affinity with the classics was by no means a new phenomenon in the fourteenth century; it can also be found in monastic authors of the twelfth century, where it has received some fine attention in Father Jean Leclercq's study of monastic culture.[68] The point here is that the sermons I have been discussing show that around 1400, English Benedictines were keenly interested in cultivating intellectual pursuits, which included reading the classics and using this knowledge in their preaching, an interest that appears not only in the sermons I have been examining but also more generally in the large collections of classical material made, for instance, by Thomas of Walsingham and John Whethamstede, who were both Oxford-trained monks living in the monastery of St. Albans.[69]

During the years in which I had the privilege of sharing Morton Bloomfield's intellectual presence and receiving his scholarly guidance, he himself was immersed in a study of medieval monasticism and its possible influence on *Piers Plowman*. This lecture is not the occasion to evaluate the book that resulted from those studies. But it is an entirely appropriate and accurate tribute to the man and his wide-ranging learning which these lectures commemorate if I conclude by stressing that, beyond the evidence Morton had at his disposition a generation ago, the material I have here surveyed certainly bears out his hunch that in the 1370s and 80s English Benedictine monasticism was anything but a dead institution and spent intellectual effort.

Notes

1. Johannes Baptist Schneyer, *Geschichte der katholischen Predigt* (Freiburg i. Br.: Seelsorge Verlag, 1969); Jean Longère, *La prédication médiévale* (Paris: Etudes augustiniennes, 1983); G. R. Owst, *Preaching in Medieval England: An Introduction to Sermon MSS of the Period c. 1350–1450* (Cambridge: Cambridge University Press, 1926; repr. 1965).

2. Owst, *Preaching*, 49.

3. See David Knowles, *The Religious Orders in England*, vol. 2, *The End of the Middle Ages* (Cambridge: Cambridge University Press, 1955), 3 ff. The bull, *Summi magistri*, has been printed in David Wilkins, *Concilia Magnae Britanniae et Hiberniae* (London, 1737), 2:588 ff.

4. These are MSS Oxford, Merton College 248 and New College 92; see G. Mifsud, "John Sheppey, Bishop of Rochester, as Preacher and Collector of Sermons," (unpublished B. Litt. thesis, Oxford, 1953). A more recent account of Sheppey is given by Alberic Stacpoole, "Jean Sheppey," in *Dictionnaire de spiritualité ascétique et mystique*, vol. 8 (Paris: G. Beauchesne et ses fils, 1974), 763–64. Further on Sheppey's preaching oeuvre see Siegfried Wenzel, *Latin Sermon Collections from Later Medieval England* (= *Collections*), (Cambridge: Cambridge University Press, 2005), 26–30.

5. *The Sermons of Thomas Brinton, Bishop of Rochester (1373–1389)*, ed. Sister Mary Aquinas Devlin, 2 vols., Camden Third Series 85–86 (London: Offices of the Royal Historical Society, 1954). See also Wenzel, *Collections*, 45–49.

6. Now British Library, MS Royal 7.E.iv (*Summa predicantium*).

7. See Margaret Jennings, ed., *The Ars Componendi Sermones of Ranulph Higden O.S.B.* (Leiden: Brill, 1991).

8. This brief account is based on the statutes issued by the provincial chapter of 1343; see W. A. Pantin, *Documents Illustrating the Activities of the General and Provincial Chapters of the English Black Monks 1215–1540*, 3 vols. (= *Chapters*), Camden Third Series 45, 47, 54 (London: Offices of the Society, 1931–37), 2:58–61. Some of the practices described are also recorded for earlier chapters, both before and after the two provinces were united in 1336.

9. See for example Pantin, *Chapters*, 2:12, 13, 15, 19–20, 26, 97, 155, 156, etc. The statutes of 1444 stipulate a fee of 40 shillings (2:216–17).

10. At St. Albans, 1326; see Thomas Walsingham, *Gesta Abbatum Monasterii Sancti Albani*, ed. Henry Thomas Riley, Rolls Series 28, pt. 4, vol. 2 (London, 1867), 183. Again, in 1396: pt. 4, vol. 3, p. 426.

11. Roy Martin Haines, *Ecclesia anglicana: Studies in the English Church of the Later Middle Ages* (Toronto: University of Toronto Press, 1989), 17, 27, 32.

12. Owst, *Preaching*, 52–54. The occasions of monastic preaching have been reviewed in Wenzel, *Collections*, 278–87. An English translation of a monastic visitation sermon (W-130) can be found in *Preaching in the Age of Chaucer: Selected Sermons*

in Translation, trans. Siegfried Wenzel (=*Preaching*) (Washington, DC: The Catholic University of America Press, 2008), chap. 23.

13. Thomas Walsingham, *Chronicon Angliae*, ed. E. M. Thompson, Rolls Series 64 (London, 1874), 203.

14. *Chronicon rerum gestarum in monasterio Sancti Albani*, in Rolls Series 28, vol. 3, pt. 5.1, p. 38.

15. "Cum iuxta laudabilem ordinis nostri consuetudinem visitacionem precedere sermo debeat salutaris," Sermon W-117, f. 222v. For the format by which I refer to sermons see below, note 37. All translations of Latin, Middle English, or macaronic texts in this paper are my own.

16. *Chronicon rerum gestarum*, p. 53.

17. Walsingham, *Gesta abbatum*, Rolls Series 28, vol. 4, pt. 3, p. 277.

18. Wilkins, *Concilia*, 3:273.

19. Knowles, *Religious Orders*, 2:14–24.

20. Chaps. 7–8 regulate study of "sciencie primitive" (grammar, logic, and philosophy) and higher studies (theology and the two laws), but do not mention preaching; Wilkins, *Concilia*, 2:594–96.

21. Pantin, *Chapters*, 2:11–12.

22. Pantin, *Chapters*, 2:76.

23. Ernest Harold Pearce, *Monks of Westminster* (Cambridge: Cambridge University Press, 1916), 27. In 1384, archbishop Courtenay had to order that monk students do not stay at home for more than two weeks: W. A. Pantin, *Canterbury College, Oxford*, 3 vols., Oxford Historical Society, n.s., 6–8 (Oxford: Clarendon, 1947–50), 3:176.

24. Knowles, *Religious Orders*, 2:58. For university preaching in general see Wenzel, *Collections*, 297–304.

25. Margaret Jennings has discussed the subject of monks and the cure of souls: "Monks and the *artes praedicandi* in the Time of Ranulph Higden," *Revue Bénédictine* 86 (1975): 119–28.

26. Joan Greatrex, "Benedictine Monk Scholars as Teachers and Preachers in the Later Middle Ages: Evidence from Worcester Cathedral Priory," in Joan Loades, ed., *Monastic Studies* II (1991): 213–25. See also Patrick J. Horner, "Benedictines and Preaching the Pastoralia in Late Medieval England: A Preliminary Inquiry," in *Medieval Monastic Preaching*, ed. Carolyn Muessig (Leiden, Boston, and Cologne: Brill, 1998), 279–92.

27. Knowles, *Religious Orders*, 2:58.

28. See the headnotes to his sermons in the edition by Devlin.

29. R-3, edited by Patrick J. Horner, FSC: "John Paunteley's Sermon at the Funeral of Walter Froucester, Abbot of Gloucester (1412)," *American Benedictine Review* 28 (1977): 147–66.

30. W-71.

31. W-2; edited by D. M. Grisdale, *Three Middle English Sermons from the Worcester Chapter Manuscript F.10* (Leeds: Kendal, 1939), 1–21.

32. British Library, MS Titus C.ix, fol. 26; and W-28, edited by W. A. Pantin, "A Sermon for a General Chapter," *Downside Review* 51 (1933): 291–308.

33. "Venerabilis pater noster Benedictus," J/5-13, fol. 67v.

34. "Monachorum legislator, sanctissimus pater Benedictus," R-5, fol. 29v.

35. "Nos religiosi, qui religionem ingressi sumus et beati Benedicti imitatores esse contendimus," R-18, fol. 88.

36. "Non simus igitur discipuli Epicuri sed . . . regulariter imitantes vestigia nostri patroni re et nomine Benedicti," R-29, fol. 143v.

37. They are, with their occasions: O-6 (3 Lent?); O-24 (Assumption, preached to Franciscans?); O-25; R-3 (funeral); R-6 (general chapter of Cistercians); R-18 (visitation); R-29 (Christmas Eve); R-31 (St. Alban); W-4 (Assumption; also in R-5); W-5 (Christmas Eve); W-13 (4 Lent, in English, to lay people?); W-28 (general chapter); W-71 (general chapter); W-102 (to clergy); W-104 (Conception or Nativity of the Blessed Virgin Mary); W-105 (Deposition of St. Benedict); W-113 (St. Benedict); W-117 (visitation); W-118 (visitation?); W-119 (St. Benedict); W-121; W-124 (Assumption); W-127; W-128; W-130 (visitation?); W-131 (St. Benedict); W-133 (Good Friday); W-134 (university); W-135; W-138? (Vigil of Assumption); W-139 (Assumption); W-143? (to clergy); W-152 (Maundy Thursday?); W-153; W-155 (Good Friday); W-156 (Assumption?); W-167 (university); J/5-13 (St. Benedict); London, British Library, MS Cotton Titus C.ix, fols. 26–27 (general chapter). The siglia used here as well as detailed inventories and discussions of the manuscripts can be found in Wenzel, *Collections*.

38. "Celestis quidem agricola, metrum et mensura tocius ordinis sublunaris et etheree mansionis, a luce prima in vesperam sue fabrice influens incrementa, vineam quandam electam in loco vberi, sanctam scilicet religionem monasticam, in vitibus sanctorum patrum nostrorum primo in Egipti partibus plantatam ad horam quam postea ab inimici lupi rapacitate sua dextera adquisitam in tocius Christianissimi [sic] terminos transtulit et transduxit. Cuius vinee monastice plantule terram orti militantis ecclesie sic firmarunt quod pre ceteris aliis religionibus in vitibus viret, in palmitibus floret, in botris fructificat incessanter, ligatur frequencius per funes obediencie, purgatur diligencius per abdicacionem proprietatis, foditur profundius per mortificacionem carnis proprie, et propagatur per salutaria statuta et consilia," W-130, fol. 249ra.

39. W-71, fol. 131rb.

40. In W-28, Abraham is considered the founder of monasticism: "Iste ergo princeps Abraham gerens tipum aptissimum prelatorum exemplare, monachatus posuit fundamentum," Pantin, "A Sermon," 298. Other references to Abraham in W-113, fol. 219; W-135, fol. 258vb.

41. "Qui estis solidiores et experti in militia religionis Christi, fratres vestros pascere, suple doctrina et exemplo, . . . nunc videlicet deuote orando, nunc vigiliis

insistendo, nunc corpus ieiuniis castigando, ac ceteris consimilibus bonis operibus semper inherendo," W-138, fol. 263 v.

42. "Sic ergo corda nostra Deo demus per silencium et sanctam meditacionem quantum ad intellectum, per amorem et compassionem quantum ad effectum [*read* affectum], per obediencam, castitatem, et proprietatis abdicacionem quantum ad effectum, ut hac triplici armatura nostre religionis armati qua nostre professionis executores effecti imitando vestigia sanctissimi patris nostri Benedicti ab hoc seculo . . . nosmetipsos securius," J/5-13, fol. 68 v.

43. "Vt igitur hec congregacio religiosa et religio congregata non tumultuosa turba sed multitudo pacata et vnum corpus misticum veraciter censeatur, sic insolubiliter caritatis compage et glucio dileccionis adinuicem colligandi sunt animi singulorum, vt ad instar diuersorum membrorum in eodem corpore que iuxta variam fortune exigenciam sibi inuicem compaciuntur eciam et congaudent quidquid vni acciderit quadam amica vicissitudine et vnione gratissima ad cumulum doloris vel gaudii omnes reputent esse suum," W-71, fol. 131vb.

44. W-130 analyzes these three groups of monks and their functions in the "vineyard" of the monastery at some length.

45. "Due quasi milicie sunt quibus regitur et protegitur ciuitas nostre religionis. Nam sicut officiales ministratores temporalium procurando et prouidendo fratribus vite necessaria et iura ordinis extrinseca defendendo mercione militant in acie sua, sic claustrales continuis oracionibus insistendo et in scripturis meditando ac eciam diuinis vacando seruiciis valde militant eciam in acie sua, sicque dum Maria vacat ocio, Martha ministrat," W-156, fol. 297.

46. "Sub claustri namque tecto, vbi iam queso reperitur Ieronimus qui per frequens virtutis studium leccionisque diligenciam ad vere sciencie lumen et litterarum noticiam nititur peruenire? Iam vix habetur aliquis qui cum Bernardo tante deuocionis sapit dulcedinem ut eterni solis splendorem, Christum Dei Filium, per interne meditacionis morulam sine graui fastidio valeat intueri," R-29, fol. 142v.

47. "Modernis namque claustralibus sacre leccionis non sapit suauitas, deuote oracionis languescit sedulitas, ac contemplatiue sanctitatis deuocio iam redditur tediosa. Vbi queso sanctorum patrum obediencia regnat sine mora? Vbi caritas perfecta seu humilitas non simulata, que quondam in uirtuoso honeste conuersacionis studio claustrali, scilicet paradiso floruerant monachorum? Certe, si verum fatear, obediencia iam moritur, humilitas proscribitur, et caritas euanescit, honorisque reuerencia que maturis seniorum etatibus foret a iuuenibus exhibenda iuuenili leuitate sepius uertitur in derisum. Iam metas modestie excedit sobrietas, sacri ieiunii violatur integritas, ac mutorum lingue claustralium qui sacris leccionibus uacantes assidue deuota seruarent silencia, circa friuolas vanitatis fabulas in claustri sacrario reserantur. Sicque scolam virtutum non ad pia contemplacionis exercicia sed ad contencionis litigia videntur frequencius exercere," W-4, fol. 17v.

48. "Nobis enim suadet regula nostra ac precipit oportunis temporibus silencium obseruare, et obstat quorundam monachorum abusio, qui nec in choro nec in

dormitorio nec in claustro curant verba scurilia et turpiloquia precauere. Precipit nobis regula nostra religiose et ordinate incedere, et obstat quorundam monachorum abusio qui in vestibus curiosi[s] operimentorum preciositate et superfluitate non modicum delectantur. Prestat nobis regula nostra victus sufficienciam et suadet in cibis et potibus modestie parcitatem; cui obstat quorundam monachorum abusio qui estimant sibi licere quocienscumque et quandocumque et quibuscumque locis indifferenter commedere et vsque ad mediam noctem suis potacionibus et aliis cantacionibus inhonestis insistere et vacare. Precipit nobis regula nostra claustrum sine abbatis aut presidentis alcius [?] non exire; cui obstat quorundam monachorum abusio qui contra canonicas sancciones presumunt in agris et siluis venacionibus clamosa voce intendere et infra ceptra monasterii canes venaticos retinere. Preterea, secundum scilicet Constitucionem Benedicti pape XII capitulo 27, tenemur nos monachos bis vel ter celebrare singulis septimanis; cui obstat quorundam monachorum abusio cuiusmodi sunt obedienciarii, qui dicunt se propter suas administraciones minus ydoneos et indispositos ad celebrandum. . . . Tales, karissimi, monachi si pro predictis abusionibus in suis capitulis pro[. . .]tur, statim contra precidentes sua peccata nituntur defendere, correcciones regulares appellare, et contra superiorum precepta et consilia murmurare et pertinaciter rebellare," W-128, fol. 243vb.

49. "Si quis studeat vel contemplacioni vacet, dicunt enim quod ypocrita est; si paciencie, timidus; si simplicitati, fatuus est; se iusticie, impaciens est; si religioni, singularis est; si predicacioni . . . , appetitor laudis; si coram hominibus acceptus fuerit, adulator est," W-124, fol. 236vb.

50. "Sed inter cetera habuit commendabilem condicionem: noluit libenter audire malum de aliqua persona, noluit credere fabulis, etsi audiret aliquam, vellet construere in partem meliorem. Et hoc fuit causa sue quietis et aliorum. Et si quisquam sibi suum reuelaret consilium, nusquam vellet detegere. Foret eciam valde difficile alicui facere ipsum male opinari de amico suo. Et siquis referret sibi malum de suo amico, responderet quandoque ad instar Socratis pro suo discipulo, 'Tu dixisti,' quasi diceret: cum verum vel non, tu ita dixisti," R-3, fol. 19. The sermon has been edited by Horner, "John Pauntley's Sermon," 147–66.

51. "Olym namque claustrales senes cum iunioribus vineas et vites librorum propriis manibus conscripserunt. Scribebant nonulli codices plures inter horas canonicas interuallis captatis, et tempora pro quiete corpori commendata fabricandis codicibus concesserunt. De quorum laboribus vsque in hodiernum diem in plerisque splendent monasteriis aliqua sacra gazophilacia diuersis libris plena ad dandam scienciam salutis studere volentibus atque lumen delectabilem semitis aliorum. . . . Sed prothdolor . . . iam fertur Liber Bachus respicitur et in ventrem . . . itur, liber codex despicitur et a manu eicitur, sicque calicibus epotandis non codicibus emendandis indulget hodie studium plurimorum," W-130, fols. 249vb-250ra. In translating the last sentence, where complaint leads to verbal punning, I have employed some poetic license in order to reproduce in English the kind of wordplay

that a modern audience is familiar with from the rhetoric of Jessie Jackson. The pun *codices /calices* appears again in W-139, fol. 265v.

52. Most recently: Roy M. Haines, *Ecclesia anglicana*, 201–21 and 333–50; earlier publications are listed on 333 n. 2. The macaronic sermons in O have now been edited with translations in Patrick J. Horner, *A Macaronic Sermon Collections from Late Medieval England: Oxford, MS Bodley 649* (= *Macaronic*) (Toronto: Pontifical Institute of Mediaeval Studies, 2006).

53. O-25, edited by Roy M. Haines, "'Our Master Mariner, Our Sovereign Lord': A Contemporary Preacher's View of King Henry V," *MS* 38 (1976): 85–96. The quoted passage appears on 89–90. Also in Horner, *Macronic*, 520–23

54. W-13, edited by Grisdale, *Three Middle English Sermons*, 41–42.

55. "Lilia enim pallent in radicibus, candent in foliis, virent in foliis, et redolent in humoribus atque granis. Sic enim claustrales psallerent [*sic;* read pallerent] in fructuosa sacre scripture recitacione, virerent in librorum composicione, et redolerent in sciencie adquisicione," W-130, fol. 250ra.

56. "Quantum in doctrina proficimus, tantum in morum honestate siue augmento virtutum succrescere et in huius incrementi protestaciones et signa ostendere obligamur. Debet namque scolasticus monachus ceteris in gestu apparere maturior, in risu suspensior, in affatu honestior, humilior in incessu, mansuecior in aspectu, religiosior in ornatu; vt quicumque talem attenderit, quasi filium sanctissimi Benedicti, quasi angelum Domini, tanquam ipsam normam viuendi se inuenisse concedat," W-134, fol. 258rb. See also Siegfried Wenzel, "Academic Sermons at Oxford in the Early Fifteenth Century," *Speculum* 79 (1995): 305–29.

57. See the account in Knowles, *Religious Orders*, 2:66, and in a privately printed thesis by M. E. Marcett, *Uhtred de Boldon, Friar William Jordan and Piers Plowman* (New York, 1938), 16–18. The event is reported in *Eulogium historiarum*, ed. Frank Scott Haydon, Rolls Series 9 (1863), vol. 3, pp. 337–39.

58. W. A. Pantin, *The English Church in the Fourteenth Century* (Cambridge, 1955; American edition, Notre Dame: Notre Dame University Press, 1963), 167.

59. Especially in R-31, fol. 154; and perhaps in W-14; W-67; W-107; W-143; and J/5-13, fol. 78v. The relevant passage from W-107 has been edited with translation in Siegfried Wenzel, "Why the Monk?" in *Words and Works: Studies in Medieval English Language and Literature in Honour of Fred C. Robinson*, ed. Peter S. Baker and Nicholas Howe (Toronto: University of Toronto Press, 1998), 265–66; to be reprinted in Siegfried Wenzel, *Elucidations: Medieval Poetry and Its Religious Backgrounds*, Synthema 6 (= *Elucidations*) (Louvain: Peeters, 2009), chap. 19.

60. R-31, fol. 154v.

61. W-143, fol. 271.

62. W-153, fol. 290vb, and W-167, fol. 336v.

63. "Vos igitur, reuerendi mei, quos iurate religionis votiua constringit professio habitusque autenticat in conuersacione monasticus, filo regulate racionis conductore harum abusionum conclusio uelocius discedite laborinto dulcedine litterarum vberius recreati," R-31, fol. 155v.

64. "Reuera si claues sciencie seculi suscepissem cum Paulo, omniumque genera linguarum hactenus taliter didicissem vt cum Mercurio mellite vocis dulcedine floridam uerborum eloquenciam Tulliani gutturis superarem, circa nostre procuratricis laudem non solum insufficiens reperirer, verum inscius et ignorans, mutus pariter et elinguis omnibus apparem," W-4, fol. 17v. The entire sermon has been translated in Wenzel, *Preaching*, chap. 16.

65. "Patres conscripti" appears in W-71, fol. 131va, and W-167, fol. 336.

66. British Library, MS Titus C.ix, fol. 26v.

67. Beryl Smalley, *English Friars and Antiquity in the Early Fourteenth Century* (Oxford: B. Blackwell, 1960). The use of pseudo-classical material studied by Smalley in later fourteenth- and fifteenth-century sermons has been discussed in Siegfried Wenzel, "The Classics in Late-Medieval Preaching," in *Mediaeval Antiquity*, ed. Andries Welkenhuysen, Herman Braet, and Werner Verbeke, Mediaevalia Lovaniensia, ser. 1, studia 24 (Leuven: Leuven University Press, 1995), 127–43; to be reprinted in Wenzel, *Elucidations*, chap. 8.

68. Jean Leclercq, *The Love of Learning and the Desire for God: A Study of Monastic Culture*, trans. Catharine Misrahi (New York: Fordham University Press, 1961), chap. 7. A more specific study of such classicizing style is R. W. Southern, "Peter of Blois: A Twelfth-Century Humanist?" in *Medieval Humanism* (New York: Harper & Row, 1970).

69. See Antonia Gransden, *Historical Writing in England*, vol. 2, *C. 1370 to the Early Sixteenth Century* (Ithaca: Cornell University Press, 1982), chaps. 5 and 12.

"Love and Do What You Will"
The Medieval History of an
Augustinian Precept [1996]

Giles Constable

St. Augustine used the precept "Love and do what you will" only twice in his known writings, but it was cited widely in the Middle Ages, and later, and has been considered one of his most characteristic sayings.[1] Taking off from Augustine, and supported by his authority, but often departing from his purpose and meaning, these citations provide an insight into some of the changing concerns of medieval theology and spirituality. Augustine first used "Love and do what you will" in 410, in his fifth sermon on the verse from Galatians 6.1 that reads (in the Douai version of the Bible) "If a man be overtaken in any fault, you, who are spiritual, instruct such a one in the spirit of meekness." To this Augustine added, as if continuing Paul's words:

> And if you speak out, love within [*intus*], you exhort; you coax; you chide; you rage; *dilige et quicquid uis fac*. For a father does not hate his son; and yet a father, if there is need, beats his son; he inflicts pain in order to protect salvation.[2]

Five years later, in his commentary on the first letter of St. John, where he was concerned specifically with the use of force against the Donatists, Augustine said that human actions are distinguished by the root of love. Some deeds that appear to be good are not based in love, and others that appear harsh and cruel are done in order to correct at the behest of love:

> A brief precept is given you once for all, *Dilige et quod uis fac*. If you are silent, you are silent with love; if you speak out, you speak with love; if you correct, you correct with love; if you spare, you spare with love; provided the root of love is within, nothing but good can come forth from this root.[3]

Augustine developed the point at other places in this treatise, as when he said that "Love alone distinguishes between the sons of God and the sons of the devil" and that although a bad man could receive the eucharist and be called a Christian, "he cannot have love and be evil [*habere . . . cari-*

65

tatem et malus esse]." Later, turning to the topic of unwillingness to use force for a good purpose, he wrote:

> Do not then think that you love your servant when you do not strike him, or that you love your son when you do not discipline him, or that you love your neighbor when you do not chide him: this is not love but laziness. Love should rise up to correct, to emend.

And citing the dominical precepts to love the Lord God and your neighbor as yourself, he wrote: "Hold therefore onto love and you will be safe. Why do you fear lest you do evil to someone? Who does evil to someone he loves? Love, and it is impossible for you to do anything but good."[4]

Augustine did not distinguish between various types of love, and at different places in his works he used the terms *dilectio, caritas,* and *amor* interchangeably, as in the Bible.[5] It is therefore uncertain whether he had in mind love of God or love of neighbor when he wrote *Dilige et quod uis fac.* William James in *The Varieties of Religious Experience* translated the precept as "If you but love [God], you may do as you incline,"[6] and Gilson said that everything done by a soul filled with the love of God "it does by pure love; each of its acts, whatever it may be, grows out of a perfect and absolute love of God, so that everything it does will be good with an infallible goodness."[7] Dihle in his study of *The Theory of Will in Classical Antiquity* paraphrased the precept as "An action which is exclusively motivated by love for God or one's neighbor can only be virtuous and in accordance with God's commandment."[8] Gallay, in contrast, who made a special study of *Dilige et quod uis fac,* said that it referred to love of neighbor and meant that "We should love our brothers; one can behave towards them as one wishes; love cannot produce evil fruits."[9] This view is confirmed by passages in some of Augustine's other works, such as his sermon *On Christian discipline,* where he remarked, after citing Paul's reference in Romans 13.10 to love of neighbor as working no evil and as "the fulfilling of the law," that he "seems to have said nothing about the love of God, but he said that the love of neighbor alone is enough to fulfill the law. . . . Behold that which was two has been made into one. In short, love your neighbor, and it will be enough."[10] In his sermon on the Lord's prayer, Augustine told his listeners to love their enemies:

> And if you cannot love him who rages, love him who asks. Love the man who says to you "Brother I have sinned, forgive me.". . . If you will then forgive, however, you will then dismiss hate from your heart: you dismiss hate,

I say, not correction from your heart. What if the man who asks forgiveness should be punished by me? Do what you will (*fac quod uis*); for I think that you love your son even when you strike.[11]

The resemblance of this passage to *Dilige et quod uis fac* in the sermon on Galatians 6.1, which was written at about the same time, shows that Augustine's precept applied to love of neighbor, above all in a familial setting, including the family of Christians, who had responsibility for one another.

Scholars are also disagreed over the meaning and purpose of the precept. Even the correct translation is in doubt. The *uis* in *quod uis fac* is usually translated "will" or "wish," but it may mean "purpose," "intend," or even "have to" or "must," which would bring out the prescriptive character of the precept. "Do what you must" is less permissive than "Do what you will." William James, who knew its use principally in post-Reformation sources, called it "Saint Augustine's antinomian saying" and "morally one of the profoundest of observations, yet . . . pregnant . . . with passports beyond the bounds of conventional morality." He compared it with Ramakrishna's maxim that "He needs no devotional practices whose heart is moved to tears at the mere mention of the name of Hari."[12] Joseph Fletcher in his book *Situation Ethics* wrote that "Augustine was right again, as situationists see it, to reduce the whole Christian ethic to a single maxim, *Dilige et quod uis fac*" which he translated as "Love with care and *then* what you will, do."[13] Robert Zaehner associated "Love and do what you will" with the Buddhist concepts of "a Oneness beyond all number and a 'Goodness' beyond good and evil" and cited a Japanese master who said, "Die while alive, and be completely dead: then do whatever you will, all is good."[14] These interpretations would have surprised Augustine, who had no idea of justifying behavior "beyond the bounds of conventional morality" or of opening a door, as Zaehner put it, to "a state beyond right and wrong, good and evil."[15] His purpose was not permissive or antinomian, to free the perfect from observance of the law. " 'Love and do what you will' in Augustine," according to John Rist, "is no license for libertinism or situation ethics."[16] It was, on the contrary, rigorist and designed to assert the responsibilities of fraternal love, which had occasionally to be severe and even harsh. For Augustine the law of love was not a dispensation from the other commandments but their fulfillment.[17]

It is not my intention, however, to study Augustine's doctrines of love and will and their relation to behavior, especially coercion, nor to enter into the age-old philosophical and ethical battle over the respective roles of the head and the heart, intellect and emotion, in motivating human actions. The idea that violence could be inspired by love, and the application to warfare of the precept to love one's enemies, were of importance later, especially during the crusades, which were sometimes seen as acts of love.[18] But so far as I know "Love and do what you will" was never specifically applied to warfare in the Middle Ages.

It may have been on account of its emphasis on interiority and its apparent voluntarism that "Love and do what you will" was very rarely cited in the early Middle Ages. Even with the assistance of CETEDOC and the Chadwyck-Healey concordance to the *Patrologia latina*, I have located only two citations before about 1100, and none between the sixth and tenth centuries. The first is in a sermon on love of neighbor and love of enemies that was long thought to be by Augustine, and was published among his works, but is now attributed to Caesarius of Arles, in the first half of the sixth century, who said:

> *Dilige ergo et quicquid uolueris fac:* love with all your heart and practice towards your neighbor what you will. If you are angry, it is sweet because it proceeds from love; if you chide, it is agreeable; if you even chastise and strike, it is acceptable.[19]

Caesarius's source is unknown. His use of *quicquid* points to the sermon in Galatians 6.1 and the subsequent list of applications to the commentary on 1 John, but it may have come from another, now lost, work by Augustine.

The second, and more interesting, citation is in Ratherius of Verona's account of the translation of St. Metro, which dates from between 961 and 968, where Ratherius urged the faithful to use Metro's relics as "an interior counsellor" and to seek advice from him about "the impulse of intention." "For if they have followed the single eye in the thing they desire," Ratherius continued, citing the single eye that makes the body full of light from Matthew 6.22 and Luke 11.34, "they can rejoice. I think that they have taken a necessary guide." He then said *Habe caritatem et quicquid uolueris facito,* and added, citing 1 Corinthians 13.5, "and O how happily I rejoice, for love, as someone else says, 'dealeth not perversely'."[20] Ratherius did not identify the source of his citation. *Quicquid uolueris* suggests Caesarius, but the future imperative *facito* appears only in Ratherius.

His use of *Habe caritatem* in place of *Dilige* is important because it anticipates the principal form of the precept in the Middle Ages and may represent a conscious change from what John Benton called "the possible ambiguity of *dilige*."[21] *Dilige* means to love or cherish generally, in a family sense. *Habe caritatem* defines the type of love and by associating it with the Gospel *caritas* sounds like a dominical precept. Alan of Lille in the twelfth century said that "to have love" implies that the love inheres in those who have it.[22] *Habe caritatem* may derive from Augustine himself, who used it in his commentary on 1 John, or possibly from Gregory the Great, who said in his commentary on Ezechiel, with reference to Solomon's litter of which the pillars were silver, the going up purple, and the middle covered with love (Song of Songs 3.10), "Have love indeed [*Habe quippe caritatem*], and you will without doubt come to that place where both the silver pillars are created and the purple going up is held."[23] Since this passage was incorporated into the commentaries on the Song of Songs by Paterius, Bede, and William of St. Thierry, *Habe caritatem* was known to medieval writers from several sources.[24]

Quod uis fac was also known from non-Augustinian sources, especially in formulations of the Golden Rule to do unto others as you would have them do unto you, which reads in the Latin version of Matthew, *Omnia ergo quaecumque uultis ut faciant uobis homines, et uos facite illis* and, in Luke, *Prout uultis ut faciant uobis homines, et uos facite illis similiter.* Isidore of Seville in his *Synonyma* wrote *Quod tibi fieri uis, fac alteri; quod uis ut faciat alius tibi, hoc et tu facito illi,* where both *quod uis fac* and *quod uis facito* appear.[25] *Quod uis fac* is found in the *Verba seniorum,* where one hermit told another that he could do what he wanted with his portion of a loaf of bread,[26] and *si uis fac* in the anonymous *Breviary on the psalms,* which was published among the works of Jerome but was written after 450, perhaps by Faustus of Riez or John the Deacon, who wrote "If you wish, do what follows, and you will see [eternal] life."[27] This was expanded to *quod si uis fac* by Bruno of Würzburg in his commentary on the psalms.[28] There is no reason to believe, however, that any of these, in spite of the verbal similarities, either derived from or influenced the later development of Augustine's precept, which at some time between the fifth and tenth centuries was reformulated into *Habe caritatem et quicquid uolueris facito* and later into *Habe caritatem et fac quicquid uis,* and was preserved probably in a florilegium or book of sentences derived from Augustine's writings.

The precept with *Dilige* was rarely used after about 1100. I know of only four examples from the twelfth century, twice in differing contexts and with a distinctive meaning, and twice in commentaries on John, where it derived, directly or indirectly, from Augustine. For Robert of Arbrissel in his letter to countess Ermengard of Brittany, written in 1109, *Dilige* referred to

God and *fac quod uis* to religious principles and behavior. Citing the dominical commandments to love God and one's neighbor, Robert wrote that:

> The blessed Augustine said "Love and do what you will [*Dilige et fac quodcunque uis*]." Do not be greatly concerned that you are married to an unbelieving man. Remember the holy woman Esther who was married to the unbelieving prince Ahasuerus and who accomplished much for the people of God. And the Apostle said "The unbelieving husband is sanctified by the believing wife" [1 Corinthians 7.14].

Amid her worldly surroundings, therefore, Ermengard always should have God in her heart. "Love and God will be with you," Robert wrote, and later, citing Psalm 36.3, "Believe, love, 'trust in the Lord and do good', and inhabit the land of your heart, and you may feast in its riches."[29] The other citations of *Dilige et quod uis fac* are in Abelard's *Sic et non*, to which I shall return; in Martin of Leon's commentary on 1 John, which derives from Augustine;[30] and in the *Glossa ordinaria*, where the verse "We ought to love one another" from 1 John 4.11 was glossed "Love and do what you will. If you are silent, you are silent with love; if you speak out, you speak out with love. Nothing except good can come forth from this root."[31] This is an abbreviation of the similar passage in Augustine's commentary on 1 John, but out of context it may convey a more permissive view than Augustine intended.

In contrast with *Dilige et fac quod uis*, the version with *Habe caritatem* was cited in the twelfth century at least twenty-five times by fifteen authors, including six secular clerics, four Cistercians (or eventual Cistercians), three regular canons, and two black monks. André Wilmart in the notes to his edition of Aelred of Rievaulx's *Disputation against someone's letter on the rule and profession of monks*, which was written in reply to a regular canon, said that the maxim was commonplace [*banale*] and that it was cited by the canons who were under the patronage of Augustine "for whom love was the basis of all morality."[32] This suggests that it was used in a permissive sense to allow Augustinian canons to do what was prohibited to stricter monks and canons. Though none of the writers in whose works it appears were in the forefront of the movement of monastic reform, with the exception of Robert of Arbrissel, who used *Dilige et fac quodcunque uis*, they represent a cross-section of the spiritual writers of the time and show both the broad appeal of the precept and the many ways in which it was used.

The first known writer to use *Habe caritatem et fac quidquid uis* was Ivo of Chartres, in the so-called prologue to his *Decretum*, where he said that the building of God was ruled by love:

which, mindful of the salvation of neighbors, orders that what everyone wants to be done to himself should be done to others. Each ecclesiastical doctor therefore interprets and moderates the ecclesiastical rules in such a way that he refers everything that he teaches and expounds to the kingdom of love and that he neither sins nor errs, since mindful of the salvation of neighbors he endeavors to reach the end that is owed to ecclesiastical institutions. Wherefore the blessed Augustine, treating ecclesiastical discipline, said "Have love and do what you will. If you chide, chide with love. If you spare, spare with love." But the greatest care should be used in these matters, and the eye of the heart should be cleansed, so that in punishing or in sparing sincere love should assist in curing these disorders, and no one in the manner of venal doctors should seek their own [1 Corinthians 1.24; etc.] and incite the blame of the prophet: "They killed souls which should not have died, and they saved souls alive which should not have lived" [cf. Ezechiel 13.19].[33]

Ivo of Chartres used the passage again in a letter concerning the administration of ecclesiastical law written to abbot Pontius of Cluny in 1109/16. Echoing the prologue to the *Decretum,* Ivo said that superiors should take care neither to permit what is harmful nor to forbid what is advantageous:

> For just as sick people are not always cured when the laws of medicine are observed and are cured when the laws are suitably put aside, so consideration must be given in curing disorders of spirits to those that will be cured by the rigor of discipline and by the moderation of indulgence. In all these matters the highest counsel is that which we have from father Augustine speaking in his treatise on ecclesiastical discipline: "Have love and do what you will. If you spare, spare with love. If you chide, chide with love."[34]

Ivo, like Augustine, used the precept to justify, and in some cases to enjoin, severity in the administration of justice. In the prologue to the *Decretum* he referred to Augustine "treating ecclesiastical discipline," and in his letter to Pontius he cited a treatise [*tractatus*] on ecclesiastical discipline, which is otherwise unknown. He may have had *On Christian discipline* in mind, but the precept is not found there. The ultimate source is probably the commentary on 1 John, which has the same general form of the precept followed by various applications, including to spare and to correct. But it had come some distance from Augustine's original before it appeared in Ivo's work. From the prologue it was taken over in its entirety, including the references to chiding and sparing, in Hildebert of Lavardin's letter 2.53.[35] As a bishop and administrator, like Ivo and Augustine, Hildebert was concerned for the proper enforcement of the law, which included both severity and leniency, provided they were rooted in love.

Abelard, in contrast, was interested in the moral content of human actions and, above all, in the importance of intention. In his discussion of the inconsistencies and errors of the prophets and apostles in his *Sic et non*, which dates from 1121/32, Abelard said that these should be attributed to ignorance rather than to lying or duplicity:

> nor should anything said out of love for edification be attributed to presumption or to sin, since it is established that before the Lord all things are distinguished according to intention, as is written "If thy eye be single, thy whole body shall be full of light." Whence there is also that [precept] of the blessed Augustine treating on ecclesiastical discipline: "Have," he says, "love, and do what you will." The same on the epistle of John: "Those who have not love are not of God. Whatever you will, have; [if] you have not this alone, nothing is of advantage to you. If you have not the others, have this, and you will fulfill the law." Likewise: "A brief precept is given to you once for all: Love and do what you will."[36]

Abelard cited the precept twice in this passage: once in the form *Habe caritatem et fac quicquid uis*, which he attributed to Augustine's hypothetical *On ecclesiastical discipline* and which probably derived from Ivo's *Decretum*, and the second time as *Dilige et quod uis fac*, which may have come directly from the commentary on 1 John, with which Abelard was certainly familiar.[37] Later in the *Sic et non*, in a section showing that man must love God for Himself and not for any material reward, Abelard cited a series of quotations from the works of Augustine, including *Habe caritatem et fac quidquid uis* as from *De disciplina ecclesiastica*, followed by three from the commentary on 1 John: "Love alone distinguishes between the sons of God and the sons of the devil," "The sons of God are distinguished from the sons of the devil only by love," and the series of qualities, cited above, ending "A man cannot have love and be evil."[38]

In his commentary on Romans, which dates from 1133/6, Abelard discussed the question of whether Christians should love and pray for everyone, including the damned and those not predestined to life, even when they know that the prayers will be without effect:

> But you say that [precept] of Augustine "Love and do what you will," and you remember that of Jerome "Love has no measure." Wherefore love often compels us to exceed measure in such a way that we wish for what is

never good or just to do and on the contrary do not wish for what it is good to do, such as to kill or afflict the saints, which even in them "work together unto good" [Romans 8.28]. But we reserve this discussion for our *Ethics*.[39]

In that work Abelard cited "Have love and do what you will" in his discussion of the question "Why we ought sometimes to punish those whom we know to be innocent?" He gave as an example a mother who accidentally smothers her child, "the one whom she holds with the greatest love [*amore summo*]," while trying to warm it with her own clothing, and who, when she is brought before the bishop, is punished not for her fault, Abelard said, "but in order that subsequently she or other women may be rendered more cautious in providing for such things."[40] Here, therefore, Abelard used the precept to justify morally a deed that is punished in the world. As Luscombe said in his note to this passage, "God and men differ in their methods of judgement."[41]

Peter the Venerable, in contrast, used "Love and do what you will" in his Letter 28 to Bernard of Clairvaux, written in about 1127, to justify the diversity of monastic observances. He replied to the Cistercian criticisms, especially the reception of novices in Cluniac houses without the delay prescribed in the rule, by saying that "We profess to follow in these and other matters the rule of mother love," upon which, he said, quoting Matthew 22.40, "dependeth the whole law and the prophets." After citing Gregory the Great that all precepts of the Lord grow from the root of love and Augustine's "Have love and do what you will," he asserted that by receiving novices without a delay the Cluniacs followed "this rule of love."[42] Towards the end of the letter, replying to the charge that the Cluniacs injured the rule of Benedict by changing it, Peter argued that on the contrary the rule should be changed precisely because it was founded on love, of which the one and only office was to seek human salvation. He supported this with three Augustinian texts, concluding with "Love and do what you will," and added that "In order to be mindful of human salvation, therefore, it does what it wills. If it is allowed to do what it wills, it is allowed to make the rule; and it is allowed to change [it]."[43] Writing to Bernard in 1144, Peter pointed out that monks who had professed the same rule did not always observe it in the same way:

> But lest you should call such monks guilty on account of these things, lest you dare accuse [them] for this reason of prevarication, hear the authority of heaven, indeed of the king of the heavens, [saying] "If thy eye be single, thy whole body shall be full of light." Hear also the Apostle: "Let all your

things be done in love" [1 Corinthians 16.14]. Hear also father Augustine: "Have love and do what you will." Hear also the very writer of the rule, indeed the holy spirit, who dictated the same rule and said that the abbot "should so arrange and temper all things that souls should be saved and that the brothers should do what they do without complaint."[44]

Peter again cited "Have love and do what you will" in conjunction with "If thy eye be single, thy whole body shall be full of light" in Letter 28, where he added "That is, if the intention will be good, all the works will also be righteous."[45] Ratherius of Verona also associated the impulse of intention and the single eye; Ivo of Chartres said that "the eye of the heart should be cleansed"; and Abelard used "Have love" and "the single eye" to support his contention that the Lord judges all things "according to intention."[46] In the English translations of this biblical verse, the Douai version has "lightsome"; the King James version has "full of light," which is used here for the sake of clarity; and the New English Bible has "If your eyes are sound, you will have light for your whole body." For medieval authors the single eye meant pure intention, sincerity, and straightforwardness. Gerard Manley Hopkins equated it with "the heart right."[47]

There were already some signs before the middle of the twelfth century, however, that "Have love and do what you will" was being misused to justify sinful behavior. In the chapter on "Whether all *dilectio* of God may be called *caritas*" in *On the sacraments of the Christian faith*, which dates from 1135/40, Hugh of St. Victor argued, first, that *dilectio* and *caritas* were the same and that "love of God is always good"; second, that the perfect love "which is not lost" differs from other types of love; and third, that manifest sinners—he used the examples of David who committed adultery and murder and St. Peter who denied Christ—do not retain the love that cannot be lost:

> If love is here, the fullness of the law is here; if there is the fullness of the law, how can there be prevarication? If they say that someone who does such things had love, why do they not also say that in doing this he committed no sin, since Scripture says "Whoever is born of God sinneth not" [1 John 5.18] and since it is again said elsewhere "Have love and do what you will." For if it is true that those who do such things can retain love, since it is allowed to those who have love to do what they will, it is perfectly proven that what they have done is not a sin. Let them therefore go with their love and do what they will, since they have great defenders, of whom some indeed defend that they do not lose love but others concede that they do whatever they want with love.[48]

Hugh then went on to demonstrate at length that when David and Peter sinned voluntarily, they indeed lost love but not the spirit of the Lord, which assured their eventual salvation. He warned in particular that sinners of this type, when they consent to sin, sometimes have a pious *affectus*, presumably meaning a feeling or attitude of piety, which, Hugh said, is not "worthy of the name of *caritas* or *dilectio* of God." "Those who place the merit of man in the I-know-not-what *affectionibus* that we sometimes see to exist, out of either nature or habit, in unbelieving and iniquitous people, should have looked on this with the eye by which alone the whole body is made light."[49]

Hugh returned to the subject of the relation of will to merit in his chapter on human will, which he equated with the power of God, saying that "All merit is therefore in the will. As much as you will, so much you merit." The precise meaning of this axiom *Quantum uis tantum mereris* was discussed by later theologians, to whom I shall return. For Hugh it meant that merit is determined by will rather than by results and that if someone is unable to carry out a sincerely willed intention, the merit is not reduced, as he explained, in a somewhat roundabout way, when he wrote that:

> All merit is in the will even if, with regard to effect [*opus*], there may or may not be an effect; nothing in the will is less, except perhaps that the will itself would become greater if an effect were achieved. If therefore you wish to have great merit, have great will, great trust.

And he concluded, reversing the order of his previous words, "You merit as much as you will."[50] Putting this together with his previous discussion of love, the fault of David and Peter lay in their voluntary consent to sin, which is incompatible with perfect love. "In that will by which they chose to consent to the flesh against God, they in no way had the love of God."[51] Hugh thus rejected the view, which some of his contemporaries were apparently proposing, that those who claimed to have love were free to do whatever they wanted.

Aelred of Rievaulx also expressed some reservations in his *Mirror of love*, which dates from 1142-43 and where he examined (perhaps in opposition to the arguments of black monks like Peter the Venerable) the strictness of the rule of Benedict, such as "the small and cheap quantity of food and drink, the roughness of the clothes, the torment of the fasts and vigils, the grinding of the daily work, and other such things," and where he stressed that the monastic profession and rule consisted of both virtues and observances. Aelred then entered into a hypothetical conversation with someone who:

> rising from the side, says "Why do you reproach me from the rule? Have love and do what you will. Therefore we eat and drink not because tomorrow we shall die but because we are filled with love." With love, I [that is, Aelred] ask, or with vanity? "Why therefore?" you ask. "Does not he who has love fulfill the rule? . . . Why . . . do you force me to those harsh things by the authority of the rule? If on the contrary you have love, it is unnecessary for you to force [me] to redeem your vows, which your lips expressed."

To this Aelred replied that divine precepts were unchangeable and that any variation must be a dispensation, not a destruction.

> For since the purpose of this institution [that is, the rule] is the preservation of love and the emendation of vices, then indeed this dispensation is reasonable if it promotes this purpose. But if vices are encouraged more by the dispensation than by the institution, love is violated, [and] this dispensation is shown to be certainly dangerous, if not perhaps damnable.[52]

A third witness to the growing caution with regard to "Have love and do what you will" was Richard of St. Victor in his *Mystical notes on the psalms*, where he stressed the importance of works as the criteria of love. Commenting on the queen in gilded clothing on the right side of God in Psalm 44.10, Richard explained that temporal goods are on the left side of God and eternal goods on His right and that love, the queen of the virtues, wants to please God by her precious clothes, which stand for works.

> The error, as I think, of some who claim that works are nothing should be condemned here. Have love, they say, and do what you will, righteously at least [*recte utique*]. For just as when [I am] full of love I commit no evil out of desire, so I do not easily pass over any good that presents itself to be done. And this is indeed what Augustine says, not what your negligence invents. For the proof of love is the display of work.[53]

Richard made this point again in his commentary on Psalm 118, where he said that the single eye that made the body full of light applied to the limbs of the body, not the vices.

> The truth does not therefore commend things that are neither the body nor part of the body, that is, evil deeds, even if they are done, if they can be done, with a good intention. But it wished rather to show that those things that really constituted the body of virtues, that is, good works, are altogether not good if they proceed from an evil intention. Since "if thy eye

be evil, thy whole body shall be full of darkness" [Matthew 6.23]. Why is it, they say, that the angel [*angelus*: presumably an error for *Augustinus*] said, "Have love and do what you will"? Do we therefore think that love is blind? Let us hear what the Apostle felt about it: "Love" he said "is the fulfilling of the law" [Romans 13.10]. . . . Perfect love enlightens fully."[54]

In spite of these reservations, "Have love" continued to be cited in a positive sense in the second half of the twelfth century. Peter Comester associated it with the final perseverance of Christ on the cross and commented that "All difficulties are easy to him who loves [*amanti*]," which echoes Augustine's view that "Love [*amor*] makes everything that is harsh and monstrous completely easy and close at hand."[55] Peter of Poitiers cited both "Have love and do what you will" and "To him who has love what can be lacking?," also from Augustine, in the discussion of perseverance in his *Sentences*, arguing that a man who has this love will be saved. At the end of the work he cited Paul's description of love as "the end of the commandment" (1 Timothy 1.5) and "Have love and do what you will" and concluded with the verse from Ecclesiastes 12.12-13 "For 'of making books there will be no end. Fear God and keep his commandments, for this is all man'."[56] Alan of Lille used "Have love" in his treatise against heretics to show that the Old Testament patriarchs, whom the heretics called evil, were saved because they fulfilled the law out of love, "for all work done out of love is deserving of eternal life," and again in his *Book on the distinctions of theological terms* as an example of the use of "to have" in the sense of inherence, since love inheres in those who have it.[57] Peter the Chanter cited "Have love," together with other biblical and patristic texts, in the chapter "On love" in his *Abbreviated word*, to show that "Love is the prince of all the virtues." Never solitary, never idle, "considering nothing human alien to itself," he said, it embraces without error and preserves without labor all the precepts.[58] And Peter of Blois in a sermon on, among other topics, the necessity of confession and penance said that "Have love and do what you will" was itself "the abbreviated word" and that it summed up the teaching of Moses and the prophets, the apostles and evangelists, and the doctors and pastors to whom Christ said "He that heareth these heareth me" (Luke 10.16).[59]

Adam Scot of Dryburgh in his treatise *On the order, habit, and profession of the Premonstratensian canons*, which was written before he became a Carthusian in about 1188, defended the variety of religious observances, and especially of clothing, by citing not only "Have love," which he attributed to Augustine, but also "What someone else said, similar to this sentence, 'Have love and wear any vestment you will',"[60] or (as a witty colleague proposed) "Love and don what you will." Whether or not this was Adam's own invention is unknown. Later in this work he stressed that whatever God or his agents establish is done because of love:

> If you have love, you know that whatever you do is salutary to you. Whence the blessed Augustine ... treating of ecclesiastical discipline said "Have love and do what you will." And this seems to be a very great permission that he allows you to do not any one thing but anything you will. But pay attention to what he puts first: "Have love." It is rightly granted that you may "do what you will," but because you previously have love.

He also pointed out that Augustine referred to love of God and neighbor "in the first chapter and in the very exordium of his rule."[61]

The primacy of love and good intention was also stressed by the Cistercians Elias of Coxida and Gunther of Pairis. Elias said in his first sermon, citing Augustine, that we should never chide the sin of another "unless our conscience will clearly bear witness for us before God that we act out of love. If you chide, chide out of love, and all things are saved: 'Have love and do what you will'."[62] Gunther made the same point with regard to giving alms. Christ's words "Give alms, and all things are clean unto you" (Luke 11.41) referred only to those who "truly and worthily" give alms, Gunther said, not to malefactors, who cannot redeem their sins by giving away temporal things. The saying "Have love and do what you will," he continued, did not mean "that someone who has love is allowed to perpetrate thefts, homicides, and adulteries, but that by having love he can do nothing that impedes obtaining [eternal] life."[63]

These writers bring us to the turn of the thirteenth century, but before leaving the twelfth we should look briefly at a few indirect references or allusions to "Have love," like that in the commentary on Matthew by Rupert of Deutz, who said "May you have a single eye, that is good intention in your heart, and do as [*quomodo*] you wish" and that "the evil eye, that is, bad intention," simply seeks the praise of men.[64] This was written in 1125/27 and is another, relatively early, association of doing what you will with the single eye and good intention. According to the chronicle of Sainte-Barbe-en-Auge, prior William, probably in the 1130s, designed a seal with the images of St. Martin and St. Barbara and the motto *Si recte uiuis fac mihi quod tibi uis*, which seems to be a conflation of "Have love" and the Golden Rule, with "If you live righteously" in place of "Have love" and "do unto me what you wish for yourself" in place of "do what you will."[65] The canon lawyer Gratian wrote in the section on penance in his *Decretum* that "Whoever once has love will henceforth be unable to sin criminally."[66] And Baldwin of Canterbury said in his treatise *On heavenly rest* "Have therefore faith, hope, and love; and you will be of the house of Jacob and of the people of Israel and the number of the elect."[67] Baldwin had in mind the theological virtues rather than the Augustinian precept, but the phrase "have love" may have echoed in the minds of his readers.

We should also look briefly at some parallel precepts or axioms that shed light on the question of the relation between love, will, and human actions. The first of these, which we have already encountered, is Hugh of St. Victor's *Quantum uis tantum mereris*, which the theologians of the twelfth and thirteenth centuries discussed and revised in several ways (especially by substituting *intendis* for *uis* and *facis* or *uis* for *mereris*) that can be roughly translated as "You merit as greatly as you will," "You merit as greatly as you intend," "You do as greatly as you intend," "You intend as greatly as you will," and "You do as great a thing as you intend." These variations, into which I cannot fully enter here, depend on whether *quantum* was interpreted as an adverb, indicating the quality of the will or intention (or, later, the quantity of the quality), or as a noun, indicating the nature of the act, as *quantum rem* makes explicit.[68] None of these related directly to "Have love," but they dealt with the same question of the relation of the internal attitude to exterior action and stressed that the merit of an action depended upon the will or intention with which it was performed. The same point is made by the maxim *Affectus tuus operi tuo nomen imponit*, which derived from St. Ambrose's treatise *On offices* and meant that "Your attitude [or feeling] determines the moral content of your action."[69] It was cited in the twelfth century by several writers, including Alan of Lille, who used it in his *Summa Quoniam homines*, which was written probably about 1160, to prove that actions are considered good or bad "from a good or bad *affectio*," which he equated with *affectus*. Citing Matthew 7.18 and 6.22, he said that:

> "A good tree cannot bring forth evil fruit, neither can an evil [tree] bring forth good [fruit]." "If thy eye be light [Alan used *lucidus* rather than *simplex*], thy whole body shall be full of light," that is, if your intention will be good, the deed proceeding from that intention will be good. God does not consider how much [*quantum*] but from how much [*ex quanto*] [this may be an allusion to *Quantum uis tantum mereris*], as if He says that a deed is not judged except from the will.[70]

The *affectus*, as Lottin pointed out, is thus informed by intention,[71] or, as Javelet put it, "Liberty receives the divine order and the intentionalized soul goes toward its transfiguration by love." The rational will or natural liberty is, he said, "the *affectus*, the order of love, of experience, of action."[72]

The appeal of "Have love and do what you will" depended upon its twin stress on love and on interiority, which were central to the thought of many theologians in the twelfth century.[73] None of those who cited "Have love," however, even those who may have known it from Augustine's own works, referred to his use of *intus* both in the sermon on Galatians 6.1, where he said "if you speak out, love within," and in the commentary on 1 John, where he wrote that "provided the root of love is within, nothing but good can come from this root."[74] By their stress on will and intention as well as love, however, they left no doubt that the determining factor in making moral judgments was the internal *affectus*, which was sometimes equated with the Holy Spirit or with direct inspiration from God. Bernard of Tiron was said to have referred everything he thought or did to the name of reason, that is, to the rational will or informed *affectus*. "He neither willed nor did anything that was not right, and he attended to human acts as if they were divine judgments."[75] More strikingly, Francis of Assisi wrote in his *Testament* that "After the Lord gave me brothers, no one showed me what I should do, but the Almighty Himself revealed to me that I should live according to the form of the holy gospel."[76]

The Cistercian Caesarius of Heisterbach included in his *Dialogue of miracles*, which was written about 1220, several stories about a good-hearted and generous dean of the church of St. Andrew in Cologne, who, when he had no fish, deceived some monks by serving pork disguised as turbot, gave to the poor money stolen under false pretenses, and distributed to the hungry loaves of bread belonging to his brother canons. When the interlocutor in the dialogue asked "How will this deed be excused?" the monk (that is, Caesarius himself) replied:

> Many things are allowed to saints that are not allowed to those who are not saints. "Where the spirit of the Lord is, there is liberty" (2 Corinthians 3.17). Whence the authority "Have love and do what you will." Love excused him; necessity excused him; authority excused him; fraternity excused him. Love, because consolation of the poor made him needy. Necessity, which knows no law. . . . Authority, because he was dean and as if the father of the brothers. Fraternity, because he considered all things ought to be common to all.

The fact that Caesarius gave such an elaborate justification shows that he was not entirely at ease with the dean's behavior or prepared to hold him up as a model for any except saints, who obey different rules from ordinary men and women. A similar lack of ease is shown by the modern translators of the *Dialogue*, who rendered "Have love" as "so long as you are in a state of grace," which distorts the sense, if not perhaps the intention, of Caesarius's words.[77]

It was this tendency to rely on internal feeling and divine inspiration that gave rise to the reservations concerning "Have love and do what you will," of which the origins can be seen in the works of Hugh and Richard of St. Victor and Aelred of Rievaulx. The only sure way to know whether the love is inspired by God or by selfish motives is visible actions. A man's internal disposition and intention, according to Augustine, are known from his actions and behavior, and for Richard of St. Victor, in the passage cited above, what was done must be done righteously and "The proof of love is in the display of work."[78] There was thus a growing reluctance to judge human behavior by a purely internal standard. The changes in the concept of love may also have contributed to a certain caution in the use of "Love and do what you will," particularly as love came to be associated, in both religious and secular works, with power rather than with will and interiority.[79] It was still cited in the thirteenth century, but I have found fewer references owing not only to the lack of general indices and concordances to late medieval literature but also, perhaps, to a real decrease in its use. Thomas of Chobham, writing at about the same time as Caesarius, used it in his *Summa on the art of preaching* to support his comparison of "the love that especially saves us" to the helmet of salvation with which Christians should arm themselves.[80] Thomas Aquinas in his *Disputed Question* on "whether or not love [*caritas*] is a special virtue distinct from other virtues" cited *Habe caritatem* on the negative side, saying that "Therefore there is no other virtue except love, and thus it is not a special virtue distinct from others."[81] And in the Middle English *Ancrene wisse* or *riwle*, of which the date and authorship are in doubt but which has recently been attributed to a Dominican writing between about 1221 and 1250, it appears in the chapter on love, where the author cited numerous precepts and examples, beginning with Paul's *pietas autem ualet ad omnia* [cf. 1 Timothy 4.8, which has *utilis est* for *ualet*] which he translated as "a sweet and clean heart is good for all things," the example of the desert father Moses from Cassian's *Collations*, the eye of the heart, and Bernard of Clairvaux's saying that a pure heart "makes you do all that you do, either for the love of God only or for the good of another and his benefit." These are followed by "Keep your heart always pure, and do all that you will," Paul's "All things are clean to the clean," and, finally, in Latin, Augustine's "Have love and do what you will," to which is added *uoluntate uidelicet rationis*, by the will of reason,[82] which corresponds to Richard of St. Victor's *recte utique* and to the "rational will" and "informed *affectus*" of the theologians. This addition shows the author's concern to emphasize that love alone does not justify unreasonable or sinful action, as does the parallel of love with a pure heart, which, he said, desires and loves only God and the things that help them come to God. "Love alone will be placed in St. Michael's scales. Those who love most will be most blessed, not those who lead the hardest life, for love weighs more than this."[83]

An anonymous author from Passau who wrote a treatise against the Waldensians in the early 1260s singled out those who said the church erred in prohibiting the marriage of priests and the promotion of illegitimate children to higher dignities in the church. "Some also say," he continued, "that what continent people do above the girdle, in kissing, touching the breasts, pressing together their bosoms, and embracing, is all done in love."[84] He did not mention "Have love and do what you will," but the passage clearly shows how in the middle of the thirteenth century the doctrine of love was being used to justify behavior, in James's words, "beyond the bounds of conventional morality."

In some cases it was used to support beliefs that were considered heretical. Margaret Porete, who was condemned as a heretic and burned at the stake in 1310, wrote in her *Mirror of simple souls* (of which the full title continues *that have been annihilated and survive only in will and the desire for love*) that Reason said that someone who has for his bow the two strings of the light of faith and the force of love "has permission to do everything that pleases him, in witness of [which is] love itself that says to the soul: 'Friend, love and do what you will'."[85] The Latin version, which was prepared probably during Margaret's lifetime, has "soul" in place of "friend" and reads *Anima, ametis et faciatis quicquid uultis*. The use here of *amare* rather than *diligere* or *habere caritatem* may reflect the form in which the precept circulated in the fourteenth century and suggests that the translator did not know the Augustinian original, while keeping its sense.[86] The Middle English version, which may have been designed to show the work's orthodoxy, has "witness of God Himself" in place of "witness of love itself" and continues "Love loveth, and doith what he wole."[87] In itself there is nothing unorthodox here, but the editors of the English translation suggest, on the basis of the translator's glosses, that among the charges brought against the *Mirror* was

"That the soul brought to nothing in the love of her creator neither desires or rejects poverty or tribulation, masses or sermons, fasting or prayers,"[88] and this corresponds to the teaching of the *Ancrene wisse* that love outweighs the hardest life and that those who love most will be most blessed.

Jean Gerson referred to Margaret Porete in his book *On the distinctions of revelations*, where he cited as evidence of the dangers of unrestrained love:

> a certain book written with almost unbelievable subtlety by a woman named Mary of Valenciennes [i.e., Margaret Porete]. This deals with the prerogative and eminence of divine love, to which according to her anyone who comes is free from the whole law of the precepts, citing in her support that taken from the Apostle "Have love and do what you will."[89]

Gerson's attribution to Paul rather than Augustine (like Richard of St. Victor's *angelus*) shows, unless it is a scribal error, that he gave the precept high authority, though unfamiliar with its origin. Master Eckhart may also have known the *Mirror of simple souls*, since he was in Paris shortly after the condemnation of Margaret Porete. In one of his sermons he explicitly condemned those who said that "If I love God and God's love, I can surely do everything I want," saying that anyone who can act against the will of God does not have His love.[90] Yet Eckhart himself cited *Habe caritatem et fac quod uis*, attributed to Augustine, both in his commentary on the Gospel of John to support "that a just and virtuous man cannot lie, sin, and generally do evil when the condition of virtue resists [*repugnante habitu virtutis*]," and in his sermons on Ecclesiastes to support that "Whoever does what the law ordains does not sin, but anyone who acts against the law sins," adding that "Love and virtue are universally always for the good and 'the end of the commandment' (1 Timothy 1.5)."[91]

These passages show that in the late Middle Ages "Love and do what you will," though still cited by mainline theologians, moved towards the margins of orthodoxy. Protected by its Augustinian origins and its use by writers of unimpeachable orthodoxy, including Thomas Aquinas, it was never, so far as I know, condemned as heretical, but it was clearly regarded as dangerous and as in need of explicit reservations to insure against its misuse. This may explain why I found no examples of its use in the later fourteenth or fifteenth centuries, even by writers with whose spiritual attitudes it would seem to fit.[92] It continued to be cited, however, in early modern times, as the comments of William James show, though he gives no references to the works of specific authors. For some writers it lost its religious content and was tainted, if not imbued, with secularism. Already in the Middle Ages the phrase *Ago quod uolo*—"I do what I will"—was associated with sensuality, concupiscence, and sin.[93] One thinks of Rabelais's *Fay ce que voudras* and of Goethe, who said "Do what you will; it is all the same" and elsewhere that "How one thinks is one thing; what one does is two; if it comes out well it is right; if it does not succeed, it remains bad."[94] The basic creed of the modern witches known as Wiccans is "An ye harm none, do what ye will."[95] This is a long way from Augustine and the medieval authors who asserted the primacy of love and intention, upon which the merit of external actions depend. At the end of the film version of *A Room with a View* (but not in Forster's book) Mr Emerson says to his son "Love and do what you will" to urge him to follow the dictates of his heart in a purely secular sense.[96] Over the centuries the precept was interpreted in different ways to suit differing purposes and needs. Above all in the twelfth century it was taken up by spiritual writers concerned with love and intention, which was applied to all spheres of human activity. It is not for us to say which (if any) of these uses and interpretations is correct in an absolute sense but to try to understand what it meant to those who used it. I have looked at only a part of this history, the medieval part, and that principally in the twelfth century, but I hope it will give an insight not only into the influence and application of a long-lived Augustinian precept but also into the minds and motives of the writers who used it.

Notes

The following abbreviations are used in the Notes:

CC	=	*Corpus Christianorum*
CC:CM	=	*Corpus Christianorum: Continuatio mediaeualis*
Clavis	=	*Clavis patrum latinorum*, 2nd ed. (Sacris Erudiri, 3; Bruges-The Hague, 1961)
CSEL	=	*Corpus scriptorum ecclesiasticorum latinorum*
PL	=	*Patrologia latina*
SC	=	*Sources chrétiennes*

In addition to the friends and scholars mentioned in the notes, I am indebted, especially for help with late medieval sources, to Larry Benson, Robert Lerner, Bernard McGinn, Brian McGuire, Heiko Oberman, Alexander Patschovsky (and his assistants at the University of Konstanz), Brian Stock, and, on points of translation, to John Callahan, Michael Curschmann, and Janet Martin.

1. Germain Morin in his edition of Augustine's *Sermones post Maurinos reperti*, Miscellanea agostiniana, 1 (Rome, 1930), p. 214, n. 13, said that "Habes heic unam ex sententiis, quibus statim dignoscatur Augustinus."

2. Augustine, *Serm. Frang.* V, 3, in PL, XLVI, 985, and *Sermones post Maurinos reperti* (n. 1 above), p. 214. See A. Kunzelmann, "Die Chronologie der Sermones des hl. Augustinus," in *Studi agostiniana*, Miscellanea agostiniana, 2 (Rome, 1931), pp. 501 and 515, on the date; Peter Brown, "St. Augustine's Attitude to Religious Coercion" (1964), in his *Religion and Society in the Age of Saint Augustine* (London, 1972), p. 277; and Pierre-Patrick Verbraken, *Études critiques sur les sermons authentiques de saint Augustin*, Instrumenta patristica, 12 (Steenbrugge, 1976), p. 166.

3. Augustine, *In Ioannis epistolam ad Parthos*, VII, 8, in PL, XXXV, 2033; and SC, LXXV, 328. Clavis, no. 279.

4. Augustine, *In Ioannis epistolam ad Parthos*, V, 7, VII, 6 and 11, and X, 7, in PL, XXXV, 2016, 2032, 2034, and 2059; and SC, LXXV, 260, 324, 332, and 426.

5. On Augustine's use of *dilectio, caritas,* and *amor*, which are all translated here as *love*, see the introduction by Paul Agaësse to his edition of Augustine's *Commentary on the First Epistle of St. John*, in *SC*, LXXV, 31-36; and, more generally, the article by Dany Dideberg on "Caritas" in the *Augustinus-Lexikon*, ed. Cornelius Mayer, I, 5-6 (Basel, 1992), pp. 730-43.

6. William James, *The Varieties of Religious Experience* (New York-London, 1902), p. 80; cf. 361, where he translated it "If you only love God enough, you may safely follow all your inclinations."

7. Etienne Gilson, *Introduction à l'étude de saint Augustin*, 2nd ed., Études de philosophie médiévale, 11 (Paris, 1943), p. 182. John M. Rist, *Augustine: Ancient Thought Baptized* (Cambridge, 1994), p. 191, said that "Love and do what you will" makes a man "wish to want what God wishes, loves and commands," which (like God Himself) is eternal and unchanging.

8. Albrecht Dihle, *The Theory of Will in Classical Antiquity*, Sather Classical Lectures, 48 (Berkeley-Los Angeles-London, 1982), p. 131.

9. Jacques Gallay, "*Dilige et quod uis fac*. Notes d'exégèse augustinienne," *Recherches de science religieuse*, 43 (1955), pp. 546-47, with references to other works. See also André Mandouze, *Saint Augustin. L'aventure de la raison et de la grâce* (Paris, 1968), p. 657, who said that the precept was often misunderstood "parce que ceux qui citent la formule n'ont cure en général d'en rétablir le contexte." John Benton, "Consciousness of Self and Perceptions of Individuality," in *Renaissance and Renewal in the Twelfth Century*, ed. Robert L. Benson and Giles Constable (Cambridge, Mass., 1982), p. 293, wrote that Augustine "put so much trust in informed Christian virtue that he could even advise, 'Love and do what you wish'."

10. Augustine, *Sermo de disciplina christiana*, 5-6, in PL, XL, 672. Clavis, no. 310.

11. Augustine, *Serm.* 56 *de oratione dominica*, 17, ed. Patrick Verbraken, "Les sermons CCXV et LVI de saint Augustin," *Revue bénédictine* 68 (1958), pp. 38-39. See Kunzelmann, "Chronologie" (n. 2 above), pp. 460-61 and 512, dating it 410/12, and Verbraken, *Études* (n. 2 above), pp. 66. Augustine also used *fac quod uis* in his *Ep.* 247,1 in *CSEL*, LVII, 586, and in *Serm.* 80, 4, in *PL*, XXXVIII, 495 (Kunzelmann, "Chronologie," pp. 500 and 512: "um 410"); 178, 10, in *PL*, XXXVIII, 965-66 (Kunzelmann, "Chronologie," pp. 491 and 513: "nach 396"); and 132, 2 (2), in *PL*, XXXVIII, 736, which was cited by Jonas of Orléans, *De institutione laicali*, II, 2, in PL, CVI, 171D. See Verbraken, *Études* (n. 2 above), pp. 80, 132, and 178.

12. James, *Varieties* (n. 6 above), pp. 80 and 361. Geoffrey Shepherd in the notes to his edition of *Ancrene wisse: Parts six and seven*, Nelson's Medieval and Renaissance Library (Edinburgh-London, 1959), p. 53, said that "the phrase could be easily put to dangerous uses."

13. Joseph Fletcher, *Situation Ethics: The New Morality* (Philadelphia, 1966), p. 79, who went on "It was not, by the way, *Ama et fac quod uis* (Love with desire and do what you will). It was not antinomianism." See p. 117 on the nature of Christian love for Augustine. I owe this reference to Richard Hunt.

14. Robert C. Zaehner, *Zen, Drugs and Mysticism* (New York, 1972), pp. 124-25.

15. Ibid., p. 162.

16. Rist, *Augustine* (n. 7 above), p. 191.

17. See Gallay, "*Dilige*" (n. 9 above), pp. 549 and 552; and Agaësse, in SC, LXXV, 80 and 328, n. 1.

18. To "slay for God's love" was the essence of crusading, according to Norman Daniel, *Islam and the West* (Edinburgh, 1960), p. 113. See also Carl Erdmann, *The Origin of the Idea of Crusade*, trans. Marshall Baldwin and Walter Goffart (Princeton, 1977), p. 245, citing Anselm of Lucca (repeated in Gratian); Jonathan Riley-Smith, "Crusading as an Act of Love," *History* 65 (1980), pp. 185-86; and Benjamin Z. Kedar, *Crusade and Mission: European Approaches toward the Muslims* (Princeton, 1984), p. 102, on the requirement to love the Jews and Muslims.

19. Caesarius of Aries, *Serm.* 29, 4, in CC, CIII, 128. Cf. Caesarius of Arles, *Sermons*, I, trans. Mary Magdeleine Mueller, Fathers of the Church, 31 (Washington, D.C., 1956), p. 146.

20. Ratherius of Verona, *De translatione S. Metronis*, 13, in *CC:CM*, XLVI, 28.

21. Benton, "Consciousness" (n. 9 above), p. 293, n. 93, referring to "the version quoted (or created?) by Ivo of Chartres."

22. See p. 77 and n. 57 below.

23. Gregory the Great, *Homilia in Hiezechihelem*, II, 3, 15, in *CC*, CXLII, 247.

24. Paterius, *Expositio veteris et novi testamenti*, 13: *Super Cantica Canticorum*, 24, in *PL*, LXXIX, 910C; Bede, *In Cantica Canticorum*, 6, in *CC*, CXIXB, 367; and William of St. Thierry, *Super Cantica Canticorum*, 3, in *PL*, CLXXX, 456B.

25. Isidore of Seville, *Synonyma*, II, 81, in *PL*, LXXXIII, 863B.

26. *Verba seniorum*, V, 13, 15, in *PL*, LXXIII, 947A.

27. *Breviarium in psalmos, ad* ps. 33, in *PL,* XXVI, 977A (among the works of Jerome). *Clavis,* no. 629.

28. Bruno of Würzburg, *Expositio psalmorum, ad* ps. 33.12, in *PL,* CXLII, 145C.

29. J. de Petigny, "Lettre inédite de Robert d'Arbrissel à la comtesse Ermengarde," *Bibliothèque de l'Ecole des Chartes* 15 (3rd S. 5; 1854), pp. 227-28 and 231.

30. Martin of Léon, *Expositio in epistolam I B. Joannis,* in *PL,* CCIX, 281 A.

31. *Glossa ordinaria, ad* 1 Joan. 4.11, in *PL,* CXIV, 701D.

32. André Wilmart, "Un court traité d'Aelred sur l'étendue et le but de la profession monastique," *Revue d'ascétique et de mystique* 23 (1947), pp. 272, n. 23 ("cette maxime devenue banale").

33. Ivo of Chartres, *Decretum, prol,* in *PL,* CLXI, 48B. According to Bruce Brasington (letter dated 16 October 1996), the prologue may have been written about 1095, before the *Decretum.* According to the index to Ivo's *Panormia* in *PL,* CLXI, 1385 (taken from the edition of 1587, which I have not seen), *Charitatem habe, et fac quod uis* also appears in the prologue to the *Panormia,* which is at this point identical with the prologue to the *Decretum* and of which only the rubrics are printed in *PL,* CLXI, 1042. See Rolf Sprandel, *Ivo von Chartres und seine Stellung in der Kirchengeschichte,* Pariser historische Studien, 1 (Stuttgart, 1962), pp. 28-31; Benton "Consciousness" (n. 9 above), p. 293, n. 93 (n. 21 above); James A. Brundage, "St. Anselm, Ivo of Chartres, and the Ideology of the First Crusade," in *Les mutations socio-culturelles au tournant des XIe-XIIe siècles. Études Anselmiennes (IVe Session).* Abbaye Notre-Dame du Bec, Le Bec-Hellouin 11-16 juillet 1982 (Paris, 1984), p. 181, on Ivo's equation of lawful coercion with love; Robert Somerville and Bruce C. Brasington, *Prefaces to Canon Law Books in Latin Christianity: Selected Translations, 500–1245* (New Haven-London, 1998), p. 134 and n. 64, calling *Habe caritatem* "a maxim with a long and complicated history"; and Bruce C. Brasington, *Ways of Mercy: The Prologue of Ivo of Chartres* (Vita Regularis: Editionen, 2; Münster, 2004), pp. 27, 116-17.

34. Ivo of Chartres, *Ep.* 231, in *PL,* CLXII, 235AB.

35. Hildebert of Lavardin, *Ep.* II, 53, in *PL,* CLXXI, 279A. See Peter von Moos, *Hildebert von Lavardin, 1056–1133,* Pariser historische Studien, 3 (Stuttgart, 1965), p. 185, on Hildebert's knowledge of law, citing this letter.

36. Abelard, *Sic et non, prol.,* ed. Blanche Boyer and Richard McKeon (Chicago-London, 1976-77), pp. 97–98. On the dates of this and Abelard's other works cited here see Constant J. Mews, *Peter Abelard,* Authors of the Middle Ages, II, 5 (Aldershot, 1995).

37. The fact that he went on to cite by name the *De disciplina christiana* (and other works by Augustine) suggests that he regarded *De disciplina ecclesiastica* as a separate work. "Fac quod uis" is also used in *The Lost Love Letters of Heloise and Abelard: Perceptions of Dialogue in Twelfth-Century France,* ed. Constant J. Mews (New York, 1999), p. 222 (Ep. 41).

38. Abelard, *Sic et non,* 138, ed. Boyer and McKeon (n. 36 above), pp. 472–73.

39. Abelard, *Commentaria in epistolam Pauli ad Romanos*, 4, *ad* 13.10, in *CC:CM*, XI, 293.

40. Abelard, *Ethica*, 5, ed. David Luscombe, Oxford Medieval Texts (Oxford, 1971), p. 38.

41. Ibid., p. 39, n. 3, citing the differing view of Robert Blomme, *La doctrine du péché dans les écoles théologiques de la première moitié du XIIe siècle*, Universitas catholica Lovaniensis. Dissertationes ad gradum magistri in Facultate Theologica uel in Facultate Iuris Canonici consequendum conscriptae, III, 6 (Louvain-Gembloux, 1958), p. 202, n. 1, who considered this an example of how Abelard reacted "contre des théories trop objectivistes qui avaient encore cours à son époque."

42. Peter the Venerable, *Ep.* 28, ed. Giles Constable, Harvard Historical Studies, 78 (Cambridge, Mass., 1967), I, 59–60 and 98.

43. Peter the Venerable, *Ep.* 28, ibid., I, 98.

44. Peter the Venerable, *Ep.* 111, ibid., I, 281, citing *Regula Benedictii*, 41.

45. Peter the Venerable, *Ep.* 28, ibid., I, 60. On the single eye see Blomme, *Doctrine du péché* (n. 41 above), pp. 73–77, and C. S. Lewis, *Studies in Words*, 2nd ed. (Cambridge, 1967), p. 171.

46. See pp. 68, 71, and 72 above.

47. Gerard Manley Hopkins, *The Wreck of the Deutschland*, 29, in his *Poems*, ed. W. H. Gardner, 3rd ed. (New York-London, 1948), p. 65. I owe this reference to Helen Vendler.

48. Hugh of St. Victor, *De sacramentis*, II, 13, 12, in *PL*, CLXXVI, 545D–46D, and trans. Roy J. Deferrari, Mediaeval Academy of America. Pub. 58 (Cambridge, Mass., 1951), p. 397.

49. Ibid., col. 548CD, and trans. Deferrari, p. 399, who translated *affectus* as both "affection" and "affectation" and proposed a somewhat different translation of this passage. On *affectus* in the works of Augustine see Brian Stock, *Augustine the Reader* (Cambridge, Mass.-London, 1996), pp. 39 and 59, who translated it "disposition."

50. Hugh, *De sacramentis*, II, 14, 6, coll. 561AD and 562BC, and trans. Deferrari, pp. 413 and 414. See Odon Lottin, *Psychologie et morale aux XIIe et XIIIe siècles* (Louvain-Gembloux, 1942–60), IV.I, 315 and 480, and Blomme, *Doctrine du péché* (n. 41 above), pp. 312–13.

51. Hugh, *De sacramentis*, II, 13, 12, col. 548B, and trans. Deferrari, p. 399.

52. Aelred of Rievaulx, *De speculo caritatis*, III, 94-95, in *CC:CM*, I, 150–51. See Anselm Hoste, *Bibliotheca Aelrediana*, Instrumenta patristica, 2 (Steenbrugge-The Hague, 1962), pp. 41–46. Aelred repeated these views, using "Have love" and much of the same language, in his *Disputacio de monacorum regula et professione*, in the notes to which Wilmart remarked that "Have love" had become a banal maxim: Wilmart, "Court traité" (n. 32 above), pp. 271–72 and n. 23. See Hoste, *Bibliotheca*, p. 46.

53. Richard of St. Victor, *Adnotationes mysticae in psalmos*, *ad* ps. 44, in *PL*, CXCVI, 322D–23A.

54. Ibid., *ad* ps. 118, coll. 358D-59A.

55. Peter Comestor, *Serm.* 16, in *PL*, CXCVIII, 1767C (= ps.-Hildebert of Lavardin, *Serm.* 20, in *PL*, CLXXI, 431D) and Augustine, *Serm.* 70, 3, in *PL*, XXXVIII, 444. Peter of Blois, *Ep.* 86, in his *Opera omnia*, ed. J. A. Giles (Oxford, 1847), I, 267, wrote: "Caritas omnia suffert, omnia sustinet. Nihil difficile est amanti." Note the apparent equation of *caritas* and *amor* in these passages. See also *Ancrene wisse*, 6, ed. Shepherd (n. 12 above), p. 18 and relevant note on p. 51.

56. Peter of Poitiers, *Sententiae*, III, 28, and V, 22, in *PL*, CCXI, 1130B and 1280D. On Peter's view of intentionality see Lottin, *Psychologie* (n. 50 above), IV.1, 347.

57. Alan of Lille, *De fide catholica contra haereticos*, I, 38, in *PL*, CCX, 342B (see n. 78 saying that the printed text has *Apostolus* in place of *Augustinus*), and *Liber de distinctionibus dictionum theologicalium*, s.v. *habere.*, ibid., col. 807C. See Marie-Thérèse d'Alverny, *Alain de Lille. Textes inédits avec une introduction sur sa vie et oeuvres*, Etudes de philosophie médiévale, 52 (Paris, 1965), pp. 71-73 and 156-62.

58. Peter the Chanter, *Verbum abbreviatum*, 95, in *PL*, CCV, 274AC.

59. Peter of Blois, *Serm.* 65, in *PL*, CCVII, 774BC. See also n. 55 above.

60. Adam of Dryburgh, *De ordine, habitu, et professione canonicorum Praemonstratensis ordinis*, III, 8, in *PL*, CXCVIII, 466D. The alternate translation was proposed by Robert Bjork of Arizona State University.

61. Ibid., VIII, 11, col. 516CD. The phrase *de disciplina tractans ecclesiastica* suggests that Adam was using Ivo's *Decretum*. For the Augustinian rule see Luc Verheijen, *La règle de saint Augustin* (Paris, 1967), I, 148. Adam's two references to "Have love" are mentioned in his seventeenth-century *Vita* by G. Ghiselbertus, in *PL*, CXCVIII, 44C and 65C. See also François Petit, *Ad viros religiosos. Quatorze sermons d'Adam Scot* (Tongerloo, 1934), pp. 37-38; and James Bulloch, *Adam of Dryburgh* (London, 1958), p. 29.

62. Elias of Coxida, *Serm.* 1, in *PL*, CCIX, 999A.

63. Gunther of Pairis, *De oratione, jejunio et eleemosyna*, 2, in *PL*, CCXII, 212A. This reference is followed by a discussion of simplicity, recalling the single eye.

64. Rupert of Deutz, *De gloria et honore filii hominis super Mattheum*, 6, in *CC:CM*, XXIX, 177.

65. R.-Norbert Sauvage, *La chronique de Sainte-Barbe-en-Auge*, Mémoires de l'Académie nationale des sciences, arts et belles-lettres de Caen, Documents (Caen, 1906), pp. 23–24.

66. Gratian, *Decretum*, II, 33 (*De penitentia*), 3, 12, in *Corpus iuris canonici*, ed. Emil Friedberg (Leipzig, 1879), I, 1193; cf. ibid., II, 33, 3, 43, col. 1207.

67. Baldwin of Canterbury, *De requie coelesti*, in *PL*, CCIV, 445A.

68. Lottin, *Psychologie* (n. 50 above), IV.1, 334, 356–60, 373, 398–99, 445–46, 454-74, and 480-82, citing the works of, among others, Stephen Langton, William of Auxerre, Albertus Magnus, Bonaventura, and Thomas Aquinas. See also M.-D. Chenu, *L'éveil de la conscience dans la civilisation médiévale*, Conférence Albert-le-Grand, 1968 (Montreal-Paris, 1969), p. 28.

69. Ambrose, *De officiis*, I, 30, in *PL*, XVI, 71B.

70. Alan of Lille, *Quoniam homines*, 193, ed. P. Glorieux, in *Archives d'histoire doctrinale et littéraire du Moyen Age* 28 (1953), p. 337 (116 on the date). See Lottin, *Psychologie* (n. 50 above), IV.1, 321, and d'Alverny, *Alain* (n.57 above), pp. 60-61. A variant form is found in the account of the preaching of the crusade in 1198 in Rigord, *Gesta Philippi Augusti*, 120, in *Oeuvres de Rigord et de Guillaume le Breton*, ed. H. François Delaborde, Société de l'histoire de France, 210 and 224 (Paris, 1882-85), I, 140, which has *affectus tuus operi tuo finem imponit*, "Your attitude determines the result of your work."

71. Lottin, *Psychologie* (n. 50 above), IV.1, 334. Chenu, *Eveil* (n. 68 above), p. 28, paraphrased the motto "C'est la volonté, la volonté intentionnelle qui décide de ton acte et le définit."

72. Robert Javelet, *Image et ressemblance au douzième siècle de saint Anselme à Alain de Lille* (Paris, 1967), I, 418; see 423–25 on Richard of St. Victor's view of love of neighbor as the image of the Holy spirit, not *in* or *ad* but *secundum imaginem*.

73. See the old but still-useful work of Pierre Rousselot, *Pour l'histoire du problème d'amour au Moyen Age*, Beiträge zur Geschichte der Philosophie des Mittelalters, VI.6 (Münster, 1908), esp. pp. 35-39 on William of St-Thierry; 43–49 on Hugh of St. Victor; and 49-55 and 76-77 on Bernard of Clairvaux.

74. See p. 65 above, and Stock, *Augustine* (n. 49 above), pp. 198 and 215, on Augustine's sense of interior renewal and knowledge of the inner self.

75. Geoffrey Grossus, *Vita Bernardi Tironiensis*, 103, in *PL*, CLXXII, 1428B.

76. Francis of Assisi, *Testamentum*, 14, in his *Opuscula*, ed. Cajetan Esser, Bibliotheca franciscana ascetica medii aevi, 12 (Grottaferrata, 1978), p. 310.

77. Caesarius of Heisterbach, *Dialogus miraculorum*, VI, 5, ed. Joseph Strange (Cologne-Bonn-Brussels, 1851), I, 352, and *The Dialogue on Miracles*, trans. H. Von E. Scott and C. C. Swinton Bland, Broadway Medieval Library (London, 1929), I, 405.

78. Augustine, *Tractatus in Evangelium Ioannis*, 90,1 (ad 15.23), in CC, XXXVI, 551; see *Contra Faustum*, 19, 11, in CSEL, XXV, 510, on the need for visible signs and sacraments for any religious association. See Rist, *Augustine* (n. 7 above), p. 244, and Stock, *Augustine* (n. 49 above), pp. 16 and 271, on the need for "corporeal signs" as an indication of intentions. For Richard of St. Victor see pp. 76–77 above.

79. See, in addition to Rousselot, *Problème de l'amour* (n. 73 above), Myrra Lot-Borodine, *De l'amour profane à l'amour sacré* (Paris, 1961); and, on love in secular literature, C. S. Lewis, *The Allegory of Love: A Study in Medieval Tradition* (Oxford, 1936); W. T. H. Jackson, *The Anatomy of Love: The "Tristan" of Gottfried von Strassburg* (New York-London, 1971), esp. pp. 64–141 on "aspects of love"; and C. Stephen Jaeger, "L'amour des rois: structure sociale d'une forme de sensibilité aristocratique," *Annales ESC* 46 (1991), pp. 547–71, who mentions among other topics "l'amour en tant que relation dominante dans la vie publique unissant le souverain et la cour, le souverain et le vassal." I owe the final point in the text to Nicholas Watson.

80. Thomas of Chobham, *Summa de arte praedicandi*, 6, in *CC:CM*, LXXXII, 154.

81. Thomas Aquinas, *Quaestio disputata de virtutibus*, 018, QDW, qu2, ar5, ag9, in his *Opera omnia*, III, ed. Roberto Busa (Rome-Stuttgart-Bad Cannstadt, 1980), 418–19.

82. *Ancrene wisse*, 6, ed. Shepherd (n. 12 above), p. 19. See also the edition (under the title *Ancren riwle*) and translation by James Morton, Camden Society, 57 (London, 1853), pp. 384-86, and the translation by Anne Savage and Nicholas Watson in *Anchoritic Spirituality*, Classics of Western Spirituality (New York-Mahwah, 1991), p. 189. On the authorship and date see the introduction to *Anchoritic Spirituality*, pp. 7–15, and Yoko Wada, *"Temptations" from "Ancrene Wisse,"* I, Kansai University, Institute of Oriental and Occidental Studies, Sources and Materials Series, 18 (Kansai, 1994), esp. pp. lxxi and lxxxix, with references to previous works.

83. *Ancrene wisse*, ed. Shepherd, p. 20, and ed. Morton, p. 387.

84. *Quellen zur Geschichte der Waldenser*, ed. Alexander Patschovsky and Kurt-Victor Selge, Texte zur Kirchen- und Theologiegeschichte, 18 (Gütersloh, 1973), p. 91.

85. Marguerite (Margarite) Porete, *Le mirouer des simples ames anienties et qui seulement demourent en vouloir et desir d'amour*, 13, ed. Romana Guarnieri (Rome, 1961), p. 24, and *CC:CM*, LXIX, 56. Cf. *The Mirror of Simple Souls*, trans. Ellen Babinsky, Classics of Western Spirituality (New York-Mahwah, 1993), p. 95, who has "My love, love and do what you will." On Margaret Porete see Alexander Patschovsky, "Freiheit der Ketzer," in *Die abendländische Freiheit von 10. zum 14. Jahrhundert*, ed. Johannes Fried, Vorträge und Forschungen, 39 (Sigmaringen, 1991), pp. 275–81.

86. Marguerite Porete, *Mirouer*, 13, in *CC:CM*, LXIX, 57.

87. Marilyn Doiron, "Margarete Porete: 'The Mirror of Simple Souls.' A Middle English Translation," *Archivio italiano per la storia della pietà*, 5 (1968): pp. 267 and 245, where it is proposed that the English translation was made by bishop Michael Northbrook, who died in 1361. Nicholas Watson, "Melting into God the English Way: Deification in the Middle English Version of Marguerite Porete's *Mirouer des simples âmes anienties*," in *Prophets Abroad: The Reception of Continental Holy Women in Late-Medieval England*, ed. Rosalynn Voaden (Woodbridge, 1996), pp. 31-33, associated the translation with "the explosion of vernacular theological writing" ca. 1370/1410.

88. Doiron, "Margarete Porete" (n. 87 above), p. 372. This passage is in the appendix by Edmund Colledge and Romana Guarnieri, who concluded (pp. 381-82) "that the *Mirror* is a work of heresy, written by a teacher of false doctrine skilled in concealing her unorthodoxy behind ambiguity and imprecision." See also Patschovsky, "Freiheit" (n. 85 above), p. 276, calling the *Mirror* "ein genuin häretisches Werk."

89. Jean Gerson, *De distinctione revelationum*, ed. Louis Ellies Du Pin (Antwerp, 1706; rpt. Hildesheim, 1987), I, 55a D, and ed. Palemon Glorieux, III (Paris, 1962), p. 51.

90. Eckhart, *Serm.* 74, in *Meister Eckhart*, ed. Franz Pfeiffer, Deutsche Mystiker des vierzehnten Jahrhunderts, 2 (Göttingen, 1857, rpt. 1906), p. 232, and as *Serm.* 29 in *Meister Eckhart. Die deutschen und lateinischen Werke* (Stuttgart, 1958-76): *Die*

deutschen Werke, II, 79; cf. Raymond B. Blakney, *Meister Eckhart: A Modern Translation* (New York-London, 1941), p. 193. See Romana Guarnieri, "Il movimento del Libero Spirito dalle origine al secolo XVI," *Archivio italiano per la storia della pietà* 4 (1965), p. 417 (citing this passage in n. 2), and Robert Lerner, *The Heresy of the Free Spirit in the Later Middle Ages* (Berkeley-Los Angeles, 1972: rpt. Notre Dame-London, 1991), p. 183.

91. Eckhart, *Expositio s. Evangelii secundum Iohannem*, V, 19, and *Sermones et lectiones super Ecclesiastici*, XXIV, 30, in *Die lateinischen Werke* (n. 90 above), III, 353, and II, 293-94. Kent Emery of Notre Dame University drew my attention to the line in *Purgatorio*, XXVII, 131, where Virgil, bidding farewell to Dante said "Lo tuo piacere omai prendi per duce" [From now take your pleasure as guide], which has been associated with Augustine's precept, as in the translation by S. W. Arndt (Lewiston-Queenston-Lampeter, 1994), p. 419, n. 28; cf. the edition by C. H. Grandgent (Boston-New York, 1933), p. 577, n. 131: "Now that Dante's soul has been cleansed and his will set free from the bondage of vice, all his impulses are necessarily good." The early commentary of Benvenuto Rambaldi of Imola, ed. J. P. Lacaita (Florence, 1887), IV, 157, interpreted *lo tuo piacere* as "will, which is in the power of the intellect." This is different from love, and in spite of the stress on doing what you will, Dante's intent seems different from Augustine's.

92. Luther came close when he said in his sermon on 5 June 1525 that someone wins love for God by recognizing the dead Christ and "Quando haec dilectio, facit, quod deus iubet," where "What God orders" may mean the same, for some writers, as "what you will": Martin Luther, *Werke*, XVI (Weimar, 1899), 285.

93. Hildegard of Bingen, *Liber vite meritorum*, IV, 30, in *CC:CM*, XC, 193, said that someone who follows his own pleasure (*placitum*) "quod uult, hoc sibi eligit, nec utilitatem sed tantum uanitatem aliorum considerat." See also James A. Brundage, "Carnal Delight: Canonistic Theories of Sexuality," in *Proceedings of the Fifth International Congress of Medieval Canon Law* (Vatican City, 1980), p. 371 and n. 39.

94. J. W. Goethe, *Die Wahlverwandtschaften*, in the *Gedenkausgabe* (Artemis Verlag), IX (Zürich, 1949), 24, and *Poetische Werke: Gedichte und Singspiele*, I. *Gedichte* (Berlin-Weimar, 1965), p. 656.

95. Margot Adler, *Drawing down the Moon: Witches, Druids, Goddess-Worshippers, and other Pagans in America Today* (Boston, 1986), p. 101.

96. The writer of the script, Ruth Prawer Jhabvala, wrote in a letter of 31 July [1986] that "I'm sure old Mr. Emerson would have been horrified to think a quote from a Bishop and Church Father had been put in his mouth, but as I meant him to mean it in its purely secular interpretation, maybe he wouldn't have minded it so much."

Postscript

Any additional references to "Love and do what you will," especially in late medieval sources, will be gratefully received (and incorporated with acknowledgment in a future edition of this essay) by the author at the Institute for Advanced Study, Princeton, NJ 08540.

Piers Plowman, the Monsters, and the Critics: Some Embarrassments of Literary History [1998]

Anne Middleton

My purpose here begins, and will end, with embarrassment—as a critical response to, and ultimately as a clarifying perspective upon—*and from within*—*Piers Plowman*. As a critical response to the poem this embarrassment is fairly easy to describe, though less easy to account for without some critical and historical distance on our own enterprises to date. Facing that complex of embarrassments squarely, however, makes it possible to see how and why the poet renders this inconvenient emotion as a crucial point of leverage upon his vast and unruly project, ultimately as his threshold of disclosure of his principles of form, and of the specifically literary character and purposes of his project.

For both of these pursuits, the poem's third vision is a key exhibit, as it has long been something of a test case for both local and total interpretation, for specifying the characteristic features of Langland's art, and for overall critical and historical understanding of its achievement. It is there that the poem stages a confrontation with the embarrassments of its own multiple ambitions, and the commonplace and humbling constituents of its making. Close attention to the sequence that ends with Ymaginatif's *paideia* is far beyond the scope of this lecture; here I can at most sketch briefly how that sequence manages to bare the device of the poem as a whole, not only as a literary innovation but as a literary-historical intervention of signal importance—and why this sequence in the poem marks the poem's pivotal disclosure of its own literary character with a significant blush, a sudden access of shame and embarrassment. I suggest that Langland's fictive staging of embarrassment at this juncture has in turn something to tell us about the "present state" of our own discipline today, and about the altered, but still vexed, relations between positive knowledge and aesthetic response in our terms of professional and pedagogical engagement with early English literature, and this poem in particular, since Morton Bloomfield raised this issue in his seminal 1939 article surveying the state of criticism on the poem.[1]

Understanding the terms and scope of its profound originality was, Bloomfield rightly insisted, the central *desideratum* for future study of the poem. To this end he proposed two scholarly enterprises that have largely defined the labors of its scholarly half-acre ever since. Considered simply as two different scales of attention for philological investigation, they ought in principle to be complementary: on the one hand, the "meaning of Langland's words and lines," and on the other, "general study of the backgrounds," in "folklore, art, theology, homilies, religious tractates, and various literatures, as well as in social and economic history"—i.e., text and context, microcosmic and macrocosmic investigation of what might be termed the poem's ingredients. In more than fifty years' hindsight, these mandates might seem to have been splendidly fulfilled on several fronts: the "cruxbusting" exegetical essay on the intricacies of a term or short passage has been a hardy and productive perennial in this field, while a larger-scale feast of contextual studies in social and intellectual history has assured that anyone who takes the trouble to make its acquaintance will be prevented from some of the more egregious errors in generic understanding that Bloomfield identified.[2] Yet the hunger for significant form that remained central to his survey remains in part unsatisfied: we seem no closer to benefiting from these efforts in the ways that Bloomfield seems to have hoped we would in understanding the poem's literary originality. And that is because in the intervening decades the estrangement between Mercury and Philology has proceeded to a largely unremarked and uncontested divorce, each of the parties having in the interim found other disciplinary identifications and domains of argument. A brief conspectus of the half-acre then and now will help to specify why Bloomfield's central *desideratum* remains a live agenda for criticism—and why his later aphoristic insight that the poem reads "like a commentary on an unknown text" remains productive.[3]

From where we stand now, the most striking aspect of Bloomfield's 1939 conspectus of our field is its referential base: his survey of secondary scholarship is confined to studies or mentions of *Piers Plowman* alone, from the earliest appropriation of it within early modern reformist scholarship, through more recent and increasingly specialized studies. The essay refers to other medieval primary texts chiefly as temporally or spatially adjacent artifacts within the poet's field of advertent knowledge, whether as material for use, as broad generic templates, or as "sources and analogues," as these were to be termed in Chaucer studies at about the same time.[4] But since under this general definition of what counted as philological scholarship, other literary objects came into view only as a possible component of the poet's lifeworld of reference, not as a repertory of formal and generic gestures that could help define the significance of specific poetic choices, the relation of comparative analysis to assessing Langland's poetic originality remained submerged. Such comparison, both within and across literary languages, remained largely circumscribed by the far stronger perimeter-fence of national languages as defining the entity of which literary history was largely written. That this model had long been ill-suited to medieval literary studies was in this decade becoming more openly acknowledged, but the 1930s were chiefly a period of brilliantly generative articulations of such intellectual discomfort. Like much prophetic discourse, Bloomfield's essay remains essential for bringing into view nodal problems whose solutions were visible only as *desiderata*; what is at issue is the relation of reference to meaning and of meaning to form. Nearly all the literary scholars we still esteem from that decade (one thinks of Auerbach and Spitzer) were engaged in the same unsettling prophetic enterprise.

A felt need for better apprehension of the "originality" of the poem (and, implicitly, its coherence and power as a work of literature) thus came most urgently from a kind of wilderness beyond the national-language terrain long considered proper to it, as Bloomfield clearly saw, citing studies that pursued possible formal resemblances to Dante and earlier French allegories; as he also noted, the few fitful attempts to date at generally appreciative criticism of the poem had been based on perceived analogies with modes of poetic fiction historically and generically inapposite to it. In this respect, his diagnosis was characteristic of its moment, in which literary studies in its first decade of modern professionalization lacked a syntax for framing the relation between questions of poetic form and aesthetic design, and the traditional forms of knowledge that the two levels of philological research Bloomfield proposed could supply concerning the materials, both verbal and referential, that informed these. (One might even say that thus described, his circumstance resembled that of Langland's poetic persona in Vision Three, in attempting to grasp the relation between an ample store of "clergial" repertory and citational competence and what he—which is to say ultimately the reader—most urgently needs for spiritual and cognitive satisfaction.) Under these circumstances, sporadic attempts at aesthetic understanding would remain monstrous and alien incursions into a specialized professional scholarly enterprise less frequent and more embarrassing at every foray.

Bloomfield's prophetic unease with the adequacy of the state of philological knowledge to the urgent and specifically literary questions presented by this poem was, within the same transitional decade, registered on behalf of other medieval long poems of enigmatic character yet compelling power, in two landmark critical essays published in 1936. I refer of course to Tolkien's pivotal essay, "Beowulf, the Monsters and the Critics," and to C. S. Lewis's almost incidental remarks on the poem in *The Allegory of Love*.[5] Though unmentioned by Bloomfield in his conspectus of scholarship—chiefly, I think, because his effort amounted to parallel testimony—each offers an indicative vantage point from which to assess what has since befallen the effort to understand the originality and beauty of *Piers Plowman* as a literary work—or, more fundamentally, *that* it was advertently designed *as* a literary work. One of these provides my title for this lecture; the other articulates the central critical plaint that has kept the poem for all the intervening decades an important exhibit in social and intellectual history (and as a poem, chiefly a repository of brilliantly pungent and evocative moments), and fixed its nameless author in literary history and pedagogy as arch-antitype to the canon-defining poet of the Middle English era, Chaucer. If Chaucer could grudgingly be allowed by critics to have left his last work in some respects unfinished, Langland would remain to literary-historical hindsight the poet whose project was not simply under continual renegotiation but interminable, because lacking a manifest "foreconceit" or discernible positive poetics that could sustain its weight and length. This differential qualitative judgment would in turn affect the choices of presentation of the printed texts of each poet that would make them available (or intractable) to modern "institutions of literary consumption."[6] Unlike his younger and putatively more genial and masterful coeval, Langland has been appreciated as a highly gifted poet whose great project is nevertheless accessible to "appreciation" only in pieces. Implicitly committed to a poetic project no less epic in scale and ambition than those of Dante or Milton, he remains to literary-historical view a writer unable fully to subordinate to his overarching purpose his almost limitless repertory of informing discourses.

What provoked Tolkien's classic essay on *Beowulf*—and later James Sledd's humorously self-conscious revival of its formula in his essay on Chaucer's Clerk's Tale—was a long-standing critical embarrassment at the center of these two poems, an embarrassment that both these scholars pointedly declined to find debilitating. That embarrassment—the "monster" of both essays—was a narrative motive and "motif" from a putatively more elementary or "primitive" level of feeling, thought, or belief than that attributed to the poem's elegantly wrought stylistic surface and narrative *ordo*: in the case of *Beowulf* the three nonhuman monsters with which the hero does battle; in the Clerk's Tale the fable or "folktale" substratum of the tale of the demonic consort which alone, it was argued, could "explain" the motiveless malignancy of Walter's repeated trying of Griselde's patience. Both critics argued that the peculiar excellence of the poem in question, the wonder it aroused and the generative provocation it issued, came not in spite of this allegedly embarrassing feature but through it: that the poem, in some non-ironized sense we would have to deal with as "modern" scholars, meant what it said. We should not attempt to resolve our admiration for the work into praise of splendid style and dignified ornament, still less translate its alien creatures into the more manageable and civilized guise of abstractions or "allegories." Rather we would have to come to terms with the monstrous actants of the fable itself—and even, if we could stay the course, the further inference that the poet might really have intended, as part of his design, to provoke the embarrassment to a sense of intellectual seriousness or propriety that his monstrous device repeatedly aroused.

A similarly euhemeristic tendency has dominated accounts of the two embarrassingly vernacular monsters whose unquenchable ardor for truth gives Langland's poem such unitary design as it has: Piers the Plowman and Will the Dreamer, the only figures who at the end of the poem remain uncompromised, untraduced, as they have been throughout the poem the only figures whose persistent animus has generated its continued incident.[7] These vernacular figures are the poem's two chief fictive inventions, and both are set in motion and lead their riveting literary lives among preexisting and variously abstract terms with a rich and varied prior existence in treatises of moral psychology and philosophy, in Scripture and in salvation history (Conscience, Reason, Scripture; Trajan, Abraham), figures from already "civilized" (in this case mostly Latinate) discourse who have therefore received the lion's share of annotational attention. Will and Piers, by contrast, long and rightly seen as central to the poem's coherence, have been understood in this role in two very different ways. In one view—the dominant form of "critical" account of the poem as a whole—the poem's two main vernacular figures function, much as the other personifications of the poem do, as signifiers. They must *mean*: assigning them meaning is the main enterprise of reading, and as the poem continues they each are asked to *stand for* more and more. And since they operate within in a loosely temporal sequence of manifestations, defining a broadly narrative trajectory, the plot traced by these manifestations, understood as the poem's chief principle of coherence, is the story of their gradually (in this case literally—in a series of steps, passūs) improving rectification and realization as Christian subjects, the beneficiaries of the ministrations of the other actants in the nominal plot. To be sure, in this account their representative roles are complementary rather than identical: Will the Dreamer as recipient of all the ministrations of ecclesiastical and philosophical instruction is by definition tainted in his understanding by original sin, as he is ardent for rectification; Piers' complementary ardor is gradually realized in the visionary sequence in his double resemblance to Christ and Peter as exemplary of all the Dreamer perpetually and ideally desires. Yet in this view they are each the products of the poem, not its fictive agents: their "development," understood as increased comprehension and self-aware self-modification, is coextensive with the poem's development; the poem exists to perfect their definitions as *characters*, inscriptions or imprints of the didactic process that is the poem. In this view, the auspices or ambitions of poetic pedagogy in itself needs little explication.

In the alternative view, which I think offers a better account of the poem's otherwise unaccountable moves—particularly those very quibbles and digressions that are especially resistant to larger formal and rhetorical explanation according to the former regimen—these two monstrous figures function not as developing characters or signifiers but as embodiments and locators of the work's chief and most distinctive "literary interest," marking it as a particular kind of action. I use the latter term in the sense recently discussed by Steven Knapp, for whom "literary interest" is rooted in the sense of a powerful if elusive analogy between authorial and readerly agency, an ethical similarity which offers "an unusually precise and concentrated analogue of what it is like to be an agent in general."[8] These two vernacular protagonists sustain the principles of formal coherence of the poem and specify the kind of agency it envisions in its users. They define the special sense in which it may be understood as, in C. S. Lewis's term, a "moral poem," without necessarily thereby proceeding as a didactic one.

Lewis's summary discussion of *Piers Plowman* in *Allegory of Love* begins from the indicative remark that "in *Piers Plowman* we see an exceptional poet adorning a species of poetry which is hardly exceptional at all" (158). Lewis does not consider himself bound to indicate, however, what that "species" is, beyond designating *Piers Plowman* a "moral poem," into which Langland "throw[s] in, as any other medieval poet might have done, a good deal of satire on various 'estates.'" While acknowledging the splendor of several major passages—the sublime drama of the liturgy, for example, or the complex theology of the Fall—Lewis seems to ascribe their conceptual and affective power to the rich traditional practices and intertexts in which these are embedded, and to the beliefs these sustain, without reference to the narrative and dialogic auspices under which the poet restages and resituates these within his own design, to which Lewis is surprisingly inattentive. Such moments, in Lewis's view, not only fail to produce coherence but exempt poetic genius from answerability to poetic design; they do not counterbalance but underwrite his famous judgment that Langland is "confused and monotonous" and "barely makes his poetry into a poem" (161).

To be sure, Lewis makes these remarks literally and explicitly *in passing*: that is, in the course of eschewing extended discussion of the poem, as, he says, "a little outside our subject"—outside, that is, his book's theme, which he defines early on as the "allegorical feudalization of love." But the purported extraneousness of Langland's poem to Lewis's topic is likewise indicative: one wonders what, if not that, he understood the Passion sequence (which he admires) to be. In other words, the nearly total *absence* from Langland's poem of any of the erotic or pathetic figurations of divine love, available in many of the works that serve the poet as sources and analogues—an absence that one might therefore regard as surprising—does not provoke Lewis into thought about the poem's designs. Rather this notable absence becomes an embarrassment, prompting not explanation but curtailment of critical interest. The poem's digressive brilliance solicits the critic's digression, which he finally declines to pursue as a temptation resisted. But it is as a temptation initially unrecognized that, as I shall suggest, the poem itself stages, at its very center, its own explicit engagement with the question of poetic design and its auspices, and the relation of beauty to the nourishment of the soul.

Lewis's admittedly perfunctory assessment points to a major tradition of subsequent critical practice upon the poem, and is the more indicative precisely because of its untroubled brevity. It tacitly subsumes the effort to discern the general intentional form or "species" of the poem in that of identifying its constituent ingredients, the rhetorical postures and generic gestures of one or more of the recognizable contributory discourses and "source" texts that the poem pervasively mimes, as Lewis seems to recognize. Since these are numerous and extremely heterogeneous, and are not easily reduced to any single coherent rhetorical program, this "catalogue" approach to form renders the poem incoherent by stipulation. Lewis differs from most of his contemporaries in this line of thought chiefly in eschewing the further critical enterprise required to pursue it: the philological labors of gathering a monstrous hoard, a critical venture in primitive accumulation, when what most urgently needs explaining, as Morton Bloomfield presciently understood, was the literary-historical significance of the poem's startling gaps and fissures.

As an answer to questions of formal intent, this enterprise is doomed in the ways that Bloomfield foresaw. The luster and occasional rarity of each item unearthed from its normal ambits of use to become part of Langland's "materials" conduces to a high estimate of the poet's learnedness, a virtue easily equated by professionalized literary scholars with poetic value and power, for it implies that much has been successfully subordinated and assimilated to achieving his effects, which remain beyond account, much as royal splendor asserts the incontestability of the hegemonic claims made simply by possessing it. The method (if one can honor it with such a term) of such a critical enterprise is, like that of Beowulf's *wyrm*, acquisition without understanding. The objects in this storehouse of explicatory lore are scarcely ever considered by their collectors in relation to the kinds of cognitive, affective, or memorial experience that this putatively primitive accumulation attests, perpetuates, *and confects*—in short, to the literary work they do in this poem. Yet the willed and often anguished turn away from this feast of literate and "clergial" lore is repeatedly a constitutive gesture of the poem, and deferred satisfaction is the formal condition and metaphoric representation of its making, as Jill Mann has provocatively suggested.[9]

How to deal, then, with not only the poem's dense texture of inclusions but its principled refusals, its notorious discontinuities—in short, its insistently proclaimed relation to what is *not there*? These gestures are those that most resist understanding as anything other than lapses, whether of taste and measure ("confusion and monotony"), of focus (quibbles, digressions, longueurs), or of argumentative or narrative continuity—the unaccountable excesses and recursions of Langland's poetic procedure. To understand the constitutive role of these purported gaps and distractions in the poem, I counterpose to Lewis's dismissive verdict the *via negativa* proposed by Morton Bloomfield's resonant observation, in a survey of the poet's formal models, that the poem is "like a commentary on an unknown text." This richly generative notion marks a founding moment for historical criticism of this poem, as it also implies a larger awareness of the historical contingency of "literature" generally as a cultural mode and historically specific formation. For it proposes that the enabling condition of the poem's initial invention and forms of realization was the perception, not of an unassimilable plenitude of knowledge or doctrine to be mastered and submitted to rhetorical form, but of a radical lack or absence, a discursive hunger.

Bloomfield's resonant dictum suggests a new approach to the place of this poem in literary history, a matter heretofore surprisingly resistant to exploration. It suggests a route to understanding not simply the realized form of Langland's poem—"digressions," monotonies and all—but also its generative role in literary history, as a poetic project that came to define the conditions of possibility and realization of "vernacular literature" as a distinct cultural category, and of "serious fiction" as a point of critical leverage upon its world. It indicates the terms in which Langland's work would come to demonstrate to its contemporaries what philosophically serious vernacular fiction could do—and would do so in ways that I think are demonstrably registered by both Chaucer's and Gower's work of the 1390s. Bloomfield's work on the poem, in tandem with Donaldson's very different kind of close diachronic attention to its variously realized states, was, and remains, prophetic of what literary history of this era—before there existed any possibility of national literary "canons"—would be about, and could do. It suggests that Langland's compositional designs and intents are in effect driven or drawn by a purpose that began, not in a primal constructive literary design, extended by piecemeal appropriation of "moral" discourses, but in the generative perception of anomaly, of a gap between past and present textual possibility, a recognition of something in which his own intervention is an act of bridge-building, and like all bridge-building an act fraught with both risk and the possibility of new projects and directions of mental travel, facilitating something beyond itself, as it is prompted by something it did not make. This authorial perception of anomaly, not a "foreconceit" of a unitary plenitude to be realized in architectonic form, is, in other words, the condition in which Langland's conception of the work of literature arises, in which its formal choices on all scales are realized, and in which "literary interest" is engaged. It is also what motivates the act and art of commentary, as a mode of dialogic inquiry.

In identifying Langland's project as commentary I mean to locate it within a tradition of philosophical practice, not simply exegesis, in which philosophizing is conducted through systematic exploration of, and distinctions from and within, what has already been argued or asserted on his subject; it is in fact the dominant medieval expository mode for developing philosophical argument. The purpose of philosophizing in this manner is not, however, simply serial local elucidation (the usual aim of marginal or running annotation), nor is it ultimately apologetic or persuasive, to "save the appearances" of, or to promulgate, the received wisdom or authoritative teachings that provide its premises and materials (usually called the writer's "sources" when the texts under discussion are considered "literary"). It is, rather, a sustained active engagement with the textual field under examination. Commentaries *de anima*, for example, enlist the several discourses on the soul in textual conversation, to produce useful distinctions to continue such exploration. Commentary as philosophic inquiry thus offers a course of pedagogy or self-improvement only inferentially, in the sense that the Socratic enterprise does: it requires to get started only the premise that knowledge, however it is defined or produced, is consequential: it has something to do with action and outcomes, and offers something more—and something other—than a thesaurus or hoard of traditional understanding and pious belief, attractively repackaged.

As a vernacular commentary on the precarious premises of its own making, framed in the serial fiction of "romanced" adventure, Langland's poem conducts a speculative exploration of the kinds of reading praxis that sustain belief, embodied in a narrative form that aligns questions of "literary interest" with those of moral edification. It thereby presents an episodic "reading lesson," examining through fictive hypothesis what the truths of faith might mean and feel like in desirous experience, and what kind of "truth" a representation of such an experience might offer. Hence the important secondary aspect of this philosophizing in Langland's poem— never displacing the "moral" urgency of its primary fictive exploration but shadowing it as a matter of the poem's nascent literary ethos and principles of form—concerns the question of in what sense the "literary interest" of the poem itself offers anything of distinctive value or use to the mind that entertains it, and (the embarrassing issue that confronts Will at the end of the third vision) what literary pleasures have to do with edification.

It is in Vision Three that Langland explores the affective and reflexive dimensions of the Dreamer's quest "to know Dowel," and thereby simultaneously discloses the poetics of the project, in Ymaginatif's discourse on the pleasures offered by "clergial" reading of world and Book to their full imaginative depths, as against (in B) mere "makyng," and (in C) in relation to the range of applied arts and sciences that comprise cosmographical "clergie." Pointedly echoing the initial earthly panorama of the Prologue, the second Middelerthe panorama of harmonious animate nature, disclosed as an "inner vision" encapsulated within the poem's third vision, this display brings into view the visionary project of the poem itself and the almost boundless hermeneutic possibility it evokes. For the first time in Vision Three, Will seems at last on the verge of becoming a sadder and wiser man, and thereby ready to wake from the inner-vision sequence, improved by what has finally become legible as an edifying and beautiful spectacle, one offered to him in the recognizable Latin literary register of Alan of Lille and other allegorists of Nature as benignly legible to a properly philosophical gaze (B.11.320–75/C.13.129–92). Yet Reason will have none of this literary sentiment: he sharply recasts Will's reading of the lovely sight as signifying his yielding to yet one more temptation, as the opening words of his rebuke (C.13.194/B.11.376), which conclude the inner-dream sequence, echo those of Rechelesnesse that began it (C.11.193/B.11.34): "recche þe neuere . . . " (never mind; don't concern yourself with. . . .).[10] Because this time unrecognized as such, the beautiful second Middelerthe display is if anything more dangerous than the first, which presented the solicitations of acquisitive and carnal desires under the aegis of Fortune, in response to Scripture's humiliating "scorn." To the eyes of desirous interpretive ambition rather than ruminative wonder, Reason suggests, the "natural" harmonies of animate nature, however beautiful, can only invite the Will once more into hermeneutic temptation. His response to this sharp final reorientation of the pedagogy presented by the inner dream is indicative, and heralds a recognition Augustine well understood: "Tho caughte I colour anoon and comsed to be ashamed / And waked therwith" (B.11.405–6/ C.13.212–13). What follows the closure of the inner vision, and concludes the third dream, is the pedagogy of Ymaginatif; still more embarrassing, it proves to have been with him for all of his life, unrecognized. Under Reason's correction, Will remains within the inner dream, suspended in the uncomfortable position of having acknowledged the stunning and potentially reformative power of beauty, but ignorant of what beyond exemplarity it has to offer him.

Central to Reason's account of what this panorama offers is the "suffraunce" with which one must behold it to understand it. In Reason's view, Will's apparently contrite lament at human excesses remains a sentimental and showy rather than edifying acknowledgment of chastisement, because it is so obviously premised on, and gratifying to, spectatorial reading; its axiomatic generality continues to exempt Will in the first person from understanding the face of Nature as divine inscription, and its solemn regularities as divine language addressed to his needs, rather than an endless source of adventitious exemplarity through rhetorically felicitous "forbisnes." It is the very plenitude of this divine inscription, its excessiveness in relation to any single human programmatic pedagogy, and a changed, imaginatively receptive, attitude of affective and cognitive response to the fullness of its gratifications ("suffraunce") that now more profoundly hail the Dreamer before he can awake satisfied from the third vision. What happens at that juncture implicitly discloses the terms of Langland's own poetic project as a sustained vernacular exercise in "deep reading" in the treasury of divine inscription, rather than as rhetorical composition. Ymaginatif's final intervention in the third vision offers a spiritual pedagogy in reading rather than "makyng," and the prospect of full "clergial" enjoyment of the beautiful order of both divine testaments, the world and the Book.

To the "clergial kynde wit" commended by Ymaginatif, figural understanding is not a trick of rhetoric, by which exemplifications may be extracted from the phenomenal world for purposes of preaching and teaching (the instrumental discourses proper to "clergie" as the class of ecclesiastical ministers), but an aptitude of the soul to the kind of perspicuity that is a property of the divinely-given "real," when approached by the soul in a state of "suffraunce," rendering it amenable to cognition of all creatures visible and invisible, by imaginative alignment with the suffering author of both world and Book. "Ymaginatif" reading and writing is thus facilitated, but not given, by the arts and sciences, which occupy most of the admittedly heterogeneous disciplinary gamut of this enigmatic figure's corrective lore.[11] Ranging from moralized bestiaries to the science of the stars, the very miscellaneity of Ymaginatif's exposition has provoked widely varied scholarly estimates of the explanatory power and role of this figure in the poetic sequence, from a rigorous and comprehensive account of Langland's general philosophical alignments, engaging advanced scholastic debates on the faculties of the soul (Kaulbach), to advocacy and illustration of the less exalted, even commonplace, figurative skills required for the effective instrumental didacticism of the ecclesiastical ministry, and other forms of applied rhetoric—i.e. the repertory of school-lore that also underwrites the composition of edifying fiction (Minnis, Hanna).[12] Yet despite their apparent disagreements on the remit and profundity of Ymaginatif's pedagogy, there need be no ultimate quarrel between these views, if what is at issue is the general form and poetics of the enterprise itself, rather than, as in most critical discussion of Vision Three, the intellectual lineages of its lore.

It is the explicitly pedagogical register of the dialogues of Vision Three, and particularly of the tutelage of Will's lifelong silent companion Ymaginatif as an informant anterior to all formal instruction, that makes explicit the vexed question of the discursive intent and mode of the work itself, and the importance of clear distinctions between it and the instrumental discourses that pervade its language and reference. This secondary task, which the poet evidently considered a *sine qua non* of the poem's extension into its two long versions, is to indicate the special, non-demonstrative, auspices under which these familiar didactic ingredients are offered as, among other things, *imaginative fiction*, requiring the reader to consider what kind of "truth" is available to a reader by a work so insistently "clergial" in matter yet literary in mode—which is to say, as all medieval expositors of the *artes* knew, deeply figurative and analogous in its manner of proceeding, and producing as its most characteristic and beneficial experience startling and pleasurable recognitions that repeatedly elude argumentative formulation.[13]

Among the many supremely learned accounts of the third vision to which my own understanding is indebted, perhaps the most comprehensive, moving, and formally trenchant is the classic essay of Joseph Wittig on the self-reflexivities of this "inward journey."[14] As Wittig notes (271), Langland's choice of names for its ultimate tutelary figure suggests that he "intended to stress the activity rather than the faculty" of imagination, and, as in the *Benjamin Minor* to which his poem is intellectually indebted, the power of Ymaginatif can only be brought into view through the enabling access of shame that marks Will's transit from the inner vision back to the pedagogical sequence of the third vision. The salient point of tangency between Wittig's penetrating account of the medieval philosophical psychology of self-knowledge and my reading of the metapoetic aspect of the sequence is Will's pivotal blush of embarrassed recognition, upon which the sequence recasts the worldly panorama of his inner vision in a perspective newly transformed by "suffraunce": from this point the inescapable sense of human insufficiency presented by the "wonders" of Nature's spectacularly beautiful unlikeness to the subject beholding it is transformed into the pleasurable plenitude of the noetic quest. To an Ymaginatif view, the beauty of the phenomenal world is shown to be of the same kind as textual divine inscription, and productive of the same spiritual joy.

Bartholomeus Anglicus, in *De proprietatibus rerum* (given here in Trevisa's English), provides an account of blushing as a physiological response to prompting in the sensible soul, as it submits its apprehensions to "resoun," a process that occurs at the point of encounter of a "natural" animal process with one of specifically human moral cognition (many ancient philosophers had observed that the other animals do not blush): "þe philosophir seiþ þat þe forhede is þe seete of schame and of worshipe, and þat is for he is nyȝe þe vertue ymaginatif. By þe vertu ymaginatif þinges þat ben elenge oþir glad, semeliche oþir unsemeliche, ben sodeinliche ibrouȝt to þe dome of resoun, and þere þey ben idemed."[15] But perhaps more germane to the metapoetic function of this blush, and its pivotal role in marking the changed auspices of the "literary interest" of the work, is Augustine's valorization of the endless pleasures of the *involucrum*. Read under "suffraunce," the various phenomenal reflections of divine cosmic inscription continue to sustain the soul after philosophy ceases: "Where the philosopher blushes, there the apostle finds treasure: not scorning the base *involucrum*, he attains the precious reality it covers."[16] One has only to apprehend both world and Book in the mode of "suffraunce," to find in them "hidden treasures of wisdom and knowledge: . . . Turn to this *involucrum*, and pray that it be unfurled for you." Peter Dronke discusses this remarkably positive and capacious Augustinian understanding of the joys to be obtained by "reading" the world as divine inscription: it is an art and mental disposition for finding, not constructing, the pleasure of the text that underlies all texts. This, and not the rhetorical use of figuration, proves to be at the core of Ymaginatif's *paideia*: it is a pleasure to be found, not "founden up" in "making." On second thought, Langland saw fit to remove Ymaginatif's problematic indictment of "making," rewriting it and moving it to a more fitting narrative juncture between the first and second visions of the C-version, as Will is held answerable to Reason and Conscience for the uses of this gift in the world's work.

Dronke's exploration of a group of medieval Latin texts "commonly grouped as 'Platonic' . . . in which the abstract and the concrete, ideas and images, are inextricably conjoined" (1) is indispensable to understanding the discursive ambitions of Langland's poem, the sense in which its episodic narrative may be seen as a running commentary on these, and the kinds of repeated generic misidentifications to which it is subject as an unprecedented vernacular venture in this mode. His account of both the theories and large-scale compositional applications of "imaginative and symbolic modes of thought" in these Latin texts (2) delineates more successfully than any critical study of *Piers Plowman* to date the fundamental literary-philosophical scope of Langland's project. More to my purpose here, it also helps to suggest the terms in which its episodic form, tracing (the) Will's encounter with a sequence of misapprehensions (alternately his own and those of his dialogic interlocutors) of the "intente" of this pursuit of divine "wonders," may accurately be regarded as a commentary on this enterprise. Proceeding narratively in the literary form of a cosmic quest-romance, differentiated (often pointedly, by local dictional markers) from the amatory and chivalric materials of English and Anglo-French antecedents in this mode, the repeatedly disrupted and redirected narrative of Will's desire enacts a continuous commentary on the unprecedented vernacular "reading" experience the poem affords.

By making the question of beauty and pleasure central to his long poem and the answer an enabling condition of its continuation, Langland poses a deeply Augustinian problem and stages its characteristically Augustinian solution as a crisis in a quest-narrative. Augustine's "breakthrough" to recognition of the suasive and comforting truths of divine revelation had consisted not in acceptance of the philosophical arguments in which he had immersed himself in the company of his friends in the process of conversion, nor even in the rhetorical beauties of Scripture, which indeed had at first seemed to him embarrassingly crude in expression, but rather in two powerful and silent confrontations with the plenitude of the text, the first facilitating the second, and both demonstrating the responsiveness of divine inscription to human need felt before it can be framed as philosophical objective. Ambrose's silent reading of Scripture, without vocalization, gave Augustine his stunning first encounter with a nonrhetorical conception of the written divine word (*Confessiones* VI.3); later (*Confessiones* VIII.11) a song audible only to the ears of the soul invited him to his second and determinative understanding of the soul-sustaining pleasures of the divine text as spoken through its apostles. Encountered in the manner of *sortes*, a random passage proved the book to be all-sufficient in every part to every human occasion and need, allowing it to address these prophetically, perspicaciously, and comfortingly. But such adventitiously nourishing plenitude can only be an embarrassment to philosophical inquiry.

Augustine's celebration of the world as given distinctively to the human mind for pleasurable rumination on its "wonders" occupies the first post-narrative book of the *Confessions*, book 10. Ymaginatif's highly miscellaneous pedagogy enacts the functional counterpart of this transitional book, retroactively ascribing to the dialogic sequence of the third vision a philosophically impoverished view of the issues at stake, insofar as it enlists the phenomenal world and clergial textuality as arsenals of argument, rather than sources of joy. It is only when Will has shown himself capable of such plenitude and satisfaction that he can be invited to the Banquet of Clergie, where once again argument (this time in the register of the ecclesiastical *magisterium*) conspicuously fails. Like Augustine's exclamatory journey through the wonders of memory, the poem proves to be a reading lesson, as well as a model of what a form and style answerable to that "suffering" apprehension of the created world might feel like.

Needless to say, a long narrative poem thus conceived as an extended "reading lesson" fitted to the habits, and designed for the interpellation, of a readership heretofore inured to romance adventure in both its secular and religious forms was an endeavor "unattempted yet in prose or rhyme" in English when Langland undertook it, at some point late in the reign of Edward III, and as a vernacular enterprise it had to be invented from the ground up and explicated by literary means. The dislocation of a philosophical enterprise from its customary language and discursive situations and sanctions, and from its familiar expository genres, brings with it, as a kind of back-formation or reflex, two secondary tasks: that of providing a rationale for such an undertaking, and that of repeatedly reframing the philosophical project in response to its vicissitudes in application and exemplification, its realization in a new discursive site. It is for this reason, and not through the desire to interpret this figuration naively as "autobiographical," that the poet's philosophical enterprise is perpetually, and *constitutively*, shadowed by this doubly self-reflexive one, a secondary scrutiny that is brought to bear upon both the initiatory premises of the commentator—that disjuncture with the already-established "texts" that prompted and continue to motivate the inquiry as it proceeds—and also upon the ways in which his novel expository methods put unexpected pressures upon that text and its application. These newly-exposed anomalies become sources of embarrassment—staged in this poem as provocative disruptions or "digressions," challenges, and seeming byways to a continuing argument—which brings us at last to the critical embarrassment with which we began: the resistance of Langland's poem to broad formal and generic accounts, and thence to a renewed appreciation for Bloomfield's deceptively simple and memorable formulation of what it feels like to read it: "like a commentary on an unknown text."

The wisdom of this perception lies in the suggestion that the author's designs and strategies are, at least in principle, legible as multiple determinations, not dispersed determinants—by means of a process in which a sense of the difference or dislocation of the refound and reused fragment from its primary site of production *necessarily and advertently* plays some part. The poetic enterprise thus understood neither trades in, nor even adds further value to, the constituent discursive materials of the poem as its "hoard" of value, but undertakes to return this treasure of wit to productive utility in sustaining the community and the individual desirous spiritual imagination. Only by imaginatively striving to recover the "unknown text" of fitfully, ardently, and awkwardly expressed desire that provoked the poet into such commentary might one become something more than a puzzled guest at the banquet, a "consumer" surrounded by a feast of unassimilable philological and argumentative nutrition fit for Tantalus's table, culled from a veritable terminal moraine of medieval thought. Only as a hungry vernacular participant in the poet's labors of production of food for thought from this daunting terrain—one who shares Piers' own appetite for such labors—can the reader of a literary text share in the harvesting practices, and the imaginatively nourishing results, by which the commentator on his own enterprise seeks to translate existing "institutions of literary consumption" into such sustaining livelihoods as could be based upon the discursive fields of his own lifetime ("al times of my time to profit shal turne"), and to model that labor as the work of literature. New corn, not old gold, was the best possible yield from labor in the fields of vernacular imagination.

Notes

1. Morton W. Bloomfield, "The Present State of *Piers Plowman* Studies," *Speculum* 14 (1939): 215–32; reprinted, with some revisions by the author, in *Style and Symbolism in Piers Plowman*, ed. Robert J. Blanch (Knoxville: University of Tennessee Press, 1969), 3–25.

2. In contrast to Skeat's parallel-text edition of the poem, whose running notes were clearly produced in the course of editing, the Athlone edition did not envision continuous annotation as part of its scope, instead surrounding its text with the rationales that led to its production as an extended act of textual criticism, and providing at the foot of the page only the versional variants deemed significant to illuminate the lections chosen by the editors, rather than running explanatory notes on substantive matters of reference, language, and register. Skeat's scholia were thus the earliest continuous annotations of the poem; it is significant that the Penn Commentary in progress, though originally intended as additional volume of running annotation of the Athlone texts in all three versions, is now freestanding as a Commentary; a similar gap between text-editing for print presentation and explanatory annotation of the text produced has widened throughout Middle English studies in the decades since Bloomfield's essay. The retreat of such running annotation from carefully-produced printed texts testifies to a growing gap between specialist and generalist capabilities for engaging medieval texts. For *Piers Plowman*, the price of entry to its expertly-elucidated textual vicissitudes has now become too high to sustain the kind of access, either to specialists in medieval culture or the vanishing "general reader," that Skeat's genial emissary work invited, or the "literary interest" it presumed in both text and reader.

In his running notes Skeat enacts the role of an ideally informed and closely attentive audience, an ambassador or envoy of the poem's peculiar local habits and felicities to our time. As he explains the poem's local reference, customs, and idioms with a wealth of apposite example, whether from dead or still-living usages, he also occasionally discloses himself in his benevolent emissary role, with little bursts of applause for piquancies of expression or observation—as in his endearing note of academic fellow-feeling at Clergy's summary rebuke to Will (A.12.6), "The were lef to lerne but loth for to stodie" (This state of mind is still common). Such ready empathy and interpretive advocacy typifies the posture of the annotator with respect to the work: it bespeaks the conviction that all will be clear, and as powerfully so to another reader as to the annotator, if only one is willing to take the trouble to become sufficiently acquainted with the customs of the country, the more local the better; to enter, with the aid and comfort of the annotator-guide, as far as possible into its language, and to think in its terms. For unlike the textual editor, the annotator can afford to dwell in the undergrowth of variance, at least partially withholding ultimate judgment in detail about authorial agency in favor of more amiable mediatory labors, not only of explicating the work to the annotator's contemporaries but also illuminating the interesting little neighborly frictions in understanding between the poem and its immediate discursive environment at various stages in its transmission history. The annotator's lot is thus a pleasant one: a genial and often very learned myopia, bemused and patient with the little communicative foibles that commonly arise in neighborhoods, a benign diplomacy energetically applied within short distances and definite spaces, and exercised to best results in the intensive cultivation of a relatively small allotment garden. In this universe of critical discourse, a so-called quibble or digression, to say nothing of a crux or variant lection, has all the charm of a volunteer seedling, to be watched with interest to see what it becomes.

Such scholia thrive with particular luxuriance around this work, and often make it seem to its more occasional visitor as if they are all there is to see there. Paradoxically—because the scholia on *Piers* are not only so dense but so interesting, encapsulating some of the most provocative work on the poem, while they often leave unstated both their larger premises and the inferences about poet and milieu that might be made from their cumulative testimony—it is more than usually difficult to see through them to a wider critical or historical vantage point. Worse still, that normative "usually," which holds out the possibility of attaining such a vantage point, is given by the work of Chaucer—the only Middle English rival to *Piers Plowman* in sheer density of accrued annotative labors, but which unlike *Piers* became the defining reference point for specifically literary canonicity, leaving its immediate alliterative predecessor in the unenviable role of an intractable obstacle, to be transcended or explained away in order to make literary history intelligible at all.

On the relation of text presentation and supporting information to the poem's critical history, see further my essay "Editing Terminable and Interminable," *Huntington Library Quarterly* 64 (2001): 161–87. Under the general editorship of

George Kane, the Athlone edition is complete in four volumes since this lecture was presented: *Piers Plowman: The A Version*, ed. George Kane (London: Athlone Press, 1960; rev. ed., London: Athlone Press; Berkeley and Los Angeles: University of California Press, 1988); *Piers Plowman: The B Version*, ed. George Kane and E. T. Donaldson (London: Athlone, 1975; rev. ed., London: Athlone Press; Berkeley and Los Angeles: University of California Press, 1988); *Piers Plowman: The C Version*, ed. George Russell and George Kane (London: Athlone Press; Berkeley: University of California, 1997); and (since Athlone Press was acquired by Continuum International in January 2001) Joseph S. Wittig, *Piers Plowman: Concordance* (London: Continuum International Publishing Group, 2001). The *Penn Commentary on Piers Plowman*, to appear in five volumes, each authored by one of the team of five engaged in this project since 1991, is keyed to the Athlone edition in all three versions. Andrew Galloway, *Volume I* and Stephen Barney, *Volume 5* (Philadelphia: University of Pennsylvania Press, 2006) have appeared; the former covers the first vision of the poem (Prologue-Passus 4), the latter the final three visions (C Passus 20–22/B Passus 18–20). Volume 2, on Vision 2 (C Passus 5–9/B Passus 5–7/A Passus 5–8) by Ralph Hanna; Volume 3, on Vision 3 (C Passus 10–14/B Passus 8–12/A Passus 9–11) by Anne Middleton; and Volume 4 , on Visions 4 and 5 (C Passus 15–19/B Passus 13–17) by Traugott Lawler, are in progress.

3. Morton W. Bloomfield, *Piers Plowman as a Fourteenth-Century Apocalypse* (New Brunswick: Rutgers University Press, 1966), 32.

4. The same general formula for such an overview remained in place into the early 1980s, when the general style sheet for the revised *Manual of Writings in Middle English* mandated that, like all other sections of this reference work, the chapter on *Piers Plowman*—a task assigned to me by Talbot Donaldson around 1970 for completion of the bibliography he had begun, and a new survey essay—was to have a nonannotated bibliography under categories already defined by the earlier edition of the Manual. See "*Piers Plowman*," chap. 18 in *A Manual of Writings in Middle English*, vol. 7, ed. Albert Hartung (New Haven: Connecticut Academy of Arts and Sciences, 1986), 2211–34 (Commentary), 2419–48 (Bibliography). When the volume was published, my addition of comparative and broader contextual categories to the Manual's general formula was remarked as anomalous. The two other bibliographies of the poem, in train simultaneously with my *Piers* chapter for the *Manual*, were annotated as well as categorized: Vincent DiMarco, *Piers Plowman: A Reference Guide* (Boston, MA: G. K. Hall, 1982), and Derek Pearsall, *An Annotated Critical Bibliography of Langland* (New York and London: Harvester, 1990); both remain works of frequent recourse for scholars of the poem. Beginning in 1987, with the founding of the *Yearbook of Langland Studies*, an annual annotated bibliography with a similarly broadened scope of reference supplanted the earlier formula.

5. J. R. R. Tolkien, "Beowulf: The Monsters and the Critics." *Proceedings of the British Academy* 22 (1936): 245–95; James Sledd, "The *Clerk's Tale*: The Monsters and

the Critics," *Modern Philology* 51.2 (1953): 73–82; C. S. Lewis, *The Allegory of Love* (Oxford: Oxford University Press, 1936; repr. New York: Oxford University Press, 1958).

6. For the latter phrase, see Lee Patterson, "The Logic of Textual Criticism and the Way of Genius: The Kane-Donaldson *Piers Plowman* in Historical Perspective," in his *Negotiating the Past: The Historical Understanding of Medieval Literature* (Madison: University of Wisconsin Press, 1987), 77–113 at 109. Patterson's reflections on "originality" as the objective of the Athlone editors' textual criticism accord with the argument of the present essay on this quality as the ultimate objective for literary historians as well. For the distinction between "unfinished" and "interminable" as inflecting the critical history of the poem, and much other helpful advice, I am indebted to my colleague Steven Justice, whose recent lectures on historicism in medieval literary studies (at Kalamazoo in May 2004, and at Princeton in spring 2006) have reanimated my own rethinking of the implications of this essay. For further discussion of the generic and formal questions attending this issue, see his essay, "The Genres of *Piers Plowman*," *Viator* 19 (1988): 29–65.

7. Anne Middleton, "Narration and the Invention of Experience," *The Wisdom of Poetry: Essays in Early English Literature in Honor of Morton W. Bloomfield*, ed. Larry D. Benson and Siegfried Wenzel (Kalamazoo: Medieval Institute Publications, 1982), 91–122.

8. Steven Knapp, *Literary Interest: The Limits of Anti-Formalism* (Cambridge, MA: Harvard University Press, 1993), 139. See also the useful discussion of historical criticism of fictive representation in Scott Dykstra, "Wordsworth's 'Solitaries' and the Problem of Literary Reference," *ELH* 63.4 (1996): 893–926. Dykstra's account (904) of the "ontological ambiguity" of these figures well captures the distinctive and compelling effects produced within Langland's populous fictive domain of personifications and nonce "personations" by the focal figures of Piers and (with increasing cogency in each successive version) Will: "Arresting our attention with all the "staged" force of an allegory or emblem, they seem to recede at some point in our reading beyond the grasp of their own figural dimension towards a more particularized and yet finally anonymous mode of existence . . . [forcing] us to "think" the public theatricality of high argument with respect to the nameless and unremembered lives of persons" (see also especially 894–96). Dykstra continues with a question that also solicits the consideration of *Piers Plowman* scholars, perhaps even more urgently now than a decade ago, when this lecture was first prepared: "What sort of 'historical imagination' is implied by such a practice?"

9. Jill Mann, "Eating and Drinking in Piers Plowman," *Essays and Studies*, n.s., 32 (1979): 26–43.

10. In both versions, the two "inner visions" that befall the Dreamer late in the third dream are depicted as temptations, though the status of the second only manifests itself as such when Will attempts to "read" it. In B, the spectacle is displayed to the Dreamer as a view from the "mountain" of Middelerthe, underscoring the analogy of this panorama to that of the "kingdoms of the world and their splendor"

shown to Jesus by the devil, just prior to the initiation of his ministry (Matthew 4:8/Luke 4:5–7). In C, the second part of the inner vision is instead presented in the "mirrour" of Middelerthe, a change which underscores the noetic pedagogy it offers.

11. Like the skill of the swimmer, which makes it more likely that one cast into "Temese" will survive the plunge, "clergial" arts confer a survival advantage (but no more than that) on the soul habituated to their proper exercise; the "suffraunce" that gives the soul the power to "row" out of danger, however, is not intrinsic to "clergial" arts (B 12.160–73/C 14.104–13). This figure in Ymaginatif's highly metaphorical tutelage in turn reprises in another register the "forbisne" of the boat in which one may stumble yet not drown, proffered in the waking preface to the third vision by the friars in answer to Will's query on the whereabouts of Dowel, and in turn echoes the *navicella* of St. Peter's salvation. On the rich argumentative resonance of this mosaic image by Giotto, originally placed over the entrance to St. Peter's in Rome, and on "monumental allegory" generally in the later Middle Ages, see Hans Belting, "The New Role of Narrative in Public Painting of the Trecento: *Historia* and Allegory," in *Pictorial Narrative in Antiquity and the Middle Ages*, ed. Herbert L. Kessler and Marianna Shreve Thompson, *Studies in the History of Art* 16 (Washington DC: National Gallery of Art, 1985), 151–68; esp. 154–57.

12. Ernest N. Kaulbach, *Imaginative Prophecy in the B-Text of Piers Plowman* (Woodbridge, Suffolk: D. S. Brewer, 1993), esp. 40–47; Alastair J. Minnis, "Langland and Late-Medieval Theories of the Imagination," *Comparative Criticism* 3 (1981): 71–103; Ralph Hanna, "Langland's Ymaginatif and the Limits of Poetry," in *Images, Idolatry, and Iconoclasm in Late Medieval England*, ed. Jeremy Dimmick, James Simpson, and Nicolette Zeeman (Oxford: Oxford University Press, 2002), 81–94, particularly 85–88 on the "scrappy" and "non-august" character of Ymaginatif's lore. For an analysis that corroborates my general sense that the "unknown text" on which the poem enacts its commentary is the poem itself, see further Hanna, "Reading Prophecy, Reading *Piers*," *YLS* 12 (1998): 153–57, and Hanna, *London Literature* (Cambridge: Cambridge University Press, 2005), chap. 6, pp. 243–304.

13. On the perpetual distrust of fable or myth as vehicle of philosophical discourse, see Peter Dronke, *Fabula* (Leiden: E. J. Brill, 1974; 2nd ed., 1985), introduction, esp. pp. 3–6 and chap. 1, esp. pp. 17–20 and 48–57. The "dream-within-a-dream" sequence of the third vision of the poem marks the point of suture where both long versions of the poem extend from the end of the A-text.

14. Joseph S. Wittig, "*Piers Plowman* B, Passus IX–XII: Elements in the Design of the Inward Journey," *Traditio* 28 (1972): 211–80.

15. Bartholomeus Anglicus, *On the Properties of Things*, ed. M. C. Seymour (Oxford: Clarendon, 1975), bk. 5, cap. 10; vol. 1, p. 188. This physiology and psychology of shame, and the account of the *vis imaginativa* with which it is associated, attributed here to "þe philosophir" (Aristotle), are derived ultimately from Avicenna's *Liber de anima* IV–V, probably as transmitted in Vincent of Beauvais, *Speculum Naturale*,

possibly via Jean de Rochelle, *Summa de Anima.* On these see Kaulbach, *Imaginative Prophecy in the B-Text of Piers Plowman,* 40 n. 2, 42 n. 3, and 47 n.5; and H. S. V. Jones "Imaginatif in *Piers Plowman,* " *JEGP* 13 (1914): 583–88.

16. Augustine, *Sermo* CLX, De verbis apostoli, I Cor. cap. I.31, Qui gloriatur, in Domino glorietur; *Patrologia Latina* 38, col. 872; cited in Peter Dronke, *Fabula,* 56 n. 1.

"THE PLACE OF THE APOCALYPTIC VIEW OF HISTORY IN THE LATER MIDDLE AGES" AND THE LEGACY OF MORTON BLOOMFIELD [1999]

KATHRYN KERBY-FULTON

I met Morton Bloomfield only near the end of his life, when he served as external examiner for my DPhil Dissertation. Having spent a fearful night in anticipation of meeting a great scholar, I met a man who was also humble to the core. He told me two things I will never forget: first, because I, too, was a Canadian, he told me that he had always regretted having to leave his native Montreal for the United States, but that in those days latent anti-Semitism would likely have prevented him from getting an academic post in Canada. We talked about how Jewish Montreal had since become the home of some of Canada's most prominent writers, and how the postwar Jewish exodus was now much studied by Canadian historians. Secondly, he told me that the title of his book, Piers Plowman as a Fourteenth-Century Apocalypse, *was not his own, but rather one the press imposed in an effort to boost sales, over his strong protestations. To anyone who knows the book, this will make immediate sense: his measured, circumspect approach to the intricate question of the poem's genre, and the complexity of apocalyptic genres themselves, have never squared with the bold title. His candor and generosity toward a young scholar continued in our correspondence—the last thing I was able to send him was a book on postwar Canadian Jewish history—but it was very quickly cut short by his death. That conversation, held in Warren House in 1986, I can remember as though it were yesterday, and I am grateful today to be able to honor Professor Bloomfield in this lecture.*

Piers Plowman as a Fourteenth-Century Apocalypse was a groundbreaking book in more than one way, but first and foremost because Bloomfield insisted on taking Langland seriously as a thinker. It remains one of the most important intellectual histories of a Middle English poem, and still indispensable, despite important advances in our knowledge of the literary culture and political history of the Ricardian court since it was written. Today I want to tackle a topic raised by one of its impressively documented appendices, each of which could launch a thousand PhD theses—or Bloomfield lectures, as the case may be. In appendix 4, "The Place of the Apocalyptic View of History in the Later Middle Ages," Bloomfield surveyed the astonishing variety of medieval opinions on Salvation History, concluding with this insight: "The apocalyptic view of history was not merely *the* Christian or medieval view; to concentrate wholeheartedly on it as Langland did represents a definite choice among possible philosophies of history. Not all fourteenth-century English thinkers or artists were so inclined—neither Occam nor Chaucer, Richard Rolle nor Bradwardine, John Gower nor Richard Bury. Langland's historical view, though not unique or original, is nevertheless a view *he could have avoided but did not.* He was fundamentally apocalyptically-minded in a way many of his distinguished contemporaries were not."[1] Like many brilliant observations, this is so simple it hurts. Bloomfield, moreover, was the first scholar to take a real interest in finding out exactly *how* Langland might have acquired the knowledge to support a passion so scarce among his colleagues. By the time he was finished, he had laid the groundwork for much more than a study of Langland: he left a legacy of scholarship that is still heavily used by historians, and today I would like to talk both about that legacy and about what further things we, sitting dwarflike on the shoulders of Bloomfield, can see from the vantage point he gave us.

From the outset, the reformist urgency of Langland's apocalypticism seemed to Bloomfield most like Joachim of Fiore's. This was, in the 1950s, virtually a counterintuitive connection—Joachimism was still largely associated in scholarly minds with Italy, southern France, and the Mediterranean. The assumption that it had never reached England was widely held. Bloomfield's work, however, changed that: he produced amazing, unnoticed, incontestable manuscript evidence for the "Penetration of Joachism into Northern Europe" (the title of a classic article he coauthored with Marjorie Reeves).[2] But he was still very cautious, even self-effacing, about advancing his thesis in relation to Langland. In the book's appendix 1, "Joachim of Flora in Fourteenth-Century England," he says "The time is not yet ripe to argue the case positively, for much more needs to be known about the intellectual life of fourteenth-century England than is possible at present. Too much important material lies buried in Latin manuscripts not well known or not easily available."[3]

I believe the time is now riper.[4] In this paper I am going to speak of just such "buried" material, newly uncovered, of which Bloomfield was not himself aware, and (since time here is short) of one manuscript in particular that clinches his case as nothing before has. It is a *Piers Plowman* manuscript, Cambridge, University Library, MS Dd.1.17, which, unnoticed to anyone so far, actually contains a learned Joachite prophecy echoing many of the apocalyptic themes of the poem. There can be no doubt about the original compiler's intentions: the prophecy and the poem are copied, as is the entire manuscript, by the same scribe.[5] The significance of this—when supported by other evidence for the spread of Joachite ideas in contemporary English reformist circles—is enormous for our understanding of both Langland's project and its impact. The prophecy is of a kind that many scholars still believe to be rare in England (the supposed rarity of this material had always been a key argument against Bloomfield's thesis). In fact, we now know this sort of *Joachitia* is not rare in England, but its circulation has been obscure to modern scholarship for the very good reason that it was considered suspect by medieval authorities, and often suppressed or anonymously or pseudonymously transmitted (as in the Cambridge Dd *Piers* MS).[6] Here, for instance, the prophecy is attributed to an authority of impeccable orthodoxy, John of Legnano, an internationally known canon law professor from Bologna whose opinions on the Schism were highly revered in Richard II's court. But the prophecy traveling under this appropriated guise is a very radical text: some of its predictions match (verbatim) those for which Johannes Hus, the reformist leader of the Hussite movement, was condemned at the Council of Constance in 1414. And this was by no means the first run-in with the law that certain sources for the Dd prophecy had had, as we are about to see.

But even this is enough information to bring us to the crucial point I would like to suggest here: that not only, as Bloomfield argued, was Langland's apocalyptic view of history a *deliberate* and passionate choice but also that it was not entirely a *safe* choice. At the precise time Langland was writing, it was less safe than Wycliffism—in fact even Wycliffite writers usually tried to distance themselves from it. No one during Langland's lifetime had yet died for espousing Wycliffite ideas, but many had died for espousing Franciscan Joachite ones—or even views that merely sounded like them. The second crucial point I would like to make is that in choosing this material Langland also made an *intellectual* choice—and a slightly unusual one, one that smacked of Continental intrigue and high drama, tainted (long before Hus's execution) by official condemnation, or, depending on one's point of view, ennobled by the innocent deaths of those who had refused to give up their belief in radical Church reform. To understand this, however, we first need some history of Joachimism and related prophetic traditions.

Experimenting in Continental Genres:
Langland, Joachimism, and the Transhistorical

The first official condemnation of Joachim's views happened in 1215, only after his death, and only on an academic point of Trinitarian theology, but it heralded an insidious and steady "criminalization" of his apocalyptic thought that finally reached a climax in the next century with the terrible persecutions of Franciscan Joachites by Pope John XXII. There is not space in this paper, unfortunately, to trace this process; nor is there time to say more than a few words about its impact in England.[7] Bloomfield's discovery of a Latin poem of the 1220s written in English monastic circles, and perhaps the earliest extant discussion of the condemnation in Europe, stunned scholars in the 1950s as evidence of the sophistication of insular discussion. A few lines from the poem may suggest the tone of the debate: in the manuscript version Bloomfield turned up, it follows a copy of the Creed, and begins rhetorically: "Do you believe, O Brothers, all these things? We believe. Therefore we condemn the writings of Abbot Joachim [which are] contrary to the writings of Master Peter Lombard." The poem then proceeds with a technical theological analysis of the conflict, and ends: "These things therefore we acknowledge, believing with . . . the sacred council *cum Petro, contra Joachim.* . . . Joachim we reject (*reprobamus*)."[8] The official condemnation had come, unfortunately for Joachim's reputation, in the Lateran Council in 1215, and, because English reformers took the tenets of the Council especially seriously, using them as the basis for a national initiative in pastoral reform, it appears that what was a minor theme elsewhere in Europe in the later reception of Joachim was sharply magnified in England. Many other references to condemnation for espousing Joachite thought or its analogues in England exist, ranging from Matthew Paris's notice (again, the first in Europe) of the Scandal of the "Eternal Evangel" in 1254 (a scandal which caused the resignation of highly placed Joachite thinkers in the Franciscan order), to that of the recantation of an Oxford lecturer, a Friar John, in 1358, and that of a Durham friar, Richard Helmyslay, in 1380, both during Langland's lifetime.[9] Moreover, English scholastic thinkers from Archbishop John Pecham to Wyclif himself participated in a dismissive denunciation of Joachite apocalypticism that stemmed largely, I believe, from their training more than from intimate knowledge of what they were condemning.[10] As a result of these various forms of disapproval, the modern scholar of Joachite reception in England is faced with the detritus of suppression or haphazard survival, surviving alongside other evidence of determined hoarding on the part of certain medieval compilers. Serious Joachimism was transmitted, and continued to come across the channel, often from and into convent libraries (where the authorities rarely went looking for problematic books), and in anonymous prophetic collections on international church politics. At least sixty manuscripts of English provenance which carry some form Joachite thought are extant today, among which is the Dd *Piers Plowman* manuscript.

Reformist apocalypticism (of which Joachimism was by no means the only type) was also associated with entirely orthodox, but sensationally high-profile, European prophetic figures (many of them women) who had famously swayed kings and threatened popes. Moreover, because of its revelatory nature, it could and did open up intellectual "spaces" for new kinds of thought, spaces where a certain freedom of expression and tolerance of doctrinal pluralism (even sometimes non-Christian) could flourish. All in all, it must have seemed rather charismatic to Langland—a man who, at least in the breakdown of the A-Text, created a narrator suffocating spiritually under a sense of Christianity's apparently arbitrary intolerances.[11] Langland's project, in borrowing from this genre, looks like a poet's attempt to infuse a tradition of continental apocalypticism into the vernacular English scene.[12]

Chaucer, I would suggest then, was not the only Ricardian author to be seduced by continental genres in an attempt to explore difficult philosophical problems unhampered by his present historical moment. In Langland's case, the large "symbolist" systems constructed by reformist apocalyptic writers would have been extremely attractive as a window on the transhistorical (just as Chaucer used classical *historiae*). Joachimism, for instance, was much more than a pack of predictions about the date of Antichrist's coming; it was a complex, majestic exegetical hermeneutic, a "system" in the Blakean sense, gleaned from Trinitarian clues hidden throughout Scripture.[13] As Bloomfield lucidly summarized it:

> Arguing on the basis of analogies that he claimed to find between the period of the Old Testament and the period of the New Testament down to his own time.... The period of the Old Testament [Joachim believed] was primarily the age of the Father; the period from the time of Jesus down to roughly Joachim's time was that of the Son; and the third age, ... would be that of the Holy Ghost under whose aegis the Saracens and Jews would be converted. The Old Testament, then, is the key to the meaning of history.[14]

Unusually empathetic to and knowledgeable of Jewish exegesis, Joachim's writings offered a powerful understanding of Christian salvation history. In this view, as Bloomfield summarizes it, "the birth throes of each age are violent and give rise to Antichrists. Each age, however, is an advance over the preceding one. The human race progressively receives a fuller revelation."[15]

The majesty of this symbolist system, along with its trajectory, however, was, in some of its manifestations at least, a great threat to established theological interests. Curt Bostick has nicely summarized the problem this way: "The appeal [of traditional apocalypticism] lay in its promise that although Antichrist will wreak havoc across the globe, one may find safe harbor in the confines of the [C]hurch."[16] But reformist apocalyptic thought was always somewhat uncomfortable to Church authorities because it usually imagines a faithful remnant (for Joachim they were the *viri spirituales*—spiritual men) in the church, hanging onto purist ideals and fighting not only demons without, but *within*. This is true of all the major thinkers: Hildegard, Joachim, William of St. Amour, Olivi, Rupescissa. And it is certainly true of Langland, vividly imagined in the battle for Unity Holy Church, itself a Schism nightmare. When Antichrist makes his attack on Unity, "Proute prestes cam with hym—passyng an hundred," armed to the teeth, "And hadden almost Vnite and holynesse adowne" (C.XXII.218, 227). The besieged "Vnite" is by this time populated only with the faithful remnant, who for Langland are the "fools" (a concept he has used earlier in the poem to invoke both St. Paul's fools for Christ, and St. Francis's *joculatores Domini*).[17] The allegory is complex. The siege is moral, historical, eschatological, and even ethnic (the attacking priests come from Ireland (C.XXII.221)), but the outlines are clear. When Antichrist wins over the friars and the religious, the "foles were wel gladere to deye / Then to lyue lengere, sethe leautee was so rebuked" (C.XXII.62–63), and they are gathered into Vnite (74–75). When these lines were first written (in B.XX.62–63), the most recent "fools" who had died for "leautee" were the radical Franciscan Joachites, and the newer "fools" under serious threat were those who dared to confront a newly schismatic pope. (Certainly by the time Langland was creating C, for instance, England's Cardinal Adam Easton, was languishing in prison). We know from manuscript evidence, to which we can now add Dd.I.17 itself, that clergy concerned with precisely these matters were owners of *Piers Plowman*. One thinks of John Wells, for instance, who was called upon as proctor of the English Benedictines to try to save Cardinal Adam Easton from Urban VI's prison, and whose *ex libris* appears in the manuscript, Oxford,

Bodleian Library, MS Bodley 851, into which the Z text of *Piers Plowman* is bound.[18]

Legal Fictions and Schism Propaganda: John of Legnano, Jacobus de Theramo's *Belial*, and the Sources of the *Regnum* Prophecy

Cambridge's Dd prophecy stems from an enormously complex world of at least three different types of sources. First, the prophecy, which I will call by its incipit *Regnum spiritus sancti* (The Kingdom of the Holy Spirit), uses genuine and full-fledged Joachite exegesis, as we will see below. It dares to take on one of the most dangerous subjects of this exegesis, the coming of the Age of the Spirit, a topic which in other contemporary manuscripts and contexts could and did come under direct censorship, even in England. Secondly, the prophecy draws upon Schism polemic, of the kind that swirled around John of Legnano's name and his legal defenses of the pontiff—its central metaphor, of marriage and adultery, springs from precisely this world. John of Legnano (1320–83), taught canon law at the University of Bologna. He had written widely on censorship and excommunication issues, which made him an ideal man to attribute a dangerous prophecy to—as other shadow writers of Schism polemic already knew.[19] Thirdly, many details of the prophecy are borrowed from the *Belial*, a daring legal and theological text written in 1382 as propaganda in support of the schismatic pope Urban VI by Jacobus de Theramo, an Italian canon lawyer.[20] The *Belial* poses as a legal textbook teaching actual courtroom procedure (and was popular as such); in fact its agenda was much more subversive: it dramatizes a court scene in which God's plan for human salvation itself is put on trial. Dd's *Regnum* is a blend of material from these diverse sources, all being invoked in legal circles in the headiness of the early Schism years. Although these are Italian figures, the readership of such texts was international—they traveled, to borrow a metaphor from Bloomfield's elegant discussion of "the monastic grapevine," via a legal professional grapevine.

We now know a good deal more not only about Joachite manuscripts but about Langland himself than when Bloomfield wrote. We know that he was almost certainly associated in some capacity with the Westminster world of legal professionals and civil servants, a group whose interests and book ownership patterns showed them to be part of international culture.[21] Westminster is also a culture in which John of Legnano, and most especially the *Belial*, were known; Joachimism, too, appears in legal manuscripts surprisingly often.²² The prophecy's attribution to Legnano must have given it serious credibility in England, which was pro-Urban in schism politics (Legnano's defence of Urban, published internationally by Urban himself, was so convincing to the English court that it never bothered to mount its own defense on Urban's behalf).²³ But the choice of Legnano as a name with which to "launder" a radical prophecy is an intriguing one for literary scholars both because of his great reputation at the court of Richard II, and because in the "Clerk's Tale," Chaucer ranks Legnano ("Lynyan") with Petrarch, as the two great luminaries of Italy:

> Frauceys Petrak, the lauriat poete,
> Highte this clerk, whos rethorike sweete
> Enlumyned at Ytaille of poetrie,
> As Lynyan dide of philosophie,
> Or lawe, or oother art particuler;
> But deeth, that wol nat suffre us dwellen heer,
> But as it were a twynklyng of an ye
> Hem bothe hath slayn, and alle shul we dye.²⁴

In fact, as McCall points out, Chaucer's tone here has a kind of confidence which suggests that Legnano was as well or better known to his audience than Petrarch was.²⁵ Chaucer's own diplomatic mission to Milan in 1378 had coincided exactly with the outbreak of the Great Schism, an event that likely altered what it could achieve. So finding Legnano's name in a Langland manuscript (given Langland's likely Westminster connections as well) is not entirely surprising.

Some of *Regnum*'s predictions are drawn verbatim from the *Belial*, which the author overtly names, and which had its own censorship history, eventually including the trial of Jan Hus. The reformist leader of the Hussite movement, Hus was charged with citing the *Belial* at the Council of Constance in 1414, prior to his execution, a charge we will examine in more detail below.²⁶ The *Belial* is also known in Latin by the more benign title, the *Consolatio Peccatorum* (*The Consolation of Sinners*), part of a fuller title claiming to be nothing less than a compendium on the redemption of the human race (*Compendium perbreve de redemptione generis humani*).²⁷ Oddly enough, this text itself appears elsewhere in the Dd manuscript, which, as all modern scholars agree, is a convent production, probably of the York Austin friars.²⁸ It is an "Olympian" compilation of works concerning salvation history and missions to the non-Christian peoples, the intertwined themes always intimately associated with medieval apocalyptic expectation.²⁹ Not only does the manuscript contain *Piers*, and the *Regnum* prophecy quoting the Belial verbatim, but under the *Consolatio* title the Dd scribe also copied the full Latin *Belial* itself, not far from where he copied the Joachite prophecy.[30] The presence of both is startling, although folio 262, which contained the very end of the *Belial* and therefore presumably its overtly partisan colophon, is gone from the manuscript, a defect supplied only by a sixteenth-century hand. There is also no rubric heading the author's address ("Universis Christi fidelibus . . . "). These things might point to some slightly later awareness of the danger of the text. By 1400–10 Jacobus was in official trouble with the papacy and prevented, even as Bishop of Florence, from traveling to the Council of Pisa. Jacobus was well known across Europe for this work, and also in Hussite circles, where Joachimism traveled as well.[31] The *Belial* citation in the inquisition records of Jan Hus[32] perhaps prompted the radical bowdlerization of the text when it was translated into the vernacular, especially in German. In its Latin form, however, the full *Belial* exists in dozens upon dozens of manuscripts on the continent, where it travels in just the kind of company as *Piers* does, that is, with works like *Mandeville's Travels* (also in Dd) and other writings concerned with the peaceful conversion of the non-Christian peoples.[33] It also travels with works concerned with the "legal" issues surrounding the redemption of humankind, with the potential for universal salvation that Christ's Harrowing of Hell seems to hold out. Jacobus's treatment is so startling because for him these "legal" issues refer to the validity of God's judgment, reminiscent of the spirit in which Langland's narrator rails himself into near unorthodoxy at the end of the A-text.

The *Belial* is constructed as a case involving the devil's claim on the souls that Christ "stole" during the Harrowing of Hell, and a debate between the Four Daughters of God. This is portrayed as a stunning courtroom drama such as Langland himself might have written if he had chosen to compose in what can often be the dialogically "roomier" forum of Latin.[34] Just to give a brief sense of why this work startled its readers, it shows Belial (acting for the Conclave of the Devils, in a scene reminiscent to modern readers of *Paradise Lost*) pointing out that God is ineligible as a judge because of his relationship with the defendant (Christ)![35] Solomon, therefore, is deputed to act for God, thus beginning a series of evolving court battles in which Moses is a lawyer for Christ, an appeal is heard before the Patriarch Joseph, and, eventually, brought to a close by the mediation of David. It is perhaps no wonder that some of the vernacular versions of *Belial* would later find their way onto the *Index*.[36] In addition to the daring theological moves that

Jacobus makes to get fair legal representation and counsel for the devil's party, the text was also suspect for the radical apocalypticism it espoused. In this context, it is interesting that the *Belial* can also be found in manuscripts with the *Ackermann aus Böhmen*, that is, the German work about a peasant-husbandman (*Ackermann*) that Konrad Burdach thought most like *Piers Plowman* in radical social thought and in chiliasm, noting especially the fight with the devil over the stolen fruit in Langland's Tree of Charity passage, the Harrowing, and the Four Daughters of God.[37] In the German version, as in others, the *Belial* was heavily propagated by the German chancery, who also, in another direct parallel with the Westminster transmission of *Piers Plowman*, propagated *Der Ackermann*.[38] These works testify to the vitality of the legal literary tradition in which Langland himself wrote, and the parallels between and among these texts, and our little Joachite prophecy that borrows overtly from *Belial*, are indeed striking.

The *Regnum spiritus sancti* prophecy uses a detailed exegetical analysis, such as one finds in the genuine works of Joachim himself, in both the positive role it gives to Old Testament women in Salvation History,[39] and to the Jewish people generally. The text opens by explaining how the different faiths arose from the children of Leah and Rachel and their handmaidens. After exhaustive exegesis, we learn that the Kingdom of the Holy Spirit had its beginning in Rachel, "through whom the seed of Abraham is saved."[40] Rachel, it says, represents the Synagogue, whose fruitfulness was not ultimately "barren" (*sterilem*) but merely delayed, conceiving spiritually by the Holy Spirit and bringing forth both the people of Israel and the people of Judah, that is, both the unfaithful and faithful.[41] What is especially striking here is the timelessness of Rachel's contribution, as present and enduring, for this writer, as we more usually find in Marian devotion itself. Mary, we should note, is not ever mentioned in the prophecy, which is a "decentering" of conventional ideas of the "Church" more radical than even Joachim's own exegesis represents (where Rachel is usually paired with Mary).[42] Through Rachel, the prophecy asserts, all salvation comes, as does the kingdom of the Holy Spirit itself, described in true Joachite fashion as coming *after* Antichrist.

What is especially interesting about the *Regnum* theme of Rachel and Leah is that another Schism prophecy, also falsely attributed to Legnano, begins, "In illo tempore erunt duo sponsi, unus legitimus et alter adulter" ("In that time there will be two spouses, one legitimate, and the other an adulterer") and then predicts that the adulterer will reign ("adulter regnabit").[43] The application to the Schism is obvious, and the Cambridge

Regnum prophecy (note even the similarity in marital diction) seems, by comparison, much more subtle and original, in giving this theme of the two wives a Joachite exegetical twist.

The "Kingdom" prophet tells us that following the abomination of Antichrist against the true Vicar of Christ in his Church and kingdom, "through the time and times and half a time, which are three and a half years, according to Daniel,"[44] the whole Church and kingdom of Christ will be renewed (*renouabitur*), and the greatest peace upon Jerusalem, through the whole world for 1000 years.[45] But before these marvelous events there will be apocalyptic horrors, and for these the author liberally plagiarizes the *Belial*: the time "from the desolation of the temple of the Jews until the Infernal Power" is complexly calculated by consulting Daniel—I spare you the mathematics—but antichrist will be vicar of the Church, against "the true vicar" some time between the years 1364 and 1409. He will persecute the holy in the worst tribulation ever seen, and will command the destruction of the Holy of Holies, and the burning of the Old and New Testament (". . . sancta sanctorum destrui ac novum & vetus testamentum concremari").[46] This last section, and the 1409 dating, is taken over entirely from the *Belial*.[47] It suggests a creative reworking both of the Joachite "angelic pope" tradition and the prophecy made infamous by the 1255 condemnation of the "Eternal Gospel," that is, regarding the superseding of the Old and New Testaments by the so-called "Eternal Gospel" in the Age of the Spirit. This alleged tenet of Joachimism (in fact a radical distortion of it) was kept alive by antimendicant polemicists, and by literary sources like *The Romance of the Rose*. It had a way of uniting everyone against Joachimism, widely regarded by writers as different from each other as the Wycliffites and their nemesis, Thomas Netter, as the essence of Joachite heresy—a phenomenon we will examine at the end of this paper.

Now, this was a convenient prophecy to present to a pope locked in schism, especially a pope one is hoping to flatter—and this is apparently just what Jacobus did when he wrote the *Belial*, the colophon of which stresses that it was composed in 1382, during the pontificate of "the most holy . . . Lord Urban VI, pope of the *Universal* Church."[48] Whoever created the Cambridge Dd manuscript's *Regnum* prophecy knew precisely what he was doing, then, in attributing it to Urban's chief apologist, Legnano, and referring directly to Jacobus's *Belial*, ("vt dictum est in tractatu Belial nuncupato compositum per urbanum sextum"). And he was clearly also well versed in genuine Joachite thought—knowledgeable enough (as we saw with his handling of Rachel) to be creative with it. The expectation of a coming Age of the Holy Spirit is a touchstone, perhaps the most reliable of any, for what distinguishes Joachite from non-Joachite apocalyptic thinkers. Elsewhere I have discussed the complexities of this argument, especially as they relate to Langland's own sense of the future, as in the blissful *pacis visio* (C.III.436 ff.), with its end to war, its "o cristene kyng," and universal illumination of Jews and Muslims, who "shal syng *Credo in spiritum sanctum.*"[49] Another such passage is his *ad pristinum statum* prophecy of C.V.168 ff., with its sweeping vision of wealth redistribution for the reform of all, and of Holy Church "clothed newe."[50] My concern here, however, is with the aspects of this expectation on record as having *worried the authorities,* and which we do find echoed in *Piers,* or, at the very least, in passages that could be mistaken for such an expectation.

By 1400 Jacobus himself was in official trouble, and by 1414 his *Belial* was too. Among the charges against Hus at the Council of Constance was that he had cited this prophecy as applying to Pope Alexander V.[51] This inquisition record runs: "Likewise, article nine, in which is contained that Joannes Hus said in the vernacular to the people ("dixit in vulgari ad populum"), 'Behold fulfilled is the prophecy which was foretold by Jacobus de Theramo, that in the year of our Lord 1409 will arise one who will persecute the Gospels and the faith of Christ,' through these things denoting Lord Alexander, who in his bulls commanded the books of Wyclif to be burned."[52] Here, the burning of the Old and New Testaments (some thirty years after Jacobus first wrote these line in the early 1380s) is associated with Wycliffism. Indeed, on the continent, the *Belial* does travel in several manuscripts with Wycliffite material.[53] But the *Belial* portion of *Regnum* in the Cambridge manuscript (the only known copy) says nothing about Wyclif. It is lifted, as we have just seen, almost verbatim from the original *Belial.* It describes the coming period of Antichrist's reign as pope during which the Church will be persecuted through temporal kings for nine years, the blood of the clergy will flow just like water, and there will be great famine and tribulation such as "has not been seen before among the people of the church of Christ," not to mention schism (of course), the destruction of "the Holy of Holies," and the burning of the Old and New Testament.[54] All this is to occur before the Kingdom of the Holy Spirit on earth, though the timing of various events after that is confused, and the prophecy eventually winds down with the Last Judgment in the vale of Jehoshaphat.

Now, there is much here that would interest a reader of Langland's own prophecies, copied in Dd, of course, not many folia away. His are not quite so sensational as this, but they were not that far off. *Piers Plowman* also envisions antichrist taking over the papal throne (a prophecy certainly *in vulgari ad populum*):

> For Auntecrist and hise al the world shal greue
> And acombre þe, Consience, bote yf Crist the helpe.
> And false profetes fele, flateres and glosares,
> Shal come and be curatours ouer kinges and erles.
> And thenne shal pryde be pope and prince of holy chirche,
> Coueytise and vnkyndenesse cardynales hym to lede. (C.XXI.219–24; B.XIX.217).

There is also the prophecy, mentioned briefly above, of a temporal king "beating" the church (C.V.168), and which forebodingly predicted famine and flood (C.VIII.343 ff.), all motifs that occur in *Belial* and in *Regnum*.[55] Langland, too, has elaborate schemes of future church history that posit patterns of tribulation and renewal, all easily—whatever his own views— *mistaken* for Joachism. And his fourfold allegory of the Harrowing of Hell scene, which rages against arid clerical intellectualism via the threatening apocalyptic image of the vintage of Jehoshaphat for which Christ thirsts (XX.410), is nearly Joachite in exegetical complexity:[56]

> Y fauht so, me fursteth 3ut, for mannes soule sake.
>   *Sicio.*
> May no pyement ne pomade ne preciouse drynkes
> Moiste me to þe fulle ne my furst slokke
> Til þe ventage valle in þe vale of Iosophat,
> And I drynke riht rype must, *resureccio mortuorum.*
> And thenne shal y come as kynge, with croune and with angeles,
> And haue out of helle alle mennes soules. (C.XX.408–14)

This same combination of apocalyptic exegesis and salvational generosity appears in various Joachite contexts.[57] Of the Schism itself, Langland had much more to say than he felt able to write: his contempt for the college of cardinals is first thinly veiled ("And power presumed in hem a pope to make"), and then tantalizingly withheld, "Forthi I can and can nau3te of courte speke more" (B.Prol.108 and 111)—a kind of toying with would-be censors that he suppressed in the C text (when, as Cardinal Adam Easton's imprisonment in the mid-80s shows, speaking out on Schism matters was becoming more dangerous—at least for those within Urban's reach!). We see in Langland's C some of the limitations of speaking "in vulgari ad populum"—but also why the Cambridge *Regnum* prophecy and the *Belial*, both couched in the safety of Latin, would be of interest to the compiler of a manuscript containing *Piers Plowman*—or vice versa.

Rival Radicalisms: Joachimism and Wyclifism

How aware was the English compiler that he was dealing with dangerous, or at least a potentially dangerous, text? And did he, like Hus's inquisitors, see the text (especially the reference to the Old and New Testament being burned) as a Wycliffite motif? Or was the impulse for copying it an interest in Joachite or Continental or Schism prophecy? The question may seem minute, but it is not: it can teach us, first of all, not to jump to conclusions that Wycliffism was the dominant mode of radical reformist thought in the last quarter of the fourteenth century. And it can help us date a long undateable manuscript (Cambridge Dd.1.17 has not been dateable more precisely than the last quarter of the fourteenth century or the first quarter of the fifteenth). In answer to the first question, we recall that neither the *Belial* nor the Cambridge prophecy mentions the burning of *Wyclif*'s books ("libros Wiclifi cremari" occurs only in the Hus inquisition records)—Jacobus, we remember, was writing on the continent in 1382. What was in Jacobus's mind was most likely a memory of the Joachite scandal of the Eternal Gospel in 1254, in which the fanatic Gerard of Borgo San Donnino claimed that the Old and New Testaments would be "superseded" in the imminent Age of the Holy Spirit—a story best known to literary scholars via *The Romance of the Rose*.[58] Nor did the English scribe of the Cambridge MS react to that particular part of the passage. We know this because he supplied marginal brackets highlighting what he thought were the two most important passages, the first beginning with the description of the coming reign of the Holy Spirit following the reign of Antichrist—the reference to the *Belial* tract and Urban VI—and ending with the description of schism and clerical desolation; the second bracket[59] highlights the passage giving the dates 1364 and 1409, and the verbatim quotation from the *Belial*. These marginal brackets strongly suggest Schism concerns and Joachite interests, not Wycliffite ones. His bracket, moreover, stops *before* the mention of the burning of the Old and New Testaments, which is unlikely to have been missed by any reader after this actually begins to happen in England (not before 1388 at the earliest). A further clue to possible dating is that he either invoked or at the very least retained the name of John of Legnano, who died in 1383, and whose currency value or topicality belongs not so much to the fifteenth century, but, earlier, to the period of the Schism from its outbreak in 1378 until Legnano's death in 1383 and shortly thereafter. Other items in the manuscript that can be dated point to about this period of ca. 1381 (for their composition, at least).[60] There is no doubt, however, that for this writer, the avant-garde way of thinking about the Schism is Joachite, which makes sense given its prominence as an *older*, radical "left-wing" reformist ideology. This is also the critical period of Langland's life—he is composing B, and perhaps beginning work on C in response to events of the early 1380s (certainly the Rising in 1381, and possibly the Blackfriar's Council in 1382).

Some further evidence for the thesis that the scribe was interested in Joachite, not Wycliffite, matters comes from Ian Doyle's evidence that it was associated with the York convent of the Austin friars (the older view that it came from Glastonbury is problematic).[61] The Joachite materials of the York Austins, in fact, are among the most extensive and exciting collection of English *Joachitia* known to us today, thanks partly to John Erghome, active there in the decades between 1360 and 1390.[62] He is, of course, most likely the author of another suspect prophetic work, a commentary on the *Bridlington Prophecies*, which can also be found in manuscript with *Piers Plowman* (Bodley 851, with Ramsey associations, another convent known today to have held *Joachita*).[63] If Dd was made among the York Austins, the scribe may well have been motivated by Joachite interests, for which he had a superb library at his fingertips, and colleagues passionate on the subject to consult.

I'd like now to turn briefly to two other contemporary texts to help flesh out this picture of attitudes toward Joachimism in England and the issue of its dangerousness during the Wycliffite period. The first is the *Opus arduum*, a Latin commentary on the Apocalypse written by an anonymous, imprisoned Wycliffite in 1389, which contains the complaint that the bishops are not only burning all the new vernacular religious works,[64] but that the friars, their procurators (*procuratores*), have taken to confiscating and locking up of the works of William of St. Amour, John of Rupescissa, William Ockham, and Peter John Olivi.[65] This is a very strange list, and too complex for full analysis here, but, for our purposes today, what all four writers had in common was that they had come into conflict with the papacy, two as Franciscan Joachites, a third suspected of being so, and a fourth for attacking Joachites in ways too much like their own. Wycliffites themselves did not really make use of such prophecy (however much they might have agreed with some of its polemical positions)—it was, for the most part, antithetical to their manner of thought.[66] The author of the *Opus arduum* in fact quite typically denounces the pseudo-Joachite view (attributing it directly to Joachim of Fiore himself) that "the gospel law" (lege ewangelica apostolica) has been superseded by the "new law of the Holy Spirit" (nova lex quam spiritus sancti appellavit) (fol. 143v, col. a). The use of word "law" (*lex*), in the medieval canonical sense of an *independent* Church or faith, is pointed.[67] This is an opinion, he says, that is condemned as the most impious of doctrinal abominations ("tamquam nephandissimum abominationibus catholicis improbatur," col. a-b). The source of this anti-Joachite charge is, of course, the 1254 Scandal of the Eternal Evangel—and it is fascinating to see an Englishman dragging this out in 1389. Clearly it was not antiquarianism for him—just as clearly his Joachimism is known mainly from hostile sources, and he had some premonition that the Wycliffite reformist project could be (and was being) mistaken for it. And his fears were well grounded (one thinks of the connection Hus's inquisitors made, which likely made Wyclif turn in his grave). So, the passage tells us that even Wycliffite writers were nervous or contemptuous about the orthodoxy of Joachim.

The *Opus* is also fascinating for the snapshot it gives of early Wycliffite ideas: the author is not at all interested in eucharistic or other "trademark" notions; his main concerns still overlap largely with those of many orthodox thinkers like Langland, that is, with issues of the abuse of temporalities and church government.[68] The death penalty is not yet in place, though the author worries about cries for it ("hereticum clamant et Lolaldum merito comburendum," fol. 157v)—"Lollard" itself is still an unwelcome term of abuse. He, too, uses apocalyptic thought to demonstrate that the current pope is antichrist ("in quo omnia misteria antichristi fuerunt impleta," fol. 76), and the author is greatly preoccupied with the Schism, indeed, obsessively exercised by the disastrous Flanders crusade Bishop Despenser mounted in 1383 on behalf of Urban VI, and against his rival pope, Clement. What is especially significant about this text is that the author is writing, and writing voluminously, from prison—Anne Hudson has canvassed two scenarios, both plausible: the first being that the author was Nicholas Hereford, whom we know to have been protected in house arrest by William Neville, one of the "Lollard knights" in the circle of Chaucer, in fact. The second, that the author was writing from the Franciscan convent in Oxford, under house arrest—the fascinating thing is that *either* scenario might account for his access to continental sources.[69]

A second author who helps us understand attitudes toward Joachism in this period is Walter Brut, also one of the few other Wycliffite thinkers with an extensive knowledge of continental apocalyptic thought. He, too, was suffered to write extensive Latin apocalyptic commentary, if not from imprisonment, at least under official surveillance. Hudson makes the point that he never cites anything but the Bible. In fact he uses and has assimilated a vast quantity of Joachite and related materials. He does *not* cite his references likely because he was in enough trouble with the authorities already without the help of Joachism. Like the author of the Cambridge prophecy, he dares to calculate numerically the coming of Antichrist, and harnesses this to an exhaustive demonstration that the present pope is Antichrist, which he does very much in a continental style. In order to do so, he has to demolish the popular "legendary" notions of Antichrist ("quod fabula illa ab errore ymaginancium"), which he does by proving that they are unbiblical, and by extending a degree of respect to non-Christian peoples which, as we have seen, is a feature of Joachite thought. So, for instance, he assures us that the Jewish people would never be so foolish as to be seduced by a messiah claiming to be from the tribe of Dan—they know, he says, that their messiah will be from the tribe of Judah, and will be peaceful, not warlike ("quod esset pacificus, non bellicosus").[70] Here he gives an eloquent and moving description, based on the Old Testament prophets, of the Messiah the Jews expect. In short, the Jews are, for Brut, a good deal more intelligent than the multitude of Christians who have fallen for such *fabulae*.[71] Like the author of the Dd prophecy, he gives a striking role to women in the church, even women preachers, something, as I have argued elsewhere, he has assimilated from the continental apocalyptic tradition—and not necessarily from Wycliffism at all (and something Langland's own female audience, as we now know from marginalia, saw in the poem's women preachers).[72] In Brut we see writ large what the Dd prophecy suggests *in parvo*—that contact with continental reformist apocalyptic thought can promote unusual tolerance in how marginalized groups are treated. The question for the authorities, of course, was how much of this freedom of expression was tolerable, and in the end, even many Wycliffite thinkers could not tolerate so much tolerance.

The writers closest to Langland in mentality among those I have discussed are the author of the *Regnum* prophecy and Walter Brut. All three strive for a kind of inclusive approach to Salvation History, all three are pushing the limits of freedom of expression—only Langland is pushing them in the vernacular, and perhaps then it is no surprise that Langland's is the most conservative of the three. But Langland was prompted by an impulse—which suited his inclusivist temperament very well—to import a charismatic and slightly dangerous continental apocalypticism, well represented by but not limited to Joachism, into his English poetic project. He was using reformist models of a much older stripe, models which, after the 1380s, would be, like his own poem, under pressure of appropriation into a Wycliffite agenda (where they went underwent a kind of censorship, too).

In conclusion I would like to suggest that both Chaucer and Langland experimented with continental models and genres—Chaucer with humanism, Langland with reformist apocalypticism (for which there was no native equivalent in England); both did so for similar reasons—to explore possibilities that couldn't otherwise be explored within a strict sense of orthodoxy. Just how strict Chaucer's sense of the confinement was may be seen finally by his "Retractions" (if they are what they seem to be) and by the medieval reception of his work.[73] Langland's literary world was more parochial, but his sense of orthodoxy seems to have been much more spacious. He, too, however, turned to a transhistorical and transcultural genre for room to breathe.

When we read Langland, we read with this hindsight—and with our decade's fascination for Lollardy. Bloomfield read Langland with the foresight of one who knew mid-fourteenth-century fascination with Joachim. And that is just another reason why Bloomfield makes such good reading today.

Notes

1. Bloomfield, *Piers Plowman as a Fourteenth-Century Apocalypse* (New Brunswick, NJ: Rutgers University Press, 1961), 178. A more detailed version of the present paper can be found in my *Books Under Suspicion: Censorship and Tolerance of Revelatory Theology in Medieval England* (Notre Dame: University of Notre Dame Press, 2006), as Case Study 1.

2. Bloomfield and Reeves, "The Penetration of Joachism into Northern Europe," *Speculum* 29 (1954): 249–311.

3. Bloomfield, *Piers Plowman*, 157.

4. For a summary of new work and the first published list of English Joachite manuscripts, see Kathryn Kerby-Fulton, "English Joachimism and Its Codicological Content, with a List of Known Joachite Manuscripts of English Origin or Provenance before 1600," in *Essays in Memory of Marjorie Reeves*, ed. Julia Wannenmacher (Burlington, VT: Ashgate Press, forthcoming). See also "English Joachite Manuscripts and Medieval Optimism about the Role of the Jews in History: A List for Future Studies," in "Essays in Honour of Sheila Delaney," special issue, *Florilegium* 23 (2006): 1–48.

5. The entire manuscript, made up of three volumes, is copied by the same scribe. The most recent description of C.U.L. Dd.I.17 is C. David Benson and Lynne Blanchfield, *The Manuscripts of the B Version of Piers Plowman* (Cambridge, 1997), 33–37, which also cites bibliography for previous descriptions (33). The manuscript is massive, written throughout by one scribe, and is comprised of three volumes (or more likely two, judging by the continuous quire signatures of the first two), joined together in "a single great book," as Kane and Donaldson put it (see *Piers Plowman: The B Version*, ed. George Kane and E. T. Donaldson (London: Athlone, 1975)). This view is not disputed by any modern scholar; see, Benson and Blanchfield, 33 n. 22.

6. Kerby-Fulton, "English Joachimism."

7. For a full chronology chart, and extensive discussion, see my *Books Under Suspicion* for 1215 and the following, p. xx.

8. For the Latin text of the poem, see Bloomfield and Reeves, "Penetration"; the translation (which only attempts a prose rendering) is my own.

9. For the primary sources of these events, see the Chronology chart in the front of Kerby-Fulton, *Books Under Suspicion*, at their respective dates, 1254 (p. xxi), 1358 (p. xxxvi), and 1380 (p. xli).

10. For the history of antifraternal and academic anti-Joachimism, see Kerby-Fulton, *Books under Suspicion*, chaps. 3 and 4. For Percham especially see pp. 192ff.

11. On Langland's treatment of the end of the A-Text, see Kerby-Fulton, *Books Under Suspicion*, chaps. 9 and 10.

12. The English tendency toward antimendicantism, antipapalism, and political fascination with disendowment made England receptive to Joachite prophecy, which had, for instance, predicted the Schism, the disendowment of the Church, envisioned the reform of the friars, and the purification of the papacy under a holy, humble figure of Peter.

13. Compare William Blake's conscious sense of creating what he calls a "system" in his epic *Jerusalem*.

14. Bloomfield, *Piers Plowman*, 65–66.

15. Ibid, 66.

16. Curtis V. Bostick, *Antichrist and the Lollards: Apocalypticism in Late Medieval and Reformation England* (Brill: Leiden, 1998), 89.

17. Langland explicitly evokes both earlier in the poem in his famous description of the "lunatyk lollares," see Pearsall's note to C.IX.105 and 136, and 1 Cor. 4:10 especially. For references to the Schism in *Piers Plowman*, other than those mentioned below, see also C.XVII.243, and XXI.428–29, and likely 443–45. When citing the C-Text, I use the edition by Derek Pearsall, *Piers Plowman by William Langland: An Edition of the C-text* (London: Edward Arnold, 1978).

18. See the discussion of Wells and Bodley 851 in my review of *Piers Plowman: A Working Facsimile of the Z-Text in Bodleian Library, Oxford, MS Bodley 851*, intro. by Charlotte Brewer and A.G. Rigg, *Modern Language Review* 91.4 (1996): 959–61. See Kerby-Fulton, *Books Under Suspicion*, 466 n. 7. For another politically active expert in

canon law who owned *Piers Plowman*, Walter de Brugges, see Rees Davies, "The Life, Travels, and Library of an Early Reader of *Piers Plowman*," *Yearbook of Langland Studies* 13 (1999): 49–64.

19. See J. McCall, "The Writings of John of Legnano with a List of Manuscripts," *Traditio* 23 (1967): 421–37, 431 for mention of our prophecy, which appears among the spurious items. Other prophecies regarding the Schism were attributed to Legnano (see McGinn, *Visions*, 254 n. 4; and see the discussion of one below, cited by Rusconi). Dozens of manuscripts survive of his *Commentaria in Clementinas, De interdicto ecclesiastico*, and *De censura ecclesiastica* (on which see McCall). A treastise entitled *De heresiis* was also ascribed to him. See also J. McCall's "Chaucer and John of Legnano," *Speculum* 40 (1965): 486.

20. I would like to thank Robert Lerner for drawing my attention to the Belial tradition and for helpful bibliography. For much of the information about Jacobus below, I follow Norbert Ott, *Rechtspraxis und Heilsgeschichte zu Uberlieferung, Ikonographie und Gebrauchssituation des deutschen Belial* (Munich: Artemis Verlag, 1983).

21. See C. T. Allmand, "The Civil Lawyers," in *Profession, Vocation, and Culture in Later Medieval England: Essays Dedicated to the Memory of A. R. Myers*, ed. Cecil H. Clough (Liverpool, Liverpool University Press, 1982), 155–80; and Kathryn Kerby-Fulton and Steven Justice, "Scribe D and the Marketing of Ricardian Literature," in *The Medieval Professional Reader at Work: Evidence from the Manuscripts of Chaucer, Langland, Kempe and Gower*, ed. Kathryn Kerby-Fulton and Maidie Hilmo (Victoria: English Literary Studies, University of Victoria, 2001), 217–38.

22. Kerby-Fulton, "English Joachimism," for evidence of legal manuscripts containing Joachite works and see also my "English Joachite Manuscripts and Medieval Optimism about the Role of the Jews in History," cited in n. 4 above.

23. McCall, "Chaucer and John of Legnano," 487.

24. A. S. Cook suggested various historical contacts Chaucer would have had with John of Legnano, "Chauceriana II: Chaucer's 'Linian,'" *Romanic Review* VIII (1971): 358–82; see also the note to this passage in the *Riverside Chaucer*.

25. McCall, "Chaucer and John of Legnano," 484.

26. For the articles of heresy charged against Hus, see Gordon Leff, *Heresy in the Later Middle Ages*, vol. 2 (Manchester: University of Manchester Press, 1967), 676–77.

27. *Compendium perbreve de redemptione generis humani, Consolatio Peccatorum nuncupatum, et apud nonnullos Belial vocitatum*, or sometimes as *Lis Christi et Belial coram judice Salomone* or *Processus Luciferi*. For these and other titles, and the translation history into multiple European medieval vernaculars, see P. B. Salmon, "Jacobus de Theramo and Belial," *London Mediaeval Studies* II (1951): 101–15.

28. Ralph Hanna, 1993, cited in Benson and Blanchfield, *Manuscripts of the B Version*, 33: following Ian Doyle's suggestion regarding the coincidence of the contents with the surviving library list of the York Austin Friars, adds "certainly the historical texts of the manuscript suggest origin among the regular clergy."

29. The adjective is Anne Middleton's; see her "The Audience and Public of '*Piers Plowman*,'" in *Middle English Alliterative Poetry and Its Literary Background*, ed. David Lawton (Cambridge: Brewer, 1982) 103–23.

30. Fol. 231ra–61vb. Jacobus was restored to favor in 1410 by a bull from John XXIII, which, however, the pope (despite his statement to the contrary) does not seem to have examined too closely. The bull refers to the *Belial* as a book called *Somnium Nabugodonosor sive Statuta Danielis*, two visions, in fact, that the *Belial* recounts, but which are, for safety's sake, censored from the German. For the bull, and the German censorship, see Salmon, "Jacobus," 108–9.

31. See the previous note. On Joachimism in Hussite circles, see Robert Lerner, *The Heresy of the Free Spirit in the Later Middle Ages* (Berkeley: University of California Press, 1972).

32. For which see Ott, *Rechtspraxis*, 22–25, and the quotations below.

33. Ibid, see Ott's appendices listing all the extant manuscripts.

34. One small free-form instance of Langland's ability to do this may survive at C.XV.51a. See Kerby-Fulton, *Books Under Suspicion*, chap. 3, for discussion and especially p. 191.

35. For the Latin text, see Melchior Goldast Haiminsfeld, *Processus Juris Joco-serius* (Hanau, 1611), from which there are also quotations in Ott. Salmon ("Jacobus," 105) mentions the comparison with *Paradise Lost* made disapprovingly by earlier critics.

36. The work is variously described: in the 1559 *Index* it is under "Auctorum incerti nominis libri prohibiti," B, "Belial sive de consolatione peccatorum" (the latter being the title under which it appears in Dd.I.17); but by 1590 it is also described as: "Belial, procurator Luciferi, contra Moysen, procuratorem Jesu Christi," (emphasizing one of the most scandalous aspects of the work). The suppression of Jacobus's name in many manuscripts clearly was effective by the sixteenth century. See *Die Indices librorum prohibitorum des sechzehnten Jahrhunderts, gesammelt*, ed. F. Heinrich Reusch, (Tübingen: Litterarischer Verein in Stuttgart, 1886) 180 and 467; for commentary, Ott, *Rechtspraxis*, 25; and Salmon ("Jacobus," 103) also for the comments of eighteenth and nineteenth-century scholars who deemed the work blasphemous.

37. See Konrad Burdach, *Der Dichter des Ackermann aus Böhmen und seine Zeit* (Berlin: Weidmannsche Buchhandlung, 1926–32), especially "Eschatologische Züge," in vol. 3, pt. 2, pp. 116–39 (which also covers the Taborites); and the fifth chapter, on *Piers Plowman*; the John Ball letters (167ff.); and the Harrowing-related themes (226ff.), with comparisons to Hussite, Wycliffite, Joachite, and radical Franciscan materials. For summarizing quotations from Burdach's argument see also Kathryn Kerby-Fulton, *Reformist Apocalypticism and Piers Plowman* (Cambridge: Cambridge University Press, 1990) 240 n. 107 and 108.

38. Salmon, "Jacobus," 112.

39. As Marjorie Reeves has pointed out, Joachim returns again and again to the fertile women of the Bible because he sees the patterns of history in terms of germination and fructification. Since Rachel, often understood to symbolize the contempla-

tive life in relation to Leah as the active life, gave birth to Joseph in the sixth year of her marriage, Joachim took this to mean that the new spiritual *ordo* would begin during the sixth age of history. Joachim also formulated his monastic reforms in the founding of his order at Fiore, with its contemplative emphasis, in terms of the conceptions of Rachel and Mary, as Stephen Wesley has shown. See Marjorie Reeves and Beatrice Hirsch-Reich, *The Figurae of Joachim of Fiore* (Oxford: Clarendon Press, 1974), 167–68 and Stephen Wesley, "Female Imagery: A Clue to the Role of Joachim's Order of Fiore," 164 and 169.

40. There is no edition of "Regnum spiritus sancti," and no other manuscripts have surfaced as yet; all quotations here come from the manuscript, C.U.L. Dd.I.17, fols. 203vb–4rb. (I have only attempted a diplomatic transcription of key passages here, with minimal emendation indicated in brackets). See also McCall, "John of Legnano," 431. The prophecy opens "Regnum spiritus sancti distingu(u)ntur in iacob filii Isaac qui duas uxores ex vno patre natas viz. lyam & aliam rachielem qui jacob ex lya prima sua vxore quatuor filios genuit & cessauit parere. Rachel vero secunda vxor videns qui infecunda est..." (203vb).

41. "Post hoc deus respiciet Rachaelem synagogam sterilem & ipsa concipie[t] spiritualiter de ipso spirit[o] sancto duos populos infideles & fideles pariet viz. israeliticum populum & populum iudaycum & sic ipse spiritus sanctus totum mundum spiritualiter in semine habrahe saluabit" (203vb).

42. For Joachim's understanding, Reeves and Hirsch-Reich, *Figurae*, 167–68.

43. Cited in Roberto Rusconi, *Attesa della fine: Crisi della società, profezia, ed Apocalisse in Italia al tempo del grande scisma d'Occidente, 1378–1417* (Rome: Istituto Storico Italiano per il Medio Evo, 1979), 166; on 164–67 he discusses the prophecies associated with John of Legnano, but does not mention the Cambridge *Regnum* prophecy.

44. "per tempus & tempora & dimidium temporis qui sunt tres anni cum dimidio secundum danielem" (203vb).

45. "tota ecclesia et regnum christi renouabitur... & pax maxima erit ierusalem ecclesie & regno christi nec non toti orbi per mille annos" (203vb).

46. "A desolacione templi iudaici vsque ad potestatem infernalem... secundum danielem xii.c. erunt anni mille CCti nonaginta que sunt in annis christi millo.ccco. lxiiijo & durabit vsque ad annos a desolacione templi computando [marginal note: CCCtos] mille xxxv. qui sunt in [quotation from Belial begins here] annis domini millo.CCCCo ix. infra quos ipsa potestas infernalis ponet in christi ecclesia antichristum qui persequitur ecclesiam christi & eius verum vicarium per temporales reges infra ix annos quibus completis ignaturus [sic] est in ecclesia christi & quam possidere debet contra verum christi vicarum annis tribus cum dimidio in graui persecucione populi sancti & sacerdotum sanguis effudetur sicut aqua & famis valida erit & tribulacione qualis non fuit ex qua die visus est in ecclesia christi postea deficiet eius potencia & siue manu conteretur que precipiet sancta sanctorum destrui & [ac—*cancelled*] nouum & vetus testamentum concremari."

47. *Processus*, ed. Goldast, 239; and Burdach, *Ackermann*, 507: "Anno domini 1409 ipsa potestas infernalis ponet in Christi ecclesiam potestatem Antichristi, qui persequetur ecclesiam Christi et eius verum Vicarium per temporales Reges infra 9 annos; quibus completis regnaturus est in Ecclesia Christi et quam possidere debet contra Christi verum Vicarium annis tribus et dimidio. Ex gravi persecutione populi sancti et sacerdotum sanguis sicut aqua effundetur, et fames valida erit et tanta erit tribulatio qualis non fuit ex qua die visus est populus in Ecclesia Christi. Postea deficiet eius potentia et sine manu contereretur, ac praecipiet Sancta Sanctorum destrui ac Novum et Vetus Testamentum concremari."

48. "Datum Adversae prope neopolim, die penultima mensis Octobris, sextae indictionis, Anno Domini MCCCLXXXII, pontificatus santissimi in Christo patris et domini Urbani et sacrosanctae ac universalis Ecclesiae Papae Sexti anno quinto aetatis meae tricesimo tercio," cited in Ott, *Rechtspraxis*, 16.

49. In this prophecy, Langland even uses arcane symbolism common to Joachite writings. See Kerby-Fulton, *Reformist Apocalypticism*, 175–76.

50. For the optimistic apocalyptic programs of both these complex passages, see Kerby-Fulton, *Reformist Apocalypticism*, 51–52.

51. I would like to thank Robert Lerner for bringing the connection with Hus to my attention.

52. "Item articulus nonus, in quo continetur, quod Joannes Hus dixit in vulgari ad populum: 'Ecce completa est Prophetia, quam praedixerat Jacobus de Theramo, quod anno Domini millesimo quadrigentesimo nono surget unus qui Evangelium Epistolas et Fidem Christi persequitur,' per haec denotandae Dominum Alexandrum, qui in suis bullis mandavit libros Wiclefi cremari." Ott, *Rechtspraxis*, 21–22; Burdach, *Ackermann*, 507.

53. At least six extant manuscripts are known to contain both (see the appendix of manuscript descriptions in Ott, *Rechtspraxis*)—a fascinating point for medievalists of England, because Wyclif denounced prophecy, thought Joachim a foolish dreamer, and genuinely took a hard scholastic line against visions of all sorts (see my *Books Under Suspicion*, chaps. 1 and 4).

54. See Lerner, *Free Spirit*, on the relations between Joachite and Hussite expectation.

55. See the passage quoted in n. 47 above.

56. For the exegetical complexity of this passage, which operates on all four levels of exegetical allegory, see the notes in Pearsall's edition to lines 402–12.

57. Joachimism and various other kinds of salvational generosity are discussed in Kerby-Fulton, *Books Under Suspicion*, chapters 1 and 10 in particular.

58. See Kerby-Fulton, *Books Under Suspicion*, chronology chart, 1254 and 1255.

59. See Kerby-Fulton, *Books Under Suspicion*, figs. 10a and 10b, showing scribal highlightings brackets in the *Regnum* prophecy.

60. Another item in the manuscript, the *Chronicon breve rerum Anglicarum*, beginning abruptly without a rubric on fol. 93, was compiled ca. 1381, because it does not

mention events after that year. See the Dd.I.17 description in *the Cambridge University Library Catalogue of Manuscripts*, vol. 2, p. 18.

61. For this consensus, see Benson and Blanchfield's entry on Dd.I.17's provenance, p. 33. I would like to thank James Carley for his advice on this as well. Glastonbury also held prophetic materials.

62. See Kerby-Fulton, *Books Under Suspicion*, pp. 101–8 and 137.

63. For the serious dangers of citing the *Bridlington Prophecies*, see my *Books Under Suspicion*, pp. 106–8.

64. "Per generale mandatum prelatorum ad comburendum, destruendum et condempnandum omnes libros, scilicet omelias ewangeliorum et epistolarum in lingwa materna conscriptos" (*Opus arduum*, fol. 174v).

65. I have read the passage in a microfilm of MS Brno University Mk 28, fol. 174v, kindly loaned to me by Penn Szittya; Curt Bostick also generously supplied me with his chapter on the *Opus arduum* from his forthcoming book. Anne Hudson, to whom I am indebted for her detailed work on the Opus, discusses this passage on p. 54 of "A Neglected Wycliffite Text," (*Lollards and their Books* (London, Ronceverte: 1985)) and reads it as saying that Oxford and Salisbury are "the places where the books of Ockham, Rupescissa, Olivi, and William of St. Amour have been *destroyed*" [my emphasis], and again on p. 49 she says that "the *bishops* have caused the destruction in Oxford and Salisbury of the works of" these writers. But the passage is ambiguous, and what exactly the role of the bishops was is not really clear; what is clear is that the friars are named as agents ("quia fratres huius negocii procuratores errant" (fol. 174v)) of the prelates who order, first, the destruction of vernacular books—described by the *Opus* author as homilies, gospels, and epistles written in the mother tongue—and, secondly, that the friars are responsible for keeping the four Latin writers named under lock and key. This seems to be how both Bostick and the Rouses have read the passage as well (see Mary A. Rouse and Richard H. Rouse, *Authentic Witnesses: Approaches to Medieval Texts and Manuscripts* (Notre Dame: Notre Dame University Press, 1991), 412). It remains to be discovered exactly what the role of the bishops of Oxford and Salisbury was; Oxford at this time was still under the diocese of Lincoln. For the whole Latin text of the passage, see Kerby-Fulton, *Books Under Suspicion*, appendix B, p. 403.

66. Note Hudson's remark that Wycliffite tradition is "largely innocent of Joachim," (*The Premature Reformation* (Oxford: Clarendon, 1988), 264), but I would suggest that antipathy played a larger role than has been suspected. Walter Brut seems to be the one further exception to this (discussed below). See Kerby-Fulton, *Books Under Suspicion*, chap. 5, for further details on the rest of the this paper.

67. I am grateful to John Van Engen for his advice about this.

68. See Hudson, "Neglected Wycliffite Text."

69. For further analysis, see Kerby-Fulton, *Books Under Suspicion*, chap. 5.

70. *Registrum Johannis Trefnant*, ed. W. W. Capes (London: Canterbury and York Society, 1916), 296–97; cf. Wyclif, *De Potestate Pape*, 118, discussed in Bostick, *Antichrist*, 61.

71. Brut is also very consciously "naturalizing" the imported apocalyptic thinking (which he handles with real security) to create a new apocalyptic role for the "British," which he does by historicizing *British* salvation history. For analysis, see Ruth Nissé, "Prophetic Nations," *New Medieval Literatures* 4 (2001): 95–115.

72. See my "*Eciam Lollardi*: Some Further Thoughts on Fiona Somerset's '*Eciam Mulier*: Women in Lollardy and the Problem of Sources,'" in *Voices in Dialogue*, ed. Linda Olson and K. Kerby-Fulton (Notre Dame: University of Notre Dame Press, 2005), 261–78. For more recent and lengthy treatment of Walter Brut, see also Alastair Minnis, *Fallible Authors* (Philadelphia: University of Pennsylvania Press, 2008).

73. See Kerby-Fulton, *Books Under Suspicion*, chap. 9.

Jewish Sages and German Schoolmen [1999]

Bernard McGinn

Ecumenism seems like such a good idea that we may wonder why it wasn't invented earlier. The story of the relations among versions of one faith (the narrow ecumenism) and attempts at understanding among different faiths (the broad ecumenism) were few and far between before the last century. In the case of the contentious history of Rabbinic Judaism and Christianity, related offspring of the same Second Temple Jewish mother, two millennia give us a story more notable for its downsides than its inspiring moments. Still, the tale is not all one of incomprehension, suspicion, and hatred, as well as their evil offspring, persecution. History rarely records friendships among common folk, personal acts of kindness, and the humane interaction of neighbors. In the record that does survive, the ecumenism that did exist between Jews and Christians before the last two centuries was largely what might be called a philosophical ecumenism. What I mean by this is that throughout the medieval and early modern periods it was on the level of the philosophical endeavor to understand God and the world that Jews, Christians, and Muslims were sometimes able to bracket their religious divisions and suspicions and engage each other with respect, if not always with agreement, given the fact that they were, after all, philosophers.

There are a number of chapters in the history of these encounters, which were almost always conducted in writing and at some historical distance, not in person. (When Jewish and Christian thinkers had real public encounters in the Middle Ages it was most often in stage-managed debates of a false and sometimes vicious nature.) One of the most intensive and interesting of these philosophical meetings was the use of the thought of two Jewish philosophers, Solomon Ibn Gabirol and Moses Maimonides, by the German Dominicans of the great age of the "School of Cologne," that is, the house of theological studies (*studium generale*) that flourished between 1250 and 1350.

First, a few remarks on the two Jewish sages of Spain and how they became accessible to the German schoolmen. Very little is known of the life of Solomon Ibn Gabirol.[1] He was born in Malaga about 1020. Taken to Saragossa while still young, he soon became famous for his poetry. There is uncertainty about the time of his death, but it was most likely between 1060 and 1070. Gabirol's poems are in Hebrew; his prose philosophical works in Arabic. The most famous of the latter is *The Fountain of Life (Meqor hayyim/ Fons vitae)*, written about 1046, and hence a remarkable achievement for a young man.[2] The Arabic original survives only in part, but Latin and Hebrew translations became popular in their respective religious communities. The Latin translation made in Spain, probably about 1150 by John of Seville and Dominic Gundissalinus, names the author as Avicebrol (Avencebrol, or sometimes Avicebron), the names he was known under during the history of scholasticism.[3]

The *Fons Vitae* was fairly well-known among Christian thinkers between 1150 and 1250.[4] Dominic Gundissalinus was not only a translator but also an independent, if eclectic, philosopher. He adopted Gabirol's distinctive form of Neoplatonism centered on the relation of the science of matter and form to the science of the Will and the science of the First Essence in a small treatise called *De unitate et uno*.[5] This work uses material from Boethius, so it often circulated under that august name, thus giving some Gabirolean teachings, such as universal hylomorphism (i.e., that all creatures are composed of matter and form), the authority of the great late Roman thinker. In another treatise, the *De processione mundi*, Gundissalinus supported Gabirol's fundamental axiom that all creation must be composed of two primal realities, matter and form—"Everything created must be different from the Creator. Since the Creator is truly one, unity ought not to belong to creatures. . . . Since the Creator is truly one, the creature which comes after him must be two."[6] Another teaching of the *Fons Vitae* that had considerable effect on scholastic debates in the thirteenth century was the doctrine of plurality of forms, i.e., that in one individual being it was possible to have many substantial forms. Avicebrol's arguments in favor of both universal hylomorphism and the plurality of forms were adopted in different ways by his scholastic readers. For instance, the Paris master William of Auvergne (d. 1249), who called Avicebrol "the single most noble of all philosophers," held to plurality of forms but denied the existence of matter in spiritual creatures, like angels. Gabirol was a considerable presence in the debates on both issues between ca. 1200 and 1250. That story has been well told by others and need not delay us here.[7]

Far too much is known about the life of the second Jewish sage, Moses Maimonides, to try to summarize his story and accomplishments.[8] Born in Cordoba in 1138, he wandered far and wrote much before his death in Egypt in 1204. The writings of Maimonides are extensive and extensively controversial. (The best wisdom I ever received about Maimonides was given to me by a philosopher in Jerusalem many years ago, who told me that when questioned about anything I said about Maimonides, I should reply, "My-monides is not Your-monides.") Here, however, we are not so much concerned with Maimonides himself as with the reception of his ideas by the medieval schoolmen.[9] Maimonides's philosophical masterpiece, the *Guide of the Perplexed* (ca. 1190), was translated into Latin under the title *Dux neutrorum* from one of the Hebrew versions, not from the original Arabic.[10] This version was apparently completed in the 1230s, though we do not know where or by whom. By the 1240s the text was being used by Paris masters, like Alexander of Hales. Not all scholastics trained at Paris were interested in the great Jewish sage, as the example of Bonaventure shows; but many were, including Thomas Aquinas. It is ironic to note that one of the first theologians to use Maimonides, though without naming him, was the same William of Auvergne who praised Avicebrol and who, as bishop of Paris, was responsible for the burning of the Talmud in 1248.

Why were the philosophers and theologians of the Latin West interested in these two Jewish thinkers?[11] The answer to this question highlights an important aspect of the philosophical ecumenism of medieval scholasticism. By the early twelfth century the schoolmen had begun to recognize that philosophical, scientific, and medical wisdom resided not so much in the Fathers, supreme authorities in theology as they were, but in the great pagan philosophers and scientists and in their heirs in Islam and Judaism. The twelfth century saw a wave of translations of ancient Greek texts that often took circuitous routes through Syriac and Arabic before making it into Latin.[12] Translations of Muslim and Jewish philosophers writing in Arabic also began. Spain and Sicily were the centers for this activity, and a small band of intrepid scholars, whose wanderings and exploits are the intellectual equivalents of the questing knights of medieval romance, were vital in this transmission of cultural knowledge. The interchange often involved errors and mistaken identities. The famous *Liber de causis*, a late twelfth-century translation of a tenth-century Arabic reworking of Proclus's *Elements of Theology*, for example, was often ascribed to Aristotle.[13] It seems likely that Gabirol came into Latin under false pretenses as a Muslim, or even a Christian Arab, rather than a Jew. John of Seville and Gundissalinus seem to have thought this on the basis of the Arabic language of the text and the fact that Gabirol gives no overt signs of his Jewish faith in the *Fountain on Life*.

In the late twelfth and first half of the thirteenth century the translation effort shifted to making available the full corpus of Aristotle and the great Muslim philosophers, especially Avicenna and Averroes. While Averroes was at first looked upon primarily as the "commentator," that is, the foremost interpreter of what Aristotle ("the philosopher") really meant, this was not the case with Avicenna. Nor does it seem that it was so with Maimonides. Avicenna and Maimonides were promptly welcomed into the arena of philosophical ecumenism because it was felt they were masters in their own right, sources of wisdom, as well as worthy opponents in the disputatious boxing ring of the struggle to attain philosophical truth through honest argument.

My metaphor of philosophical discussion as a boxing ring may seem far-fetched, but it is not totally off the mark, if you recall those depictions of Thomas Aquinas, such as that of Filippino Lippi in the Caraffa Chapel in Santa Maria sopra Minerva in Rome, which show the friar triumphing over Averroes prone at his feet after a knockout blow. I have not found any scenes of Maimonides in a similar position, perhaps because while Aquinas often disagreed with *Rabbi Moyses*, he treated him with respect—more courtesy and understanding than he reserved for the Greek Orthodox Christians he engaged in controversy. The literature on Thomas's relation to Maimonides is extensive, particularly on such issues as knowledge of God, the duration of creation, and the nature of spiritual creatures; but, given my concentration on the German Dominicans, I will not comment on it here.[14] Before moving on to Germany, however, I should note that Thomas also studied Gabirol's *Fons Vitae*, though his reaction to Gabirol's distinctive form of Neoplatonism was largely negative.[15] (C. Vansteenkiste's lists of Aquinas's direct citations from Jewish and Arab authors find 86 references to Maimonides versus 23 to Gabirol.)[16]

In order to get some understanding of how Gabirol and Maimonides were taken up by the German Dominicans and the effect of this philosophical encounter we need to look briefly at the world of German Dominican thought during the period 1250 to 1350. In 1248 the Dominican *magister actu regens* at the University of Paris, the learned polymath Albertus teutonicus, was commanded by the order to leave his chair and set up a *studium generale*, or what we might call today a degree-granting divinity school, for the Dominicans at Cologne. (Albert took with him his star student, a corpulent young Italian friar named Thomas.) On the basis of recent work by historians of medieval thought, this event has emerged as one of the most significant moments in German intellectual history. Though Albert was only at Cologne for a scant five years, his teaching and inspiration, as well as the genius of his first students and the several generations that succeeded them, made the Cologne Dominican *studium* the focus of an intellectual florescence whose full extent is only now being revealed through the publication of the ongoing *Corpus Philosophorum Teutonicorum Medii Aevi* and other research and writing.[17]

The greatest name among Albert's students was Meister Eckhart (ca. 1260–1328), though he was a student in the broad sense, since he only met Albert and heard some of the aged master's aphorisms when Albert returned to Cologne in his declining years. Two friars much influenced by Eckhart who apparently did not study in Cologne, John Tauler (d. 1361) and Henry Suso (d. 1365), were strongly marked by some of the major philosophical and mystical themes emanating from the great *studium*. In the past few decades, other figures, some who were probably formed by Albert himself, like Hugh Ripelin (d. 1268), Ulrich of Strasbourg (d. 1277), Dietrich of Freiberg (d. 1320), have emerged from the shadows as major thinkers. They were followed by a considerable number of lesser folk (e.g., John of Sterngassen, John Picardi of Lichtenberg, Nicholas of Strasbourg, Henry of Lübeck, etc.). Though there were real philosophical and theological differences among the German Dominicans, they shared a commitment to deep speculative thought of a Neoplatonic cast and a devotion to mystical preaching and teaching in the vernacular. Following Albert's lead, their investigations centered on the role of the intellect in attaining happiness, though to reduce such a group of important thinkers to any single theme is somewhat artificial.

The German Dominicans were also notable among medieval scholastics for a wide-ranging philosophical ecumenism that incorporated pagan, Muslim, and Jewish philosophers into their thinking and writing, though naturally this was more true of some than of others. In the 1320s, however, the attack on Eckhart's attempt to weld philosophy, theology, and what we today call mysticism into a new synthesis dealt a severe blow to the ambition and creativity of the Cologne School. In the wake of Eckhart's condemnation by papal bull in 1329, his followers, especially Suso and Tauler, continued to show sympathy for the philosophical ecumenism of their forebears, but they turned their backs on the academic concerns of their contemporaries in Cologne and Paris. They preferred to use their learning to continue Eckhart's mission of mystical preaching. One of their contemporaries, however, Berthold of Moosburg (ca. 1300–ca. 1365), kept the ecumenical philosophical agenda of the founders of Cologne alive through the 1330s and 1340s. By the time of the onslaught of the Black Death, a century after Albert came to Cologne, the golden age of German Dominican learning was already dead.

Albert the Great was responsible for setting the intellectual program of the Cologne *studium*. The great polymath sought to synthesize a number of philosophical and theological traditions that today seem scarcely compatible, perhaps because we have lost the medieval sense of the unity of truth. During his period at Cologne he continued the intensive study and commentary on Aristotle he had begun at Paris (the early thirteenth-century condemnation of Aristotle's writings had become a dead letter by the 1240s).[18] At the same time Albert pioneered a new intellective interpretation of the corpus of the Pseudo-Dionysius, commenting on all four treatises of the collection, as well as the letters, between 1248 and 1254. Albert was also engaged in the study of Avicenna, as is shown by the many Avicennan features in his writings. Alain de Libera contends that Augustine's theology of beatitude, Avicenna's noetic of emanation, and Dionysius's presentation of mystical union constitute the three basic building blocks of Albert's thought.[19] A fourth significant source for Albert was the *Liber de causis*. Indeed, Albert's most important metaphysical treatise, the *De causis et processu universitatis*, written in the late 1260s, is a paraphrase, commentary, and expansion of the *Liber de causis* in light of his understanding of Dionysius. Although Albert was not alone among the scholastics in mining the *Liber de causis*, his interest in this Proclean book seems to have been at least partly responsible for the revival of the study of Proclus among the German Dominicans. The spate of translations of the Neoplatonic philosopher's treatises and Platonic commentaries, and the frequent use of this last great pagan (and anti-Christian) Neoplatonist, has led scholars to speak of this as an era of *Proclus Latinus*.[20]

Among the wide range of sources used by Albert both Maimonides and Gabirol can be included, although Albert treated them more critically than did most of his successors. Albert's use of Maimonides is relatively restricted.[21] On some issues, he was happy to cite Rabbi Moses as an authority, such as in his attack against Aristotle's arguments for the eternity of the world.[22] Albert also used Maimonides in arguing against those philosophers, like Avicenna and Averroes, who held that the world was a necessary product of the First Cause. Like Maimonides, he emphasized that God does not cause the way natural things do by the necessity of their being but by way of his own being, which is Intellect and Will.[23] Nevertheless, Albert often criticized Maimonides. For instance, he disagreed with Rabbi Moses's identification of the angels with the Aristotelian separate intelligences;[24] he also felt that Maimonides's doctrine of prophecy was too naturalistic, not allowing sufficiently for the role of supernatural gifts from God.[25]

Albert's attitude toward Gabirol is particularly revealing. Given the fact that the Dominican's basic philosophical position has been described as a metaphysics of flow (*fluxus*),[26] one might have expected him to have welcomed Gabirol's monotheistic re-interpretation of the Neoplatonic paradigm of emanation and return. But there is "flow" and "real flow," Albert might have said. Ever the trenchant critic, he discerned essential differences between his own revised Proclean-Dionysian metaphysics of flow and the Jewish version proposed by Avicebrol. Three chapters in his *De causis et processu universitatis* are devoted to a detailed examination and refutation of the *Fons Vitae*, which the acerbic Dominican in one place dismisses as the product of "a sophomore" (*quidem sophistarum*). Sophomore or not, Albert's concern with the *Fons Vitae* is a good example of critical philosophical dialogue and is important for highlighting the fundamentals of his metaphysics.[27]

Gabirol based his system on his interpretation of two fundamental principles of Neoplatonic metaphysics: first, the principle of mediation, that is, two extremes cannot be related apart from a third mediating reality; and second, the principle of coinherence, or as the Platonist Numenius once put it, "all in all, but each according to its nature."[28] To these Gabirol joined the third principle noted above—the axiom that the Absolute must be one and therefore can only produce a duality, something that is different from Itself and therefore inherently twofold (e.g., FV IV.6). In using these principles to forge a synthesis between Jewish belief in an omnipotent Creator and a Neoplatonic universe constituted by coinherent levels of the emanation of the fundamental duality of matter and form, Gabirol emphasized the role of the Creative Will (*voluntas creatrix*) as the essential medium between the one God and the dual creation. Thus, in Gabirol's thought, the Creative Will plays a role analogous to what we find in Philo's conception of the Logos, as well as in Christian Neoplatonic Logos theology.

Albert detected an essential opposition between this view of creation and his own metaphysics founded on God as the immediate Creator of all things, including particular beings, and the necessary role of the Logos, or Divine Intellect, in the creative process. For Albert, following Aristotle, will is always specified to act by intellect, so in creation it is God as Intellect not as Will (though these two are really one) that must take the essential role. According to the Dominican, Gabirol's insistence on the priority of the Creative Will threatened to undermine the intelligibility implanted in the universe by the Creator and therefore the role of philosophy itself. Albert also argued that Gabirol's principles of mediation and coinherence compromised a free and immediate divine creation. Finally, he noted that all good philosophers held that "from what is one only what is one can come," an axiom thought to go back to Aristotle, and, of course, in direct opposition to Gabirol's third principle.[29]

Albert's broad use of so many philosophical resources was of importance in launching the philosophical ecumenism of his German Dominican followers. Several of these thinkers were more open than he to the influence of the two Jewish sages, Gabirol and Maimonides. Meister Eckhart is too original a thinker to be characterized as anybody's disciple or follower, but for at least some aspects of his thought it is not illegitimate to speak of him as a Latin Maimonidean.[30] His knowledge of the *Guide*, or *Dux neutrorum*, was extensive and it is interesting to note that nowhere in his works does he disagree with Maimonides by name, the way Aquinas and Albert did.[31] References to Maimonides appear rarely in Eckhart's vernacular preaching, perhaps five or six times, and usually as a part of the group of *heidnische meister* that would include the ancient philosophers, as well as Jews and Muslims. It is quite different in Eckhart's Latin works. Although the indices to the critical edition works are not yet complete, it seems that Eckhart mentions Maimonides second only to Aristotle among his non-Christian sources.[32] In his *Commentary on Exodus* it is surprising to see him using Maimonides about as often as he does Augustine.

Why was Eckhart so drawn to the Jewish sage? Two fundamental reasons were: (1) the importance of philosophical exegesis, and (2) the supremacy of negative theology. Eckhart adopted many details of his reading of Old Testament texts from Maimonides, but the influence of the Jewish philosopher was more fundamental than providing this or that detail—Eckhart found in Maimonides a model of the kind of philosophical reading of the Bible that he thought essential to good preaching.[33] Eckhart's conviction of the unity of all truth, natural (i.e, philosophical), moral, and theological, meant that although scripture was not written in a philosophical way (*demonstrative*), it could, and even should, be read that way, as Maimonides had shown. Since there could be no conflict between reason and revelation, philosophical reasoning was an essential tool for correctly interpreting the Bible. As Eckhart says at the beginning of his *Commentary on John*, "In interpreting this Word (Jn 1:1) and everything else that follows my intention is the same as in all my works—to explain what the holy Christian faith and the two Testaments maintain through the help of the natural arguments of the philosophers."[34] In the prologue to the second Genesis commentary (the *Liber parabolorum Genesis*) he emphasizes that his purpose in this work is "to show that what the truth of holy scripture parabolically intimates in hidden fashion agrees with what we prove and declare [i.e., philosophically] about matters divine, ethical, and natural."[35]

In line with this principle, it is obvious that a good exegete needs to know how to treat the parables, that is, the metaphors and stories that make up so much of the scriptural text. Here, Eckhart explicitly turns to Maimonides. In the same prologue to the aptly-named *Liber parabolorum Genesis*, he cites Maimonides's *Guide* to show that, as he puts it, "the whole of the Old Testament is either natural science or spiritual wisdom," summarizing the sage's distinction between two kinds of parables, those in which "every . . . word of the parable separately stands for something," and those in which "the whole parable is the likeness and expression of the whole matter of which it is a parable."[36] Eckhart does not really use this distinction very much in the course of his exegesis, but it is noteworthy that he cited Maimonides, along with the Augustine of the *Confessions*, as models for engaging in a philosophical reading of Scripture.

Eckhart invoked Maimonides for many particular readings during the course of his biblical commentaries, especially on Genesis and Exodus. For example, in discussing God's relation to creation, Eckhart in several places explores how God, although he is without location (*illocalis*), can for that very reason be called the "place of all things" (*locus omnium*).[37] Although John Scottus Eriugena had also experimented with such formulae, it is more likely that Maimonides was the source for Eckhart's explorations of this theme, although he is not mentioned by name.[38] Eckhart does, however, specifically refer to Maimonides for corroboration of a theme central to his anthropology (and that of the Dominican order in general): the soul's intellect as the place of union with God. Latin Sermon IX says, "In the essence [of the soul] as intellective, it is joined to what is higher than itself, God, just as Rabbi Moses has said: 'And thus it is an offspring of God.'"[39] This is not a throwaway reference, because intellective and indeed supraintellective union with God is at the heart of Eckhart's message. As he put it in Sermon XXIX: "The one God is intellect and intellect is the one God . . . . Therefore, to rise up to intellect, and to be subordinated to it, is to be united to God."[40]

Surveying all aspects of Eckhart's use of Maimonides is not possible in a brief essay. It may be useful, however, to comment on the second main reason that the Dominican had such a strong affinity with the Jewish philosopher: their mutual preference for a rigorous negative theology, the delicate task of using language to transcend itself in a trajectory pointed toward the ultimate mystery of God. In the history of Western speculation on the naming and unnaming of God there were, of course, many authorities for the primacy of negative theology: Plotinus and Proclus among the Greeks; Avicenna among the Muslims; and Dionysius, Boethius, Eriugena, and even Thomas Aquinas among the Latins. Eckhart uses them all, but when he undertook his most detailed examination of the problem of naming God in the two long sections of his *Commentary on Exodus* that together constitute a minitreatise on the divine names, Maimonides emerges, along with Aquinas, as the primary conversation partner.[41]

A brief look at the structure of this treatise will cast light on Eckhart's appreciation for Maimonides. The treatise comprises four parts, of which three involve extensive use of the Jewish philosopher's teaching on the impossibility of predicating positive attributes of God, especially as found in *Guide* 1.51–64 (Eckhart's chapter numbers are usually one higher than modern editions). At times, Eckhart gives long quotations from the *Guide* (e.g., nn. 171–74); in other places he engages in what might be called a philosophical conversation with Maimonides and his Christian authorities, most notably Thomas Aquinas, but also Augustine, Dionysius, and Boethius. The first part of the treatise (nn. 34–53) deals with "what some philosophers and Jewish authors think of this question [i.e., the divine names] and of the attributes which name God." Although Avicenna is cited, the basic discussion is with Rabbi Moses, first by detailing what the sage directly taught about the question (nn. 37–44), and then by discussing "the root and reason the Greek and Arab philosophers and the Jewish sages give why nothing may be positively or affirmatively said to be in God or fittingly predicated of him" (nn. 45–53). Eckhart concludes this section by drawing parallels between Augustine and Maimondes on why the identity of all attributes with the unknown divine substance prove that, as Rabbi Moses has it, "all positive statements about God are improper expressions, since they posit nothing in him. . . . All things that are positively said of God, even though they are perfections in us, are no longer so in God and are not more perfect than their opposites" (n. 44, citing *Guide* 1.53).

This, of course, is not really Augustine's view but it is typical of Eckhart's approach, as we see in the three remaining parts of the treatise, where the Dominican, like Eriugena before him, attempts to contrive an agreement (*consensum machinari*) among his authorities, even if it meant twisting some arms. The second part of the treatise (nn. 54–61) is supposed to deal with what the Christian authors hold on these issues. It begins, however, with a philosophical analysis of modes of predication and analogy and moves on to a treatment of how trinitarian language does not negate the oneness of the divine essence (nn. 56–57). Oddly enough, but fully in accord with Eckhart's conviction of the unity of philosophy and theology, he calls in the authority of both Maimonides and also Gabirol to support his teaching that there is no real distinction of attributes in God, as Thomas Aquinas and other Christian theologians held, but that all distinction rests on the side of the human intellect. His quotation from *Guide* 1.51 here was later included as article 23 in the bull of condemnation against Eckhart issued by John XXII in 1329—giving Maimonides the unusual distinction of being the only Jewish philosopher condemned for Christian error!

The third part of Eckhart's treatise (nn. 62–78) is the only section where Maimonides does not feature. This is because the discussion involves the Boethian teaching that only substance and relation language are fittingly used in relation to the trinitarian God. The main authorities are Boethius, Augustine, and Thomas Aquinas. In this section Eckhart seems to side more with Aquinas's teaching that the *via eminentiae* is the best form of language about God, rather than the *via negationis* of Maimonides.[42] (The issue of Eckhart's final position on divine predication cannot delay us here.) Distinctly Eckhartian, and again not in Maimonides, is his appeal to God as the *negatio negationis*, the highest form of affirmation, as the solution to the difficulty of the best way to name God (n. 74).

The fourth part of the treatise (nn. 143–84) returns to a strong engagement with Maimonides, as Eckhart discusses "the name more proper and especially peculiar of God, that is, the Tetragrammaton." This section contains three parts. The first (nn. 143–60) is a disquisition on eight scriptural names for God, basically drawn from *Guide* 1.60–64. The second (nn. 161–69) tries to show how Christian understanding of the name "He Who Is" (*qui est*) taken from Exodus 3:14 is a proper name for God and is in conformity with the teaching of Avicenna and Maimonides (n. 164). Finally, the last part (nn. 170–84) deals with the hermeneutics of the divine names, both the positive names (nn. 170–77) and the negative names (nn. 178–84). In this section Eckhart once again relies heavily on Maimonides as his main authority for emphasizing the supremacy of negation. As the Dominican summarizes, "The stronger the argument by which a person removes these [positive] attributes from God, the more perfect he is in divine knowledge" (n. 183). Without attempting to deal with all the issues involved in Eckhart's dense treatise, especially whether there is the kind of final coherence among his authorities that he seems to suppose, this brief sketch does give some sense of how extensive the engagement between Eckhart and Maimonides really was.

Eckhart also knew Gabirol's *Fons Vitae* and quoted it favorably, although less frequently than he did Maimonides.[43] Eckhart rejected Gabirol's teaching on the plurality of substantial forms, as well as the principle that only duality can come from absolute unity,[44] but he never attacked the *Fons Vitae*, as Albert had. Rather, he used the work in areas where he found it helpful, especially in its teaching on the nature of the One. Even here, however, Eckhart does not engage Gabirol in a detailed way, as he had Maimonides, but rather employs the text in standard scholastic fashion for proof texting a position already decided upon. For example, a passage from the second section of the "Treatise on the Divine Names" combines Gabirol and Maimonides with Boethius as testifying to the absolute unity of the divine nature: "No difference at all is or can be in the One, but 'All difference is below the One,' as it says in the *Fountain of Life*, book 5. 'That is truly one in which there is no number,' as Boethius says. And Rabbi Moses, as mentioned above, says that God is one 'in all ways and according to every respect,' so that any 'multiplicity either in intellect or in reality' is not found in him."[45]

If Eckhart is the most positive of the scholastics toward Maimonides, the last of the major thinkers of the German Dominican School may be described as the most Gabirolean. Berthold of Moosburg, a contemporary of Tauler and Suso, is not exactly a household name, but the ongoing edition of his masterwork, a vast commentary on Proclus's *Elements of Theology* (about two thousand pages when complete),[46] has begun to reveal him as the most ambitious of the medieval students of Proclus and an original philosopher who combed the resources of pagan, Christian, Islamic, and Jewish philosophy in his exposition of a revised Proclean metaphysics. His work, as Stephen Gersh puts it, is "a major contribution to the medieval tradition of Platonism."[47] Berthold possessed wide learning, making considerable use of all the standard ancient philosophers known to the scholastics, as well as Al-Ghazzali, Averroes, and Avicenna among the Muslims. To a large extent he reads Proclus through the lens of the Dionysian corpus, but other Christian Neoplatonists are also important for him, notably Boethius and John Scottus Eriugena, as known through Honorius Augustodunensis's paraphrase of the *Periphyseon*, the *Clavis Physicae*.[48] Among the German Dominicans he cites Albert and Dietrich of Freiberg extensively, but not Meister Eckhart, perhaps due to Eckhart's condemnation. Berthold uses Maimonides sparingly (twelve times in the edition thus far), but Gabirol is quoted and discussed frequently—298 times![49] No other Latin author uses Gabirol more, or more positively.[50]

What did Berthold find in Gabirol that was so important for his massive commentary on Proclus? It is difficult to give a complete answer to this, since the edition of the *Expositio* is still underway. On the basis of my partial readings in the 1500 pages published thus far (comprising the commentary on 158 of the 211 propositions of Proclus's *Elementatio*), it may be possible to provide at least some sense of Berthold's project and the role that Avicebrol plays in it by a look at the opening of the work, specifically the prologue, the commentary on Proclus's title, and the exposition of the first five propositions.

Berthold's *prologus* is an extended and at times eloquent Platonic meditation on how the created universe reveals God, and therefore also a defense of the legitimacy of the study of natural philosophy for the Christian thinker.[51] The prologue takes the form of a comment on that cornerstone of Christian philosophy, Paul's declaration in Romans 1:20, "The invisible things of God are beheld by the creature of the world through the understanding of the things that have been made" (Invisibilia enim ipsius a creatura mundi per ea quae facta sunt intellecta conspiciuntur). The first part briefly deals with God as the object to be understood (*invisibilia dei*). The longer and more important second part concerns the subject of the knowing, the "creature of the world" (*a creatura mundi*), i.e., the human being who philosophizes to raise himself to God. Here Berthold describes the human person as a microcosm, a model of the universe, or macrocosm.[52] This is scarcely new, but the Dominican's fourfold analysis of the microcosm as "corporeal, spiritual, intellectual, and 'uniale' subject" is distinctive.[53] Finally, he concludes the prologue with a brief treatment of Paul's "per ea quae facta sunt," that is, the four ways in which created things serve as instruments for knowing God. This consideration of the cosmos as a beautiful manifestation of God closes with a fitting hymn, in which Berthold calls himself the *humilis theoricus* (the humble contemplative).

Gabirol does not play any part in this largely Dionysian-inspired prologue, but in the exposition of the title of Proclus's treatise he begins to appear and to show why Berthold found the *Fons Vitae* so helpful for his project. This exposition forms a short treatise on Berthold's view of the content and method of philosophico-theological discourse.[54] The Dominican begins with a typically scholastic analysis of the author and subject matter of the book, the latter dealing with its material, formal, and final causes of the work. In this section, as Stephen Gersh has shown, Berthold introduces a "totally un-Proclean" ontological structure "in the form of a contrast between God viewed as substance and things subsequent to God viewed as attributes of the deity." He does so on the authority of axioms drawn from the mysterious *Book of the Twenty-Four Philosophers* and also from Gabirol.[55] In Berthold's words, "any kind of substance is an accident by reason of its dependence on the First, to which alone belongs the essence of subject, not insofar as it exists in passive potency, but as active in the sense that he who made the universe sustains it. Avencebrol speaks of this kind of accident in the *Fountain of Life*, book 3, chapters 36 and 54."[56] At the end of the exposition of the title Berthold returns to Gabirol, creating a concord between a series of quotations from book 1 of the *Fountain* and passages from Boethius and Augustine on the role of philosophical investigation in attaining beatitude and final perfection. For Berthold, then, Avicebrol was not only a model for the philosophical enterprise as such, but also a source for some of the distinctive aspects of his own philosophico-theological system.

Some important aspects of this influence also emerge from the role Gabirol plays in the exposition of the first five propositions. Berthold analyzes each axiom from Proclus's *Elements* in terms of what it presupposes philosophically (*quod supponitur*) and what it proposes as teaching (*quod proponitur*). The five initial axioms concern the foundational issue of the relation of the One and the many.[57] Gabirol plays a restricted role in Berthold's exposition of the first two axioms—"Every multitude participates in the One in some fashion," and "Everything that participates in the One is both one and not-one."[58] In the third and fourth axioms, however, the Jewish Neoplatonist emerges as a major voice, along with his translator and student Gundissalinus.[59] The third proposition declares that "Everything that becomes one does so by participation in the One." Berthold explains both the *suppositum* and the *propositum* of this axiom by a threefold distinction of modes of "becoming" (*fieri*)—becoming by creation, becoming by determination, and becoming by generation. Participated union by generation is analyzed in fundamentally Gabirolean terms, because the union of matter and form that is at the heart of the *Fons Vitae* is based upon the action of the generating First Cause—"It is necessary that besides matter and form there be a third thing, a Generative Principle that draws them out from the possibility of existing and makes them one in act."[60] In response to the objection that only similar things can be joined together, while matter and form are dissimilar, Berthold calls upon a half dozen texts from Gabirol to show that although the two are different, "nonetheless they come together in a union on the basis of the essential habitude that matter has to form by means of which it desires to be united to it as its perfection."[61] When he turns to the *propositum* side of this threefold distinction, Berthold again employs Gabirol to argue against those who contend that there is some kind of third nature that is needed to unite matter and form—no, he says, they become one without any medium by the attraction of nature set in them by the First, or Generative, Cause.[62]

Proposition 4, "Everything that is only united is different from the Absolute One (*unum per se*)," features even heavier use of texts from Gabirol (sixteen in all) and from his student Gundissalinus (ten citations).[63] Although the Jewish philosopher is quoted only four times in proposition 5 ("Every multitude is second to the One"), this axiom clearly reveals Berthold's deeply Gabirolean perspective and his disagreement with Albert's critique of the Jewish philosopher.[64] The *suppositum* section of this axiom takes up a central difference between Aristotelianism and Platonism, as Berthold sees it: that is, whether from what is absolutely one only one thing can come, as the Aristotelians, or *Peripatetici*, hold; or whether the Platonic view about the procession of the multitude from the One is correct. The first part sets out the Peripatetic view, largely depending on a passage from Avicenna's *Metaphysica* 9.4 about the emanation of the universe from the First Intelligence (113.12–115.70). "But this position does not please the Platonists," begins the second section, "who, though they concede and often demonstrate that the First Principle [of creation] is not at this point the *per se unum*, but is One simply, absolutely, and the same according to itself, . . . still say that from such a One a multitude immediately proceeds."[65] Dionysius and Boethius are cited in support of this teaching, though Berthold recognizes that weighty authorities, such as Albert, and even perhaps Plato himself (*Timaeus* 31ab is cited), seem to hold the opposite.

The third part of the *suppositum* is devoted to hoisting the Peripatetics on their own petard, as Berthold argues for the position "That a multitude proceeds immediately from the One can be shown on the basis of three propositions set down and admitted by the Peripatetics themselves!" (117.143–44). In this section Berthold turns to Gabirol and Aristotle to show how multitude in potency exists the mind of the one Creator (117.147–118.192), before engaging in a lengthy debate with Albert, showing that his intellectual forebear's arguments actually support the opposing view—namely, the position of Gabirol that duality and multiplicity must follow from the creative activity of the One (118.193–120.240).

At the end of the *propositum*, Berthold again appeals to Gabirol, along with other authorities, to summarize the henological core of his revised

Proclean metaphysics. Perhaps a Latin quotation from this section, dealing with the supremacy and plenitude of the One, may provide something of the flavor of this foremost of Gabirol's Latin admirers. In his hymn to the One, Berthold adopts a rapturous style: "Est quippe unum omnium perfectivum, bonificativum, conservativum, mensurativum, aequativum, aequalificativum, convenientiae et similtudinis operativum, appetitus excitativum, amabile et amoris attractivum, delectabile et complacentiae generativum, dignum existens et dignificativum, singularitatis possessivum, indivisibilitatis praeacceptivum, communicabile et communicativum. Amplius secundum Avencebrol (FV IV.11) unum est multitudinis effectivum, effectae sustentativum, sustentatae retentivum et contentivum."[66]

Philosophical ecumenism, at least in Germany, seems to have become dormant with the fading of the Cologne School of Dominicans. In the 1440s, however, it began to revive as Nicholas of Cusa once again turned to reading Maimonides, perhaps under the influence of Meister Eckhart. But that chapter, as well as the subsequent encounters between Jewish and Christian thinkers of the later fifteenth and sixteenth centuries, are another part of the story.

NOTES

This essay was first given at a colloquium for the retirement of my friend and colleague, Joel Kraemer, Professor of Jewish Studies at the Divinity School of the University of Chicago. I am very happy to have it appear in this volume dedicated to the accomplishments of another friend, Morton J. Bloomfield, as a replacement for the already published Bloomfield lecture that I delivered in 1999.

1. For an introduction to Gabirol, see Raphael Loewe, *Ibn Gabirol* (London: Weidenfeld & Nicolson, 1989).

2. The title is taken from Ps 36:10. For an introduction to the text and its versions, see Loewe, *Ibn Gabirol*, chap. 3.

3. The standard edition of the Latin text of the *Fons Vitae* (hereafter FV) is that of Clemens Baeumker, *Avencebrolis Fons Vitae ex Arabico in Latinum translatus ab Iohanne Hispano et Domenico Gundissalino*, in *Beiträge zur Geschichte der Philosophie des Mittelalters* 1.2–4 (Münster: Aschendorff, 1892–95).

4. For some aspects of the influence of the FV, see Bernard McGinn, "Ibn Gabirol: The Sage among the Schoolmen," in *Neoplatonism and Jewish Thought*, ed. Lenn E. Goodman (Albany: SUNY, 1992), 77–110.

5. The work was edited by Paul Correns, *Die dem Boethius fälschlich zugeschriebene Abhandlung des Dominicus Gundisalvi De Unitate*, in *Beiträge zur Geschichte der Philosophie*

des Mittelalters 1.1 (Münster: Aschendorff, 1891). For a recent discussion and partial translation, see *Von Einen zum Vielen: Der neue Aufbruch der Metaphysik im 12. Jahrhundert. Ein Auswahl zeitgenössischer Texte der Neuplatonismus,* ed. Alexander Fidora and Andreas Niederberger (Frankfurt: Klostermann, 2002), 66–79, and 136–44.

6. This passage from the *De processione mundi* can be found in the edition in Menendez Pelayo, *Historia de los Heterodoxos Espanoles,* vol. 1 (Madrid, 1880), 698. It paraphrases a text from FV IV.6, p. 222, lines 24–28.

7. See Erich Kleinedam, *Das Problem der hylomorphen Zusammenhang der geistigen Substanzen im 13. Jahrhundert behandelt bis zum Thomas von Aquin* (Breslau: Universität, 1930); D. O. Lottin, "Le composition hylémorphique des substances: Les débuts de la controverse," *Revue néoscolastique de Philosophie* 34 (1932): 21–41; and Paul Bissels, "Die sachliche Begrundung und philosophie-geschichtlicher Stellung der Lehre von der materia spiritualis in der Scholastik," *Franziskanische Studien* 38 (1956): 241–95.

8. For a detailed introduction to the life and writings of Maimonides, see Herbert A. Davidson, *Moses Maimonides: The Man and His Works* (Oxford: Oxford University Press, 2005); and Joel L. Kraemer, *Maimonides: The Life and World of One of Civilization's Greatest Minds* (New York: Doubleday, 2008).

9. The most recent study of Maimonides's medieval Western reception is that of Görge K. Hasselhoff, *Dicit Rabbi Moyses: Studien zum Bild von Moses Maimonides im lateinischen Westen vom 13. bis 15. Jahrhundert* (Würzburg: Ergon, 2004). For the wider reception history, see Görge K. Hasselhoff and Otfried Fraisee, ed., *Moses Maimonides (1138–1204): His Religious, Scientific, and Philosophical Wirkungsgeschichte in Different Cultural Contexts* (Würzburg: Ergon, 2004).

10. Since there is no modern critical edition of the Latin version, we must depend on the Paris 1520 printing, *Rabbi Mossei Aegyptii Dux seu Director dubitantium aut perplexorum,* ed. Giustiniani (repr. Paris, 1964). The best studies of the translation and its influence are those of Wolfgang Kluxen: "Literargeschichtliches zum lateinischen Moses Maimonides," *Recherches de théologie ancienne et médiévale* 21 (1954): 23–50; and "Die Geschichte des Maimonides im lateinischen Abendland als Beispiel einer christlich-jüdischen Begegnung," in *Miscellanea Mediaevalia 4: Judentum im Mittelalter,* ed. Paul Wilpert (Berlin: Walter de Gruyter, 1966), 146–66.

11. A few other Jewish philosophers became available in Latin, notably Isaac Israeli, but they were not as extensively used.

12. There is also a large literature on the translation effort. For a recent summary, see Peter Schulthess and Ruedi Imbach, *Die Philosophie im lateinischen Mittelalter: Ein Handbuch mit einem bio-bibliographischen Repertorium* (Düsseldorf and Zürich: Artemis & Winkler, 2000), 133–40. See also Jean Jolivet, "The Arabic Inheritance," in Peter Dronke, ed., *A History of Twelfth-Century Western Philosophy* (Cambridge: Cambridge University Press, 1988), 113–48.

13. Two new editions with German translations and studies have recently appeared: Alexander Fidora and Andreas Niederberger, *Von Bagdad nach Toledo: Das "Buch der Ursachen" und seine Rezeption im Mittelalter* (Mainz: Dieterich'sche Verlags-

buchhandlung, 2001); and *Liber de causis: Das Buch von den Ursachen*, ed. Andreas Schönfeld and Rolf Schönberger (Hamburg: Felix Meiner, 2003). For some discussion of the use of the book by the German Dominicans, see Bernard McGinn, *The Harvest of Mysticism in Medieval Germany (1300–1500)* (New York: Crossroad-Herder, 2005), 39–42.

14. Among the important treatments in recent decades are David B. Burrell, *Knowing the Unknowable God: Ibn-Sina, Maimonides, Aquinas* (Notre Dame: University of Notre Dame, 1986); Idit Dobbs-Weinstein, *Maimonides and St. Thomas on the Limits of Reason* (Albany: SUNY, 1995); and Avital Wohlmann, *Maimonide et Thomas d'Aquin: Un dialogue impossible* (Fribourg: Éditions Universitaires, 1995).

15. For a full account, see Fernand Brunner, *Platonisme et Aristotelisme: La critique d'Ibn Gabirol par saint Thomas d'Aquin* (Louvain: Université de Louvain, 1965).

16. C. Vansteenkiste, OP, "Autori Arabi e Giudei nell'opera di San Tommaso," *Angelicum* 37 (1960): 336–401.

17. The *Corpus Philosophorum Teutonicorum Medii Aevi*, under the general editorship of Kurt Flasch and Loris Sturlese (Hamburg: Felix Meiner, 1977–) is dedicated to producing critical editions of the following major German Dominican thinkers: 1. Ulrich of Strasbourg; 2. Dietrich of Freiberg; 3. Johannes Picardi of Lichtenberg; 4. Henry of Lübeck; 5. Nicholas of Strasbourg; and 6. Berthold of Moosburg. The best current study of this group, despite its misleading title, is Alain de Libera, *La mystique rhénane d'Albert le Grand à Maître Eckhart* (Paris: Éditions Seuil, 1994).

18. For an introduction to the role of Aristotle in the medieval scholasticism, see the still useful work of Fernand Van Steenberghen, *Aristotle in the West: The Origins of Latin Aristotelianism* (Louvain: Nauwelaerts, 1955).

19. See de Libera, *La mystique rhénane*, 33–56; and in more detail in his *Albert le Grand et la philosophie* (Paris: Vrin, 1990).

20. For an introduction to the role of the *Proclus Latinus* among the German Dominicans, see McGinn, *Harvest of Mysticism*, 45–47. Among the important studies of the influence of Proclus in the Middle Ages and Renaissance, consult Paul Oskar Kristeller, "Proclus as a Reader of Plato and Plotinus, and His Influence in the Middle Ages and the Renaissance," in *Proclus: Lecture et interprète des Anciens* (Paris: CNRS, 1987), 191–211; Loris Sturlese, "Proclo ed Ermete in Germania da Alberto Magno a Bertoldo di Moosburg," in *Von Meister Dietrich zu Meister Eckhart*, ed. Kurt Flasch (Hamburg: Felix Meiner, 1984), 22–33; and Loris Sturlese, "Il dibattito sul Proclo Latino nel medioevo fra l'università di Parigi e lo studium di Colonia," in *Proclus et son influence: Actes du Colloque de Neuchâtel*, ed. G. Boss and G. Seel (Neuchâtel: Éditions du Grand Midi, 1987), 261–85.

21. See C. Rigo, "Zur Rezeption des Moses Maimonides im Werk des Albertus Magnus," in Walter Senner, ed., *Albertus Magnus nach 800 Jahren: Neue Zugänge, Aspekte und Prospektiven* (Berlin: Akademie Verlag, 2001), 29–66; and the old work of Jacob Guttmann, "Der Einfluss der maimonidischen Philosophie auf das christliche Abend-

land," in *Moses ben Maimon: Sein Leben, seine Werke und sein Einfluss*, ed. W. Bachmann et al. (Leipzig: Foch, 1908), 153–75.

22. Albert the Great, *Physica* VIII, tr. 1, cap. 11; *In II Sent.* d. 1, art. 10; and *Summa theologiae* Ia, tr. 1, q. 4, m. 2, a. 5. These passages often appeal to *Guide* 2.14.

23. E.g., *Physica* VIII, tr. 1, cap. 13, citing *Guide* 2.19.

24. *Summa theologiae* Ia, tr. 2, q. 53, m. 3; and *De causis et processu universitatis* Ia, tr. 4, cap. 7. Eckhart alone agreed with Maimonides and Avicenna on this point.

25. For a discussion, see Guttmann, "Der Einfluss," 169–75.

26. See de Libera, *Albert le Grand et la philosophie*, chap. IV.

27. The three chapters discussing Gabirol are *De causis et processu universitatis*, Liber I, tr. 1, cap. 3; tr. 3, cap. 4; tr. 4, cap. 8. For a longer discussion of Albert's refutation of Gabirol, see Bernard McGinn, "Ibn Gabirol: The Sage Among the Schoolmen"; and Bernard McGinn, "*Sapientia Judaeorum*: The Role of Jewish Philosophers in Some Scholastic Thinkers," in *Continuity and Change: The Harvest of Late-Medieval and Reformation History; Essays presented to Heiko A. Oberman on his 70th Birthday*, ed. Robert J. Bast and Andrew C. Gow (Leiden: Brill, 2000), 216–17.

28. Numenius, *Fragments*, ed. Eduard des Places (Paris: Les Belles Lettres, 1973), 90 (Fr. 41).

29. See *De causis et processu universitatis*, Liber I, tr. 4, cap. 8. The principle actually was first enunciated by Avicenna, and was not universally held. Maimonides, for example, questioned it in *Guide* 2.22. For a history, see Arthur Hyman, "From What Is One and Simple only What Is One and Simple Can Come to Be," in *Jewish Neoplatonism*, 111–35.

30. Much of the extensive literature on the relation between Maimonides and Eckhart is cited in the most recent study of the two thinkers: Yossef Schwartz, "Zwischen Einheitsmetaphysik und Einheits-hermenuetik: Eckharts Maimonides-Lektüre und das Datierungsproblem des 'Opus tripartitum,'" in *Meister Eckhart in Erfurt*, ed. Andreas Speer and Lydia Wegener (Berlin: Walter de Gruyter, 2005), 259–79, which includes a chart of how many times Eckhart cites Maimonides in comparison to other major sources. See also Hasselhoff, *Dicit Rabbi Moyses*, 205–14.

31. One passage in a Middle High German sermon does take issue with a Maimonidean position, without naming Rabbi Moses.

32. Schwartz, "Zwischen Einheitsmetaphysik und Einheitshermeneutik," 279, counts 119 references to Maimonides compared to 206 to Aristotle, but these are provisional figures.

33. For a brief survey of Eckhart's principles and practice of exegesis and the literature on it, see Bernard McGinn, *The Mystical Thought of Meister Eckhart* (New York: Crossroad-Herder, 2001), 23–29. The most detailed recent study of Maimonides's impact on Eckhart's exegesis is Yossef Schwartz, "Meister Eckharts Schriftauslegung als maimonidisches Projekt," in Hasselhoff and Fraisse, *Moses Maimonides*, 173–208.

34. Eckhart's works will be cited according to the critical edition, *Meister Eckhart: Die deutschen und lateinischen Werke* (Stuttgart and Berlin: W. Kohlhammer, 1936–),

with various editors. The German works will be cited as DW with appropriate volume, page, and line number where required. The Latin works appear as LW with volume, page, and line. The Latin works are divided into number sections (e.g., n. 2), which also will be given. The text quoted here comes from the *Expositio s. evangelii secundum Iohannem*, n. 2 (hereafter abbreviated as In Io.) (LW 3:4.4–6).

35. *Liber parabolorum Genesis* n. 4 (hereafter Par. Gen.) (LW 1:454.6–10).

36. Par. Gen. n. 5 (LW 1:454.11–455.6), citing *Guide*, Preface.

37. See, e.g., In Io. nn. 199–205 (LW 3:168–73); *Expositio libri Sapientiae* (hereafter In Sap.) n. 133 (LW 2:471); and Sermo (hereafter S.) V n. 51 (LW 4:48).

38. See Yossef Schwartz, "'Ecce locus est apud me': Maimonides und Eckharts Raumvorstellung als Begriff des Göttlichen," in *Raum und Raumvorstellungen im Mittelalter*, ed. Jan A. Aertsen and Andreas Speer (Berlin: Walter de Gruyter, 1998), 348–64.

39. S. IX n. 115 (LW 4:109). Eckhart is referring to *Guide* 3.53. This was a favorite Maimonides text for Eckhart, since he also refers to it his *Expositio libri Exodi* (hereafter In Ex.) n. 277 (LW 2:223), Par. Gen. n. 139 (LW 1:606), and in the first Genesis commentary, *Expositio libri Genesis* n. 185 (LW 1:328–29).

40. S. XXIX n. 304 (LW 4:270).

41. Eckhart's "Treatise on the Divine Names" is found in In Ex. nn. 34–78 and 143–84 (LW 2:40–82 and 130–58), commenting on Ex 15:30 and 20:7. For a more detailed discussion, see Bernard McGinn, ed., *Meister Eckhart: Teacher and Preacher* (New York: Paulist Press, 1986), 15–30. This work also contains a translation of the text on 53–70, and 90–102.

42. See especially In Ex. n. 78 (LW 2:81) and its use of a classic text of Aquinas on the *via eminentiae* from *Summa theologiae* Ia, q. 13, a. 3.

43. Schwartz, "Zwischen Einheitsmetaphysik und Einheistshermeneutik," 279, calculates 13 uses; my own calculations give 17. The only study of the relation of Eckhart and Gabirol is Fernand Brunner, "Maître Eckhart et Avicébron," in *Lectionum Varietates: Hommages à Paul Vignaux* (Paris: Vrin, 1991), 133–52.

44. E.g., In Ex. n. 52 (LW 2:56) argues for the unity of substantial form. *Expositio libri Genesis* nn. 12–13 (LW 1:195–98) demonstrates how the one universe comes from the one God. Eckhart's position on universal hylomorphism is more ambiguous, especially in light of his analysis of matter and form as the intrinsic principles of the universe, which forms the third parabolical understanding of the "heaven and earth" of Genesis 1:1; see Par. Gen. nn. 28–33 (LW 1:497–501).

45. In Ex. n. 58 (LW 2:64–65). The references are FV V.23; Boethius, *De Trin.* 2; and Maimonides, *Guide* 1.51.

46. The work is in process of a critical editing by a team led by Loris Sturlese, *Berthold von Moosburg: Expositio super Elementationem theologicam Procli* (Hamburg: Felix Meiner, 1984–), as Volume 6 of the *Corpus Philosophorum Teutonicorum Medii Aevi*. Thus far published are: 6.1, *Prologue: Propositiones 1–13* (1984); 6.2, *Propositiones 14–34* (1986); 6.3, *Propositiones 35–65* (2001); 6.4, *Propositiones 66–107* (2003); and 6.7, *Propositiones 160–183* (2003). In addition, Loris Sturlese previously published the comment

on the final propositions: *Expositio super Elementationem theologicam Procli 184–211: De animabus* (Rome: Edizioni di storia e letteratura, 1974).

47. Stephen E. Gersh, "Berthold von Moosburg and the Content and Method of Platonic Theology," in *Nach der Verurteilung von 1277: Philosophie und Theologie an der Universität von Paris im letzten Viertel des 13. Jahrhunderts; Studien und Texte*, ed. Jan A. Aertsen, Kent Emery Jr., and Andreas Speer (Berlin: Walter de Gruyter, 2001), 493–503. The best introduction to Berthold is de Libera, *La mystique rhénane*, chap. 7. See also Kurt Flasch, introduction to *Expositio super Elementationem* 1:xi–xxxviii.

48. See the edition of this important work by Paolo Lucentini, *Honorius Augustodunensis: Clavis Physicae* (Rome: Edizioni di Storia e Letteratura, 1974).

49. Among the philosophical resources this puts him behind only Proclus himself, as well as Aristotle and Averroes (357 times). For comparison, Plato is cited 125 times (mostly the Timaeus), while Avicenna appears 123 times.

50. Gabirol also appears in the writings of other German Dominicans, though not always positively, given Albert's attack on him. Positive uses include an appearance in a vernacular sermon of Heinrich von Ekkewint, on which see Kurt Ruh, *Geschichte der abendländische Mystik*, vol. 3, *Die Mystik des deutschen Predigerordens und ihre Grundlegung durch die Hochscholastik* (Munich: Beck, 1996), 409. The FV is also cited in the Latin commentary on the "Granum sinapis" poem sometimes ascribed to Eckhart; see Maria Bindschedler, ed., *Der lateinische Kommentar zum Granum Sinapis* (Basel: Benno Schwabe, 1949), 106.

51. The "Prologus" is found in *Expositio super Elementatio* VI.1: 5–35.

52. The section on the world as macrocosm (14–22) is deeply Platonic and an eloquent expression of a form of cosmic piety.

53. "Subiectum specialiter contuendum est quadruplex, scilicet corporale, spirituale, intellectuale et uniale" (7.71–72). Berthold's conception of the "uniale" subject, that is, the *unum anime*, or deepest aspect of the human person as capable of unification with God, is developed on the basis of Proclus and Dionysius (see, e.g., 23.583–600; 25.650–659; 26.675–27.726; and 31.840–45).

54. My remarks here follow the analysis by Gersh, "Berthold von Moosburg," 497–500.

55. On the *Liber XXIV Philosophorum* and its influence on the German Dominicans, see McGinn, *Harvest of Mysticism*, 42–45.

56. *Expositio tituli* J (46.335–47.339).

57. On Berthold's doctrine of the One, or henology, see Jan A. Aertsen, "Ontology and Henology in Medieval Philosophy (Thomas Aquinas, Meister Eckhart, and Berthold of Moosburg)," in *On Proclus and His Influence in Medieval Philosophy*, ed. E. P. Bos and P. A. Meijer (Leiden: Brill, 1992), 120–40.

58. In the analysis of Prop. 1A, Gabirol is cited to provide one of the six definitions given for *multitudo* (72.43), and there is a brief reference in Prop. 2A (84.74–77) to the discussion in the *titulus* of how all things can be described as accidents in relation to God's substance.

59. Berthold recognized that the treatise ascribed to Boethius and now known to be from Gundissalinus was based on Gabirol, e.g., Prop. 1E (78.247–48): "Auctor vero tractatus, qui intitulatur *De unitate et uno*, qui totus excerptus est de libro Avencebrol *Fontis vitae.*"

60. *Expositio*, prop. 3C (95.134–36; cf. 138–39).

61. *Expositio*, prop. 3C (96.156–58).

62. *Expositio*, prop. 3F (99.269–86).

63. *Expositio*, prop. 4 (101–12). Berthold uses Gabirol and Gundissalinus in the *suppositum* section of the exposition, which is divided into three parts. The first is entitled "De unito aliorum opinione," and begins by citing Gabirol extensively on the duality of the first intrinsic principles of matter and form (101.20–102.58), as well as using three of his definitions of matter among the fourteen that are given (102.60–103.87). The discussion of the two operations of the Creator (*creatio* and *compositio*) that follows largely depends on Gundissalinus. The second part, "De distinctione unibilium," uses Gabirol's teaching on the descent and multiplication of prime matter (106.200–107.211). The third part, "Diversitas unitorum," does not cite Gabirol.

64. *Expositio*, prop. 5 (113–26).

65. Prop. 5B (115.72–78). Berthold here is distinguishing between God the One in himself (*per se unum*) and the One as the creative cause.

66. Prop. 5D (122.309–16).

Imagining and Imaging the End: Universal and Individual Eschatology in Two Carthusian Illustrated Manuscripts [1999]

Richard K. Emmerson

I am delighted to contribute to this lecture series honoring Morton W. Bloomfield, one of the great medievalists of his generation. It gives me the opportunity to acknowledge to his family, friends, and colleagues my scholarly debt to him, which I trace to a late summer day in 1972 when discussing *Piers Plowman* with George H. Brown, my advisor at Stanford University. When I expressed puzzlement about the role played by the figure of Antichrist in the poem's concluding passus, George straight away recommended the book by his Harvard professor, Morton Bloomfield: *Piers Plowman as a Fourteenth-Century Apocalypse*.[1] I was fascinated by the wide learning and critical insights of this wonderful book, which introduced me to Joachim of Fiore and helped make sense of that most enigmatic of Middle English poems. It also launched my dissertation research on the figure of Antichrist, which led to my first book.[2] Although not his student, I think of Morton as a valued teacher who sparked my early interest in things apocalyptic and am truly honored to contribute to a collection honoring his memory.

Like the pioneering work of Norman Cohn and Marjorie Reeves, Bloomfield's scholarship highlighted medieval apocalyptic beliefs and thinkers that had been overlooked by historians of medieval history, literature, and religion.[3] This relative neglect during the first half of the twentieth century was due to the nature of the apocalyptic subject matter, which was personally distasteful to many scholars and judged by others to be of insufficient importance to merit extensive research.[4] Thanks to the groundbreaking work of Bloomfield, Cohn, and Reeves, however, over the past four decades scholars have studied late medieval apocalypticism in depth.[5] Much scholarship has stressed its more radical forms, particularly those associated with Joachim of Fiore, his heterodox followers, and later revolutionaries citing his name if not his genuine works.[6] As a result, the continuing influence of orthodox apocalypticism during the later Middle Ages has sometimes been ignored, perhaps because it was so prevalent that it is now taken for granted. Its traditional nature has perhaps also made it less attractive to recent trends in scholarship stressing the heretical and oppositional, trends that mistakenly equate apocalypticism with millenarianism rather than recognizing it as a central component of mainstream eschatology, the doctrine of the last things.[7]

My scholarship over the past quarter century has sought to balance knowledge of late medieval apocalypticism by emphasizing its more prevalent and traditional forms and above all its influence on medieval literature, including didactic and visionary poems, allegories and romances, saints' lives and sermons.[8] I use the term "traditional" not because medieval apocalypticism did not develop with the times, adapting to political, social, and religious circumstances and responding to cataclysmic events such as the plague,[9] but because it comprised a fluid mixture of dogmas (for example, the creedal conviction in Christ's return to judge the living and the dead) and legendary beliefs never encoded as doctrine but widely inculcated—especially in vernacular texts—and regularly represented on stage and in art. Based on enigmatic biblical sources, ingenious exegetical explanations, inventive visionary reports, and disquieting folkloristic motifs, the legendary supported and expanded the dogmatic and provided dynamic and imaginative, yet remarkably consistent, accounts of what would happen in the Last Days. The role of apocalypticism within late medieval eschatology is a perfect example of that aspect of "late medieval religious culture" that, as James Simpson has shown, Tyndale and other sixteenth-century polemicists attacked "as wholly constructed by the accretive, inventive practice of human imagination. . . ."[10]

Expectations regarding Antichrist exemplify the fecundity of this imaginative process. A name only briefly mentioned in the New Testament (1 and 2 John) over time became attached to a legendary life of a dreaded deceiver and persecutor who took a leading role in the Last Days.[11] In vernacular accounts, especially drama, the impetus to relate a coherent narrative or to stage a compelling play led to imaginative elaboration, novel details, and inclusion of related eschatological themes, thus injecting vitality into an expanding tradition.[12] On stage the figure of Antichrist plays a striking dramatic role in the medieval reenactment of salvation history, since his persona claims to be the same Christ ("Ego sum Christus," Matt. 24:5) whose life the great mystery plays had enacted earlier in their cycles.[13] Antichrist, by definition, is a bombastic actor who will mimic—often in a parodic way—miraculous events from the life of Christ, even while deceiving, bribing, and persecuting the faithful. His full life, which Christians expected to witness in the near future, is staged by the mid-fourteenth-century French play *Jour du Jugement,* which begins with a sermon outlining salvation history and concludes with Doomsday.[14] It is an elaborate play that, as I've shown elsewhere, is accompanied in its unique manuscript (Besançon, Bibliothèque Municipale, MS 579) by eighty-nine miniatures that depict its major scenes, providing visual clues to how it may have been staged.[15] These represent the largest and most developed sequence of images detailing the life of Antichrist from any period and in any medium.[16]

This rich illuminated manuscript also reminds us that apocalypticism had a profound and pervasive influence on medieval art.[17] Not surprisingly, given the ideology of patronage, few works of art represent radical strands of apocalypticism, even during the later Middle Ages.[18] Medieval art—whether manuscript illustrations, woodcuts, sculptures, stained glass, or panel and wall paintings—usually draws upon and portrays an apocalypticism that is both orthodox and popular, widely held and available in the vernacular.[19] This paper demonstrates the way medieval art imagined widely held eschatological beliefs by examining two illustrated manuscripts that exemplify the varied ways traditional apocalypticism continued to influence late medieval eschatology, even as newer forms of radical apocalypticism—such as Lollard and other antiecclesiastic polemic—became increasingly strident.[20] One manuscript is French, the other English, and both were produced in the 1460s. Although they differ in their contents, designs, and aesthetics, both are Carthusian manuscripts reflecting that order's imaginative emphasis on the last things, persecution, mortality, punishment, and the ultimate role to be played by supernatural agents, whether divine, demonic, or allegorical.

These manuscripts also reveal the personal, individual, and allegorical as well as the cosmic, universal, and historical elements of traditional eschatology.[21] For in addition to imagining future events in the Last Days, medieval eschatology also detailed the fate of the individual when facing death in the present. As is well known, death and events surrounding death were obsessive anxieties during the late Middle Ages, especially after the pestilence of the mid-fourteenth century.[22] This obsession was articulated in numerous treatises such as the *Ars Moriendi,* expressed in popular verse developing *contemptus mundi, memento mori,* and *ubi sunt* topoi, and staged by morality plays such as *Everyman.*[23] This fascination was also visualized in the most popular illuminated manuscripts, the books of hours. For example, a miniature illustrating the Office of the Dead in a contemporary Burgundian manuscript pictures Death standing at the foot of a deathbed.[24] Differently from *Everyman,* where the title character is deserted by all except

Good Deeds, the dying Christian is comforted by two men as his soul flees upward through an open window toward Michael. The archangel fights two flying demons by wielding his scepter, which visually replaces the lance held by Death. This depiction of the fate of the individual soul recalls Michael's role during the universal judgment of Doomsday. A more explicit example connecting individual to universal eschatology is narrated near the conclusion of *Piers Plowman*. As Antichrist assaults the few remaining faithful who have taken shelter in Unity, Elde assails the poem's protagonist, Will.[25] The attack links the end of the visionary's long personal quest to the end of church history narrated in the poem's concluding two passus, so that the Dreamer's physical decline and approaching death become analogous to the moral decline of Holy Church in the last days preceding Doomsday. As Bloomfield writes, Langland pictures his time as "the age of Antichrist. . . ."[26]

The first of the two Carthusian manuscripts, Oxford, Bodleian Library, MS Douce 134, emphasizes cosmic and universal eschatology, events anticipated at the end of human history. It was copied in southeastern France, perhaps at the Grande Chartreuse, in the early 1460s, probably before 1463.[27] It contains the second part of the *Livre de la vigne nostre Seigneur*, that is, *The Book of Our Lord's Vineyard*. A French prose collection of didactic and moralized texts with biblical quotations in Latin, it provides an orthodox compendium of Christian doctrine. The first part of this anonymous text, which treats the first advent of Christ—from Incarnation to Resurrection—has been identified as Bibliothèque Municipale de Grenoble, MS 337 (408).[28] Its colophon, dated to 5 March 1463, refers to the manuscript as the first book of "la Vigne Nostre Seigneur" and adds that the second book—probably Douce 134—was already finished.[29] Covering 166 folios illustrated with seventy-five miniatures, it imagines events related to the second advent of Christ: the persecutions of Antichrist, Fifteen Signs of Doomsday, trumpets of judgment calling forth all souls at the General Resurrection (fol. 50v), the virtuous and vicious awaiting judgment (fol. 52v), and the eternal punishment of the damned in Hell and the reward of the righteous saved in Heaven.[30]

The central event of medieval eschatology is the Last Judgment, which the *Vigne* illustrates in several miniatures. These begin with the appearance of Christ in majesty (fol. 57v), surrounded by the hosts of heaven (Matt. 24:30). The resurrected saved (depicted as white souls with prayerful hands) and damned (shown twisted and with dark skin) await on earth. Specific judgment scenes then follow, in which, for example, Michael weighs good and evil deeds with scales (fol. 73r), the universal counterpart of his defense of the individual soul in the Office of the Dead. Christ, shown seated on a rainbow, displays his wounds as the wicked turn away in shame (fol. 74r), and then is joined by the apostles to judge the damned, including a bishop (fol. 75r). The scene is reminiscent of Doomsday plays and other late medieval eschatological themes—both literary and artistic, such as the Three Living and Three Dead and the Dance of Death—emphasizing that everyone, no matter their rank or status, will inevitably face death and stand before their judge.[31] Finally, Christ, still seated on the rainbow and flanked by saints (fol. 76r, Fig. 1), condemns the reprobate, pronouncing the dreaded "Discedite maledicti in igne eternum" (Depart from me, you cursed, into everlasting fire which was prepared for the devil and his angels) (Matt. 25:41). In the foreground two elongated dark bodies fall backwards as if buffeted by the scroll containing Christ's curse.

Attention then turns to the punishment of evil in Hell.[32] Although the manuscript pictures Heaven and numerous angels, the demonic receives its imaginative emphasis. Almost a third of its 166 folios (fols. 77r–129v) describe Hell, and these are illustrated with twenty-six detailed images picturing devils delighting in their infernal duties—including a portrait gallery of twelve hook-wielding demons (fol. 99r).[33] The miniatures depict in excruciating detail the punishments of numerous damned souls, stressing their pain, for example, as grinning demons pour lead into the mouths of two naked bodies (fol. 95v).[34] Particularly ghastly is a miniature (fol. 91v, Fig. 2) showing worms and snakes slowly devouring six burning souls by wriggling through their mouths and ears and from huge ruptures in their cadavers. The text (fols. 82r–86r) incorporates a French version of the *Vision of Lazarus*, an account popular in the later Middle Ages that, as Bloomfield comments, "gives us an elaborate picture of torture in hell, deadly sin by deadly sin."[35] For example, the proud are tied to a giant wheel turned by a devil (fol. 83r), and the wrathful are stoned and stabbed by six demons (fol. 84r).[36] Among the greedy punished in two enormous burning cauldrons are a pope, cardinal, bishop, king, and other representatives of all mankind (fol. 85r).[37] Dagmar Eichberger, in his comparative study of hellish imagery, notes that the cycle of infernal miniatures in Douce 134 "in sheer number, realism, and obsession with devils and hell, surpasses most of the imagery produced in the first half of the fifteenth century."[38]

If, then, the first part of the *Vigne* in Grenoble emphasizes Christ, the second part at the Bodleian is presided over by Satan. In what is probably the manuscript's best-known miniature, he bursts through its frame and is surrounded by his minions (fol. 98r).[39] As Martin Kauffmann notes, the image closely illustrates the text's description of Leviathan as having terrible teeth, body "like molten shields," and fiery mouth.[40] The association of Satan with Leviathan is based on its identification as the "king over all the children of pride" (Job 41:25) and interpretations allegorized by Gregory the Great's *Moralia*.[41] To enhance the apocalyptic resonance of Satan's portrait, the artist has added details, such as seven heads and ten horns, alluding to the great red dragon of the Apocalypse, which the biblical text identifies as the Devil and Satan (Rev. 12:9). It harasses the Woman dressed in the sun, who in medieval exegesis is identified with both the Virgin Mary and Ecclesia, Satan's enemies stretching from the first coming of Christ until his return in judgment, that is, throughout the entire historical range encapsulated by the two parts of the *Vigne*. The miniature's frontal larger-than-life portrait of Satan must have disturbed its fifteenth-century viewers.[42]

The manuscript further imagines universal eschatology by including a prose French account of the Fifteen Signs of Doomsday, which emphasizes the cosmic marvels expected to precede Christ's Second Coming. This popular legend, attributed in the Middle Ages to Jerome, circulated in three Latin recensions and translations in English, Flemish, French, Frisian, German, Irish, Italian, Provencal, Spanish, and Welsh. The Fifteen Signs were included in vernacular sermons and integrated into longer dramatic and didactic works such as the *Jeu d'Adam*, the Chester "Prophets of Antichrist," and the *Pricke of Conscience*.[43] More than fifty years ago William Heist identified eighty-nine versions of the legend, and others have since come to light, including that in Douce 134, which is based on the recension in Peter Comestor's *Historia scholastica*.[44] The legend was illustrated in manuscripts, such as the Holkham Bible, and stained glass, such as at All Saints Church, York.[45] It was also popularized in Jacobus de Voragine's *Legenda aurea*, which details the Fifteen Signs as a traditional component of universal eschatology in its discussion of the "Advent of Our Lord"—advent referring to both the first and second comings of Christ, as savior and judge.[46]

The *Vigne* manuscript devotes a large miniature to each sign. Some signs are based on biblical prophecy, such as earthquakes and falling stars as Jesus warns in Matthew 24:29. But most, such as the third sign, in which fish and sea monsters are expected to rise up, are not biblical but imaginative nightmares regarding the cosmic horrors of the Last Days. For this sign the large framed miniature (fol. 42v, Fig. 3) shows monstrous fish, along with two mermaids, floating above a landscape of trees and castles, depicting how "the sea beasts will come out above the surface and will roar to the heavens, and God alone will understand their bellowing."[47] To understand their supernatural character, it is necessary to realize that these are universal signs of the end, to be witnessed everywhere by everyone. They are associated with Antichrist and often illustrated following his death, as in the fifteenth-century German block book lives of Antichrist.[48] The signs are generally expected to take place during a short period of forty or forty-five days after the deceiver's death when those whom the false Christ has mislead will have the opportunity to repent and return to the true Christ.[49] The Fifteen Signs are, in other words, the cosmic culmination of the Antichrist tradition.

The *Vigne* uses Antichrist to introduce its treatment of eschatology. Douce 134 includes four images illustrating his life. The opening portrait (fol. 4r) pictures the deceiver of the Last Days standing in a mountainous landscape before a large lake while two men and a woman converse in the foreground.[50] Antichrist is depicted as a demonically inspired human wearing above his head a large two-horned devil's mask that breaks the miniature's frame. This is the artist's imaginative interpretation of Antichrist's dual nature as both man and devil. The text states that although some people say Antichrist will be born of a holy nun, his parentage is normal, but he is possessed by the devil.[51] The *Vigne* thus adopts an orthodox position in comparison with folkloristic accounts that Antichrist will be conceived through incest or that his mother will be impregnated by a devil. For example, the fourteenth-century *Jour du Jugement* stages a devil transformed into a man who conceives Antichrist on a whore living in Babylon, whereas the fifteenth-century block book *Der Antichrist* depicts a father and daughter in bed, their incestuous union orchestrated by devils.[52] The *Vigne* similarly captures Antichrist's double nature while remaining within the more orthodox tradition.

In one image, however, Douce 134 is potentially radical. Its text details the birthplace of Antichrist in Babylon and his ability to convert many kings and Jews.[53] Then follows the invasion of Gog and Magog (Rev. 20:7), the peoples associated with the lost tribes of Israel and with barbaric hordes enclosed behind the Caucasus by Alexander the Great.[54] According to the tradition, they become Antichrist's military allies, conquering Europe and destroying Christianity. In the manuscript's next miniature (fol. 6r, Fig. 4), Gog and Magog are depicted in the upper left background emerging from mountains. This is standard within the Antichrist tradition, as is the depiction in the near foreground of a triumphant Antichrist welcomed at the gates of Jerusalem. But the devil's mask Antichrist wears in the first miniature has now been replaced with a three-part hat, which led Rosemary Muir

Wright to identify him as the pope.[55] Since the text makes no such identification, it is not clear that he should be so understood, especially since the pope in medieval tradition usually remains faithful when confronted by Antichrist. Perhaps the artist of the Carthusian manuscript employs the symbolism of the vicar of Christ to picture how Antichrist parodies Christ's entry into Jerusalem and claims, "Ego sum Christus" (Matt. 24:5). Whatever the intention, the interpretation is the artist's and its effect is potentially unorthodox.

The first two Antichrist miniatures in Douce 134 imagine ways to understand his ambiguous nature—as man and devil, leader of barbaric forces and preacher of false doctrine—thus visualizing Christ's warning that "even the elect will be deceived" (Matt. 24:24). After a lengthy text, however, the third miniature (fol. 30r) abandons such subtlety, emphasizing his true nature as a vicious persecutor.[56] Picturing several horrendous tortures, it recalls the suffering of the damned in the images depicting hellish punishments, but now the suffering is shockingly experienced by the faithful. The bloody projection of future suffering is a regular feature of the Antichrist tradition.[57] The *Vigne* text fills nine folios discussing this suffering and why it is allowed by God. Text and image together provide dire warnings of future persecution and the need to remain faithful in such dire circumstances. Yet the image's vividness and portrayal of grotesque violence overwhelms the sober theological explanation, which seems abstract in comparison to the specificity and immediacy of the image.

The last miniature (fol. 36r) portraying Antichrist is placed after the text that warns he will imitate Christ's Ascension by rising from the Mount of Olives.[58] Rather than rising to heaven, however, he is struck down by the "spirit of Christ's mouth" (2 Thess. 2:8).[59] The spectacle is set among mountains, perhaps to recall the landscape of the manuscript's provenance. In the upper right corner, Christ is in a cloud, from which flames fall diagonally across the landscape onto Antichrist and his followers. The flames, the "spirit of Christ's mouth," may also allude to Antichrist's ability to call fire from heaven. This parodic Pentecost is based on interpretations of the two-horned beast who "did great signs, so that he made also fire to come down from heaven unto the earth in the sight of men" (Rev. 13:13).[60] If the *Vigne* miniature alludes to the pseudo-Pentecost, then the artist has skillfully conflated in this one image a series of expectations related to the end of Antichrist's life. The soul of the pseudo-Christ is now captured by a devil hovering over his head, who in this full-page miniature recalls the devil's mask worn by Antichrist in his introductory portrait. Antichrist's followers shown in the foreground also suffer from the falling heavenly flames.[61]

Although a compilation of several eschatological texts and the work of more than one artist, the *Vigne* has a clear unity of purpose in imagining universal eschatology and of design in imaging its texts with large framed miniatures. The second Carthusian manuscript lacks such clear unity, however. One of the most fascinating of late medieval miscellanies, London, British Library, MS Additional 37049 comprises a remarkable range of texts and images that set forth and picture biblical, geographic, historical, devotional, mystical, penitential, hagiographic, and eschatological texts, "illustrating," as Douglas Gray has noted, "nearly all the themes of Middle English religious literature."[62] Contemporary with Douce 134, it was produced, probably in a Carthusian house in northern England, circa 1460–70.[63] In its heterogeneity, it exemplifies the miscellaneity of many Middle English religious manuscripts, which, as Ralph Hanna has noted, "represent defiantly individual impulses—appropriations of works for the use of particular persons in particular situations."[64] The situations and persons implied by its numerous, relatively short, vernacular texts and copious accompanying images[65]—probably drawn by the manuscript's scribe—are lessons for Carthusian novices or lay brothers.[66] Included are important Carthusian works such as a poem on the foundation of charterhouses, illustrated by the life of St. Hugh (fol. 22r), and the Charter of Redemption (fol. 23r).[67] The manuscript's penitential and devotional aspects, particularly noteworthy, have received in-depth study.[68] Its texts and images representing the last things, furthermore, are similarly important, providing a unifying theme woven throughout the manuscript's rich diversity.

In addition to imagining future aspects of universal eschatology, the Carthusian Miscellany depicts present anxieties negotiated by personal eschatology, especially those related to the moments preceding and following death. As Marlene Villalobos Hennessy notes, "Illustrations of death, the Last Judgment, purgatory, and hell mouths appear on thirty-two pages in the manuscript, which contains a total of ninety-six folios."[69] The manuscript includes numerous texts addressing the individual reader, cautioning, for example, to "þinke ay wele þat þu sal dye." They accompany such verbal warnings with pictures depicting death, leading the editor of Additional 37049 to note its "morbid preoccupation with mortality."[70] There is a close relationship between word and image throughout. Usually the verbal and visual texts are tightly interwoven on the manuscript page, and even when the Middle English is set in a distinct text block, an accompanying drawing often directs attention to it. Thus to illustrate "Thynke on þine ending day," the manuscript pictures a skeleton holding five arrows as it menaces a rich man, who reaches out to the inscribed words directed at him: "þou sal dye þu wote neuer when, / Ne in whatt state þou sal be þen . . ." (fol. 69r).

The miscellany's imaginative mixture of universal and personal is evident in two symbolic depictions of the world, its history and mankind's position within it. The first is a *mappamundi* introducing the manuscript's universal and historical concerns (fol. 2v).[71] In the form of an Isidorean T-O world map, Asia is located above the T formed by water, Africa to the right, Europe to the left, and Rome near the center. A text below explains the division of the world by Noah's sons and the origins of countries, so that the image blends, as typical of *mappaemundi*, "historical events and geographical places, a projection of history onto a geographical framework."[72] The map represents the three continents, four corners of the world, and four elements. The manuscripts's individual counterpart of this universal symbol is a drawing of a tree inscribed "þe warlde" (fol. 19v, Fig. 5).[73] A man stands on its lower branches, while above his head a branch is inscribed "mans lyfe." Over his outstretched hand another branch holds a honeycomb, signifying mankind's worldly desires. The eschatological is introduced into the allegory by Death, symbolized by a unicorn and underscored by the gaping Hell's mouth below.[74] At the foot of the tree, white and black mice, inscribed "day" and "nyght," gnaw relentlessly through the trunk, suggesting life's imminent end. As in the opening image of the world, the four elements are represented, this time by four serpents protruding as roots from the tree. The universal has now become individual, however, for the elements, according to the accompanying text, betoken "mans body in þis warld here." The personal nature of the allegory is emphasized by the poem's opening words commanding the reader's attention and making it clear that the image's moral is aimed directly at the individual Christian: "Behalde here as þou may se / A man standing in a tree . . . ."[75]

This allegorical scene comes later, after the opening texts and images that focus both temporally and geographically on salvation history. For example, facing the *mappamundi* is a picture of Jerusalem (fol. 3r) inscribed "civitas sancta" and accompanied by an extract from *Mandeville's Travels*.[76] These two images show the world and its center in Jerusalem and set the parameters of salvation history. Jonathan Lanman has demonstrated that the "T" of a T-O world map symbolizes a cross,[77] so that these facing images may recall the Crucifixion in Jerusalem. Because *mappaemundi* also allude to Creation and Doomsday, as David Woodward notes, "A *mappamundi* could thus represent simultaneously the complete history of the Christian world: its creation, salvation, and final judgment."[78] Salvation history is as concerned with origins, such as the division of the world among the sons of Noah, as it is with endings. The *Mandeville* passage, for example, not only discusses an entrance of Hell in a valley "ful of duels" (fol. 9r) but also the location of the Earthly Paradise.[79] Just as in the *Vigne* manuscript—with its emphasis on good and evil, Christ and Antichrist, the saved and the damned—the miscellany's eschatology is thoroughly dualistic, tracing the history of the two cities. It is therefore not surprising that the very next illustrations in the manuscript (fol. 9v) picture the two earthly cities that symbolize the city of man and of God: Babylon—"þe toure of confusion," and the apocalyptic birthplace of Antichrist—represented here as a tower, and Rome, a walled city inscribed "caput Mundi," which alludes to the *mappamundi*, where Rome is pictured at the crossing of the T (fol. 2v).[80]

The English miscellany emphasizes salvation history in the next sequence of twenty-three scenes drawn over six folios, which illustrate the Middle English *Pseudo-Methodius Revelations*.[81] This seventh-century text, falsely attributed to the fourth-century bishop Methodius and written in response to the rise of Islam, became an important early medieval source of the Antichrist tradition.[82] Its range is noted at its beginning, which explains that it is translated from Latin although originally written in Hebrew and Greek and that "it tretys of þe begynnyng of þe warld and of þe endyng and also of þinges þat fallen and sal falle" (fol. 11r). It thus traces salvation history from Creation to Doomsday, moving from the past to the present to the future. The miscellany illustrates the *Pseudo-Methodius* with a series of tinted pen drawings placed two or three to a folio side in strips above the text. The first series depict the origins and results of sin from the creation of Eve, to the expulsion from the Garden and Cain's bloody murder of Abel (fol. 11r). These are followed by the generation of Seth and the Flood (fol. 11v) and the death of Noah, whose family is shown next to his tomb praying to Christ, who holds an orb marked with a T (fol. 12r). This is a biblical and historical reminder of the world's division depicted by the *mappamundi* (fol. 2v). The picture next to Noah's family also recalls the earlier Tower of Babel (fol. 9v), now depicted as "a tower of whos hyghnes suld towche vn-to heuennes" (fol. 12r).

After describing Old Testament battles (fol. 12v), the *Pseudo-Methodius* introduces the "sonnes of Ysmael" (fol. 13r) and claims that "þe kyngdom of rome sal be gret abowve al kyngdoms of folk" (fol. 13v). The symbolic two cities of Babylon and Rome are transfigured into two armies as history moves from the distant biblical to the near medieval past. Drawing on the belief that the world will last six thousand years, which is based on the scheme of the Seven Ages of the World,[83] the text notes that "In þe laste sext þowsand ȝere of þe warld, sal þe childer of Ysmael go out of wildernes . . ." (fol. 13v). They are able to conquer the world because Christians have broken God's laws. Drawings of violent battles are placed above the text here and on the following folios, concluding when Christians, portrayed as crusaders, triumph over the sons of Ishmael, who are identified as Saracens. With a promise that "þe kingdom of Cristen pepyll sal be exaltyd abowve al oþer kingdoms," resulting in "pese & gret reste opon earth" (fol. 15r), the text sets the stage for the eschatological scenes that follow in the remaining six images illustrating the *Pseudo-Methodius*.

The first image (Fig. 6) depicts people in the present who are unprepared for the trials preceding Doomsday. In a reminder that universal judgment is imminent, people eat, drink, and marry "as it was in þe dayes of Noe" (fol. 15v). This scene alludes to Christ's description of the Last Days (Matt. 24:37–39) and to the earlier pictures of Noah and the Flood (fol. 11v), a traditional type of Doomsday. Suddenly, as shown in the adjacent image, the prophecy moves into the apocalyptic future with the release of Gog and Magog. As in the French manuscript (Fig. 4), they are associated with Antichrist's armies. They are shown first as armies enclosed behind the Caucasus and then as barbaric cannibals: "And þai ete þe flesche of men, & serpents, & bestes, & women with childer þai sal ete" (fol. 15v).[84] The facing folio then depicts their annihilation. The image differs from the *Pseudo-Methodius* text, which states that Gog and Magog will be defeated by a Last World Emperor, "þe kyng of Romaynes & of Greke" (fol. 16r). Instead, the victor is Christ, pictured above holding a crossed orb while fire falls from a cloud onto the naked bodies below.[85] Antichrist now establishes his reign, ordering his armies to kill faithful Christians who oppose him, and on the next page (fol. 16v) he orders the execution of Enoch and Elijah, the apocalyptic Two Witnesses (Rev. 11:3–12).[86] As evident in the next scene, this will be Antichrist's last deed, for the "spirit of Christ's mouth"— again understood as fire from heaven, as in Douce 134 (fol. 36r)—will kill the man of iniquity.[87] Antichrist is then shoved from his throne by Michael, the defender of individual Christian souls who now plays his apocalyptic role at the end of world history, just as he does on stage at the conclusion of the near contemporary Chester "Coming of Antichrist."[88]

The *Pseudo-Methodius* images end here, but not the miscellany's account of salvation history. The text below Antichrist's death describes Doomsday and how "Þe wykkyd men sal descende with þe beste Antecriste in-to helle" (fol. 16v). A new text on the Last Judgment follows, calling on Christ's mercy. It leads to a powerful three-quarter-page image on the facing folio that depicts the judgment of all mankind (fol. 17r, Fig. 7). Drawn above the meditation on the Last Judgment, it includes many elements of universal eschatology, such as the resurrection, demons hooking the damned into Hell, and angels ushering the saved up a path to the gate of Heaven. Unlike the judgment scene in the *Vigne* (Fig. 1), however, the condemnation of the damned inscribed on the scroll to the left of Christ ("Go ȝe cursed into euerlastyng fyre" [Matt. 25:41]) does not stand alone, but is accompanied by Christ's salvific invitation at the top of the page: "Cum þe blyst into þe kingdom of my fader" (Matt. 25:34).

After two further texts on Doomsday, one stressing its unpredictability ("Whan þe day of dome sall be / It is in gods priuyte" [fol. 18v]), the miscellany reinterprets universal eschatology in personal terms, moving from cosmic and historical events to personal and present concerns by depicting individual death and judgment (fol. 19r, Fig. 8). Significantly, this full-page Trinitarian image alludes to Last Judgment imagery, thus imaginatively linking cosmic and personal eschatology. At its upper center and recalling the portrayal of Christ in the previous image (Fig. 7), God the Father, shown with a cruciform nimbus, sits on a throne with his feet resting on an orb marked with a *T*. On the upper right, a dove symbolizing the Holy Spirit flies toward God, taking the place of the flying angel who blows a trumpet in the previous image. Below and to God's right, Jesus hangs on the cross, which alludes to the cross held by a saint on Christ's right in the Doomsday image. At the bottom of the image a skeleton shoves its lance at the dying man. Death and the horned demon standing at the foot of the deathbed call to mind the horned devil and the damned in the lower right quadrant of the Doomsday image, just as the angel standing by the head of the dying man is reminiscent of the angel escorting the saved. Although visually alluding to the previous image and thereby to the judgment of universal eschatology, the image nevertheless focuses on personal eschatology, the death and judgment of the individual Christian. His soul rises from the dead body, just as the saved souls in the Doomsday scene rise into heaven.

The reading order of the image's captions similarly "rise," from the Soul's request ("O hope in nede þu help me. Gods moder I pray þe"), to Mary's reference to her right breast which she shows Jesus ("For þis þu souke in þi childhede. Son forgyf hym his mysdede"), to the Son's appeal that his Father grant his mother's request ("I pray þe fader graunte þi son for my sake my moder bone"), and finally to God's response ("Son als þu byddes sal al be. No thyng wil I denye þe"). These scrolls inscribe a dialogue found in contemporary manuscripts that share other texts with the miscellany.[89] But elsewhere the dialogue is visualized quite differently, as spoken by figures standing and kneeling in a row, so that its design does not allude to Doomsday iconography. In contrast, the representation of the dialogue in the Carthusian Miscellany (Fig. 8) explicitly recalls the Last Judgment image (Fig. 7).[90] It reminds the reader that just as the individual can make a good death and be saved, so it is possible to be saved at Doomsday. An emphasis upon judgment, in other words, need not be negative, implying damnation and the pains of Hell, for vernacular eschatology also includes an optimist strain.[91] The devil may hover at the foot of the deathbed, but the angel and the departing soul are at its head and on the right hand of God. To be on the right hand of God in medieval iconography, of course, is to be saved and rewarded with eternal life in Heaven.

The deathbed scene serves as a transition from the universal eschatology of the opening folios to the individual eschatology of the next image, the man in the tree (fol. 19v, Fig. 5). Allegorical pictures now recall the best-known medieval accounts of individual eschatology, morality plays staging the life of Mankind such as the *Castle of Perseverance*.[92] In a facing-page interweaving of word and image, the Carthusian Miscellany represents the Seven Ages of Man (fols. 28v–29r), a humanized version of the Seven Ages of the World.[93] Introduced by a titulus, "Of þe seven ages note wele. Þe sayng of þe gode angel and þe yll," these pages depict a dialogue between a man, angel, and fiend which traces the stages of the individual Christian's life from childhood to death. At its conclusion, personal judgment has clearly already taken place, because the angel pulls the soul from the mouth of the man lying naked in bed while the devil on the right turns away. As Denise L. Despres notes, "this dramatic portrayal of sin and redemption was used as a personal meditation, requiring the reader to identify with the characters who chart life's pilgrimage."[94] Such deathbed scenes are prominent in the miscellany's focus on individual eschatology. The manuscript also helps the reader imagine what will happen after death by including a debate between the body and worms, which begins by referring to "þe ceson of huge mortalite / Of sondre disseses with þe pestilence" (fol. 33r).[95] Its four images of skeletons responding to worms, although much cruder than the more practiced image of the soul filled with worms and serpents in Douce 134 (Fig. 2), are nevertheless quite effective, as are the three drawings accompanying

"A dysputacion betwyx þe saule & þe body when it is past oute of þe body" (fols. 82r–84r).[96]

Towards its conclusion, the Carthusian Miscellany links universal and individual eschatology in a crowded facing-page allegory of salvation history (fols. 72v–73r). Words, inscribed above, around, and between pictures, are subordinate to the overall visual effect but guide the eye as they move in tandem with the complex series of detailed drawings.[97] In the upper left scene (Fig. 9), Adam and Eve are expelled from a walled garden containing the serpent and the Tree of Knowledge. As in the *Pseudo-Methodius* cycle (fol. 11r), this allegory sets forth the origins and results of sin, beginning mankind's long exile in this world. It will culminate, at the end of time, either at Heaven, shown in the upper right (Fig. 10), or at Hell, symbolized by the double Hell's mouth in the lower right corner. The two mouths represent both the origin and conclusion of universal eschatology. The first engulfs the evil angels pushed from Heaven who fall down along the right edge of the illustration, a primordial event in cosmic eschatology symbolized by the stars the Dragon's tail drags from Heaven (Rev. 12:4). The second devours the damned at the end of time. They move relentlessly across the lower page from the symbol of their sin, the "meretrix magna" or Great Whore (Rev. 17). She recalls the city of Babylon, which the *Pseudo-Methodius* cycle (fol. 9v) contrasted with Rome.

Salvation history is interwoven with the life of the individual Christian, furthermore, for a baptismal font is depicted next to the expulsion from the garden and directly above the Whore of Babylon (Fig. 9). Like the other five sacraments pictured along the top register of the image—confirmation, matrimony, holy orders, the mass, and extreme unction—baptism is linked directly by red lines drawn to the bloody wound of Christ on the cross.[98] In this allegory of personal eschatology, "þe last anoyntynge of þe seke" (Fig. 10) and its placement next to heaven promises salvation for those who make a good death within the Church. The sacraments and those officiating represent Ecclesia, opposed to the false church of Babylon. This apocalyptic image also calls to mind the scene's universal eschatology and Doomsday. Thus the Whore's followers move along the drawing's bottom plane into Hell's mouth. In contrast to the damned, others reject sin and participate in the seventh sacrament, confession, represented to the right of the "meretrix magna" by three figures kneeling before a priest, who is also linked by a red line to Christ's wound (Fig. 9). The repentant then head along a rising diagonal into Heaven, paralleling the Five Wise Virgins of Christ's apocalyptic parable (Matt. 25:1–13), whose oil lamps mirror the chalice employed in the mass depicted above.[99] Those who must do further penance before earning heaven are shown in the band directly above Hell suffering the pangs of Purgatory (Fig. 10), another doctrine crucial to late medieval eschatology.[100] They are ultimately raised up by angels into heaven.

This two-page scene, a compelling interweaving of text and image, knots the strands of personal and cosmic eschatology developed earlier and separately in the manuscript. It understands salvation history from the perspective of eschatology, which provides a unifying theme for the manuscript's varied textual and visual contents. The Carthusian Miscellany connects apocalyptic, devotional, emblematic, historical, and hagiographic elements into a larger framework that underscores the importance of eschatology both from the point of view of eternity and for the individual in the here and now. In this didactic function, the miscellany resembles the French Carthusian manuscript. Both assume that knowing what to expect in the future is crucial, for as the Vigne emphasizes, Christ will surely appear in the clouds at the end of history to judge all. The two Carthusian manuscripts differ, however, in important ways. The French manuscript focuses entirely on universal eschatology, and its varied texts are inscribed uniformly to generate a coherent treatise in which framed and distinct images illustrate sometimes long passages of doctrinal text. In contrast, the English manuscript is more personal, both in its understanding of eschatology and in its sometimes rudimentary pictures. The numerous images crowded on its pages are often primary, with its texts explicating or even speaking the pictures. Nevertheless, although differing in their layout, illustrations, and texts, both manuscripts exemplify what James Simpson has called "the irreducibly visual focus of visionary writing" in the later Middle Ages,[101] and both not only imagined but also imaged many traditional expectations of late medieval eschatology.

NOTES

1. Morton W. Bloomfield, *Piers Plowman as a Fourteenth-Century Apocalypse* (New Brunswick, NJ: Rutgers University Press, 1962).

2. Richard K. Emmerson, *Antichrist in the Middle Ages: A Study of Medieval Apocalypticism, Art, and Literature* (Seattle: University of Washington Press, 1981).

3. See especially Norman Cohn, *The Pursuit of the Millennium* (London: Secker and Warburg, 1957), with its most widely quoted edition adding the subtitle, *Revolutionary Millenarians and Mystical Anarchists of the Middle Ages* (New York: Oxford University Press, 1970); Marjorie Reeves, *The Influence of Prophecy in the Later Middle*

Ages: A Study of Joachimism (Oxford: Clarendon Press, 1969); and Marjorie Reeves, *Joachim of Fiore and the Prophetic Future* (London: S.P.C.K, 1976). Bloomfield's early contributions include the still valuable essay, "Joachim of Flora: A Critical Survey of His Canon, Teaching, Sources, Bibliography, and Influence," *Traditio* 13 (1957): 249–311, and, with Marjorie Reeves, "The Penetration of Joachimism into Northern Europe," *Speculum* 29 (1954): 772–93.

4. An important exception is the work of Herbert Grundmann, including *Studien über Joachim von Floris*, Beiträge zur Kulturgeschichte des Mittelalters und der Renaissance 32 (Leipzig: Teubner, 1927; repr. 1966); and *Neue Forschungen über Joachim von Floris* (Marburg: Simons Verlag, 1950).

5. For important contributions see Robert E. Lerner, *The Powers of Prophecy: The Cedar of Lebanon Vision from the Mongol Onslaught to the Dawn of the Enlightenment* (Berkeley: University of California Press, 1983), and *The Feast of Saint Abraham: Medieval Millenarians and the Jews* (Philadelphia: University of Pennsylvania Press, 2001); Bernard McGinn, *Visions of the End: Apocalyptic Traditions in the Middle Ages* (New York: Columbia University Press, 1979; paperback edition with added bibliography, 1998), *The Calabrian Abbot: Joachim of Fiore in the History of Western Thought* (New York: Macmillan, 1985), and *Antichrist: Two Thousand Years of the Human Fascination with Evil* (San Francisco: Harper, 1994; paperback edition, Columbia University Press, 2000); and the essays in *The Apocalyptic Year 1000: Religious Expectation and Social Change, 950–1050*, ed. Richard Landes, Andrew Gow, and David C. Van Meter (New York: Oxford University Press, 2003).

6. Important contributions have been made by Roberto Rusconi, *L'attesa della fine: Crisi della società, profezia ed Apocalisse in Italia al tempo del grande Scisma d'Occidente (1378–1417)* (Rome: Istituto storico italiano per il Medio Evo, 1979); and David Burr, *Olivi's Peaceable Kingdom: A Reading of the Apocalypse Commentary* (Philadelphia: University of Pennsylvania Press, 1993). Kathryn Kerby-Fulton's notion of a "reformist apocalypticism" in *Piers Plowman* argues for Joachim's influence; see *Reformist Apocalypticism and Piers Plowman* (Cambridge: Cambridge University Press, 1990). For my response see "'Or Yernen to Rede Redels?' *Piers Plowman* and Prophecy," *Yearbook of Langland Studies* 7 (1993): 27–76, esp. 41–49.

7. On this and other methodological problems, see Richard K. Emmerson, "The Secret," a response to the *AHR Forum*, "Millenniums," *American Historical Review* 104 (1999): 1512–1628, esp. 1603–14. For collections that attend to the full range of medieval apocalypticism, see Richard K. Emmerson and Bernard McGinn, eds., *The Apocalypse in the Middle Ages* (Ithaca, NY: Cornell University Press, 1992); and *The Encyclopedia of Apocalypticism*, vol. 2, *Apocalypticism in Western History and Culture*, ed. Bernard McGinn (New York: Continuum, 1998).

8. In addition to *Antichrist in the Middle Ages*, 146–203, see my "The Prophetic, the Apocalyptic, and the Study of Medieval Literature," in *Poetic Prophecy in Western Literature*, ed. Jan Wojcik and Raymond Jean Frontain (Rutherford, NJ: Fairleigh Dickinson University Press, 1984), 40–54; "Apocalyptic Themes and Imagery in Me-

dieval and Renaissance Literature," in *Apocalypticism in Western History and Culture*, ed. McGinn, 402–44; and especially Richard K. Emmerson and Ronald B. Herzman, *The Apocalyptic Imagination in Medieval Literature* (Philadelphia: University of Pennsylvania Press, 1992).

9. See Laura Smoller, "Of Earthquakes, Hail, Frogs, and Geography: Plague and the Investigation of the Apocalypse in Later Middle Ages," in *Last Things: Death and the Apocalypse in the Middle Ages*, ed. Caroline Walker Bynum and Paul Freedman (Philadelphia: University of Pennsylvania Press, 2000), 156–87.

10. James Simpson, "The Rule of Medieval Imagination," in *Images, Idolatry, and Iconoclasm in Late Medieval England: Textuality and the Visual Image*, ed. Jeremy Dimmick, James Simpson, and Nicolette Zeeman (Oxford: Oxford University Press, 2002), 12.

11. On the figure of Antichrist in medieval thought, see Horst Dieter Rauh, *Das Bild des Antichrist im Mittelalter: Von Tyconius zum deutschen Symbolismus*, Beiträge zur Geschichte der Philosophie und Theologie des Mittelalters n.F. 9, 2nd ed. (Münster: Aschendorff, 1979); Emmerson, *Antichrist in the Middle Ages*, 11–107; Robert E. Lerner, "Antichrists and Antichrist in Joachim of Fiore," *Speculum* 60 (1985): 553–70; and McGinn, *Antichrist*, 79–200.

12. On Antichrist in medieval drama, see Klaus Aichele, *Das Antichristdrama des Mittelalters, der Reformation und Gegenreformation* (The Hague: Martinus Nijhoff, 1974); and Emmerson, *Antichrist in the Middle Ages*, 163–87. Despite its title, John Parker's *The Aesthetics of Antichrist: From Christian Drama to Christopher Marlowe* (Ithaca, NY: Cornell University Press, 2007), provides only brief discussions of Antichrist in medieval plays. Its treatment of Marlowe, however, is more valuable; see my review in *Review of English Studies* 60 (2009): 134–36.

13. See, for example, the "Coming of Antichrist" in *The Chester Mystery Cycle*, ed. R. M. Lumiansky and David Mills, EETS, supp. ser. 3 (London: Oxford University Press, 1974), play XXIII. For analysis see Richard K. Emmerson, "Contextualizing Performance: The Reception of the Chester 'Antichrist,'" *Journal of Medieval and Early Modern Studies* 29 (1999): 89–119, and "Antichrist on Page and Stage in the Later Middle Ages," in *Spectacle and Public Performance in the Late Middle Ages and the Renaissance*, ed. Robert E. Stillman (Leiden: Brill, 2006), 1–29.

14. Edited by Emile Roy, *Jour du Jugement: Mystère français sur le Grand Schisme*, Ètudes sur le theatre français au xvie siècle (Paris: Emile Bouillon, 1902); for a translation see Richard K. Emmerson and David Hult, *Antichrist and Judgment Day: The Middle French Jour du Jugement*, Early European Drama in Translation Series 2 (Asheville, NC: Pegasus Press, 1998). This notion of Antichrist's career is ultimately based on the *Libellus de Antichristo* written by the tenth-century Benedictine abbot, Adso of Montier-en-Der. See *Adso Dervensis, De ortu et tempore Antichristi*, ed. Daniel Verhelst, Corpus Christianorum Continuatio Mediaevalis 45 (Turnholt: Brepols, 1976); trans. Bernard McGinn, *Apocalyptic Spirituality*, Classics of Western Spirituality (New York: Paulist, 1979), 81–96. Drawing upon a wide range of biblical, patristic, sybilline, and

legendary materials, which he arranged following hagiographic conventions, Adso created an anti-saint's legend, portraying Antichrist's future life as a parodic inversion of the life of Christ. See Richard K. Emmerson, "Antichrist as Anti-Saint: The Significance of Abbot Adso's *Libellus de Antichristo*," *American Benedictine Review* 30 (1979): 175–90.

15. See Richard K. Emmerson, "Visualizing Performance: The Miniatures of Besançon MS 579 (*Jour du Jugement*)," *Exemplaria* 11 (1999): 245–72; and Jean-Pierre Perrot, "La Mise en Scène de L'Apocalypse au Moyen Âge: *Le Mystère du Jour du Jugement*; Espace théâtral et espace intérieur," in *L'Imaginaire des apocalypses*, ed. Jean Burgos (Paris-Caen: Lettres Modernes Minard, 2003), 113–42.

16. For an excellent study of these miniatures, see Karlyn Griffith, "Illustrating *Antichrist and the Day of Judgment* in the Eighty-Nine Minatures of Besançon, Bibliothèque Municipale MS 579" (master's thesis, Florida State University, 2008). Twenty-nine miniatures are reproduced in Jean-Pierre Perrot and Jean-Jacques Nonot, *Le Jour du Jugement: Mystère du XIVe siècle* (Chambéry: Éditions Comp'Act, 2000); all the miniatures are reproduced on the Enluminures website at http://www.enluminures.culture.fr. On Antichrist in art, see Jessie Poesch, "Antichrist Imagery in Anglo-French Apocalypse Manuscripts" (Ph.D. diss, Univ. of Pennsylvania, 1966); Emmerson, *Antichrist in the Middle Ages*, 108–45; Bernard McGinn, "Portraying Antichrist in the Middle Ages," in *The Use and Abuse of Eschatology in the Middle Ages*, ed. Werner Verbeke, et al., Mediaevalia Lovaniensia 1.15 (Leuven: Leuven University Press, 1988), 1–48; and Rosemary Muir Wright, *Art and Antichrist in Medieval Europe* (Manchester: Manchester University Press, 1995).

17. For many reproductions in color, see Frederik van der Meer, *Apocalypse: Visions from the Book of Revelation in Western Art* (London: Thames and Hudson, 1978). For scholarly studies, see the essays in *L'Apocalypse de Jean: Traditions exégétiques et iconographiques IIIe–XIIIe siècles*, ed. Renzo Petraglio, Etudes et documents publiés par la section d'historie de la Faculté des Lettres de l'Université de Genève 11 (Geneva: Librairie Droz, 1979); in David Bevington et al., *Homo, Memento Finis: The Iconography of Just Judgment in Medieval Art and Drama*, Early Drama, Art and Music Monograph Series 5 (Kalamazoo: Medieval Institute Publications, 1985), and in Emmerson and McGinn, *Apocalypse in the Middle Ages*, 105–289. See also Suzanne Lewis, *Reading Images: Narrative Discourse and Reception in the Thirteenth-Century Illuminated Apocalypse* (Cambridge: Cambridge University Press, 1995).

18. Artistic representations of more radical forms of apocalypticism usually accompanied learned Latin texts. See, for example, Marjorie Reeves and Beatrice Hirsch-Reich, *The Figurae of Joachim of Fiore* (Oxford: Clarendon Press, 1972); Martha H. Fleming, *The Late Medieval Pope Prophecies: The Genus nequam Group* (Tempe: Arizona Center for Medieval and Renaissance Studies, 1999); and Richard K. Emmerson, "The Representation of Antichrist in Hildegard of Bingen's *Scivias*: Image, Word, Commentary, and Visionary Experience," *Gesta* 41 (2002): 95–110.

19. See Richard K. Emmerson, "The Apocalypse Cycle in the Bedford Book

of Hours," *Traditio* 50 (1995): 173–98; "Beyond the Apocalypse: The Human Antichrist in Late Medieval Illustrated Manuscripts," in *Waiting in Fearful Hope: Approaching a New Millennium*, ed. Christopher Kleinhenz and Fannie LeMoine (Madison: University of Wisconsin Press, 1999), 102–30; and "Visualizing the Apocalypse in Late Medieval England: The York Minster Great East Window," in *Cross, Crown and Community: Religion, Government and Culture in Early Modern England 1400–1800*, ed. David J. B. Trim and Peter J. Balderstone (Bern: Peter Lang, 2004), 39–75.

20. Just as Lollards opposed religious images and theater, so they developed a distinctly polemical apocalypticism; see Curtis V. Bostick, *The Antichrist and the Lollards: Apocalypticism in Late Medieval and Reformation England* (Leiden: Brill, 1998). For Lollard opposition to the playing "of Antichrist and of the Day of Dome," see *A Tretise of Miraclis Pleyinge*, ed. Clifford Davidson (Kalamazoo: Medieval Institute Publications, 1993), 101–2.

21. See the discussion of the first "key" of medieval apocalypticism in Emmerson and Herzman, *Apocalyptic Imagination*, 23–25.

22. A classic study of the artistic response to the plague is Millard Meiss, *Painting in Florence and Siena after the Black Death* (Princeton: Princeton University Press, 1951); reprinted with the subtitle *The Arts, Religion, and Society in the Mid-Fourteenth Century* (1978).

23. On this aspect of late medieval religious culture, see Philippe Ariès, *The Hour of Our Death*, trans. Helen Weaver (New York: Oxford University Press, 1981), esp. 95–139; Eamon Duffy, *The Stripping of the Altars: Traditional Religion in England 1400–1580* (New Haven, CT: Yale University Press, 1992), 301–37; Paul Binski, *Medieval Death: Ritual and Representation* (London: British Museum Press, 1996); and Ashby Kinch, "The *Danse Macabre* and the Medieval Community of Death," *Medievalia* 23 (2002): 159–202. A popular account with many illustrations is T. S. R. Boase, *Death in the Middle Ages: Mortality, Judgment, and Remembrance* (New York: McGraw-Hill, 1972).

24. Baltimore, Walters Art Museum, MS 457 (ca. 1480–90), fol. 117r; see Roger S. Wieck, *Time Sanctified: The Book of Hours in Medieval Art and Life* (New York: George Braziller, 1988), pl. 37.

25. *Piers Plowman*, B.20.165–98, ed. E. T. Donaldson and George Kane (London: Athlone Press, 1975). On Antichrist's role in the poem, see Emmerson, *Antichrist in the Middle Ages*, 196–203.

26. Bloomfield, *Piers Plowman as a Fourteenth-Century Apocalypse*, 146.

27. See Otto Pächt and J. J. G. Alexander, *Illuminated Manuscripts in the Bodleian Library*, vol. 1, *German, Dutch, Flemish, French and Spanish Schools* (Oxford: Oxford University Press, 1966), no. 710; and Bodleian Library, *The Douce Legacy: An Exhibition to Commemorate the 150th Anniversary of the Bequest of Francis Douce (1757–1834)* (Oxford: Bodleian Library, 1984), 172, no. 248.

28. See *Catalogue général des manuscrits des bibliothèques publiques de France: Départements*, vol. 7, *Grenoble*, ed. P. Fournier, E. Maignien, and A. Prudhomme (Paris: Librerie Plon, 1889), no. 408; and M. E. Shields, "An Old French Book of Legends and

Its Apocalyptic Background" (Ph.D. diss., Trinity College, Dublin, 1967), 200–203, 489–93.

29. "Cy finist le premier livre de la Vigne Nostre Seigneur / et fut accompli le ve jou de mars l'an m cccc lxiii / Et est a savoir que le second livre fut premierement fait et accompli que cestuy qui est le premier . . ." (fol. 171v); quoted by Thomas Kren, "Some Illuminated Manuscripts of *The Vision of Lazarus* from the Time of Margaret of York," in *Margaret of York, Simon Marmion, and The Visions of Tondal*, ed. Thomas Kren (Malibu, CA: J. Paul Getty Museum, 1992), 155 n. 21.

30. The manuscript's Carthusian connection is evident in its representation of Heaven in an opening (fols. 144v–145r) that pictures two Carthusians among the saints who adore the Lord as described in Apoc. 4; see Martin Kauffmann's catalogue entry in *The Apocalypse and the Shape of Things to Come*, ed. Frances Carey (London: British Museum Press, 1999), 94. On the theology of resurrection and heavenly reward, see Caroline Walker Bynum, *The Resurrection of the Body in Western Christianity, 200–1336* (New York: Columbia University Press, 1995).

31. On these literary and artistic themes, see Willy Rotzler, *Die Begegnung der drei Lebenden und der drei Toten* (Winterthur: P. G. Keller, 1961); James M. Clark, *The Dance of Death in the Middle Ages and Renaissance* (Glasgow: Jackson & Son, 1950); and Philippa Tristram, *Figures of Life and Death in Medieval English Literature* (London: Paul Elek, 1976), 162–73.

32. On theological backgrounds, see Alan E. Bernstein, *The Formation of Hell: Death and Retribution in the Ancient and Early Christian Worlds* (Ithaca, NY: Cornell University Press, 1993). On this theme in medieval drama and art, see *The Iconography of Hell*, ed. Clifford Davidson and Thomas H. Seiler, Early Drama, Art, and Music Monograph Series 17 (Kalamazoo: Medieval Institute Publications, 1992); and Nigel Morgan, "The Torments of the Damned in Hell in Texts and Images in England in the Thirteenth and Fourteenth Centuries," in *Prophecy, Apocalypse and the Day of Doom: Proceedings of the 2000 Harlaxton Symposium*, ed. Nigel Morgan (Donington: Shaun Tyas, 2004), 250–60, pls. 46–56.

33. See Debra Higgs Strickland, *Saracens, Demons, and Jews: Making Monsters in Medieval Art* (Princeton: Princeton University Press, 2003), fig. 21.

34. See ibid., 67–68 and fig. 19.

35. Morton W. Bloomfield, *The Seven Deadly Sins: An Introduction to the History of a Religious Concept, with Special Reference to Medieval English Literature* (East Lansing: Michigan State College Press, 1952), 433 n. 123. For the *Vision of Lazarus*, see Max Voigt, *Beiträge zur Geschichte der Visionenliteratur im Mittelalter I, II*, Untersuchungen und Texte aus der deutschen und englischen Philologie 146 (Leipzig: Mayer & Müller, 1924; repr. New York: Johnson Reprint, 1967), 1–42; and D. D. R. Owen, *The Vision of Hell: Infernal Journeys in Medieval French Literature* (Edinburgh: Scottish Academic Press, 1970), 243–46. The text in Douce 134 is transcribed by Kren, "Some Illuminated Manuscripts," 151–52.

36. See Kren, "Some Illuminated Manuscripts," figs. 107 and 105. An English translation of the Lazarus vision included in Wynkyn de Worde's *Arte or Crafte to*

Lyue well, printed in 1505 (STC 792), includes woodcuts also depicting these punishments; see Duffy, *Stripping of the Altars,* figs. 127–28.

37. See Kren, "Some Illuminated Manuscripts," fig. 108. Kren comments that this iconography may derive "from a type of infernal punishment illustration where society's various stations, especially its clergy and ruling class, suffer the same ignominious punishment as ordinary damned souls" (148).

38. Dagmar Eichberger, "Image Follows Text: *The Visions of Tondal* and Its Relationship to Depictions of Hell and Purgatory in Fifteenth-Century Illuminated Manuscripts," in *Margaret of York,* ed. Kren, 133. Eichberger publishes miniatures depicting devils scourging the damned (fig. 87, fol. 101r) and the punishment of thieves (fig. 88, fol. 121v).

39. See A. G. Hassall and W. O. Hassall, *Treasures from the Bodleian Library* (New York: Columbia University Press, 1976), pl. 32; and the color frontispiece to *Apocalypse and the Shape of Things to Come,* ed. Carey.

40. Kauffmann, in *Apocalypse and the Shape of Things to Come,* ed. Carey, 93.

41. A well-known image based on this exegetical tradition is in the *Liber floridus,* a twelfth-century spiritual encyclopedia by Lambert of St. Omer, which depicts Antichrist riding the tail of Leviathan. See Jessie Poesch, "The Beasts from Job in the *Liber Floridus* Manuscripts," *Journal of the Warburg and Courtauld Institutes* 33 (1970): 41–51; Emmerson, *Antichrist,* 117–18, fig. 1; and Wright, *Art and Antichrist,* 62–70, figs. 13–14.

42. It is unlikely that a medieval viewer would agree with the Hassalls that Lucifer as here depicted "looks mildly pleased with himself like a masked child 'dressing up'" (*Treasures from the Bodleian Library,* 138).

43. See *Chester Mystery Cycle,* ed. Lumiansky and Mills, 405–7; and *Pricke of Conscience,* ed. Richard Morris (London: Asher, 1865), 125–27. Wolfgang van Emden, *Jeu d'Adam: English and Old French* (Edinburgh: Société Rencesvals British Branch, 1996), argues that the *Quinze signes,* generally understood as concluding the *Play of Adam,* are not part of the original play, but a scribal addition to its manuscript, Tours, Bibliothèque Municipale, MS 927 (vi–vii).

44. William W. Heist, *The Fifteen Signs before Doomsday* (East Lansing: Michigan State College Press, 1952), appendix A.

45. See W. O. Hassall, *The Holkham Bible Picture Book* (London: Dropmore Press, 1954), fols. 40v–42r; Michelle P. Brown, *The Holkham Bible: A Facsimile* (London: British Library, 2007), 86–87 and fols. 40v–42r; J. T. Fowler, "The Fifteen Last Days of the World in Medieval Art and Literature," *The Yorkshire Archaeological Journal* 23 (1914–15): 313–37; and Sue Powell, "All Saints' Church, North Street, York: Text and Image in the *Pricke of Conscience* Window," in *Prophecy, Apocalypse, and the Day of Doom,* ed. Morgan, 292–316.

46. See *The Golden Legend: Readings on the Saints,* trans. William Granger Ryan, 2 vols. (Princeton: Princeton University Press, 1993), 1:7–12. Cambridge, Fitzwilliam Museum, MS 22, an illustrated *Légende dorée* (the French version of the *Legenda au-*

rea), pictures the Fifteen Signs in a series of column miniatures followed by scenes depicting the life of Antichrist and then Doomsday. See Emmerson, "Beyond the Apocalypse," 105–8, fig. 5.10; and Martha W. Driver, "Picturing the Apocalypse in the Printed Book of Hours," in *Prophecy, Apocalypse and the Day of Doom*, ed. Morgan, 62–63, pls. 10–11.

47. *Golden Legend*, trans. Ryan, 1:8.

48. See Karin Boveland et al., *Der Antichrist und Die Fünfzehn Zeichen vor dem Jüngsten Gericht*, 2 vols. (Hamburg: Friedrich Wittig, 1979), facs. vol., pp. 28–36, where they are depicted two scenes to a page.

49. On this brief period following the destruction of Antichrist, see Robert E. Lerner, "Refreshment of the Saints: The Time After Antichrist as a Station for Earthly Progress in Medieval Thought," *Traditio* 32 (1976): 97–144; and Emmerson, *Antichrist in the Middle Ages*, 103–7. The illustrated vita of Antichrist included in the Wellcome Apocalypse on one folio depicts the fall of Antichrist when he attempts to rise from the Mount of Olives, the return of Enoch and Elijah to preach repentance, and the first of the Fifteen Signs. See London, Wellcome Institute for the History of Medicine, MS 49, fol. 13r (published in Wright, *Art and Antichrist*, fig. 50, and *Apocalypse and the Shape of Things to Come*, ed. Carey, 91). This manuscript, traditionally dated ca. 1420, has recently been redated by Jeffrey Hamburger to ca. 1470, making it contemporary with the two Carthusian manuscripts here discussed; see Hamburger's entry no. 19 in *The Splendor of the Word: Medieval and Renaissance Illuminated Manuscripts at The New York Public Library*, ed. Jonathan J. G. Alexander, James H. Marrow, and Lucy Freeman Sandler (London: Harvey Miller, 2006), 92.

50. For this miniature, see Wright, *Art and Antichrist*, fig. 47.

51. Adso's *Libellus*, the ultimate basis for the *Vigne*'s version of Antichrist, similarly wants it both ways: "He will be born from the union of a mother and father, like other men, not, as some say, from a virgin alone. . . . At the very beginning of his conception the devil will enter his mother's womb at the same moment" (McGinn, trans., in *Apocalyptic Spirituality*, 90).

52. See Boveland, et al., *Antichrist*, facs. vol., p. 3. For an English translation of the German text accompanying the block book *vita Antichristi* (based on the 1480 Strasbourg edition), see Andrew Colin Gow, *The Red Jews: Antisemitism in an Apocalyptic Age, 1200–1600* (Leiden: E. J. Brill, 1995), 238–46. For the *Jour du Jugement*, see Emmerson, "Visualizing Performance," 261–62, figs. 4, 6.

53. For Antichrist's birthplace and the role of the Jews in his career, see Emmerson, *Antichrist in the Middle Ages*, 79–81, 90–91. The relationship between Jews and Antichrist was one crucial factor in late medieval anti-Semitism; see Gow, *Red Jews*; and Strickland, *Saracens, Demons, and Jews*, 212–21.

54. See Andrew Runni Anderson, *Alexander's Gate, Gog and Magog, and the Inclosed Nations* (Cambridge, MA: Mediaeval Academy of America, 1932); Emmerson, *Antichrist in the Middle Ages*, 84–88; Paul J. Alexander, *The Byzantine Apocalyptic Tradition*, ed. Dorothy deF. Abrahamse (Berkeley: University of California Press, 1985), 185–92; and Strickland, *Saracens, Demons, and Jews*, 228–39.

55. Wright, *Art and Antichrist*, 170.

56. See ibid., fig. 6; and Emmerson, "Beyond the Apocalypse," fig. 5.9.

57. For example, Fitzwilliam MS 22, fol. 17, shows Antichrist's men torturing the faithful, who are tied to a tree; see Emmerson, "Beyond the Apocalypse," fig. 5.11.

58. See Wright, *Art and Antichrist*, fig. 48. On this feature of the legend see Emmerson, *Antichrist in the Middle Ages*, 101–3.

59. This feature of Pauline eschatology is central to Antichrist exegesis; see Kevin L. Hughes, *Constructing Antichrist: Paul, Biblical Commentary, and the Development of Doctrine in the Early Middle Ages* (Washington, DC: Catholic University of America Press, 2005).

60. On this expectation, see Emmerson, *Antichrist in the Middle Ages*, 132–33, figs. 2, 9; and Emmerson and Herzman, *Apocalyptic Imagination*, 16–18, fig. 2.

61. Wright is mistaken in arguing that the miniature identifies Antichrist as the pope because "one of his followers is a mitred bishop" (*Art and Antichrist*, 171). Throughout medieval art and literature, Antichrist's followers often include ecclesiastics as well as kings and other aristocrats, and there is no sense that these works identify him as a pope. For instance, in the *Jour du Jugement*, although a bad bishop is one of Antichrist's earliest advisors and two cardinals are converted by bribes, the pope remains steadfast and is imprisoned for his opposition to Antichrist; see Emmerson and Hult, *Antichrist and Judgment Day*, 51–52, lines 1368–1409.

62. Douglas Gray, "London, British Library, Additional MS 37049—A Spiritual Encyclopedia," in *Text and Controversy from Wyclif to Bale: Essays in Honour of Anne Hudson*, ed. Helen Barr and Ann M. Hutchison (Turnhout, 2005), 99–116, at 115.

63. For the manuscript see *Catalogue of Additions to the Manuscripts in the British Museum, 1900–1905* (London: British Museum, 1907), 324–32; Ian Doyle, "English Carthusian Books Not Yet Linked with a Charterhouse," in *A Miracle of Learning: Studies in Manuscripts and Irish Learning; Essays in Honour of William O'Sullivan*, ed. Toby Barnard et al. (Aldershot: Ashgate, 1998), 122–36; and Kathleen L. Scott, *Later Gothic Manuscripts, 1390–1490*, 2 vols. (London: Harvey Miller, 1996), 2:193.

64. Ralph Hanna III, "Miscellaneity and Vernacularity: Conditions of Literary Production in Late Medieval England," in *The Whole Book: Cultural Perspectives on the Medieval Miscellany*, ed. Stephen G. Nichols and Siegfried Wenzel (Ann Arbor: University of Michigan Press, 1996), 37–51, at 37.

65. Most of the images are reproduced in James Hogg, ed., *An Illustrated Yorkshire Carthusian Religious Miscellany: British Library Additional MS 37049*, Analecta Cartusiana 95 (Salzburg: Institut für Anglistik und Amerikanistik Universität Salzburg, 1981). See also Jessica Brantley, "The Visual Environment of Carthusian Texts: Decoration and Illustration in Notre Dame 67," in *The Text in the Community: Essays on Medieval Works, Manuscripts, Authors, and Readers*, ed. Jill Mann and Maura Nolan (Notre Dame, IN: University of Notre Dame Press, 2006), 191–96.

Imagining and Imaging the End 187

66. The Basel charterhouse, for example, although continuing to privilege Latin, produced vernacular German collections for its lay brothers; see Wolfram D. Sexauer, *Frühneuhochdeutsche Schriften in Kartäuserbibliotheken: Untersuchungen zur Pflege der volkssprachlichen Literatur in Kartäusenklöstern des oberdeutschen Raums bis zum Einsetzen der Reformation* (Frankfurt: Peter Lang, 1978), 181–92. The manuscript may also have had a pastoral purpose beyond the charterhouse, since English Carthusians, as Vincent Gillespie has shown, "had direct experience of vernacular instruction of a pastoral catechetic nature which predated by some years the concern for similar vernacular instruction for the laity as a whole." See Gillespie, "*Cura Pastoralis in Deserto,*" in *De Cella in Seculum: Religious and Secular Life and Devotion in Late Medieval England*, ed. Michael G. Sargent (Cambridge: D. S. Brewer, 1989), 161–82, at 166.

67. See James Hogg, "Unpublished Texts in the Carthusian Northern Middle English Religious Miscellany British Library MS Add. 37049," in *Essays in Honour of Erwin Stürzl*, Salzburger Studien zur Anglistik und Amerikanistik 10 (Salzburg: Institut für Anglistik und Amerikanistik, 1980), 259–62; and M. C. Spalding, *The Middle English Charters of Christ*, Bryn Mawr Monographs 15 (Bryn Mawr, PA: Bryn Mawr College, 1914).

68. For an excellent study see Marlene Villalobos Hennessy, "Passion Devotion, Penitential Reading, and the Manuscript Page: 'The Hours of the Cross' in London, British Library Additional 37049," *Mediaeval Studies* 66 (2004): 213–52. See also Jessica Brantley, *Reading in the Wilderness: Private Devotion and Public Performance in Late Medieval England* (Chicago: University of Chicago Press, 2007), which unfortunately was published after the completion of the present essay.

69. Marlene Villalobos Hennessy, "The Remains of the Royal Dead in an English Carthusian Manuscript, London, British Library, MS Additional 37049," *Viator* 33 (2002): 310–49, at 312.

70. James Hogg, "A Morbid Preoccupation with Mortality? The Carthusian London British Library MS. Add. 37049," in *Zeit, Tod und Ewigkeit in der Renaissance Literatur*, Analecta Cartusiana 117, vol. 2 (Salzburg: Institut für Anglistik und Amerikanistik, 1986), 139–89; for an edition of "Thynke on þine ending day," see 148–49.

71. The map is the manuscript's first image following two Byzantine-style portraits of Mary and Christ (fols. 1v, 2r) drawn by a different artist.

72. David Woodward, "Medieval *Mappaemundi*," in *The History of Cartography*, ed. J. B. Harley and David Woodward, vol. 1, *Cartography in Prehistoric, Ancient, and Medieval Europe and the Mediterranean* (Chicago: University of Chicago Press, 1987), 326.

73. On this allegory, taken from *Barlam and Iosaphat*, see Ruth Pitman and John Scattergood, "Some Illustrations of the Unicorn Apologue from Barlaam and Ioasaph," *Scriptorium* 31 (1977): 85–90, 89–90 on Add. 37049.

74. For the unicorn as a figure of death, see Jürgen W. Einhorn, *Spiritualis unicornis: Das Einhorn als Bedeutungsträger in Literatur und Kunst des Mittelalters* (Munich: W. Fink, 1976), 219–31.

75. Its text is edited in Karl Brunner, "Mittelenglische Todesgedichte," *Archiv für das Studium der neueren Sprachen* 90, band 167, n.s. 67 (1935): 23–24. T. W. Ross ("Five Fifteenth-Century 'Emblem' Verses from Brit. Mus. Addit. Ms. 37049," *Speculum* 37 (1957)) is mistaken when he states that "There is no drawing to accompany the poem in the manuscript" (275 n. 8).

76. See M. C. Seymour, "The English Epitome of *Mandeville's Travels*," *Anglia* 84 (1966): 27–58.

77. On the significance of these maps see Jonathan T. Lanman, "The Religious Symbolism of the T in T-O Maps," *Cartographica* 18 (1981): 18–22.

78. Woodward, "Medieval *Mappaemundi*," 335.

79. See Seymour, "English Epitome," 47.

80. The accompanying text has been mistakenly identified as an extract from Higden's *Polychronicon*, but Dan Embree ("The Fragmentary Chronicle in British Library, Additional MS 37049," *Manuscripta* 37 (1993): 193–200) shows that it "is composed entirely of excerpts translated from the thirteenth-century *Chronicon pontificum et imperatorum* by Martinus Polonus or Oppaviensis" (193). I thank Marlene Villalobos Hennessy for bringing this article to my attention and for much other help on bibliography.

81. See *Dialogus inter Militem et Clericum, Richard FitzRalph's Sermon: "Defensio Curatorum" and Methodius: "Þe Bygynnyng of þe World and þe Ende of Worldes,"* ed. A. J. Perry, EETS 167 (London: Oxford University Press, 1925), 94–112.

82. See Emmerson, *Antichrist in the Middle Ages*, 48. On its origins and relation to the apocalyptic tradition, see Paul Alexander, *Byzantine Apocalyptic Tradition*, 13–60, and G. J. Reinink, "Ps.-Methodius: A Concept of History in Response to the Rise of Islam," *The Byzantine and Early Islamic Near East*, vol. 1, *Problems in the Literary Source Material*, ed. Averil Cameron and Lawrence I. Conrad (Princeton: Darwin Press, 1992), 149–87.

83. Outlined by Augustine at the conclusion of his *City of God* 22.30; see David Knowles, ed., *City of God*, trans. Henry Bettenson (Baltimore: Penguin, 1972), 1091; on this tradition, see Emmerson, *Antichrist in the Middle Ages*, 16–19.

84. On Gog and Magog as gruesome cannibals, see Bettina Bildhauer, "Blood, Jews and Monsters in Medieval Culture," in *The Monstrous Middle Ages*, ed. Bettina Bildhauer and Robert Mills (Toronto: University of Toronto Press, 2003), 75–96, esp. 77–85; and Strickland, *Saracens, Demons, and Jews*, fig. 125.

85. As I have argued elsewhere, the manuscript's visual treatment of the destruction of Gog and Magog seems "hyper-orthodox," perhaps indicating "the artist's concern to avoid the potential heretical misuse of the legend of the Last World Emperor"; see Emmerson, "Beyond the Apocalypse," 102, and fig. 5.7. On the Last World Emperor see Hannes Möhring, *Der Weltkaiser der Endzeit: Entstehung, Wandel und Wirkung einer tausendjährigen Weissagung* (Stuttgart: Jan Thorbecke Verlag, 2000).

86. On the Two Witnesses see Emmerson, *Antichrist in the Middle Ages*, 95–101.

87. See Emmerson, "Beyond the Apocalypse," 100, fig. 5.8.

88. See Richard K. Emmerson, "'Nowe Ys Common This Daye': Enoch and Elias, Antichrist, and the Structure of the Chester Cycle," in Bevington et al., *Homo, Memento Finis*, 89–120, esp. 108–10. For early forms of Michael's eschatological role, see Daniel F. Callahan, "The Cult of St. Michael the Archangel and the 'Terrors of the Year 1000,'" in *The Apocalyptic Year 1000*, ed. Landes, Gow, and Van Meter, 181–204.

89. British Library, Stowe 39 (fol. 32v); see *Catalogue of the Stowe Manuscripts in the British Museum*, 2 vols. (London: British Museum, 1895–96), vol. 1, pp. 23–25. The dialogue also appears in British Library, Cotton Faustina, B VI, fol. 2r; for an edition see Brunner, "Mittelenglische Todesgedichte," 22–23.

90. Although I disagree with Pamela M. King ("Doomsday as Hypertext: Contexts of Doomsday in Fifteenth-Century Northern Manuscripts, 2: British Library Add. MS 37049," in *Prophecy, Apocalypse and the Day of Doom*, ed. Morgan, 391–403), who ingeniously argues that "All texts in the manuscript can, then, be related to the Doomsday image more or less directly" (403), the visual relationship between these two specific images of universal and individual judgment is definitely close.

91. See Nicholas Watson, "Visions of Inclusion: Universal Salvation and Vernacular Theology in Pre-Reformation England," *Journal of Medieval and Early Modern Studies* 27 (1997): 145–87.

92. See David Bevington, "'Man, Thinke on Thine Endinge Day': Stage Pictures of Just Judgment in *The Castle of Perseverance*," in *Homo, Memento Finis*, ed. Bevington et al., 147–77; and Richard K. Emmerson, "The Morality Character as Sign: A Semiotic Approach to *The Castle of Perseverance*," *Mediaevalia* 18 (1995, for 1992): 191–220.

93. See Elizabeth Sears (*The Ages of Man: Medieval Interpretations of the Life Cycle* (Princeton: Princeton University Press, 1986), 54–79) on the relationship of the two seven-fold schemes; on Add. 37049, see 139–40, fig. 81.

94. Denise L. Despres, "Visual Heuristics," in Kathryn Kerby-Fulton and Denise L. Despres, *Iconography and the Professional Reader: The Politics of Book Production in the Douce Piers Plowman* (Minneapolis: University of Minnesota Press, 1999), 157, and fig. 59.

95. See Marjorie M. Malvern, "An Earnest 'Monyscyon' and 'Þinge Delectabyll' Realized Verbally and Visually in 'A Disputacion Betwyx þe Body and Wormes,'" a Middle English Poem Inspired by Tomb Art and Northern Spirituality," *Viator* 13 (1982): 415–43.

96. See James Hogg, "Selected Texts on Heaven and Hell from the Carthusian Miscellany, British Library Additional MS. 37049," in *Zeit, Tod und Ewigkeit*, 85–89.

97. The inscriptions are transcribed and discussed in Francis Wormald, "Some Popular Miniatures and their Rich Relations," in *Francis Wormald: Collected Writings*, vol. 2, *Studies in English and Continental Art of the Later Middle Ages* (London: Harvey Miller, 1988), 141–44.

98. See Ann Eljenholm Nichols, *Seeable Signs: The Iconography of the Seven Sacraments 1350–1544* (Woodbridge: Boydell, 1994), 52–55 and pl. 20; Nichols mistakenly cites the folios as 27v–28r.

99. The manuscript also depicts the parable of the Wise and Foolish Virgins on fol. 80v.

100. See Jacques Le Goff, *The Birth of Purgatory*, trans. Arthur Goldhammer (Chicago: University of Chicago Press, 1984); and Duffy, *Stripping of the Altars*, 338–76.

101. James Simpson, *The Oxford English Literary History*, vol. 2, *1350–1547: Reform and Cultural Revolution* (Oxford: Oxford University Press, 2002), 429.

Fig. 1. Christ sends damned to hell. *Livre de la vigne nostre Seigneur*, Oxford, Bodleian Library, Douce 134, fol. 76r.

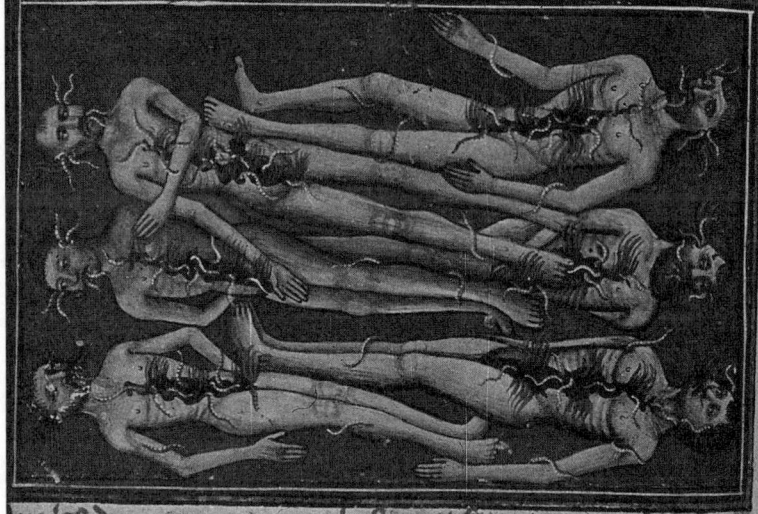

Fig. 2. Worms and serpents devour the damned. *Livre de la vigne nostre Seigneur*, Oxford, Bodleian Library, Douce 134, fol. 91v.

Imagining and Imaging the End 193

noix et gemissemens que nul nenteroza [...] Les monstres de mer sont les balaines et les serrames et aultres mueilleux poissons qui seront assebles par lieux sur la mer. ainsi que dit le prophete. O see m[...] Sed et pisces maris cogregabit[...] Et [...] et plaindront [...] on sappete. qui sera une mer[...]

Fig. 3. Fifteen Signs of Doomsday, third sign: Fish and sea monsters rise. *Livre de la vigne nostre Seigneur*, Oxford, Bodleian Library, Douce 134, fol. 42v.

Fig. 4. Antichrist, with forces of Gog and Magog, approach Jerusalem. *Livre de la vigne nostre Seigneur*, Oxford, Bodleian Library, Douce 134, fol. 6r.

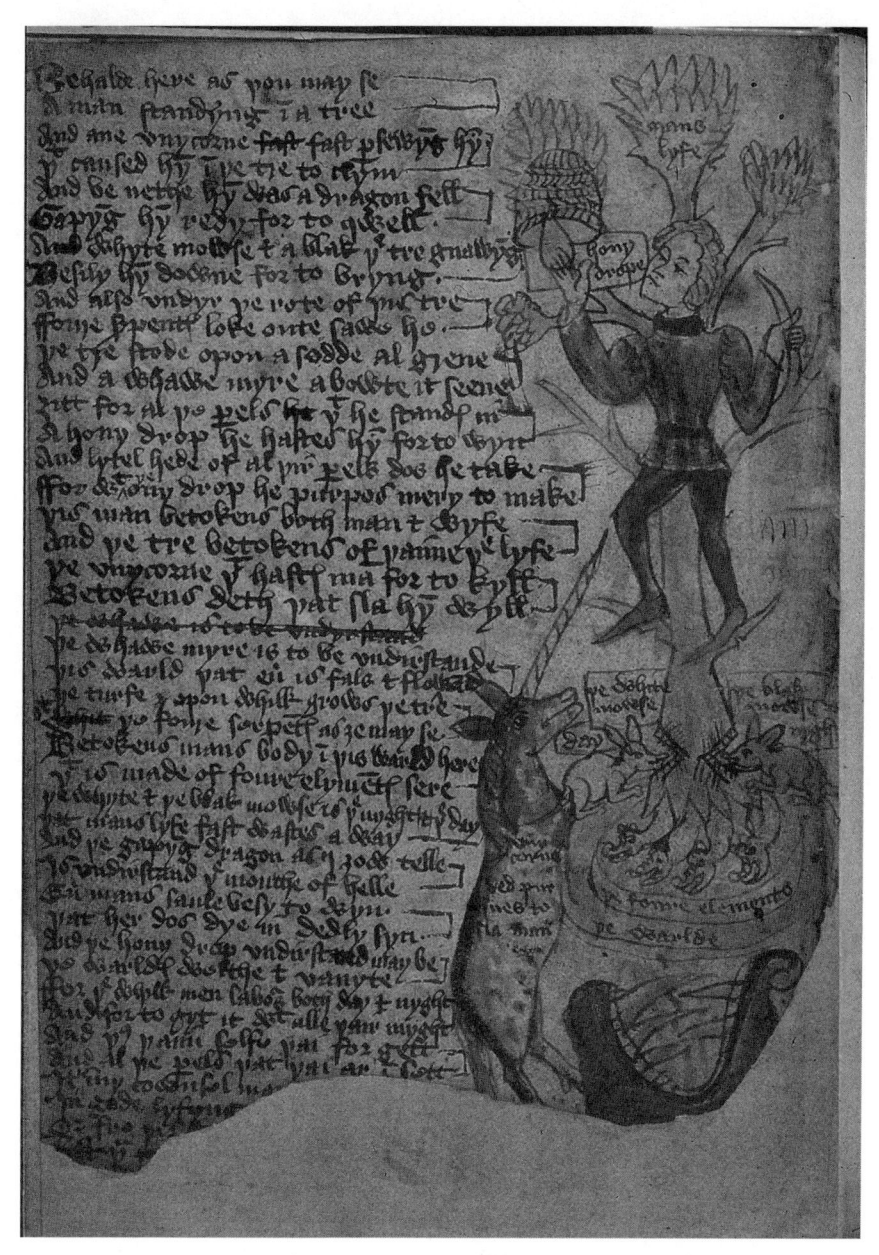

Fig. 5. Allegory of "Man's Lyfe." Carthusian Miscellany; London, British Library, Additional 37049, fol. 19v.

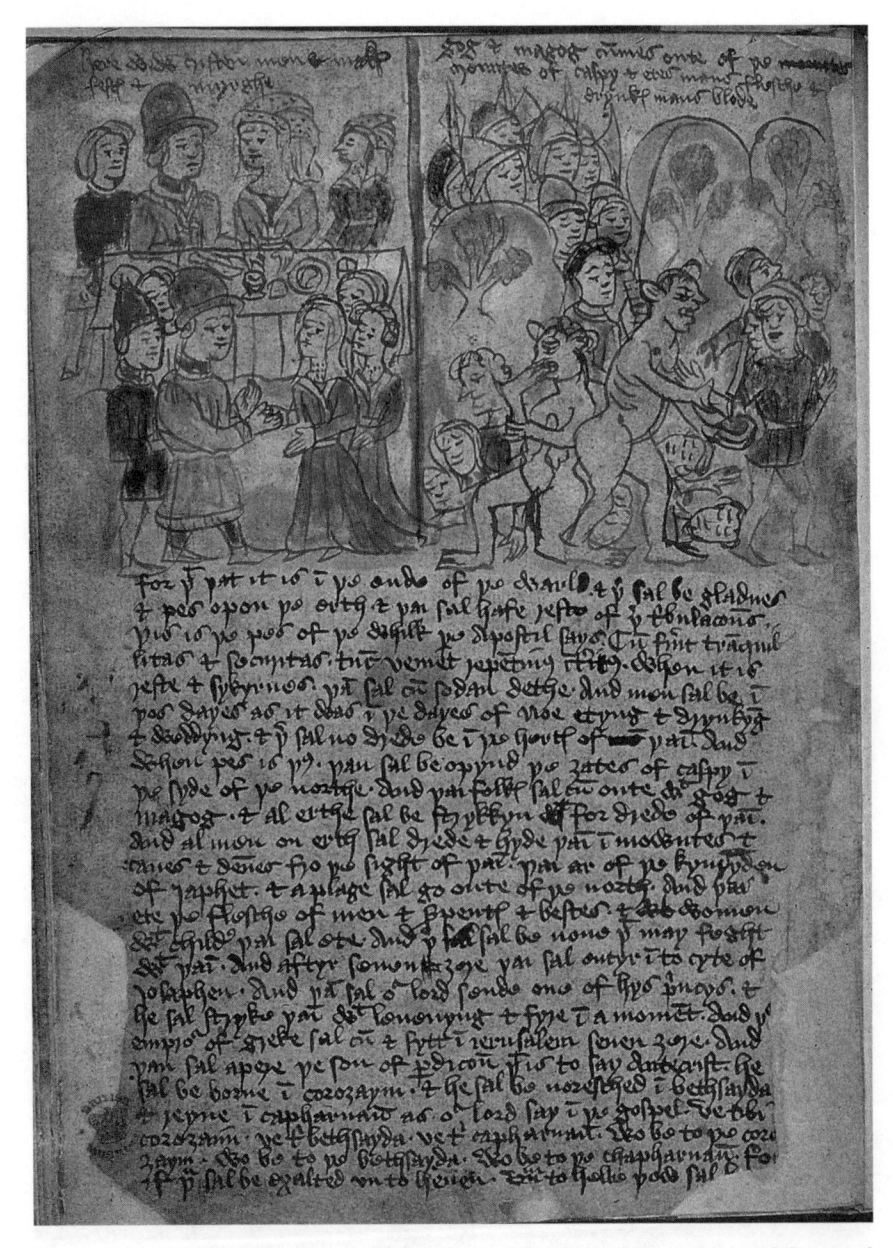

Fig. 6. Feasting and marrying as in the days of Noah, and the release of Gog and Magog. Carthusian Miscellany; London, British Library, Additional 37049, fol. 15v.

Fig. 7. Universal Judgment. Carthusian Miscellany; London, British Library, Additional 37049, fol. 17r.

Fig. 8. Personal Judgment. Carthusian Miscellany; London, British Library, Additional 37049, fol. 19r.

Fig. 9. Origins of salvation history and the life of mankind. Carthusian Miscellany; London, British Library, Additional 37049, fol. 72v.

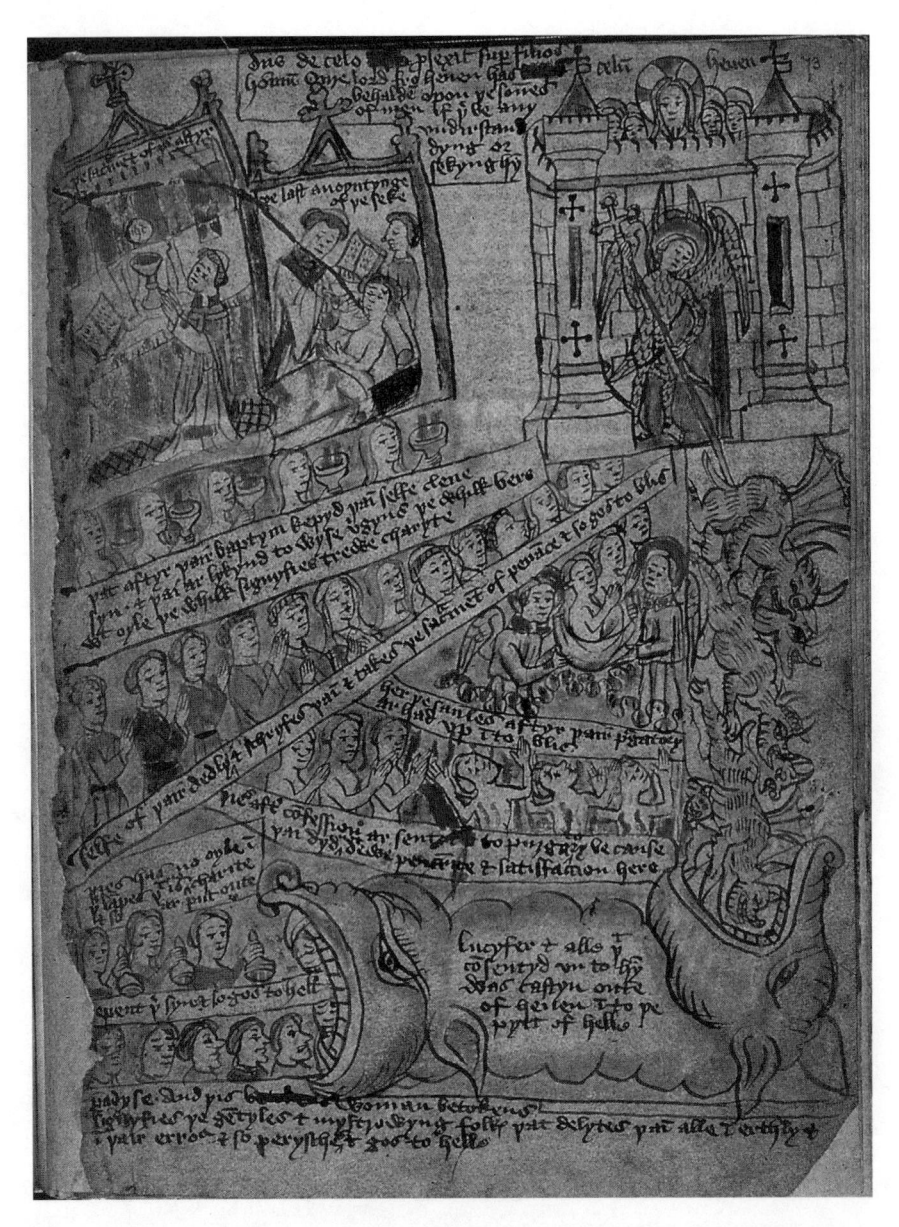

Fig. 10. The end of salvation history, death, Heaven, and Hell. Carthusian Miscellany; London, British Library, Additional 37049, fol. 73r.

William Langland, William Blake, and the Poetry of Hope [2001]

Derek Pearsall

It was impossible for me not to choose on this occasion to speak on *Piers Plowman*, the subject of what I think to be Morton Bloomfield's finest book, *Piers Plowman as a Fourteenth-Century Apocalypse*,[1] and the principal subject of our own early conversations. It is a book that much influenced my own reading of the poem, and it is present as what Blake would have called an Emanation of the body of this talk. What I shall try to do is to make some sense of the notion I have long had that Blake is a kind of brother poet-prophet of Langland, not a spiritual heir, since he had no knowledge of Langland's poem, but someone who had the same view of poetry as the instrument of the spiritual regeneration of England and of mankind, who worked at poetry in similar ways and used many of the same techniques and procedures, who had the same kind of vision of the eternal in the material, the same unquenchable hope that the constant hard work of battering against the doors of error will eventually open them to a fuller humanity, and the same crankiness. The two poets have, for me, come to seem extraordinarily alike.

There are dangers as well as satisfactions in making such comparisons, of course. If I said, for instance, that the resemblances I see between the two poets have a historical basis, that Blake was a London radical imbued with spiritual and millenarian impulses—and so was Langland; that Blake was appalled at the materialism and money-grubbing of his age—and so was Langland; that Blake lived his mature life at a time when orthodoxy was reasserting itself in the repressions that followed the first reactions to the French Revolution, after the moment of freedom in the 1780s—and that Langland lived to see a similar repressiveness in English society, with the hunting out of the Lollards, after the comparative freedoms of the 1370s; that the movement in Blake from political prophecy in his early poems on the American and French Revolutions to allegorized biblical prophecy may have been a way for him of dissociating himself from the volatile and more confusing politics of the Napoleonic years—and that the same motive may have inspired Langland to distance himself from sectarian reformism when he was writing the latest version of his poem. If I said these things, I would have to acknowledge also the historical differences over four centuries that make such comparisons inappropriate. But I think the two poets can be compared as visionaries and as poets; the comparisons do provide insight. Their poems are commentaries on each other: Blake's poems can be read through Langland's; Blake's vocabulary gives us another language in which to talk about Langland.

Since there are not many people who are regular readers of both Langland and Blake, I shall begin by offering an introductory account of *The Vision of Piers Plowman*, the one poem by which Langland is known. Subsequently, comparisons between the two poets will be most often projected from the discussion of Blake, which will be confined to the three long "prophetic books," *The Four Zoas* (first called *Vala*), *Milton*, and *Jerusalem*.

PIERS PLOWMAN

Langland's poem of *Piers Plowman* is framed as a series of eight consecutive dreams. In the first part, called "The Vision of Piers Plowman" (the *Visio*), the dreamer (Will) sees the Field Full of Folk, which is England at its work mostly of moneymaking—greedy, self-interested, the priesthood complicit in the pursuit of gain. The allegorical episode of Lady Meed, beautiful, seductive, powerful, shows how money works to corrupt the Christian community and alienate men from their true spiritual selves. But social reform seems possible, and Piers Plowman, as the type of the simple honest life of the true Christian, offers himself as a guide in setting about the reestablishment of the true Christian community on earth. In the famous scene of the Ploughing of the Half Acre we are shown how this hopeful enterprise comes to grief because of the apparently ineradicable individual greed and selfishness of the people whose lives are to be changed by reform. Like Tolstoy, Langland came to believe that only inward reform can transform people's lives: "There can be no political change of the social system. The only change can be a moral one, within men and women."[2]

So Piers Plowman gives up his attempt to reform society, and in the poem's second part, called "The Life of Dowel, Dobet, and Dobest" (the *Vita*), the dreamer becomes again the protagonist, going out in his dream in search of Dowel (the good Christian life), meeting a variety of allegorical characters personifying his own inner being and faculties and facets of his experience—Thought, Study, Learning, Imagination, Patience—and struggling through doubt, crisis and setback to understand what Dowel means. Piers Plowman appears mysteriously from time to time as the human embodiment of that life, drawing the dreamer onward in hope, until eventually, in the transfiguring climax of the poem, Piers Plowman is revealed as Christ incarnate. The great vision of the Crucifixion and the Harrowing of Hell is followed by Christ's enigmatic promise of universal salvation:

> For holy writ wol that I be wreke of hem that wrouhte ille . . .
> And so of alle wykkede I wol here take venjaunce.
> And yut my kynde in my kene ire shal constrayne my will . . .
> To be merciable to monye of my halve-bretherne. . . .
> Ac my rihtwysnesse and rihte shal regnen in helle,
> And mercy al mankynde bifore me in hevene.[3]

The poem concludes with the story of the establishment of Christ's church on earth—or in the human soul, since Langland's allegory is always simultaneously cosmic and psychological—and the characteristically grim honesty of the return to the world of fourteenth-century England where the poem began. The whole experiment seems to have failed.

Piers Plowman exists in at least three versions, representing successive revisions by the poet. There may be other partial intermediate versions. The A-text goes as far as the giving up of the plan for political reform and the beginning of the search for Dowel. The B-text revises all of A and adds more, altogether trebling the length of the poem. The C-text revises the whole of B except for the last two *passūs*.[4] In the processes of revision, portions of text are frequently added or removed, or inserted elsewhere sometimes without too much care for contextual coherence, while a revision of some minor detail will sometimes spread out into the surrounding text as Langland catches sight of something else that causes him dissatisfaction. The complexities of revision are sometimes almost inextricable: when he was doing the C-revision, Langland found himself working with a corrupt scribal copy of his own B-text, of which he seems to have had no fair copy, so that he sometimes finds himself revising text that he did not write, groping toward what he might have wanted to say.[5]

Piers Plowman is not a poem in the usual sense of the word. It has no formal construction, no ambition to be a poem, no sense of itself as a poem. It shifts and transforms through its three texts and their variants without coming nearer to achieved poetic form. Langland began it when he came of age, imaginatively, and he went on writing and rewriting it till he died. It is not a poem but a mortal combat with all that threatens the life of the spirit and the imagination.

Blake and Langland: Structure, Narrative, Form

The preceding account of *Piers Plowman* has not been consciously framed to prompt comparison with Blake, but the resemblances are constantly suggestive. Blake's poetry is all one poem, in different forms, and the three great prophetic books are reworkings of one central theme, the regeneration of man through the working of the imaginative energy of the artist and through the sacrifice and forgiveness of Jesus. They are his A, B, and C texts. *The Four Zoas*, which exists only in a single manuscript, is like the chaos from which the other two were formed. Begun in 1797, and continually raided for material for *Milton* and *Jerusalem*, it was still being added to as late as 1810.[6] Indeed, if one wished to have an idea of what Langland's working copy might have looked like, with all its erasures, partial erasures, writings over erasures, additions on inserted leaves or on scraps of paper or parchment or squeezed into the margins of existing copy, then the manuscript of *The Four Zoas*, as described by Blake's editor, would provide a suggestive model.[7] The subject of *The Four Zoas* is the regeneration of man—who is also the world, since Blake's visions, like Langland's, always have both psychological and cosmic meaning—with his elements represented as fragments of his whole being and also assuming human form. There are a great many of these in addition to the four Zoas (broadly representative of such elements as Passion, Reason, and Compassion), and each has not only its Emanation, that is, the contrary through which it is made whole (its "other half," so to speak, since Blake tends to regard the Emanation as female), but also its Spectre, that aspect of a divided self that attaches it to reason and the material order.[8] The profusion of personages, all with newly coined names, can be quite confusing, but the overall movement is towards endlessly prolonged and repeated violent struggle between these characters (that is, within man, or within the world) leading to final regeneration and harmony.

The most consistently recognizable and memorable of these characters is Urizen, the agent of regulation, limitation, analytic process, the deliverer of fixed form, the one who sets horizons to human imagination (Urīzen) and orders things by reason (Urĭzen, with the non-diphthongal pronunciation of long ī).[9] Some of Blake's most extraordinary poetry portrays the petrification, the literal turning into stone, of Urizen as the divine energy of imagination ceases to flow through him.[10] He appears in all three poems, as well as in his own early prophetic book, *The First Book of Urizen of the Bible of Hell*, Blake's version of Genesis, the first book of Moses the Law-Giver.

It is hard, with this immensely powerful figure, not to believe that he projects something of Blake's own fearful self-imagining, or not to think how close Langland is to Blake in his denunciation of the analytic power of reason. The delusion that the dreamer falls under at the beginning of the *Vita* that he can discover the nature of the true Christian life by asking questions of his intellectual faculties is mercilessly exposed. His disastrous little excursion into syllogistic scholastic reasoning, in his puerile attempt to prove that a man who sins seven times a day cannot "do well"—"'*Contra*,' quod I as a clerk, and comsed to dispute" (C.X.20)—is made to sound both silly and pompous. Another "Blakeian" feature of Langland is his contempt for the formalized procedures of institutionalized religion, what Blake in his usual paradoxical way calls "Natural Religion." Priests and religious play surprisingly little part in Langland's poem, and when they do appear they are usually fat, lazy, corrupt, or avaricious. He would perhaps have been tempted again to agree with Tolstoy, "Why is it necessary for the promotion of goodness to wear gowns and sing certain songs in certain houses?"[11]

Langland also distrusts the mechanized agencies of priestly exchange—pardons, indulgences, biennials, triennials (C.IX.319–47)—as a betrayal of the divine in man, which is the full humanity of man. It is this descent into fixities of form which he saw, like Blake, as the denial of the spirit of the divine. Metaphorically, the incessant hammering of both poets at their poems, like Los before his furnaces—

> Los beheld undaunted furious
> His heavd Hammer—he swung it round & at one blow,
> In unpitying ruin driving down the pyramids of pride,
> Smiting the Spectre on his Anvil—[12]

is a way of holding back fixity and finality and conveying through the poetic form the ever-continuing process of becoming. No text reaches final form, or expresses what editors are obliged to call "a final intention."

Milton and *Jerusalem* share with *The Four Zoas* and *Piers Plowman* the character of being perpetually in process, seeking and searching, untiring in their attention to the furnaces of the imagination, the hard *work* of the poetic visionary. *Milton* is in a continual state of revision, as if Blake were in the process of reinventing his own life as he worked upon it, just as Langland could be seen as writing and rewriting his spiritual autobiography throughout the different versions of *Piers Plowman*. *Jerusalem* was begun around 1801, much worked on 1804–7, constantly laid aside (so that Blake could earn his living), taken up again to accommodate new ideas and allegorize new outrages committed by Blake's enemies, and not completed before 1820. Nothing is cast aside or eliminated: Blake believed that nothing of creation can be destroyed.

The continuous nature of composition gives to all these poems an intense connectivity—they are bound tightly together by echoes, anticipations, repetitions, recursions, recapitulations with variation—but it also presents challenges to the reader. The immersion of a writer in a lengthy continuing imaginative operation of considerable complexity gives him a familiar inwardness with its detail that can never be fully shared by the reader, and a full understanding of the subtleties of structure and intratextual allusion is liable to remain tantalizingly elusive. This is true of both Langland and Blake. Neither, furthermore, tries to make things easier for the reader. Blake introduces new plates with accompanying text which seems to digress from the narrative or hold back its progress for hundreds of lines (as does Langland's famous analysis of *mede* and *mercede* in C.III.290–405). In *The Four Zoas*, a passage spoken by Blake is inserted (92:17–33) but the previous speaker continues without comment when the original text resumes: so in the C-text of *Piers Plowman* it is impossible to tell where the speech of the character Rechelesnesse leaves off and rebegins.[13] When long passages are spoken by someone other than the poet, as with Rechelesnesse in *Piers Plowman* or the Bard at the beginning of *Milton*, it is difficult to remember who is speaking, since there is rarely any dramatic differentiation in the mode of address. This can sometimes be imaginatively quite successful in producing an elusive metamorphosis of poet-persona into personification or vice versa (as with Rechelesnesse), but it can be exasperating when a discrepancy thrown up in the flurry of compositional revision might be understood as an indication that the author has changed his mind or equally that he intends to show a character, willfully or not, getting things wrong.[14] It is not surprising that both Langland and Blake have acquired a reputation for not being perspicuous.

Prophecy

But as these poems move towards their final climax they seem to draw closer together than ever before. In *Milton* the poet Milton comes back to earth to waken Albion from his sleep, to restore mankind through the power of his imagination. Milton was Blake's hero because he had written poetry of great power expressing the energy of opposition to a repressive and omnipotent deity. Milton's Satan was not a hero for Blake, but Milton's God was certainly the enemy, seen as a vengeful regulator and often identified with Urizen, for example in the prose address "To the Deists" in *Jerusalem* (52). Blake, though recognizing the overwhelming significance of the sacrifice and forgiveness of Jesus, rarely mentions God: he is always the Ever-Pitying One, or the Lamb, or the Divine Vision, or the Countenance Divine. Blake is unwilling to invoke the Jehovah of the Law or the vengeful God of repression and punishment. One would not expect to find a parallel suppression of the name God in Langland, but it is remarkable how often he tries to find a substitute term, such as Truth, and how overwhelmingly Christocentric his whole poem is.

In *Jerusalem*, subtitled "The Emanation of the Giant Albion," the narrative is of how the divine inspiration eventually wakens Albion, whose sick self, bound in the chains of custom, regulation and government, is annihilated and his true self is reunited with Jerusalem in the harmony of their contraries. The poem is, in non-Blakeian terms, a vision of the regeneration of corrupted England through the restoration of unity and the removal of division among all its people. It is essentially a reworking of *The Four Zoas* and *Milton* with the agencies of regeneration reshuffled. Los is, throughout *Jerusalem*, with a consistency not found in the other poems, the chief such agency. It is he (or strictly speaking his Spectre Urthona) who "kept the Divine Vision in time of trouble," and who said, "'I must Create a System, or be enslav'd by another Mans.'"[15] It is worth pausing on this statement, since it provides the clue to Blake's most characteristic procedure, the manner in which he invents new systems by inverting old ones. It is necessary, for instance, when reading Blake, to have clearly in mind that the Elect, the Redeemed, and the Reprobate (for example in *Milton*, 7:1–3) are to be understood in the opposite signification from what we are used to. Blake demands the sloughing off of conventional ways of thinking and seeing that blind one to the truth as he sees it. Langland can be compared, though the language of paradox and inversion that he employs usually has biblical precedent. Those who are faithful Christians are "fools" to the world (C.XXII.61), and "lunatyk lollares" are the true possessors of Christian wisdom, who wander the streets half-naked without a care for food or money, rapt in the ecstasy of prophecy (C.IX.105–127). Blake too suspected that "there are probably men shut up as mad in Bedlam, who are not so; that possibly the madmen outside have shut up the sane people."[16]

Los remains faithful at his furnaces throughout, the embodiment of the true artist and the work of imaginative vision. He is the divine potential in man, and he is of course William Blake—which explains some of his unusual domestic relations with his Emanation Enitharmon.[17] But at the final regeneration of Albion, he is also revealed as Jesus:

> Then Jesus appeared standing by Albion as the Good Shepherd
> By the lost Sheep that he hath found & Albion knew that it
> Was the Lord, the Universal Humanity, & Albion saw his form
> A Man. & they conversed as Man with Man, in Ages of Eternity
> And the Divine Appearance was the likeness & similitude of Los.
> (*Jerusalem*, 96:3–7)

I find it remarkable that Piers Plowman fulfils exactly the same role in Langland's poem, as the representative of the divine potential in man, and that he too is finally recognized as Jesus. When Jesus comes to do battle against Eternal Death at the Crucifixion it is in Piers Plowman's coat of arms (that is, human flesh) that he comes:

> "*Liberum-dei-arbitrium* for love hath undertake
> That this Jesus of his gentrice shal jouste in Pers armes,
> In his helm and in his haberjon, *humana natura*,
> That Crist be nat yknowe for *consummatus deus*;
> In Pers plates the plouhman this prikiare shal ryde."[18]

It is unthinkable that Langland could mean that the divine, the incarnate Christ, is the expression of man in his fullest humanity, that the divine is found in the fulfillment of the human, and through the agency of the human, but then, Langland was the kind of poet who could think the unthinkable.[19] Earlier, when the search for Saint Truth had taken the pilgrims through the landscape of the Ten Commandments and to the court of Truth, Truth is found dwelling within the human heart (C.VII.255). That is where it was all the time.

Another remarkable kinship between the prophetic visions of Langland and Blake is in the climactic scenes of harvest and vintage. Both *Milton* and *Jerusalem* end with the preparation of the reapers and winepresses for the harvest of human souls, and the first activity of the regenerated Urizen in *The Four Zoas* is to turn to the plough—"The noise of rural work resounded" (*Four Zoas*, 124:14)—in preparation for the sowing and reaping of souls and the gathering of them into barns:

> This sickle Urizen took the scythe his sons embracd
> And went forth & began to reap & all his joyful sons
> Reapd the wide Universe & bound in Sheaves a wondrous harvest
> They took them into the wide barns with loud rejoicings and triumph
> Of flute & harp & drum & trumpet horn & clarion. (132:5-9)

The scene is closely paralleled in the great allegorical vision of plowing, sowing, and reaping in the penultimate passus of *Piers Plowman*, and the gathering of the harvest of souls into the barn of Unity.

We should of course be less surprised than we are by these extraordinary resemblances, since both Langland and Blake drew their inspiration from the same source, the Old Testament prophecies of the Last Judgment and the final vintage of the resurrected souls in the Book of Joel. Both these writers were steeped in the Scriptures, especially the historical and prophetic books of the Old Testament and the New Testament Gospels, though Langland makes more use of the Psalms, being a professional beadsman, and Blake more use of the Book of Revelation, being perhaps only slightly less crazy than its author. Both respond to the apocalyptic urgency of the prophets—"Six Thousand years are passd away the end approaches fast," says Blake[20]—and Morton Bloomfield made special remark of this in respect of Langland in the book already cited; but both foresee the establishment of Christ's community on earth, not in heaven (for Blake, earth *is* heaven). In Blake, there is something more of the Old Testament—the way his poetry echoes the half-line structures of Old Testament verse, especially as they appear in contemporary verse translations of the Book of Isaiah, and in Ossianic imitations.[21] Langland's use of the unrhymed long alliterative line with strong caesura is not similarly derived, but it is similar in its nonuse of rhyme, in its loose-limbed cadences, and in the impression it creates of irresistible onward momentum, even if not, as in Blake, of a torrential lava flow of the imagination that can hardly be controlled by the form of the verse.[22]

Visionaries

Both poets were visionaries, and seers of visions that were as real to them as the material world. The evidence is documentary for Blake—famous stories like that told by his wife Catherine (one hopes that Langland's wife, who had the same name, Kit, had the same gentle and faithful forbearance as Blake's with her equally unusual husband[23]: "You know, dear, the first time you saw God was when You were four years old And he put his head to the window and set you ascreaming."[24] And again: "Even when a Child his mother beat him for running in & saying that he saw the Prophet Ezekiel under a Tree in the Fields."[25] In later years he conversed freely with Socrates, Jesus, Milton, the prophet Isaiah, the spirit of his dead brother Robert, and many others. He saw always the eternal in the material and visible: "What it will be Questiond When the Sun rises do you not see a round Disk of fire somewhat like a Guinea O no no I see an Innumerable company of the Heavenly host crying Holy Holy Holy is the Lord God Almighty."[26] His poems work out from moments of epiphany, like the shaft of light that struck his foot as he was fastening his shoe in Lambeth and that made him feel he wore the prophetic mantle of Los and was the poetic heir of Milton; or the lark-song and smell of wild thyme in the garden at Felpham that he returns to again and again in *Milton*; or Ololon descending through Beulah to seek Milton seen in the real twelve-year-old girl coming into the same garden.[27] The material and the spiritual are always simultaneously present ("To see a World in a Grain of Sand . . . ");[28] the inchoate and visionary suddenly materialize in the real world. Real historical people appear in the same imaginative frame as allegorical personifications—Milton, Newton, Locke, and Blake's personal enemies like Hayley and Schofield; sudden shifts of perspective collapse the London of South Molton Street and Stratford Place (*Jerusalem*, 74:55) into the apocalyptic "heaps of smoking ruins" of the city of Los:

> The Corner of Broad Street weeps; Poland Street languishes
> To Great Queen Street & Lincolns Inn, all is distress & woe.
> (Jerusalem, 84:15–16)

A walk in the town with Blake would obviously have been a sensational experience.

Langland too stalked the streets of London in his long coat, his head in his visions, not remarking or saluting those who passed him by, even if they were eminent persons in fine furs with silver pendants round their necks,[29] and though there is no biographical evidence—nothing is known of his life outside what he tells of the life of Will in the poem except that he was the son of Stacy de Rokayle and was probably ordained in the 1330s[30]—it is hard to believe that his poetry did not derive its inspiration, like Blake's, from remembered visions. It was Geoffrey Shepherd who first speculated that Langland, like Julian of Norwich in the *Revelations of Divine Love* (or, one might add, like Wordsworth, with his "spots of time," or James Joyce, with his "epiphanies"), meditated upon "real" visionary experiences and wove the work of memory into a narrative.[31] As with Julian, what he saw in his visions was arbitrary and inexplicable in itself—a field full of folk swarming about their business, the tearing of a document of pardon, "a man in a dirty coat selling wafers . . . a propped-up tree in an orchard"[32]—and needed the work of meditation if they were to make sense and be useful. These meditations take the form that they are bound to take in the imagination of a medieval Christian, and become the engines of vision in the poem, the ladder that leads the journeyer upward (and that may be kicked aside later—two of the episodes mentioned are altered or discarded in the C-text).

As with Blake, Langland's own personal biography, as it is represented in the poem, is woven into and inseparable from the narrative of the world's fall and regeneration—his wife and daughter at their home in Cornhill, or setting out to church to celebrate Easter, his justification of himself and his way of life before Conscience and Reason (or before the justices of the peace interrogating itinerants who may be violating the 1388 Statute of Labourers),[33] his middle years fall into the worldly thrall of Fortune, his growing old and bald and impotent.[34] As in Blake, real historical characters or characters from the bible or Jesus's parables suddenly break into the world of allegorical personifications—Abraham, Moses, the Good Samaritan, or the Emperor Trajan, bursting in to pour scorn on those who debate in scholarly fashion whether the righteous heathen shall be saved. "I am here to prove it," he says, "so to hell with your books!" (Ye? bawe for bokes!) (C.XII.73).

Langland is with Blake above all other English poets apart from Shakespeare in the immediacy with which the spiritual and the concrete are made simultaneously manifest in his poetry. In Langland, there is no spiritual meaning that is not made concrete, no realism that does not have symbolic significance.[35] Real acts of eating, drinking, gnawing, driveling, plowing, piercing, kissing, vomiting, are suddenly opened up into spiritual meaning, while the central Christian mysteries become vivid physical realities:

> Love is plonte of pees, most precious of vertues,
> For hevene holde hit ne myghte, so hevy hit first semede,
> Til hit hadde of erthe ygoten hitsilve.
> Was never lef uppon lynde lyhtere ther-aftur,
> As when hit hadde of the folde flesch and blode taken.

Tho was hit portatif and persaunt as is the poynt of a nelde,
May non armure hit lette ne none heye walles.
(C.I.148–54)

Love, says Holy Church, is like an irresistible force of gravity that draws God down to beget himself upon an earthly body; weightless once it has consummated itself in the act of Incarnation, love is drawn back to its source in God and becomes mobile and penetrative so that no armed soldiers or walled tomb may resist it.

THE POETRY OF HOPE

And what about the poetry of hope? Hope is a hard thing, hope is hard as Hell, as Richard Rolle might have put it, a constant battering against the temptations to quietism, despair, cynicism, other-worldly transcendence, but in both poets it is unquenchable. Blake's whole homespun "philosophy," as he cobbled it together from Swedenborg and later from the writings of Paracelsus and Jakob Boehme, is constructed to make hope spring eternal. Human beings are not inherently sinful but may fall into states of error from which they will always be purified;[36] they fall into these states so that they may be saved from eternal death. Urizen himself is granted his power by Jesus so that man may in the end be regenerated:

> For the Divine Lamb Even Jesus who is the Divine Vision
> Permitted all lest Man should fall into Eternal Death.[37]

Blake's places of pain and suffering are hedged around with rehabilitation areas where human beings, like troops from the front line, may rest and be peaceful—the great city of art and science, Golgonooza, built by Los as a barrier against death and despair; or the land of Beulah (Bunyan's holiday land just outside heaven), a kind of holding area where human beings who have fallen into disaster or division are cocooned until they may be made whole through time—not of course through repentance. Blake did not believe in repentance but in active forgiveness.[38]

Langland does of course believe in repentance, as well as in righteousness and sin and the payment of the debt of sin, but he also struggles to free man from the burden and consequences of such belief. He returns persistently to the idea of a universal forgiveness and salvation, trying it out first of all with the familiar knotty problem of the salvation of the righteous heathen, then seizing on the text "His mercy is above all his works" in the allegory of the Trinity, and finally, in Christ's speech prophesying the Last Judgment, imagining the unimaginable, salvation granted to all those who are brothers in Christ through their very humanity even though not through baptism.[39] At the very end of the poem, when the barn of Christian Unity has been besieged and broken into and all seems lost, Conscience gathers himself once more and goes out again in search of the grace that lies within:

> "By Crist," quod Consience tho, "I wol bicome a pilgrime,
> And wenden as wyde as the world regneth
> To seke Peres the plouhman, that Pruyde myhte destruye,
> And that freres hadde a fyndynge, that for nede flateren
> And countrepledeth me, Consience. Now Kynde me avenge,
> And sende me hap and hele til I have Peres plouhman."
> And sethe he gradde after Grace tyl I gan awake.[40]

Often regarded as pessimistic, this ending is in fact a determined expression of hope, of renewal, of continuation. Langland's great editor, Walter William Skeat, answered the view that the ending of the poem was unsatisfactory, being so suggestive of disappointment and gloom, thus: "What other ending can there be? or rather, the end is not yet. We may be defeated, yet not cast down; we may be dying, and behold, we live. We are all still pilgrims on earth."[41]

This constant striving, seeking, journeying, is the character of hope, and Blake too, in a wonderful sketch he did in his Notebook, shows himself as a traveler, striding energetically, with his stick and wearing his old-fashioned broad-brimmed hat, across a wide landscape. In 1799, as he became lost to the world, poor and dirty and despised as a complete crank, he wrote, "I laugh at Fortune & Go on & on. I think I foresee better Things than I have ever seen."[42]

Blake's doctrine of contraries is another form of affirmation. Wholeness is not achieved through negation, denial, elimination, but through the harmonization of the contraries which make up human beings: "The Negation must be destroyd to redeem the Contraries."[43] Blake always works through incorporation, inclusion, reconciliation, forgiveness, and Los's words in *Jerusalem* have a newly revealed relevance in our present troubled times:

> "What shall I do! What could I do, if I could find these Criminals
> I could not dare to take vengeance; for all things are so constructed

And builded by the Divine Hand, that the sinner shall always escape,
And he who takes vengeance alone is the criminal of Providence."
                                                (*Jerusalem,* 45:29–32)

Langland, like Blake, refuses to work by denial and exclusion, or by yes-no syllogistic reasoning ("God keep me from the Divinity of Yes & No too," said Blake in 1827, "The Yea Nay Creeping Jesus").[44] He refuses to work by any process that consists in contradiction and elimination, or progressive, point-by-point denial-by-denial dialectic. He uses an accretive, associative mode of discourse, building up by incorporation. When he is debating the question of poverty and the rights and wrongs of relieving the distress of the poor in Passus IX, his method is to spiral round the issue with endless excruciating precision of qualification, lifting the discussion into a larger and larger context by his constant reiteration of "but . . . but . . . " ("but," not "thus," is his favorite connective) so that in the end a larger truth is revealed—that human beings must give so that other human beings need not ask. Langland's analysis of the hypocrisies of "official" charity towards the poor, and the self-serving discrimination between the deserving and the undeserving poor on which it is based, is well matched in Blake's denunciation of the sanctimoniousness of the systems of poor relief in operation in his day, designed to make the rich feel complacent about their kindness more than to relieve the sufferings of the poor:

> Compell the poor to live upon a Crust of bread by soft mild arts
> Smile when they frown frown when they smile & when a man looks pale
> With labour & abstinence say he looks healthy & happy
> And when his children sicken let them die there are enough
> Born even too many & our Earth will be overrun
> Without these arts.   (*Four Zoas,* 80:9–14)

These are the instructions given by Urizen to his daughters, who work incessantly at the labor of the material world.

Since Blake's ideas about "contraries" have been alluded to, it may also be pertinent to mention a passage later in Langland's poem, often regarded as theologically naive, where he invokes a doctrine of contraries to argue that the Incarnation was necessary not just for man's sake but for God's sake too—that God was not complete in his divinity until he had partaken of humanity and learnt what hot and cold, joy and sorrow, pain and pleasure were, and what might be the sorrow of death (C.XX.217–38). The human, in Blake's terms, is an emanation of the divine, and perhaps for Blake vice versa too.

"Minute Particulars"

As poet-visionaries, both Langland and Blake live much of the time in an imagined futurity. But they are rooted too in the reality of what Blake calls the "minute particulars" of human experience.[45] If they have hope it is not because they have withdrawn their eyes from the horror. They have what the Italian Marxist Gramsci described, in a memorable phrase, as what all ameliorists must have—"optimism of the will, pessimism of the intelligence."[46]

Let me conclude by demonstrating this in drawing attention to another striking kinship between Langland and Blake, in the fact that for both poets the fullest bitterest experience of what man has made of man in the unpitying materialistic world of law and reason is in the suffering visited upon oppressed workers, especially women. For Blake the visionary experience of their pain is in the coal and iron mines of the Industrial Revolution, where "multitudes were shut / Up in the solid mountains & in rocks which heaved with their torments" (*Four Zoas*, 70:28–29), and above all among the women working in the brick-factories around London as the city advances street upon squalid street into the countryside around. Their voice is heard in the lamentation by Vala, the emanation of Luvah, before Urizen, king of light, who presides over this strict world of regulation:

> "O Lord wilt thou not look upon our sore afflictions
> Among these flames incessant labouring, our hard masters laugh
> At all our sorrow. We are made to turn the wheel for water
> To carry the heavy basket on our scorched shoulders, to sift
> The sand and ashes, & to mix the clay with tears & repentance"
> (*Four Zoas*, 31:4–8)

So too Langland, his compassion rubbed raw by the indignities and oppressions to which workers were subjected in the little industrial revolution of his day, the rapid expansion of the cloth-making industry in London, focuses on the plight of women who are pressed into service doing the worst and worst-paid jobs, spending nearly all they earn as clothworkers on their rent, and eking out a living doing odd jobs of carding and combing, patching and washing clothes, peeling reeds to make tapers, meantime feeding their children on thin gruel and porridge—cold in winter, hungry always,

>   That reuthe is to rede or in ryme shewe
>   The wo of this wommen that wonyeth in cotes. (C.IX.82–83)

These people do not appear again in English poetry until Blake. These two poets knew how the tyranny of the materialistic order worked, and who paid the price. As Blake asked, through the mouth of Enion,

> "What is the price of Experience do men buy it for a song
> Or wisdom for a dance in the street? No it is bought with the price
> Of all that a man hath his house his wife his children
> Wisdom is sold in the desolate market where none come to buy
> And in the witherd field where the farmer plows for bread in vain."
>   (*Four Zoas*, 35:11–15)

Pushed to the margins of the literary canon, these two poets seem to me to have uniquely and extraordinarily in common what all poets must desire to have—the power to see clearly, to speak eloquently of what they see, and yet to remain hopeful.

Notes

This essay is the substance of the sixth Morton W. Bloomfield Memorial Lecture, which I gave in the Barker Center at Harvard University on Wednesday 17 October 2001. I was very honored to be invited to give the lecture. I had known Morton Bloomfield for many years before I arrived to take up my post at Harvard in 1985. He welcomed me warmly, was generous to me in every way, and I looked forward to many more years of close friendship.

1. Morton W. Bloomfield, *Piers Plowman as a Fourteenth-Century Apocalypse* (New Brunswick, NJ: Rutgers University Press, 1961).

2. *Tolstoy's Diaries*, ed. and trans. by R. F. Christian, 2 vols. (London: Athlone Press, 1985), 1:241 (February 25, 1889).

3. *Piers Plowman*, C-text, XX.432–40. The edition used (with some modernization of spelling in the quotations) is *Piers Plowman, by William Langland: An Edition of the C-text*, by Derek Pearsall, York Medieval Texts, 2nd series (London: Edward Arnold, 1978). N.B., *wreke*, 'revenged'; *kynde*, 'nature'; *halve-bretherne* are brothers in blood (that is, all human beings) but not in baptism; *mercy*, 'impose a proper fine on' (but with an ambiguous alternative syntax, 'mercy [shall reign over]').

4. *Passus* (plural *passūs*), 'paces' or 'steps,' is the word used by the poet or by scribes to divide the poem into sections.

5. The fullest account of the evidence for the corrupt state of the archetypal B-text, and of the B-text that Langland used in revision, is in *Piers Plowman: The B Version*, ed. George Kane and E. Talbot Donaldson (University of London: Athlone Press, 1975), introduction, 98–127.

6. Bibliographical and other information about Blake's poems is taken from the edition of *The Poems of William Blake* by W. H. Stevenson, text by David V. Erdman (London: Longman, 1971), and from *The Poetry and Prose of William Blake*, ed. David V. Erdman, commentary by Harold Bloom, rev. ed. (Garden City, NY: Doubleday, 1970). The latter is used for citation.

7. Erdman, in *Poetry and Prose*, 737–39.

8. For some of the meanings that Blake attaches to "Emanation" and "Spectre," see *The Four Zoas*, 4:7, 49:11; *Jerusalem*, 4:14, 6:3, 74:10. *The Four Zoas* is cited by manuscript page number and line number, *Milton* and *Jerusalem* by line number of the text that accompanies the successive plates.

9. The reasoning power is described in *Jerusalem*, pl. 64.20, as that which divides human beings as individuals and breaks the bonds of love.

10. A powerful example is *The Four Zoas*, 106:18–40.

11. *Tolstoy's Diaries* (see n. 2 above), 1:240 (February 23–26, 1889).

12. *Jerusalem*, 91:41–44. Los is fairly consistently in Blake the representative of the Imagination, which is the divine in man.

13. See C.XII.11–XIII.128, and the notes in the edition cited. Medieval scribes, of course, did not mark direct speech with speech-marks, and neither did Blake.

14. See, for example, *The Four Zoas*, 82:23–34.

15. *Jerusalem*, 44:15 and 95:20; *Jerusalem*, 10:20.

16. *Blake Records*, ed. G. E. Bentley (Oxford: Clarendon Press, 1969), 268.

17. See, for example, *Jerusalem*, 86:50–88:48. There is also a charming allusion to the help that Blake's wife Catherine gave him with his engravings in the tincturing that Enitharmon does "with beams of blushing love" for the line that Los draws upon "the walls of shining heaven" (*Four Zoas*, 90:36).

18. C.XX.20–24. N.B., *of his gentrice*, 'in accordance with his noble birth'; *haberjon*, 'coat of mail'; *yknowe*, 'recognized'; *plates*, 'armor'; *prikiare*, 'horseman.'

19. It is a matter of poetic metaphor, not theology: Langland would draw the line at this in Blake: "Hence thou art cloth'd with human beauty O thou mortal man. / Seek not thy heavenly father then beyond the skies" (*Milton*, 20:31–32).

20. *Milton*, 23:55. Compare *Jerusalem*, 40:17–18: "Albions Western Gate is clos'd: his death is coming apace! / Jesus alone can save him."

21. See Peter Ackroyd, *Blake* (London: Sinclair-Stevenson, 1995), 174.

22. See, for example, *Jerusalem*, 98:28–35. Blake describes, in the opening "Address to the Public" in *Jerusalem* (3:36–48), how he first threw off the "bondage of Rhyming" but then also the monotony of isochronous metrical intervals, and produced instead "a variety in every line, both of cadences & number of syllables . . . Poetry Fetter'd, Fetters the Human Race!"

23. The references to the poet's wife in *Piers Plowman* are at C.V.2 and C.XX.472. Some scholars regard them as the "generic" wife-references of a poet-persona.

24. *Blake Records*, ed. Bentley, 543.

25. *Blake Records*, ed. Bentley, 519.

26. "A Vision of the Last Judgment," in Blake's Notebook, printed in *Poetry and Prose*, ed. Erdman, 555.

27. See *Milton*, 22:4–14; 35:42–67 and 42:29–30; 36:16–17.

28. "Auguries of Innocence," 1–2, in *Poetry and Prose*, ed. Erdman, 481. Compare *Jerusalem*, 71:15–19.

29. See B.XV.3–10. For the B-text (this passage is not in the C-text) the edition used is that of A. V. C. Schmidt, *William Langland, Piers Plowman: A Parallel-Text Edition*, vol. 1 (London: Longman, 1995).

30. For a summary account of what is known and supposed of Langland's life, see Ralph Hanna III, *William Langland*, Authors of the Middle Ages 3 (Aldershot: Ashgate/Variorum, 1993), 1–24. The information about Langland's parentage is on a blank leaf at the end of a manuscript of *Piers Plowman*, Trinity College, Dublin, MS 212 (D.4.1). The information about the ordination of "William de Rokayle" is in a document discovered by Lister Matheson and reported by him in a paper so far unpublished: see the note by Ralph Hanna in "Emendations to a 1993 'Vita de Ne'erdowel,'" *Yearbook of Langland Studies* 14 (2000): 185–98 at 187.

31. Geoffrey Shepherd, "The Nature of Alliterative Poetry in Late Medieval England," in *Proceedings of the British Academy* (1970): 56; (1972): 57–76 (see pp. 69–76).

32. The episodes based on these "showings" are to be found at C.Prol.19, B.VII.15, B.XIII.227 and 315, C.XVIII.20. See Shepherd, "Nature of Alliterative Poetry," 73.

33. This striking interpretation of the "autobiographical" apologia in C.V is made by Anne Middleton in "Acts of Vagrancy: The C Version 'Autobiography' and the Statute of 1388," in *Written Work: Langland, Labor, and Authorship*, ed. Steven Justice and Kathryn Kerby-Fulton (Philadelphia: University of Pennsylvania Press, 1997), 208–317. For an explanation in precisely autobiographical terms of Ymaginatif's claim, "I have folwed thee, in feith, thise fyve and fourty wynter" (B.XII.3), see John Burrow, "Langland *Nel Mezzo del Cammin*," in *Medieval Studies for J. A. W. Bennett*, ed. P. L. Heyworth (Oxford: Clarendon Press, 1981), 21–41.

34. See C.V.2 and XX.472, C.V.5–104, C.XI.167–95, C.XXII.189–98. Some scholars, it must be said, read the "autobiographical" references in the poem as functions of an authorial persona. There may be some that work in this way, but it would be an oversimplification to suppose that all do.

35. I adapt here a famous observation made by Panofsky about Jan van Eyck: "No residue remains of either objectivity without significance or significance without disguise." See Erwin Panofsky, *Early Netherlandish Painting: Its Origins and Character*, 2 vols. (Cambridge, MA: Harvard University Press, 1953), 1:180.

36. See *Milton*, 32:10–38; *Jerusalem*, 25:12, 31:13, 49:65–71.

37. *Four Zoas*, 33:11–12. Compare 105:17–19.

38. See *Jerusalem*, 43:11–15.

39. See C.XIV.131–217, C.XIX.274–329, C.XX.403–42.

40. C.XXII.380–86. N.B., *fyndynge*, 'provision for livelihood'; *hap and hele*, 'good fortune and good health'; *gradde*, 'cried out aloud.'

41. *The Vision of William concerning Piers the Plowman, in Three Parallel Texts*, ed. Walter W. Skeat, 2 vols., Early English Text Society (Oxford: Oxford University Press: 1886), 2:285.

42. *The Letters of William Blake*, ed. Geoffrey Keynes (London: Hart-Davis, 1968), 11. The picture appears on p. 15 of *Blake's Notebook*, edited in facsimile with transcription by Geoffrey Keynes (New York: Cooper Square Publishers, 1970). There is a reproduction of the picture in Peter Ackroyd, *Blake*, plate between pp. 336 and 337 (see also p. 334).

43. *Milton*, 40:33. For Blake's ideas about "contraries," see *Jerusalem*, 10:7–16, 17:33–47.

44. *Letters of Willam Blake*, ed. Keynes, 168–69.

45. It is a common phrase in Blake's writing. A particularly clear exposition of its meaning can be found in *Jerusalem*, 55:60–66.

46. A phrase attributed to Antonio Gramsci in an essay by Perry Anderson on Sebastiano Timpanaro in the *London Review of Books*, 5 Oct. 2001.

WHAT WAS THE *MAIDEN IN THE MOOR* MADE FOR?
[2004]

RICHARD FIRTH GREEN

Maiden in the mor lay,
in the mor lay,
    seuenyst fulle,
    seuenist fulle.
Maiden in the mor lay—
in the mor lay—
    seuenistes fulle ant a day.

Welle wa[s] hire mete.   MS: *wat*
Wat was hire mete?
    Þe primerole ant the—
    Þe primerole ant the—
Welle was hire mete.
Wat was hire mete?
    Þe primerole ant the violet.

Welle wa[s] hire dryng.   MS: *wat*
Wat was hire dryng?
    Þe chelde water of [þe]—   MS: gap at þe
    Þe chelde water of þe—
Welle was hire dryng.
Wat was hire dryng?
    Þe chelde water of þe welle-spring.

Welle was hire bour.
Wat was hire bour?
    Þe rede rose an te—
    Þe rede rose an te—
Welle was hire bour.
Wat was hire bour?
    Þe rede rose an te lilie flour.

    Maiden in the moor lay has probably attracted more discussion than any other Middle English lyric of comparable length, yet on the surface it is the most transparent of medieval poems. Philologically speaking, it presents virtually no problems for a modern reader once due allowance has been made for its fourteenth-century spelling. In terms of its lexicon, only one word, *primerole* (referring apparently to either a "field daisy" or, more probably, a "cowslip"),[1] has not survived down to standard modern English, and only two others, *meat* and *well*, have undergone significant semantic change, both having more specialized senses now than in the fourteenth century. *Meat*, indeed, is a textbook example of such specialization, while *well*, as an adjective, is now restricted to contexts involving health (we can say "my brother is well," but not "my dinner is well"). The situation is much the same syntactically: *full*, in the sense of "whole," can no longer follow the noun or phrase it qualifies (we say "a full day's work," but not "a day's work full"). Similarly we can only begin a sentence with an adjectival complement (*wel was her mete*) in self-consciously poetic or emphatic contexts: "black is the color of my true love's hair"; "obtuse is what he was!" Apart from Ronald Waldron's attempt to gloss "in the mor lay" as "lay dead in a moorland grave,"[2] I know of no interpretation of the poem that depends, even partially, upon a philological explanation. Indeed, *Maiden in the moor lay* is a poem that can safely be placed before even the most inexperienced undergradates with the reasonable expectation that they will be able to work out its denotative meaning for themselves.

Nor is *Maiden in the moor lay* very much more difficult textually, if by this we mean the deciphering of the words as they were originally copied down. True, it appears in a unique manuscript (a single detached leaf bound at the beginning of Oxford, Bodleian Library, MS Rawlinson D.913), heavily abbreviated and written out as prose, but, unlike a number of the other items on the same leaf, it is reasonably legible and its general form is quite clear.[3] The only real editorial debate concerns the number of repetitions to be accorded to its various elements. A contemporary Latin *contrafactum* of *Maiden in the moor lay* has long been known, and Thomas G. Duncan has recently used its comparatively more formal manuscript presentation to reconstruct an original version of the English poem with nine-line stanzas,[4] as against the traditional seven-line-stanza version printed by Rossel Hope Robbins and others.[5] The main difference involves a division and partial repetition of Robbins's seventh line, so that "þe primerole ant the violet" becomes

>   þe primerole ant the—
>   þe primerole ant the—
>   Ant the violet.

Duncan's case for the curious stutter in his last line depends upon our accepting that the three-syllable phrase *violet* could not have been accommodated to the same musical phrase as the six-syllable Latin *cantando gloria*—an argument probably best left for the musicologists.

Maiden in the moor lay does certainly present textual problems in the sense that the original copy is difficult to contextualize. A single detached leaf cannot tell us a great deal, particularly when we know nothing of how Richard Rawlinson, the man who donated it to the Bodleian Library, first acquired it. The paleographers date it to the first half of the fourteenth century, and the dialectologists, with even less to go on, tell us that its language is southern,[6] but these are very meager scraps of information. The one specific topographical detail on the leaf is a reference to Coggeshall in Essex, a thriving wool town with an annual fair and a wealthy Cistercian Abbey nearby. Though John Burrow is right in suggesting that R. L. Greene's claim that the Rawlinson poems were written down in this abbey is "purely speculative,"[7] I do believe this reference can help us narrow down the leaf's source to some degree. The sentence in question is "Ne sey neruer suchaman a Iordan was and wente he to gogeshale panyles" (I never saw such a man as Jordan was and he went to Coggeshall penniless).[8] Burrow comments: "a man who goes to a fair without money is either a rogue or a fool; so perhaps these lines introduced some comic or picaresque narrative" (3). However, the sentence could equally well be complete as it stands—a satirical squib directed against some well-known local figure, a *parvenu* who from humble beginnings had risen to become a man of consequence, possibly in the wool trade, or in the abbey. In this regard it is perhaps worth noting that the Abbot of Coggeshall in 1341 was a man named William Joldayn.[9] If this identification is correct, the Rawlinson poems need not have been written down in Coggeshall itself, but the leaf can probably be ascribed to the area delimited by Jordan's reputation.

If (to adapt I. A. Richards's terminology) the vehicle of *Maiden in the moor lay* is largely transparent, it will be immediately obvious that its tenor is by contrast completely opaque. This is a relatively unusual situation for readers of medieval poems to find themselves in; our labors are often directed to deciphering an intransigent vehicle in the expectation that its tenor will prove relatively unproblematic. This fact would hardly in itself be sufficient to explain the critical attention *Maiden in the moor lay* has attracted were it not that its vehicle is of a kind we have long been conditioned to respond to: reclining young women, moorland settings, wild flowers, and crystal springs are likely to fire our poetic synapses, particularly when these things are presented to us in such mesmeric rhythms. I suspect that many critics, confronted with this mysterious little poem, have experienced the kind of discomfort so amusingly articulated by Richards's pupil William Empson: "unexplained beauty arouses an irritation in me, a sense that this would be a good place to scratch."[10]

Perhaps the best place for us to start scratching would be with one of the most notorious attempts to wrest a meaning from *Maiden in the moor lay*, that of D. W. Robertson, Jr. In a seminal article called "Historical Criticism," published in the *English Institute Essays* for 1950,[11] Robertson made *Maiden in the moor lay* the subject of a "historical" *explication de texte*: "On the surface, although the poem is attractive, it cannot be said to make much sense. Why should a maiden lie on a moor for seven nights and a day? And if she did, why should she eat primroses and violets? Or again how does it happen that she has a bower of lilies and roses on the moor? The poem makes perfectly good sense, however, if we take note of the figures and signs in it." For Robertson, then, the poem was written in a kind of elaborate code (he, indeed, refers to it as an *aenigma*, "a riddle"):

> The number seven indicates life on earth, but life in this instance went on at night, or before the Light of the World dawned. The day is this light, or Christ, who said "I am the day." . . . The moor is the wilderness under the Old Law before Christ came. . . . The maiden drank the cool water of God's grace, and her bower consisted of the roses of martyrdom or charity and the lilies of purity with which late medieval and early renaissance artists adorned pictures of the Blessed Virgin Mary, and, indeed, she is the Maiden in the Moor.

I omit from this quotation Robertson's solution to the primroses and violets; the first, somewhat surprisingly, is "a figure of fleshly beauty" while the second is "a Scriptural sign of humility"—an apparent self-contradiction that Robertson blithely ignores. Fifty years later one might suppose that such a reading would be little more than a historical curiosity, but historical criticism has cast a surprisingly long shadow: for example, Karen Saupe's 1998 edition of *Middle English Marian Lyrics* includes *Maiden in the moor lay* in a section devoted to Marian *chanson d'aventure* and love quests, and her notes are taken straight from Robertson.[12]

Only eight years after "Historical Criticism," and at a time when Robertson's star was still very much in the ascendant, E. Talbot Donaldson challenged his reading before the same English Institute:

> I cannot find that the poem, as a poem, makes any more sense after exegesis than it did before, and I think it makes rather more sense as it stands than the critic allows it. Maidens in poetry often receive curiously privileged treatment from nature, and readers seem to find the situation agreeable.... It seems no more legitimate to inquire what the maiden was doing on the moor than it would be to ask Wordsworth's Lucy why she did not remove to a more populous environment where she might experience a greater measure of praise and love.[13]

After nearly a page in the much same vein, Donaldson concludes: "Robertson asks the question why should she eat primroses? I hope that if I answer, 'Because she was hungry,' it will not be said of me that a primrose by the river's brim a yellow primrose was to him, and it was nothing more."

In retrospect, the Robertson/Donaldson exchange over *Maiden in the moor lay* has come to epitomize the whole controversy over Historical Criticism, and I suspect that relatively few scholars nowadays would be ready to defend Robertson's reductive pedantry against Donaldson's irreverent belle-lettrism, but in some ways it is a pity that the job of responding to Robertson on this particular public stage did not fall to someone with a more analytical turn of mind. In fact, Morton Bloomfield's essay "Symbolism in Medieval Literature," written a year or so earlier, offers a far more cogent rebuttal of the Robertsonian method.[14] Donaldson had begun his essay with the words, "I am not aware of any valid theoretical objection to the use of patristic exegesis in the criticism of medieval literature," apparently unaware of Bloomfield's telling argument that "the multileveled system of symbolism provides no criterion of corrigibility except, as in the case of biblical exegesis, tradition" (94). Given that there was no "science of symbolism" in the middle ages and that "the commonest objects and animals embrace a wide variety of meanings, often contradictory" (88), there is no way, Bloomfield points out, "to correct any particular interpretation" (94). "With sixteen meanings for the peacock," he asks, "who is to decide between them" (95)? To give a comparatively simple example: if I wished to employ Robertson's own methods to defend a quite different reading of *Maiden in the mor lay*, I might begin with the fact that in Prudentius's *Psychomachia* (an allegory of Christian charity if ever there was one) Luxuria does battle with Sobrietas armed with violets, roses, and flower-buds,[15] and go on to argue that the Maiden is thus an allegorical representation of worldliness. In fact, R. J. Schoeck, in a piece published in the same year as "Historical Criticism," and apparently quite independently,[16] had used the exegetical method to show that the *welle-springe* was "Christus irrigans *or* the

Holy Spirit, *or* true doctrine *or* baptism [my italics]," and to interpret the maiden herself as "any member of the church, who is of pure faith, regardless of sex." All this, to adapt Robert Frost, begins to look rather like a game of tennis without a net.

Bloomfield's other major objection to the exegetical method was that it was emphatically not, despite Robertson's own appropriation of the term, "historical." At no period is there much evidence that medieval readers in general approached secular, as opposed to scriptural, material exegetically (or that secular writers would have expected them to do so), but for the later middle ages in particular, even with the Bible, "the symbolic as opposed to the literal approach . . . is [un]characteristic, . . . except perhaps in sermons" (87). Bloomfield's singling out of sermons is astute, since we know that medieval preachers, like modern ones, did sometimes allegorize secular subjects for the moral edification their congregations, including popular lyrics as well as folktales. One conspicuous example is a poem that in some ways resembles *Maiden in the moor lay*: "At a sprynge-wel vnder a þorn, . . . Þer by-syde stant a mayde." An early fifteenth-century priest called John Dygoun told his parishioners that "the bubbling fountain beneath the hawthorn is Christ's open side whence blood and water issued forth . . . the maiden standing there is the Blessed Virgin Mary,"[17] and as a result Carleton Brown felt quite justified in printing this poem in his *Religious Lyrics of the Fourteenth Century*.[18] But, as Siegfried Wenzel puts it, the real question is not "whether such poems were *interpreted* spiritually; we know that they were, by medieval preachers and by their modern successors. Rather, we should like to know whether they were *originally made* and used for purposes other than religious and moral teaching."[19] Bloomfield would certainly have agreed that, *pace* Robertson, this is the real task of the historical critic: "the really serious reason for opposing this procedure," he had written, "is the historical exactitude which is claimed or implied. One can, if one chooses, interpret a work of literature in any way whatsoever, provided that one does not claim to be thereby revealing the conscious intention of the author" (92).

Now that it has once more become respectable to talk about authorial intention, even if no longer quite in Bloomfield's sense,[20] how might we set about fulfilling his demand for historical exactitude in respect to *Maiden in the moor lay*? One obvious solution is to look for contemporary references to the poem. Barely a year after Robertson published his reading of the poem, R. L. Greene laid a historicist mine that threatened to demolish it far more effectively than anything in Donaldson's much better-known rebuttal, and twenty-two years later, after Siegfried Wenzel had laid a second one, this particular channel became effectively closed to exegetical traffic. Greene pointed out that Richard de Ledrede, bishop of Ossory (1317–60), had composed a Marian hymn, *Peperit virgo*, to be sung to the tune of *Maiden in the moor lay*.[21] This might not seem to affect the situation either way, were it not that the bishop had supplied his collection of hymns with a brief preface:

> Be advised, reader, that the Bishop of Ossory has made these songs for the vicars of the cathedral church, for the priests, and for the clerks, to be sung on the important holidays and at celebrations in order that their throats and mouths, consecrated to God, may not be polluted by songs which are lewd, secular, and associated with revelry, and, since they are trained singers, let them provide themselves with suitable tunes according to what these sets of words require. (Greene, 1974, p. iv)

This preface certainly seems to imply that Richard de Ledrede regarded *Maiden in the moor lay* as one of these lewd, secular songs associated with revelry, for which his own *Peperit virgo* would make a decorous substitute, and Greene himself had no hesitation in claiming that *Maiden in the moor lay* was "in its own time . . . definitely and explicitly regarded as secular and indeed profane" (Greene, 1952, p. 504).

This conclusion has not gone unchallenged. Joseph Harris, who, as we shall see, had his own reasons for rejecting Greene's conclusion, argued that the phrase "mayde y[n] the moor [l]ay" scribbled in the margin of the Red Book of Ossory opposite the first line of *Peperit virgo* indicates nothing more than the tune that the Marian hymn was to be sung to, and that it did not necessarily imply that *Maiden in the moor lay* was one of the lewd and secular songs to which the bishop had referred.[22] This is, of course, a possibility, if a rather difficult one. Most surviving *contrafacta* form contrasting secular/religious pairs (though it is certainly not always the case that the secular version is the earlier); a surviving English example is the two lyrics written one after the other in BL, London, British Library, MS Harley 2253: "Lytel wot hit any mon / how loue hym haueþ ybounde" (a poem about the Redemption) and "Lutel wot hit any mon / hou derne loue may stonde" (a poem of unrequited love). However, there *are* pairs of *contrafacta* in which both are secular or both are religious, particularly when, as here, the language differs between the original and its copy.[23] R. L. Greene himself was unconvinced by Harris's argument,[24] and most subsequent critics, perhaps glad of a convenient stick with which to beat D. W. Robertson, have accepted his position.

Three years after Harris's article appeared, Siegfried Wenzel supplied an important final piece of evidence.[25] In a Worcester Cathedral manuscript (MS F.126), he came across a sermon (copied ca. 1360) on the text "the stone was rolled away" (Mark 16:4), which began with a description of the Golden Age, drawn from Ovid and Boethius:

> In the first age, that of gold, men lived in mutual love, innocence, moderation, and peace. Their food was fruit that grows of its own: figs and dates, apples, nuts, and acorns. And what was their drink? The answer appears in a certain song, namely a *karole* that is called "þe mayde be wode lay." Note in the margin: "þe cold water of þe well spryng" (72)

Though it is an argument from silence, Wenzel claimed that this passage scotched any identification of this maid with either the Virgin Mary or Mary Magdalene since both are mentioned in quite different terms elsewhere in the sermon. He also pointed out that world *karole*, even though it is not used in the precise metrical sense defined by R. L. Greene, must mean that *Maiden in the moor lay* was thought of as a dance song (the primary meaning of *carol* at this period). The variant "be wode lay" for "in the mor" he explained, convincingly, as being due to oral circulation. And finally, he ventured his own identification of the maiden: "[the preacher's] use of a single line from the song, as well as the general character of the sermon collection make it most likely that she is a figure of medieval folk belief, perhaps some woodland or water sprite or *fée*" (74). In this he aligns himself with a suggestion that had first been made by John Speirs.[26]

If the Ossory and Worcester references provide the only direct medieval evidence we have about the earliest reception of *Maiden in the moor lay*, there still remain two potential indirect sources to be explored: its manuscript context, and its contemporary analogues.

Quite apart from the Jordan reference, the Rawlinson leaf offers a suggestive context for understanding *Maiden in the moor lay*; it contains ten other poems or fragments of poems, a number of which have been regularly anthologized, particularly: *Of everykune tre* (number 1), *Icham of Irlaund* (7), *Alnist by þe rose* (10), and *Al gold Jonet is þin her* (11). "Can we not take the other Rawlinson pieces as themselves providing the necessary context within which to consider this particularly difficult case?" asks John Burrow,[27] and with this in mind continues, "the general character of the collection . . . seems to be secular, even popular, with a predominance of songlike or danceable pieces mostly concerned with food or drink or love" (18). His conclusion, however, if admirably circumspect, is somewhat anticlimactic: "it is certainly true to say that 'Maiden in the mor lay' *sounds* as if it were the same sort of poem as the other Rawlinson pieces. . . . But similarity of manner does not exclude difference of meaning." The furthest Burrow is prepared to go is that its immediate context "does lend some circumstantial support to secular interpretations of *Maiden in the mor lay*. So far as this argument is concerned, Robertson is more likely to be wrong than right but one can say no more than that." Burrow himself does not consider contemporary analogues to the central figure in *Maiden in the moor lay* perhaps because other maidens in medieval literature portrayed in situations that resemble hers are few and far between; indeed neither of the two that have been proposed offers a very compelling parallel.

In 1951, E. M. Tillyard was so struck by a resemblance between *Maiden in the moor lay* and a passage in the B-text of William Langland's *Piers Plowman* describing Mary Magdalene, that he wrote a letter to the *Times Literary Supplement* about it:[28]

> And also Marie Maudeleyne by mores lyvede and dewes,
> Ac moost thorugh devocion and mynde of God Almyghty.
> I sholde noght thise seven daies siggen hem alle
> That lyveden thus for Oure Lordes love many longe yeres.
>   (B-text, 15:294–97)[29]

In the corresponding passage of his C-text Langland also mentions Mary of Egypt in this same situation (C.17:23–24). Unfortunately, the Middle English word *mores* in Langland's passage is clearly a word meaning "the root of a plant" (MED *mōr(e* n.(1), 1.(a)), not "wasteland, moor, heath" (MED *mōr* n.(1), 1.(a)), a prosaic fact that undermines much of the force of the comparison. A second problem is that neither Mary Magdalene nor Mary of Egypt can easily be thought of as maidens; not only were both notoriously licentious in youth (Mary of Egypt indeed was a prostitute), but by the time of their exiles to the wilderness both were mature, not to say elderly, women. In the third place, neither lived in the wilderness for a mere seven nights (Mary Magdalene was there for thirty years and Mary of Egypt for forty-eight).[30] Finally, as Tillyard himself admits, "the lyric is so fragile that one hesitates to make its subject penitential."

Similar problems are raised by John Speirs's attempt to link the *Maiden in the moor lay* with the mother of *Sir Percyvell of Galles*,[31] who, while her son is away for a year dallying with a *femme fatale* called Lufamour,

> Drynkes of welles ther thay spryng,
> And gresse etys, withowt lesyng—
> Scho liffede with none othir thyng
> In the holtes hare. (1776—79)[32]

Again, and self-evidently, we are not dealing with a maiden here, nor, more to the point, with someone who finds her exile in the wilderness in any way a pleasant experience. Speirs had earlier argued that Percyvell's mother is a supernatural creature (122), but this is surely wrong. If the young knight has fairy blood in his veins it seems far more likely to come from his father's side (as is the case with such romance heroes as Degaré, Le Bel Inconnu, and Tyolet).

With Tillyard and Speirs we exhaust attempts to discover a contemporary medieval analogue for *Maiden in the moor lay*, but others, not to be outdone, have looked further afield—searching for her in the recorded folklore of later centuries: Peter Dronke and Ronald Waldron in the world of folk dance and games; Joseph Harris and Karl Reichl among folksongs and ballads. Peter Dronke looks furthest afield (both geographically and rhetorically):

> What is a moor-maiden? She is a kind of water sprite living in the moors; she appears in a number of German legends, especially from Franconia. It is appropriate that the English song should be a dance-song, as one of the commonest legends associates the moor-maiden with a dance. She tends to appear at village dances in the guise of a beautiful human girl, and to fascinate young men there, but she must always return to the moor at a fixed hour, or else she dies. Sometimes it is only for one hour in the week that she is allowed to leave the moor and mingle with human beings—this perhaps is also why in the song she waits in the moor "sevenistes fulle ant a day."[33]

It is difficult to know where to begin with all this: I suppose by pointing out that the moor maiden does *not* appear in *a number* of German legends, from Franconia or anywhere else, and that even if she did there is no reason to suppose that she could tell us much about a *karole* copied down in fourteenth century England somewhere near Essex. The fact is that the Grimm brothers and their successors record many stories of water spirits (*Nixen*) behaving much as Dronke describes (though they generally arrive at their village dances in trios or pairs, rather than as single maidens), but in only a very few cases are they specifically called moor maidens (*Moorjungfern*).[34] The Grimms tells us there are moor maidens from Poppenrode in the Rhön Mountains, but *they* don't count because they're really will-o'-the-wisps (*Irrlichtern*), and they are very definitely plural in any case.[35] From the same area Wolf tells of three *Moorjungfern* visiting a festive dance in Wüstensachsen,[36] and Fensch has a story of a single dance-loving *Moorjungfer* from Oberelsbach, though he regards a local folksong about her as inauthentic.[37] It is upon such slender foundations as this that Dronke builds his extraordinary reconstruction of a medieval performance of *Maiden in the moor lay*:

> At the start of the song a girl playing the moor-maiden would have lain as if asleep. The dancers approach her, admiring her beauty, and some of the young men try to wake her, at first in vain. Then, perhaps, a bell strikes: suddenly "sevenistes fulle ant a day" are up, she comes of her own accord into the centre of the round, and is at once the acknowledged queen of the dance. An admirer offers her dainties to eat, which she refuses; he offers her primroses and violets, and these she pretends to eat. Another admirer offers her wine—again she makes a gesture of refusal; instead she goes to drink at her well. All the dancers make her a bed of flowers; she reclines on it; the bell sounds once more, and she falls back into sleep, again as out of reach as at the beginning. (196)

After this, it seems almost churlish, even sacrilegious, to step into the circle and point out that there isn't a shred of evidence for any of it.

A quick word about water sprites, since not only Peter Dronke but John Speirs (63), raise the possibility that the maiden in the moor was one, and subsequent commentators have usually at least paid lip service to their suggestion. Unlike Germany (and Scotland, Ireland, and Wales), England has a rather meager tradition of water-spirit stories and beliefs. Neither Ernest Baughman nor Katherine Briggs, each using the Stith Thompson system of cataloguing folk types and motifs, can find enough under F420 (*Water-spirits*) to fill much more than a page;[38] indeed, if one were to exclude Celtic material and (in Baughman's case) stories that may well have arrived in North America from Germany, there would only be a few lines. Gerald Bordman's *Motif-Index of the English Metrical Romances* has *no* entry under F420.[39] Furthermore, there is no recorded Middle English word that means "water spirit" (the nearest is *nicker*, from OE *nicor*, a "sea monster," and in Middle English that means "a mermaid"), and very few stories about water spirits survive from Medieval England. There is the Lady of the Lake, of course, but she is part of a common stock of Arthurian material; Walter

Map tells a story about a water spirit, but he clearly got it from Wales,[40] and Gervase of Tilbury has a fascinating account of water spirits called *draci* who carry off mortal women, but he locates these in the Rhone.[41] There is some evidence for local superstitions concerning wells and springs (though no more so than on the Continent), but water spirits, it must be said, generally inhabit lakes and rivers; that the central figure in *Maiden in the moor lay* merely drinks "þe chelde water of þe welle-spring" rather counts against her being a *Nixe* than otherwise.

Joseph Harris supplies our second folkloric interpretation (though he prefers to see *Maiden in the moor lay* as an art song rather than a folksong). His interpretation depends upon a ballad known all over Europe which treats a period of penance in the wilderness assigned to Mary Magdalene by Jesus; its only English representative is a rather debased version, called *The Maid and the Palmer* (Child 21). The parallels that Harris adduces between this ballad figure and the maiden in the moor, however, are certainly far closer than anything in Dronke. Almost everything about Mary Magdalene's life is of course apocryphal, but this ballad, judged at least against the orthodoxy of the *Golden Legend*, is apocryphal apocrypha. If Jesus is a flesh and blood figure, as he clearly is in many versions of the ballad, then the seven years of penance contradicts the biblical account in which Mary is granted instant absolution: "And he said unto her, 'thy sins are forgiven'" (Luke 7:47); if, on the other hand, Jesus is a posthumous vision, then the conventional account of Mary's period in the wilderness has been radically altered:

> In the meantime Saint Mary Magdalene, moved by her wish to live in contemplation of the things of God, retired to a mountain cave which the hands of angels had made ready for her, *and there she dwelt for thirty years*, unknown to anyone. *There she found neither water, nor herb, nor tree, whereby she knew that Jesus wished to sustain her with heavenly meats* [my italics], allowing her no earthly satisfaction. But every day the angels bore her aloft at the seven canonical hours, and with her bodily ears she heard the glorious chants of the heavenly host. Then, being filled with this delightful repast, she came down to her grotto, and needed no bodily food.[42]

In the ballad, however, both the time period and nature of the sustenance are changed. Here, for instance, is a French version:

> Mary Magdalene,
>   You will spend seven years in the woods of Beaune.

My lord and father,
> On what shall I live there?

Mary Magdalene,
> On roots in the wood.

My lord and father,
> What shall I drink there?

Mary Magdalene,
> The dew of the wood.

My lord and father,
> What shall I sleep on?

Mary Magdalene,
> Upon juniper.

At the end of this period, Jesus returns to find out how she has managed:

Mary Magdalene,
> How are you doing?

My lord and father,
> I'm doing very well.[43]

The parallels between this ballad and *Maiden in the moor lay*, if not exact, seem very close. There still remain, of course, the old problems that Mary is not a maiden and the fact that the period is seven years not seven days (though in one version of the ballad it is as short as six weeks), but the real difficulty lies elsewhere: after Greene and Wenzel, is it still possible to read *Maiden in the moor lay* as a religious poem, even one whose religious basis is as folkloric as this?

Though the Ossory and Worcester references seem to rule out our reading *Maiden in the moor lay* (at least in its original form) as a conventional religious poem, this is not to say that a connection between the poem and later Mary Magdalene ballads is impossible. Medieval folk beliefs were sometimes incorporated into more orthodox religious settings, and it is entirely credible that ballads about Mary Magdalene might have drawn on popular motifs. The wide-spread medieval exemplum of the monk and the bird, which makes use of the popular tradition that time passes more slowly in fairyland to illustrate the Christian concept of eternity, provides an excellent illustration of this principle at work.[44] In Jacques de Vitry's version a very devout abbot struggling to understand how it is that the saints are not bored in heaven is carried away by the beautiful singing of a bird in the monastery garden; in the evening he returns to his cloister only to find that no one recognizes him and after consulting the monastic archives discovers that three hundred years have passed since he first entered the garden.[45] The notion that what seems like a brief stay in fairyland is really a lengthy passage of time on earth is well attested in medieval sources (it occurs in Walter Map's story of King Herla, for instance, as well as the French romance of *Guingamour* and in the English *Thomas of Ercledoune*), and there is even a later Welsh folktale that preserves a specifically fairy version of the monk and the bird.[46] In these terms, it might well be argued that the striking parallels that Harris points to between *Maiden in the moor lay* and later Mary Magdalene ballads can better be explained as the deliberate religious incorporation of originally popular and traditional motifs.

The third of our folkloric interpreters of *Maiden in the moor lay* is Ronald Waldron.[47] Waldron believes that the maiden is dead (an idea that also appeared in Schoeck's letter to the TLS) and he cites a number of nineteenth-century children's singing games (*Boorman, Green Gravel, Jenny Jones, Old Roger, Wallflowers*) to support this view. While it is true that some of these make use of a question-and-answer pattern similar to *Maiden in the moor lay*, the actual questions are quite different, and his overall interpretation seems inherently unlikely. Corpses are not usually portrayed as eating and drinking, even metaphorically—as Hamlet says of the dead Polonius, "not where he eats but where he is eaten"—and it is also difficult to understand why a dead girl should lie in her grave for only seven nights and a day.

A final folkloric parallel is adduced by Karl Reichl, in an essay on popular strains in early Middle English love lyric; he notes a number of similarities between *Maiden in the moor lay* and a ballad called the *Enchanted Maiden* from Spain and Portugal.[48] The central figure in this ballad is a girl who has been bewitched and forced to live in the wilderness until rescued by a knight (who in some cases turns out to be her brother). Here, too, we have the question-and-answer motif, though the content of the questions is rather more distant from the Middle English poem:

> "What did you eat, my daughter,
>   What did you eat, my life?"
> "I ate with the wolves,
>   I ate what they ate." (55)

After all, such sets of questions and answers, even ones concerning food and drink, are not uncommon in the ballad tradition:

"And what did she give you, Lord Randal, My son?
And what did she give you, my handsome young man?"
"Eels fried in a pan; mother, mak my bed soon,
For I'm wearied wi huntin, and fein wad lie down."[49]

My other reservation concerns a too-easy elision of seven years with seven days: while seven years seems an entirely appropriate period to suffer enchantment, seven days does not. In fact, Reichl is not really arguing for any direct connection between this Iberian ballad and the Middle English poem, but merely using it to show how *Maiden in the moor lay* "'makes sense' in a context of folk poetry," and his conclusion, that "the Portuguese parallel does however point, to my mind unambiguously, to an interpretation of the poem as a folksong, as a specimen of popular poetry, popular in origin rather than simply popular in style" (56), is one which carries conviction.

The value of all four of the folkloric interpretations we have discussed (and particularly those of Harris and Reichl) lies less in any specific parallels they adduce than in a contextual idiom they help to establish. Karin Boklund-Lagopoulou, the poem's most recent commentator, shares Reichl's conviction that *Maiden in the moor lay* is a medieval folk song, and she neatly spells out this logic for us:

> If *Maiden in the mor lay* is quoted casually in a sermon and specifically mentioned as the melody for one of Bishop Ledrede's songs, then it itself must have been a well-known song; if the same poem shows up as one of the Rawlinson lyrics, then we have good reason to believe that other Rawlinson lyrics are also popular songs. If these medieval popular songs show the same internal stylistic traits as more recent material gathered from oral tradition, we are justified in guessing that they are folksongs.[50]

Boklund-Lagopoulou might be accused of eliding two distinct senses of the word *popular* here ("widely known" and "of the people"), and none of her propositions, except perhaps the first, is entirely watertight (certainly they would be unlikely to convince the skeptic). Nevertheless, it seems fair to say that, insofar as there is one, her position represents the current orthodoxy on *Maiden in the moor lay*.

The difficulty with most folkloric interpretations of medieval texts is that they must attribute a quite unprovable antiquity to surviving popular beliefs. There is no way to demonstrate that any given ballad, folktale, or children's game recorded in the nineteenth century (or even two or three hundred years earlier) preserves anything at all from the Middle Ages unless a clear medieval analogue for it still survives. Mere suggestive similarities, as Bella Millett has argued, are susceptible to all kinds of ideological manipulation.[51] That said, the only medieval "maidens" I know of who fulfill the dual criteria of being associated with the natural world and being disapproved of by the church are fairies, and I believe that Siegfried Wenzel is quite justified in reading *Maiden in the moor lay* as a *fée* (1974, p. 74). The disapproval of the church is easily illustrated: "what shall we say of those superstitious wretches," asks a fourteenth-century English preacher's manual, "who claim that at night they see the most beautiful queens and other girls dancing in the ring with Lady Diana, the goddess of the heathens, who in our native tongue are called *elves*?"[52] The natural setting is less unchallengeable since romances often portray fairies as courtly, urbane figures, living in elegant dwellings; even Launval, when he first encounters his fairy mistress, Triamour, "vnder a fayr forest" (222), finds her lying in a splendid pavilion, "all of werk of Sarsynys" (266), adorned with gold and precious stones.[53] The late thirteenth-century English chronicler, Robert of Gloucester, however, probably better represents popular tradition when he speaks of "a kind of spirit, or perhaps creature [a maner gostes, wiȝtes as it be]" that "is often seen on earth in wild places, . . . and that men call elves" (2748–54).[54] Thus the relatively uncourtly *Thomas of Ercledoune* locates its hero's fairy encounter "by Huntley Banks" under the mysterious "Eldone tree":

> Thomas rathely vpe he rase,
> And he rane ouer þat Mountayne hye;
> Gyff it be als the storye sayes,
> he hir mette at Eldone tree.
> He knelyde downe appone his knee,
> vndirnethe þat grenwode spraye,
> And sayde, "lufly ladye, rewe on mee,
> Qwene of heuene, als þou wele maye."
> Than spake þat lady, Milde of thoghte,
> "Thomas, late swylke Wordes bee;
> Qwene of heuene ne am I noghte,
> ffor I tuke neuer so heghe degre.
> Bot I am of ane oþer countree."[55]

It is amusing to note that if Robertson errs in taking a fairy maiden in the moor to be the Virgin Mary, he is in good company; Thomas of Ercledoune makes the same mistake.

I am not sure that we can go much further than this in terms of a detailed identification of the central figure of *Maiden in the moor lay*, but perhaps some progress may be made with Siegfried Wenzel's question about the purposes for which such poems were originally made and used. And if we are to confine ourselves strictly to medieval folkloric sources, there is one rather unlikely place where we might look for an answer: the trial of Joan of Arc in 1430 and its nullification twenty-five years later.

During her third interrogation session, in Rouen on Saturday, February 24, Joan was asked about a certain tree near Domremy, the village of her birth. Here is the record of her response:

> She replies that quite close to the village of Domremy is a tree called "the Ladies' Tree"—others call it "the Fairies' Tree" (in French *des Fées*)—near to which there is a spring. And she has heard tell that people sick with fever drink from this spring and go there in search of water to recover their health. She has seen that herself, but she does not know whether they were healed by it or not. Further, she says that she has heard that invalids, if they are able to walk, divert themselves at this tree. It is a beautiful tree called a beech, from which there comes the may (in French *le beau may*), and it used to belong to the Sir Peter de Bourlement, Knight. Further, she said that she sometimes went to divert herself there with other young girls and at that tree she made garlands for the image of the blessed Mary of Domremy. She has often heard from the old people—though not from anyone in her own family—that the fairies used to frequent this tree. And she says that she has heard a woman called Joan, wife of Aubery, the Mayor of the village, and her own godmother, say that *she* has seen the said fairies there; Joan herself says she does not know whether that is true or not. Further, she says that she has never seen the said fairies at the tree, as far as she knows, and as for seeing them elsewhere, she does not know whether she has seen them or not. Further, she says she has seen garlands hung on the branches of the tree by young girls, and that she herself sometimes hung them there with the other young girls; sometimes they took them away with them, and sometimes they left them. Further, she says that after she knew that she was called to go to France, she spent little time on games and diversions—as little as she could. And she doesn't know that since reaching maturity she ever danced near the tree, but she might well have danced there a few times with the children, or sang there more than danced.[56]

Her accusers incorporate this account into two of the articles with which she is later proposed to be charged, accusing her first of conversing with evil spirits at the tree (1:197–98; 2:164–65); and second of going there alone, often at night (or if by day during the times of divine service), and dancing about the tree and the spring, weaving garlands of various herbs and flowers, while uttering various songs and incantations—these garlands when hung in the branches of the tree would always mysteriously disappear by morning (1:198–99; 2:165–66). The thrust of these accusations seems to be, not only to associate Joan with the practice of witchcraft but to imply that she engaged in morally questionable activities, such as might undermine her claim to be a virgin. Joan indignantly denies the construction put on her behavior, but her response to these articles adds little to her previous testimony.

Valuable as Joan's testimony itself is, it pales beside the interrogation of the villagers of Domremy and the surrounding area, held in January and February 1455 as part of the process of nullifying Joan's original condemnation.[57] As a detailed medieval account of a folk ritual, it is completely unparalleled. The witnesses appear before a formal inquisition, but in relatively benign circumstances: neither they nor any of their neighbors are on trial and, indeed, their interrogators are eager to hear that their activities were quite innocent. While they can be evasive at times, they are generally far franker than they would be if they had been involved in a formal indictment. Altogether thirty-four people appear before the commission. Ten of them know, or affect to know, nothing at all about the so-called Ladies' Tree. By and large these are the well-to-do and the educated: three are priests, two are esquires, and there is a nobleman and a king's sergeant among the others; the status of one married couple is not given, but only one member of this group identifies himself as a laborer. Of the remaining twenty-four, only eight admit to hearing that fairies once frequented the tree and six of these are laborers or their wives; the other two are an artisan (a roofer) and a knight called Sir Albert D'Ourches. Here is Sir Albert's testimony: "He said that he has heard others say that in the old days fairies (*fées*) used to go beneath the tree, although he has never heard that anyone has seen them. He also said that he has never heard tell that Joan went beneath the tree, since it was before she was spoken about—twenty or thirty years before— that he'd heard that the *fées* used to go to divert themselves beneath the tree" (301). A seventy-year-old laborer called Jean Morel adds that "he had heard others say that women and fairy creatures, called *fées*, went in the old days to dance under that tree, but it is said that after St. John's Gospel was read and spoken they didn't go there any more" (254). Beatrice D'Estellin says that they do not go there nowadays, "because of their sins" (258). No one, predictably enough, is prepared to say that fairies are still seen at the tree, though Michel Le Buin does say that he doesn't know whether they went away, because they are not accustomed to go there now (293). Many of the witnesses who know the tree as the Ladies' Tree (the *arbre des dames*) adopt an obvious folk etymology to account for its name: it is called the Ladies' Tree, they explain, because the wife of the Lord of Bourlemont used to go there with her ladies-in-waiting. Whether they all believed this blatant rationalization is of course another matter.[58] Perhaps the most remarkable testimony of this kind comes from Jeannette, the widow of a clerk:

> She said on oath that the tree in question was called the Ladies' Tree, because it is said that in the old days a certain lord, called Sir Peter Gravier, Knight, Lord of Bourlemont, used to meet with a certain lady who was called *Fée* beneath that tree, and they spoke together. And she said that she heard this read in a romance. (264–65)

It is intriguing to imagine that the Lords of Bourlemont may have had their own version of the Melusine legend, though Jeannette is perhaps not the most reliable of witnesses to this.

From a number of testimonies we can form a clear idea of the appearance of the tree itself. It was a beech tree, greatly bowed down (270), standing near a grove (262); an ancient tree—"no one has heard tell of a time when it was not there" (285); a wonderful tree, of lovely appearance (256); a beautiful tree (258). Gérardin d'Épinal, a sixty-year-old laborer, waxes positively lyrical: "He has once or twice seen the temporal lords and ladies of Domremy in springtime take bread and wine and go to eat beneath the tree, because then it is as beautiful as lilies; it covers a large area [*est dispersa*] and its leaves and branches come right to the ground" (279). While most know this tree as the Ladies' Tree, five have a different name for it; they call it "the Ladies' Portals"; the Latin is *ad lobias dominarum* or the *lobie dominarum*—no vernacular equivalent is provided (283, 285, 288, 292, and 308). The implication of this may well be that some saw, or at one time had seen, the tree as a gateway to fairyland.

Except for Sir Albert D'Ourches and a priest called Henri Arnolin, all the witnesses, whether or not they know anything about stories of fairies, know about the festivities connected with the tree; most, indeed, had participated in them personally. From these twenty-two accounts it is not difficult to assemble a composite picture of what actually went on.[59] At various times in the Spring and Summer but particularly on the fourth Sunday in Lent, known as *Laetare Sunday*, or, locally, as the *Sunday of the Springs*, the young people, and probably the children, *infantes* (256), from Domremy and from of the surrounding villages (305), would go on excursions to the tree. There, they would sing, dance, and picnic. Jean Morel adds that they picked flowers (254), a detail repeated as hearsay by Nicholas Bailly (302), a local notary and hence a particularly good witness. The Lord of Bourlemont and his wife may well have presided over the festivities, particularly the main one on *Laetare Sunday*. Isabelle de Gérardin, who was in service to them, remembers this clearly (283), and perhaps it was they who provided the tablecloth that so impressed itself on Mengette Joyart's memory (285). The picnic consisted mainly of bread, apparently small loaves that the mothers baked specially (279), and the Bourlements brought wine and eggs (272).[60] After their feasting, singing, and dancing, the young people made their way back to the village by way of a local spring, called the *Fons Rannorum*,[61] where they paused to drink the waters. The notary, Nicholas Bailly, recalls once seeing the young girls return and how happy they were ("semel vidit ipsas filias dicte ville redire jocose de illa arbore") (302). Though members of both sexes participated, the depositions leave a strong impression that the festivities were dominated by the young women and their mothers.

There are three depositions, however, that seem to point to something rather more ritualized than a mere springtime picnic. Though their details are far from clear and their cultural significance is now somewhat opaque they provide a fascinating glimpse of another world. Michel le Buin, a forty-four-year-old laborer, says that the young men and women of the village go to the tree on the *Sunday of the Springs* "and make their springs for play and diversion" ("suos fontes ludendo et spaciando faciunt"); a little later he adds that Joan herself, when she was little, would go there to "make her springs" ("ad faciendum suos fontes") (293). This phrase is repeated by Gérard Guillemette, a forty-year-old laborer: the young people, he says, go to "make their springs" and divert themselves at the tree (274). It has been plausibly suggested that this refers to some kind of ceremonial decoration of the spring (*Procès en nullité*, 5:149), perhaps similar to later English well-dressing rituals.[62] Even more curious is a phrase used by another middle-aged laborer, Colin Colin: sometimes, he says, they "make a man of May" ("et aliquando faciunt unum hominem de maio") (288). We might guess that this was some kind of effigy made of branches and flowers, but what significance was attached to it and how it was employed remains a mystery. In this context, however, we might recall that Joan herself remarked that the tree was the source of *le beau may*, and guess that we are dealing here with some form of the common custom of young people's gathering greenery in the Spring with which to adorn their houses.[63]

These documents furnish irrefutable evidence that in early fifteenth-century Lorraine young people went out into the woods in the Spring, they picked flowers, they drank springwater, they ate, they danced, and they sang; we cannot be sure that they made a bower (perhaps the overarching beech tree made such a thing unnecessary), but we know from other sources that such bowers, or *feuillées*, were sometimes constructed.[64] All this was done in a space belonging to *dames*, whom Joan herself may have associated with St. Catherine and St. Margaret, but whom others certainly thought of as fairies. The imagery of *Maiden in the moor lay* resonates strongly with such details, and, *mutatis mutandis*, it is not difficult to imagine it as one of the songs that Joan and her friends might have sung and danced to.

I am not, of course, suggesting that we can make a wholesale transposition of these springtime rites from Joan's birthplace to early fourteenth-century Essex, but their broad outlines are suggestive. The practice of maying in particular seems to have been very widespread and very long lasting. We might, for instance, compare Joan's recollection of making garlands for the Blessed Mary of Domremy with John Aubrey's observation that in seventeenth-century Oxford, "on May-day the young maids of every parish carry about their parish Garlands of Flowers, w[ch] afterwards they hang up in their Churches."[65] There are few nonliterary references to maying in England before the Tudor period,[66] but a passage in Robert Mannyng of Brunne's *Handlyng Synne* (1303) suggests that something like this practice must certainly have been known at the time of our lyric:

> 3yf þou euer yn feld or yn towne
> Dedyst floure gerlaund or corowne,
> To make women gadere þere
> To se whyche þat feyrer were,
> Þys ys a3ens þe comoundement
> And þe halyday for þe ys shent.
> Hyt ys a gaderyng for lecherye
> And ful gret pryde & herte hye.[67]

We may also catch occasional glimpses of such a practice in the distorting mirror of courtly romance. In Chaucer's *Knight's Tale*, Arcite, for instance, sings a snatch of song whilst performing "his observaunce to May" (1500):

May, with alle thy floures and thy grene,
Welcome be thou, faire, fresshe May,
On hope that I some grene gete may (1510–12).[68]

This does not sound much like *Maiden in the moor lay*, but since it has been transposed into a courtly idiom that is hardly surprising. The same might be said of a lyric inserted into a detailed description of maying in the town of Mainz in the early thirteenth century given by Jean Renart in his *Roman de Guillaume de Dole*:

Down there by the shore,
My friends, now let us sing.
Ladies are dancing there
And my heart is very light.
My friends, now let us sing
In honor of May.[69]

In part, it is the very fact that *Maiden in the moor lay* sounds so different from these courtly refashionings that might lead one to conclude that its origins are genuinely popular.

I am not finally claiming that *Maiden in the moor lay* is an actual medieval maying song; I do not think we have sufficient evidence to make anything like so precise an identification. I have merely been trying here to paint a general picture of the kind of social and cultural context in which the poem might be imagined. It belongs, I believe, with a group of popular festive dance songs (in which I would include *Of everykunne tree* and *At a wellspring under a thorn*), songs that were inevitably sanitized when they were transposed into a courtly idiom. What the Domremy inquisition offers us is a comparatively unretouched source: it tells us that young people in the late middle ages went out into the countryside to sing and dance together, but, more importantly, that when they did so they were quite aware that they might be penetrating a magical, fairy world. To imagine *Maiden in the moor lay* as one of their songs is not to solve its riddles, still less to dispel its mysteries, but it is, I hope, to bring its magic into clearer focus.

Notes

1. Joseph Harris, "'Maiden in the Moor Lay' and the Medieval Magdalene Tradition," *Journal of Medieval and Renaissance Studies* 1 (1971): 59–87 at 78.

2. Ronald Waldron, "'Maiden in the Mor Lay' and the Religious Imagination," *UNISA English Studies* 29 (1991): 8–12 at 10.

3. See Peter Dronke, "The Rawlinson Lyrics," *Notes and Queries* 206 (1961): 245–46 at 245.

4. Thomas G. Duncan, "The Maid in the Moor and the Rawlinson Text," *Review of English Studies*, n.s., 47 (1996): 151–62.

5. *Secular Lyrics of the XIVth and XVth Centuries*, ed. Rossell Hope Robbins, 2nd ed. (Oxford: Clarendon Press, 1955), 12–13 (no. 18); Robbins himself prints the poem with a six-line first stanza, but seven-line versions of stanzas 2, 3, and 4.

6. W. Heuser, "Fragmente von unbekannten Spielmannsliedern des 14. Jahrhunderts, aus MS. Rawl, D. 913," *Anglia* 30 (1907): 173–79 ("der dialekt des schreibers ist zweifellos südlich," 178).

7. J. A. Burrow, "Poems without Contexts," in *Essays on Medieval Literature* (Oxford: Clarendon Press, 1984): 1–26 at 4; (originally published in *Essays in Criticism* 29 (1979): 6–32).

8. Dronke, Rawlinson Lyrics, 245.

9. G. F. Beaumont, *A History of Coggeshall, in Essex* (London: Marshall Brothers, 1890), 106.

10. William Empson, *Seven Types of Ambiguity*, 3rd ed. (Harmondsworth, Penguin Books, 1961), 9.

11. D. W. Robertson, "Historical Criticism," in *English Institute Essays*, 1950, ed. A.S. Downer (New York: Columbia University Press, 1951), 3–31 at 26–27.

12. *Middle English Marian Lyrics*, ed. Karen Saupe (Kalamazoo: Medieval Institute Publications, 1998), 154–55 (no. 81).

13. E. T. Donaldson, "Patristic Exegesis: The Opposition," in *Critical Approaches to Medieval Literature; Selected Papers from the English Institute, 1958-1959*, ed. Dorothy Bethurum (New York: Columbia University Press, 1960), 1–26 at 20–24.

14. Morton W. Bloomfield, "Symbolism in Medieval Literature," in Morton W. Bloomfield, *Essays and Explorations: Studies in Ideas, Language and Literature* (Cambridge, MA: Harvard University Press, 1970), 82–95 (reprinted from *Modern Philology* 56 (1958): 73–81).

15. *Prudentius [Oeuvres]*, ed. M. Lavarenne, 4 vols. (Paris: Société d'édition 'Belles lettres,' 1943–51), 3:62 (ll. 326–27).

16. R. J. Schoeck, "The Maid of the Moor," *Times Literary Supplement* 2575 (June 8, 1951): 357.

17. Siegfried Wenzel, *Preachers, Poets, and the Early English Lyric* (Princeton: Princeton University Press, 1986), 231.

18. Carleton Brown, *Religious Lyrics of the Fourteenth Century*, 2nd corrected ed. (Oxford: Clarendon Press, 1957), 229 (no. 130).

19. Wenzel, *Preachers, Poets*, 211.

20. See, for example, William Irwin, ed., *The Death and Resurrection of the Author*

(Greenwood, 2002).

21. R. L. Greene, "'*The Maid of the Moor*' in the *Red Book of Ossory*," *Speculum* 27 (1952): 504–6. See also *The Lyrics in the Red Book of Ossory*, ed. Richard L. Greene, *Medium Ævum Monographs*, n.s., 5 (Oxford: Blackwell, 1974), esp. ix–xiii and 15–17, and Theo Stemmler, "The Vernacular Snatches in the Red Book of Ossory: A Textual Case History," *Anglia* 95 (1977): 122–29.

22. Harris, "'Maiden in the Moor Lay,'" 61–63.

23. See R. F. Green, "The Two 'Litel Wot Hit Any Mon' Lyrics in Harley 2253," *Mediaeval Studies* 51 (1989): 304–12.

24. *Lyrics of the Red Book*, ed. Greene, xii.

25. Siegfried Wenzel, "The Moor Maiden—A Contemporary View," *Speculum* 49 (1974): 69–74

26. John Speirs, *Medieval English Poetry, the Non-Chaucerian Tradition* (London: Faber and Faber, 1957), 63.

27. Burrow, "Poems without Contexts," 17.

28. E. M. Tillyard, *Times Literary Supplement* 2571 (May 11, 1951): 293.

29. William Langland, *The Vision of Piers Plowman*, ed. A. V. C. Schmidt, 2nd ed. (London: J. M. Dent, 1995), 260.

30. Both, moreover, were sustained by miraculous food: Mary of Egypt by three small loaves and Mary Magdalene by experiencing the joy of heaven. *Jacobus de Voragine, The Golden Legend*, trans. Granger Ryan and Helmut Ripperger (New York: Longmans Green, 1941), 228–30 and 355–64.

31. Speirs, *Medieval English Poetry*, 134–35.

32. *Ywain and Gawain, Sir Percyvell of Gales, The Anturs of Arther*, ed. Maldwyn Mills (London: J. M. Dent, 1992), 147.

33. Peter Dronke, *The Medieval Lyric*, 3rd ed. (Woodbridge: D.S. Brewer, 1996), 195–96.

34. See *Handwörterbuch des Deutschen Aberglaubens*, ed. Hanns Bächtold-Stäubli and Eduard Hoffman-Krayer, vol. 6 (Berlin: De Gruyter, 1934/1935), 566 (*Moorjungfern*); and Vol. 9 (Berlin: De Gruyter, 1938/1941), 135–39 (*Wassergeister: Irrlichter*) and 156–59 (*Wassergeister: Tanz des Nixen*).

35. *Deutsche Sagen herausgeben von den Brüdern Grimm*, ed. Heinz Rölleke (Frank-furt: Deutscher Klassiker, 1994), 161.

36. J. W. Wolf, *Beiträge zur deutschen Mythologie*, vol. 2 (Göttingen: Dieterichsche, 1857), 284.

37. E. Fensch, "*Volkssage und Volksglaube in Unterfranken*," in *Bavaria*, ed. Joseph Heyberger, vol. 4, i (Munich: Cotta'schen: 1866), 204.

38. Ernest W. Baughman, *Type and Motif-Index of the Folktales of England and North America*, Indiana University Folklore Series 20 (The Hague: Mouton, 1966), 224–26, and Katherine Briggs, *A Dictionary of Fairies* (London: Allen Lane, 1976), 477.

39. Gerald Bordman, *Motif-Index of the English Metrical Romances*, FF Communications 190 (Helsinki: Suomalainen Tiedakatemia, 1963).

40. Walter Map, *De Nugis Curialium*, ed. and trans. M. R. James, revised by C. N. L. Brooke and R. A. B. Mynors (Oxford: Clarendon Press, 1983), 149ff.

41. Gervase of Tilbury, *Otia Imperialia: Recreation for an Emperor*, ed. and trans. S. E. Banks and J. W. Binns (Oxford: Clarendon Press, 2002), 718–21.

42. *Golden Legend*, 360–61.

43. Harris, "'Maiden in the moor lay,'" 64–65 (my translation).

44. Frederic C. Tubach, *Index Exemplorum*, FF Communications 205 (Helsinki: Suomalainen Tiedeakatemia, 1981), 268 (no 3378).

45. Jakob von Vitry, *Die Exempla aus den Sermones feriales et communes*, ed. Joseph Greven (Hiedelberg: Carl Winter, 1914), 18.

46. T. Gwynn Jones, *Welsh Folklore and Folk-Custom* (Cambridge: D. S. Brewer, 1930; repr. 1979), 59–60.

47. See above, n. 2.

48. "The 'Charms of Simplicity': Popular Strains in the Early Middle English Love Lyric," in *Individuality and Achievement in Middle English Poetry*, ed. O. S. Pickering (Woodbridge: D. S. Brewer), 50–56.

49. *The English and Scottish Popular Ballads*, ed. Francis James Child, 5 vols. (Boston and New York: Houghton, Mifflin, 1882–98), vol. 1, p. 158 (12A:3).

50. Karin Boklund-Lagopoulou, *"I have a yong suster": Popular Song and the Middle English Lyric* (Dublin: Four Courts, 2002), 46–47.

51. Bella Millett, "How Green Is the Green Knight," *Nottingham Medieval Studies* 38 (1994): 138–51.

52. *Fasciculus morum: A Fourteenth-Century Preacher's Handbook*, ed. and trans. Siegfried Wenzel (University Park: Pennsylvania State University Press, 1989), 579.

53. Thomas Chestre, *Sir Launfal*, ed. A. J. Bliss (London: Nelson, 1960), 59–60.

54. *The Metrical Chronicle of Robert of Gloucester*, ed. W. A. Wright, 2 vols., Rolls Series (London, 1887), 1:196.

55. *Thomas of Erceldoune*, ed. Ingeborg Nixon, 2 vols. (Copenhagen: Akademisk Forlag, 1980–1983), vol. 1, p. 32 (Thornton, ll. 81–93).

56. *Procès de Condamnation de Jeanne d'Arc*, ed. Pierre Tisset and Yvonne Lanhers, 3 vols. (Paris: Société de l'histoire de France, 1960–1971), vol. 1, pp. 65–66 [Latin] and vol. 2, pp. 65–68 [French].

57. *Procès en nullité de la condamnation de Jeanne d'Arc*, ed. Pierre Duparc, 5 vols. (Paris: Société de l'histoire de France, 1977–1988), vol. 1, pp. 244–315.

58. Cf. nineteenth-century references to fairies as *demoiselles* in the Ariège; Peter Sahlins, *Forest Rites: The War of the Demoiselles in Nineteenth-Century France* (Cambridge, MA: Harvard University Press, 1994), esp. 41–48.

59. Where at least four witnesses agree on a detail, I have not felt it necessary to give page references.

60. These eggs are particularly interesting, since they were officially forbidden in Lent.

61. This seems to be a Latinization of a local name, "Fontaine aux Rains," whose meaning is far from clear. *Spring of the Redcurrant Bushes* has been suggested, but it

may equally well mean *Boundary Spring* (see *Procès en nullité*, vol. 5, p. 149, n.1).

62. This activity was known elsewhere in France in the Middle Ages, see Roger Vaultier, *Le folklore pendant la guerre de Cent Ans d'après les Lettres de rémission du Trésor des chartes* (Paris: Guénégaud, 1965), 52 and xviii–xix.

63. See Vaultier, *Folklore*, 64–69.

64. See Jean Dufornet, *Adam de la Halle à la recherche de lui-même ou le Jeu dramatique de la Feuillée* (Paris: Enseignement supérieure, 1974), 59–60, and *Tobler-Lommatzsch, Altfranzösisches Wörterbuch*, 11 vols. (Stuttgart: Steiner Verlag, 1915–2002), s.v. *foillie*.

65. John Aubrey, *Remaines of Gentilisme and Judaisme*, ed. James Britten (London: Folklore Society, 1881), 18.

66. See Ronald Hutton, *The Rise and Fall of Merry England* (Oxford: Oxford University Press, 1994), 29–30. Similar ceremonies were associated with Midsummer Eve (39); compare Reginald Pecock, *The Repressor of Over Much Blaming of the Clergy*, ed. Churchill Babington, 2 vols., Rolls Series (London: Longman, Green, Longman, and Roberts, 1860): "men of the cuntre yplond bringen into Londoun in Mydsomer eue braunchis of trees fro Bishopis wode and flouris fro the feeld, and bitaken tho to citeseins of Londoun forto therwith araie her housis" (1:18). The *Repressor* was written ca. 1440.

67. Robert Mannyng of Brunne, *Handlyng Synne*, ed. Idelle Sullens, Medieval Texts and Studies 14 (Binghamton, NY: State University of New York Press, 1983), p. 27, lines 997–10,004. The commandment referred to is the third, but the holiday is not specified.

68. Geoffrey Chaucer, *The Riverside Chaucer*, general ed. Larry D. Benson (Boston: Houghton Mifflin, 1987).

69. "Tout la gieus, sor rive mer, / conpaignon, our dou chanter! / Dames i ont bauz levez, / mout ai le cuer gai. / Conpaignon, or dou chanter / en l'onor de mai!" (4164–69); Jean Renart, *Le Roman de la rose ou de Guillaume de Dole*, ed. Félix Lecoy (Paris: Champion, 1979), 128.

Marketing Óðinn's Mead in a Strange Land
[2005]

Roberta Frank

Of Odin's mead let draught
In England now be quaff'd.
    Egill, *Hǫfuðlausn* (ca. 936)[1]

Have you ever heard a poem worth more?
    Gunnlaugr, *Sigtryggsdrápa* (ca. 1002)[2]

In 1960, an official at the Vatican Library, glancing at the signature on the letter of introduction before her, sighed tenderly: "Ah, il Bloomfield!" "Molto intelligente, un uomo molto profondo, molto (squinting her eyes) fi-lo-so-fi-co."[3] But what exactly did she mean? Not the everyday Italian sense of the word—"calm, serene"—nor the academy's "adept in philosophical discourse," though both would have been true; no, she was using the adjective in its etymological sense, recalling—as we have been over the past three days—a scholar filled with a love of wisdom, who had a poet's instinct for true relationships, who sought to see things whole. Or as the apocryphal book of Ben Sira put it two millennia earlier: "A mind firmly backed by intelligent thought is like the stucco decoration on the wall of a colonnade" (22.17). Such a thinker, perceiving an absence in what others find a full and satisfactory now, responds with an act of creation, completing, as an ornament does, the designer's plan. How Morton Bloomfield would have delighted in the energy and flow of this gathering, the interweavings that Al-Andalus called *iqtibas* "the kindling of one flame from another," twenty-nine finely constructed stations of power strung out unpredictably across a much trampled field, tiny turbines spinning this way and that, first one, then another area catching the light.[4]

    A Bloomfield seminar could produce similar sparks. He once opened a discussion of Cynewulf's signed poetry by asking when, in what contexts, could a medieval poet say "I" or attach his own name to his work. And then we were off, on a dizzying, exhilarating journey from Pindar, Virgil, Ephrem the Syrian, Orientius, and seventh-century Hebrew liturgical poets, past the courtly Carolingians, the satirical Normans, Turoldus, Chrétien de Troyes, Marie de France, and Gottfried von Strassburg, not stopping until we had reached the first-person voices of Dante, the anagrams of Guillaume de Machaut and Thomas Usk, and Rembrandt's several score self-portraits. This was the company I wanted to keep.

The skalds came later. And what a boastful bunch they were—emphatically non-anonymous, full of self-praise and bragging relentlessly about their liquid assets.[5] For only they possessed Óðinn's regurgitated mead of poetry, spirits filched by the one-eyed god himself. No water boys they, but suppliers and servers of an otherworldly drink; its recipe, devised by some very naughty dwarfs, called for a mixture of blood, honey, and divine spittle. In their asides about verse making, skalds sometimes allude to this myth, a story of multiple murders, shape-shifting, sex with a giantess, and at least five types of bodily fluids, a narrative focused on Óðinn's theft of the mead from the giants and his sharing it with skilled poets.[6]

This potent drink is named in many mythological kennings, or circumlocutions, for poetry.[7] "I am mightily proud," says the skald Steinþórr, "of the anciently made waterfall of horns [drink, mead] of the mediocrity-shy cargo of Gunnlǫð's [giantess's] arms [Óðinn], scanty as it is" (387). "I give Grímnir's gift to gracious Óláfr" (128.1); "I pay him the reward of the fetter-looser" (69.5). The coveted mead is called "Kvasir's blood," "Hrauðnir's payment," "Falr's cup," "ship of the dwarfs," "Dvalinn's strong drink," "Dáinn's mind-wave," "Heiðr's wave," "the swallow of the race of Surtr," "cup of the giant's sons," "the ale of Lóðurr's friend," "Reginn's straight drink," "cargo of Óðinn," "Hrímnir's horn-stream," "fjord of the gods," and "rivers of the joy-hill [breast] of Mímir's friend." In performance, it is figured not as a fresh mountain spring, something a gently reared Muse might sip, but as the upchuck of a bulemic: "Hear the stream of Óðinn's breast rush from my mouth; the find of Þundr is given to me" (93.1); "I let come forth my yeast-river of the husbands of the sea-cliff women [drink of giants]" (69.1); "I make the drizzle of the spears of the aurochs cow pour over my moustache" (43.4). The Mediterranean was a tideless sea; the skald's poetry comes with the force of the Atlantic behind it: "All-father's mash-surf roars" (316.4). The warriors in the hall are all ears, drinking it in: "I dared to bear the bed-price of Óðinn to the prince, so that Yggr's cup came spilling over into the mouths of hearing [ears] of each man" (38.6). In England as elsewhere, this strong drink becomes a kind of weather: "And now it starts to rain with the rain of Óðinn's servants" (43.4); "the rain of the dwarf's comrades ran over the thingmen" (206.11).[8] The more drenched a patron and his entourage, the richer his gifts. The skald's art was marketed within a complex system of exchange, an economy of necessary generosity, whose delicate workings we can only imagine.

The Norse court poet, both friend and employee of his royal host, was an image-maker, a shaper of public opinion; he advertised a prince's ideological platform, showing him as he wished to be seen. Like panegyrists from Simonides on down, the skald sought to catch and keep moments of triumphant joy, of heightened consciousness, in which a ruler seemed illumined by a divine force and his whole person enveloped in a new confidence. Between 935 and 1035, Norse court poets, trimmed to power, made their way to the Scandinavian colonies of Ireland and Britain as well as to Anglo-Saxon England. Kings Æthelstan, Æthelred, Eiríkr of York, and Sigtryggr Silkbeard were early treated to skaldic tributes; during the eighteen years of Cnut's rule, his court at Winchester was probably *the* center in the North for the production and distribution of vernacular panegyrics.[9] Only a small portion of the Norse verse produced in the British Isles, in the century between Æthelstan's expeditions north and Cnut's death, has come down to us. The fragments that survive—datable and localized voices from the conversion-age North—don't always say much, but their very existence points to that of a Norse-accented secular culture in Anglo-Scandinavian England, about which contemporary English records are silent.[10]

By the end of the tenth century, Icelanders had a virtual monopoly as the court poets of the North Sea littoral, a situation reminiscent of the fourth and fifth centuries when Egypt provided the Empire with a stream of professional poets, panegyrists such as Ammonius, Andronicus, Apollo, Claudian, Cleobulus, Collouthos, Christodorus, Eudaemon, Harpocration, Helladius, Heraclides, Horapollon, Olympiodorus, Pallades, Pamprepius, and Triphiodorus, many of them pagan, some Christian or agnostic, who wandered from city to city reciting the praises of emperors and generals.[11] It is difficult to measure the impact of Christianity on poets who, whatever their personal beliefs, engaged passionately with traditional Hellenistic motifs and myths. The final posting of the panegyrist Cyrus of Panopolis, no stranger to the Muses, was as bishop of Cotyaeum in Phrygia; his townsman and contemporary Nonnus composed a forty-eight book mythological epic, *The Dionysiaca*, as well as a hexameter version of St. John's Gospel.[12] "Epi poiêtikêi men sphodra mainontai": "The Egyptians," wrote Eunapius of Sardis in about the year 400, "are mad on poetry."[13] By 1200, historians in Norway and Denmark were applauding, less superciliously, tenth- and early eleventh-century Icelanders for their poetic industry.[14] But, like St. Augustine in North Africa, these skalds did not live in a wholly Christian world.

Around 990, the Icelandic poet Einarr Helgason composed *Vellekla*, a eulogy for the great Jarl Hákon Sigurðarson of Hlaðir, lord of northern Norway. In stanzas rich in mythological lore (I count thirty god names), the jarl, hailed by the poet as a rebuilder of native shrines, is asked to hearken to the boat of the dwarves, the surf of the shelter of the giant, the brine the skald is furiously bailing out of his wine-ship—all expressions for Óðinn's mighty drink (117–24).[15] Ten years later, Iceland, possibly under pressure from Óláfr Tryggvason's proselytizing regime in Norway, agreed to a peaceful mass conversion, one of the stranger events in the history of Christian missions. Those who recommended accepting the new religion seem not to have been greatly worried or affected by the decision either way. It would take time—another generation, or two or three—for the Norse church to establish itself, to develop an organization and a hierarchy where there was none before.[16] But abroad was different.

King Æthelstan, who ruled England between 924 and 939, ran an emphatically Christian shop, restoring monasteries, trading in relics, establishing new bishoprics, and giving generously to religious houses. On the Norse side, he had extensive financial dealings with *pagani* settled in England, married one sister to the Hiberno-Scandinavian king of Northumbria, was accompanied on his Scottish forays by six jarls bearing Scandinavian names, fostered in his household the future king of Norway, Hákon *inn góði* "the Good," and in a charter issued early in his reign styled himself "King of the Anglo-Saxons and the Danes." Like his famous grandfather, Alfred the Great, he attracted foreign scholars and dignitaries to his court, among whom was the Icelandic poet Egill Skallagrímsson. One stanza and a refrain survive from this skald's praise poem for Æthelstan (30):

> Nú hefr foldgnárr fellda,
> fellr jǫrð und nið Ellu,
> hjaldrsnerrandi, harra
> hǫfuðbaðmr, þría jǫfra;
> Aðalsteinn of vann annat,
> allt's lægra kynfrægjum,
> hér sverjum þess, hyrjar
> hrannbrjótr, konungmanni.
>
> Nú liggr hæst und hraustum
> hreinbraut Aðalsteini.

[The battle-sharpener (warrior = Æthelstan), the chief offspring of kings, towering over the land, has now felled three princes; the earth falls under the descendant of Ælle; Æthelstan has done more; all is lower than the king of illustrious birth—this I swear here—O breaker (distributor) of the fire of the wave (gold = generous prince).

Now the highest reindeer path (mountain) lies under the bold Æthelstan.]

Egill's focus on verticality is unusual in Norse court poetry. The English king towers over his land (the adjective *foldgnárr* occurs nowhere else and seems to paint more than words need to say); earth falls under the prince; everyone and everything is lower than he is. Even the highest mountain, over which reindeer move, silently and very fast, now lies under Æthelstan. (A similar over-the-top eulogy in eleventh-century Spain prompted one patron to retort: "I am beneath what you say but above what you think.")[17] Egill's imagery advertises hierarchy, the imperial majesty of his "highness" who, on coins minted after 927 and in charters after 931, styled himself "king of all Britain." But the skald may also have been playing on the king's dithematic name—Aðalsteinn "chief stone," the first element, *aðal-* "chief," represented by *hǫfuðbaðmr* "chief offspring" and the second, *-steinn* "stone, rock, boulder," by "high towering" and "highest mountain." In a Latin acrostic poem, John the Old Saxon, monk and abbot, is thought to have addressed the young prince as *archale saxum* "chief stone," *augusta rupis* "majestic cliff," and *petrinum agmen* "craggy mass."[18] These two onomastic reworkings, one in biblically flavored Latin, the other in mythologically pointed Norse, straddle the Christian/secular divide as evocatively as the tenth-century soapstone mold found in Trendgården, Jutland, from which both crosses and a Þórr's hammer could be cast according to taste.

Neither Dunstan or Æthelwold, who spent formative years at Æthelstan's court, nor a Latin-educated anglicized Dane such as Oda, whom the king made bishop of Ramsbury, would have scented any whiff of pagan ritual in Egill's stanza, or glimpsed even subliminally the spoor of a giant or dwarf. There is no Óðinn, no Freyr, no poetic mead or swarm of valkyries to offend the Christian majority at court; nor is there any Christological imagery to alienate the king's Norse retainers. Still, the poet tries to hedge his patron with divinity as best he can. Egill's parenthetical comment—"Jǫrð [earth] falls under Ella's descendant"—probably called up an erotic image long familiar to both the Mediterranean and North Sea imagination, that of a desirable territory lying under a victorious conqueror.

Skalds from the tenth century on played on the homonymy of lower- and upper-case *jǫrð*: the common feminine noun "earth" and also the giantess-name Jǫrð, Óðinn's much put-upon consort. Egill could have avoided the innuendo by using a metrically suitable neuter or masculine term for "land," such as *lond* "land" itself; but he chose instead to insert the mythologically loaded *jǫrð*. The double entendre surfaces in no fewer than three skaldic praise poems from the tenth century. The first, by Guþormr sindri, composed for Hákon the Good, foster-son of Æthelstan, reports that that king did not abandon "Ónarr's daughter [Jǫrð 'the land'], covered with oak forest" (55.5). The second, by Eyvindr Finnsson, confirms the military seizure of Norway by Hákon Sigurðarson, jarl of Hlaðir, "under whose arm the bride of Val-Týr [Jǫrð 'land'] lies" (62.15). The third, by Hallfreðr Óttarsson and probably for the same jarl, inserts among his mythological kennings for Óðinn's wife a one-line parenthesis echoing Egill's: "Jǫrð ['the land'] goes under [= submits to] the necklace-diminisher [= generous man]" (147.4).[19] The image of conquest as piratical rape continues into the eleventh century and beyond. In 1010, Eyjólfr dáðaskáld reports that the Danish king had set Jarl Hákon's young son Eiríkr over "Óðinn's bride [Jǫrð 'the land']" (191.3)—clearly a chip off the old block. And around 1018, Óttarr svarti praises Óláfr Skötkonung of Sweden in similar terms for seizing a kingdom: "The ruler takes Óðinn's desirable wife [Jǫrð 'the land'], loveless, in the east" (267.2).[20] Egill was more discreet, preferring, like our own marketers, to keep the sex subliminal. It was Edward Bernays, Freud's (double) nephew, who in the 1920s showed advertisers how to tap into the public's unconscious. Betty Crocker cake mix was going nowhere, housewives were resistant, until Bernays had instructions put on the package urging women to add one of their own eggs to the prepared ingredients. The rest is history. Egill promoted Æthelstan as a winner not only by making him the biggest thing on the horizon, but also by encoding his compelling, irresistible virility.

In Egill's parenthesis "Jǫrð falls under Ella's descendant," the two-fold meaning of *jǫrð*—both 'earth' and Óðinn's consort—is followed by the parallel ambiguity of "descendant of Ella." From an English genealogical perspective, Æthelstan's ancestor would have to be Ella, ruler of the South Saxons in the late fifth century; from a Norse point of view, Ella is the ninth-century ruler of the Anglo-Saxon kingdom of Northumbria, slain in 867 by her viking conquerors.[21] Æthelstan had his eyes and hands on that independent province for much of his reign. Egill's words to the king may have been like Pindar's "sharp arrows in the quiver that speak to those that understand," a reminder perhaps that within living memory English rule had been curtailed by Scandinavian force. The skald, like a good salesman, pretends that he has no particular ax to grind, that he is just repeating what everyone already knows.

Toward the end of the stanza Egill makes his own presence known—"I swear to this"—before addressing Æthelstan directly as "breaker of the fire of the wave [gold]"; the English king is a gold-distributor or generous man. The skald's gold-kenning alludes both to Norse myth (the sea-god Ægir at whose feasts glowing gold stood in for firelight) and to legend (the Burgundians who, hounded by the Huns, hid their hoard in the Rhine), stories that shed radiance and glory on his prince. Rulers in skaldic verse are wealth-wounders, gold-scatterers, silver-foes, ring-tossers, and haters of gold, circumlocutions predicated on the notion that wealth, called by Marx "solidified light brought up from the netherworld," should be put into circulation, even onto a poet's arms.

A decade or so later Egill composed a strikingly different panegyric for Eiríkr, the on-and-off-again Scandinavian king of York in the mid tenth century. The skald gives prominence both to the English setting and Óðinn's mead in the two opening stanzas of the poem:

1
Vestr komk of ver,
en ek Viðris ber
munstrandar mar,
svá's mitt of far;
drók eik á flot
við ísabrot;
hlóðk mærðar hlut
munknarrar skut.

[I came west over the sea and I bring the sea of Viðrir's (Óðinn's) mind-shore (breast = mead of poetry); such is my situation/voyage. I launched the oak (ship) at ice-break (spring); I loaded the stern of my trading vessel (breast) with a catch of praise.]

2
Buðumk hilmir lǫð,
ák hróðrs of kvǫð,
berk Óðins mjǫð
á Engla bjǫð;
lofat vísa vann,

víst mærik þann;
hljóðs biðjum hann,
þvíat hróðr of fann.

[The prince offered me hospitality; I have a summons for a praise-poem; I bring Óðinn's mead (poetry) onto the lands of the English. I got the prince praised, certainly I laud him; I ask him for a hearing, because I have set out a praise poem.]

Egill brings Óðinn's mead west from Norway in the stern of a seagoing trading vessel, the hold in which fishermen might store their catch. The skald's breast, figured as this enclosure, contains, as Óðinn's did, a valuable liquid cargo. The patter of first-person pronouns—thirteen in these two opening stanzas—establishes an origin and provenance for the poet's product, while dramatizing his own role as purveyor to royalty. The king who purchases such wares is getting a bargain, a eulogy that would confirm his glory. The leitmotif of Óðinn's mead is heard again toward the close of the poem, as the poet tactfully links his artistry to that of the prince:

20
hrœrðak munni
af munar grunni
Óðins ægi
of jǫru fægi.

[With my mouth I stirred Óðinn's ocean (mead of poetry) from my mind's sea-bed (breast) concerning the polisher of battle (warrior).]

In Old Norse, the same word—*hróðr, lof*—may be used of the king's glory and of the eulogy itself. Praise poetry addresses itself to an individual whose flame is burning very bright, who is in a position to scatter gold in all directions:

17
Brýtr bógvita
bjóðr hrammþvita,
muna hringdofa
hodd-Freyr lofa;
mjǫk's hǫnum fǫl
haukstrandar mǫl;
glaðar flotna fjǫl
við Fróða mjǫl.

[The offerer of hand-stone (gold) breaks (distributes) arm-fire (gold); the treasure-Freyr (prince) will not praise torpor with respect to rings; the smooth pebbles of the hawk's strand (arm) are for him disposable; he gladdens a multitude of sea-men with Fróði's meal (gold).]

Egill depicts Eiríkr's generosity in mythological terms. This "scatterer of river-flames" (gold) is a treasure-Freyr (king) who enriches sea-warriors with Fróði's meal, the gold ground for that legendary Danish ruler by two unhappy giantesses. In earlier stanzas, Eiríkr is portrayed as an athlete in competition, a victor freshly come from battle in the east, a "sword-Freyr," a warrior who fights in person, an effective CEO. With his blade he cuts down an "oak-forest of Óðinn" (troops), as that grim god looks on with approval. Other mythological kennings in Egill's poem name the legendary sea king Haki; Hel, Nari's sister; and Gjǫlp, a giantess; the gods Bragi and Vílir, the goddess Freyja, and a trollwoman and a valkyrie. Beasts of battle—the raven, eagle, and wolf—prowl like hungry athelings through the poem's midsection. These companions twice join forces, three to a stanza:

10
Rauð hilmir hjǫr,
þar vas hrafna gǫr,
fleinn sótti fjǫr;
flugu dreyrug spjǫr;
ól flagðs gota
fárbjóðr Skota;
trað nipt Nara
náttverð ara.

[The prince reddened the sword; there was a lure for ravens; the javelin sought life; bloody spears flew. The offerer of harm to the Scots (Eiríkr) fed the trollwoman's steed (wolf); Nari's sister (Hel, goddess of death) trod the eagle's supper (the slain).]

11
Flugu hjaldrs tranar
of hræs lanar;
órut blóðs vanar
benmǫs granar;
sleit und freki,
en oddbreki
gnúði hrafni
á hǫfuðstafni.

[The cranes of battle (eagles) flew over the stacks of corpses; the lips of the wound-gull (raven) were not lacking in blood. The greedy one (wolf) ripped open a wound, and the wave of the weapon-point (blood) slapped at the raven's head-stem (prow = beak).]

War made good copy, and skalds searched for royal skirmishes that could be blown up into stirring verse.

The mythological bearings of Egill's poem gave a viking prince at odds with the West-Saxon imperium a political alternative, a way of demonstrating difference. Eiríkr is not called "king," as Æthelstan was, but *gramr, jǫfurr, hilmir, vísi, skati, fylkir, þengill, folkhagi,* and *hringbrjótr,* poetic epithets for "prince" evoking an older, more regional model of leadership. Viking rulers at York, Christian and non-Christian alike, worked in close partnership with the Northumbrian church. Æthelstan's appointee as archbishop of York, Wulfstan I (931–56), appears to have welcomed Eiríkr as king in 947, dismissed him under West-Saxon pressure in 948, then invited him back in 950. The thirteenth-century accounts that affirm that Eiríkr was baptized may well be right, on the model of Sir Walter Scott's *Harold the Dauntless,* in which a viking leader, responding to the bishop of Durham's concern for the state of his soul, says simply:

Give me broad lands on the Wear and the Tyne,
My faith I will leave, and I'll cleave unto thine.[22]

Nevertheless, back in Norway, conversion could be a risky move, as Hákon the Good quickly discovered, bringing with it short reigns, nasty ends, and few sociopolitical benefits.[23] (Eiríkr himself was assassinated in 954.)[24] Egill, with excruciatingly good manners, praises his viking king without mentioning sacerdotal duties, the restoration of ruined sanctuaries, or the tending of shrines, pagan or Christian; there is not a single "Gott mit uns" or "Deus vult" or "gods save the king." Apparently the number of deities Eiríkr believed in was not something he or his contemporaries thought a gentleman in his position should advertise.

But mythology was something people had to know, like chess, claret, or cricket, if they wanted to be thought cultured. The Emperor Tiberius famously pressed his grammarians to tell him who Hecuba's mother was, what name Achilles went under when he was among the virgins, and what songs the sirens sang.[25] Egill seems confident that the household troops at Eiríkr's court would be able to identify Nari's sister and Viðrir's sea. In eleventh-century Andalusia, Moses ibn Ezra's most famous wine song included the opaque phrase "Aner's brother's boy," alluding to Genesis 14:13 and 24, which names Aner's brother Eshkol; in Hebrew the common noun "eshkol" means "cluster," whose "boy" or offspring is wine.[26] Eiríkr's retainers had similarly to decipher kennings such as "the steed of the trollwoman" or "the fence of the ski of Haki." This was strangely atavistic language emanating from a king's hall in the shadow of York Minster, but that may have been the point.[27] By calling gold "Fróði's meal" and "river-gleams," the skald was helping Eiríkr mine his viking chic, his skeptical, scrappy, outlaw grace.

A praise poem for a prince had to have one or more refrains, naming him and his chief selling point. Their importance is underlined by the numerous saga-anecdotes about Scandinavian rulers who became homicidal when such refrains were missing. The best are as catchy and memorable as 1950s advertising jingles, and have much the same purpose. Some of us still remember:

> Dirt can't hide
> From intensified Tide.

Or the ditty for M&M candy:

> Melts in your mouth,
> Not in your hands.

Skalds, too, strove to distill the excellence of their product into a single image, what Rosser Reeves called a USP or Unique Selling Proposition, the quality that lets a brand stand out against the competition. Egill's refrain for Æthelstan focused on height, placing that king firmly on top of the food chain. Refrains advertising tenth-century Norwegian princes ruling in the British Isles promoted, instead, courage and carnage. Glúmr Geirason's refrain for Eiríkr Bloodaxe, praising his martial prowess, manages to encompass earth, sea, and fire, three of the four elements, in a single phrase: "The sword gives Eiríkr land and sea-flame [gold]" (65). Egill's two refrains for the same prince also refer to battle success:

> Orðstír of gat
> Eiríkr at þat. (31.6; 32.9)

> [Eiríkr got glory from that.]

Bauð ulfum hræ
Eiríkr of sæ. (32.12; 33.15)

[Eiríkr by the sea offered corpses to wolves.]

In a poem for Sigtryggr Silkbeard, the baptized viking king of Dublin, the skald Gunnlaugr appears to echo Egill's last refrain:

Elr svǫru skæ
Sigtryggr við hræ (185.3)

[Sigtryggr feeds the steed of the giantess (wolf) with corpses.]

Battle prowess was apparently not all-important when touting an Anglo-Saxon king. Gunnlaugr's couplet for Æthelred, the kindest compliment on record concerning that monarch, has but a glancing reference to warfare:

Herr sésk allr við ǫrva
Englands sem goð þengil;
ætt lýtr grams ok gumna
gunnbráðs Aðalráði. (184)

[All the troops stand in awe of the munificent king of England as of God; the race of men and of the war-swift king bow to Æthelred.]

For the first time in skaldic poetry, a king has moved into God's neighborhood. *Sem goð* may mean "as well as" or "as much as God"—or the gods; but the ambiguity probably would not have gnawed at Norse audiences any more than William Ernest Henley's thanking, plurally and agnostically, "whatever gods may be" troubles the virulently individualistic, militantly Christian, American terrorists who have taken to quoting his poem when sentenced. What mattered to the skald and his patron was the appearance of invincibility, of an outsized kingly sense of self. In earlier verse, Norsemen bowed down only before swords or in death; later they will bend to God. Here they kowtow to a ruler, and an English one to boot. Beginning in 994, Æthelred regularly employed vikings as mercenaries to defend his land against other raiding armies.[28] Gunnlaugr's refrain seems to be reassuring the king that his Norse mercenaries, the *herr*, remained loyal and obedient, that they would not turn on their employer. The St. Brice's Day massacre of Danes in 1002 suggests that the king's advisers remained unconvinced.

The sheer quantity of skaldic verse composed for Æthelred's successor, Cnut the Great, during his eighteen-year reign as king of England (1017–35) is remarkable, as is its mythological coloration. This great-grandson of the pagan Danish king Gormr the Old and the grandson of the Haraldr Bluetooth "who made the Danes Christian" is depicted in his skalds' refrains in cosmic high relief:

1. Þórarinn loftunga, *Tøgdrápa*
   Knútr's und solar . . . (298)

   [Cnut is under the sun's (seat the best prince)]

2. Sighvatr Þórðarson, *Knútsdrápa*
   Knútr's und himnum [. . .]
   hǫfuð- fremstr -jǫfurr. (232–34)

   [Cnut is under heaven the foremost great prince.]

3. Þórarinn loftunga, *Hǫfuðlausn*
   Knútr verr grund sem gætir
   Gríklands himinríki (298)

   [Cnut protects the land as the guardian of Byzantium (God) (does) heaven.]

4. Hallvarðr Háreksblesi, *Knútsdrápa*
   Knútr verr jǫrð sem ítran
   alls dróttinn sal fjalla. (294.8)

   [Cnut protects the land as the Lord of all (does) the splendid hall of the mountains (heaven).]

England's king, her Christian champion, is a terrestrial counterpart to the Ruler above; he looks after his realm just as the monarchic ruler of all protects heaven. Eusebius, the early fourth-century bishop at Caesarea in Palestine, wrote in honor of Constantine the Great: "Thus outfitted in the likeness of the kingdom of heaven, he pilots affairs below with an upward gaze to steer by the archetypal form."[29] Cnut's skalds do not commit themselves, as Eusebius does, as to which king is modeling himself on the other: they confirm only that their king rules like a kind of god and their god, like a kind of ruler, nothing more complicated; the higher hall and the lower one mirror one another—that is all you need to know. The idea of a cosmic sphere of influence split between God and prince seems to have been a Cnutian leitmotif. The *Encomium Emmae*, composed around 1041–42, quotes a pseudo-Virgilian tag to illustrate Cnut's closeness to God: "Divisum imperium cum Iove Cesar habes" (You, Caesar, have divided sovereignty with Jove)—a classicization of the skaldic refrains.[30] The presentation miniature in the New Minster *Liber Vitae*, produced in Winchester between 1020 and 1030 (probably the same time and place as the four fragmentary Norse poems), says something similar in visual terms, placing Cnut, sword-in-hand, in the lower register, while Christ in the upper extends a crown through an angelic intermediary.[31] The reference to God or Christ in Þórarinn's refrain as "guardian of Byzantium" recalls another full-page illuminated frontispiece depicting the Byzantine emperor Basil II (976–1025), Cnut's contemporary: the emperor stands, sword-in-hand, at the center of the drawing; Christ above extends a crown; and Greek verses in gold on a facing page explain that the ruler is God's representative on earth.[32] The refrains of Cnut's skalds express this relationship with characteristic literalness, making it intelligible to an audience of aristocratic jarls, restless housecarls, and ax murderers in their cups, some of whom may not have been Christian before their immigration, or—if they were—only lightly or recently so. The effectiveness of the repeated political slogan—Cnut protects the land—would have been reinforced by its underlying marriage metaphor: the king looks after a female land or consort (the feminine nouns *jǫrð* and *grund* again), an image from the pagan past with a Christian future. George Lakoff has recently argued that people relate to political ideologies on an unconscious level, through metaphorical frames already imbedded in their minds.[33] An abstract idea or argument resonates, or so he has been coaching politicians, only when retrofitted into a preexisting cognitive structure. The skalds were early masters of this kind of conversion.

Two praise poems composed in England early in Cnut's reign—Þórðr Kolbeinsson's *Eiríksdrápa* (or *Belgskakadrápa*) and the anonymous *Liðsmannaflokkr*[34]—are particularly rich in Norse mythological imagery. The first, in joint honor of Cnut and his powerful brother-in-law, Earl Eiríkr, son of the pagan Hákon Sigurðarson of Hlaðir, indicates that it was delivered to the king's military retainers. Earl Eiríkr, to whom Cnut gave Northumbria, is addressed as "Týr of the fire of the land of ships"—a kenning whose base word is the name of a primary heathen god and whose determiner "fire of the land of ships [sea = gold]" alludes to old lore. The skald uses three other god names to refer to the earl: "Ullr of the sword," "Þundr (Óðinn) of the horse of the sea [ship]," and "Freyr of the battle-prow [shield]." Additional figures from Norse story in Þórðr's poem include the sea king Sveiði, whose plain is the ocean; the god Hroptr or Óðinn, whose walls or homesteads are shields; and the giantess Gjǫlp, whose stud of horses is a wolf pack. Beasts of battle roam through the stanzas and the skald, after noting the death of Eiríkr's father, offers the earl that lowest-common-denominator consolation: "the fates of men prompt much" (202.2).

The anonymous *Liðsmannaflokkr* "poem of the warriors" ends with Cnut's successful siege of London in 1016. The speaker portrays this victory not so much as a political triumph as a colorful courtship display, a chance for the soldiers to show off in front of the ladies. A warrior is called "Ullr of battle," a raven, "bird of Óðinn," gold, "glowing fires of the Rhine" and "daylight of the sea," and a shield, "Hǫgni's door." The poem, composed in the voice of the rank and file, has a strong interest in female figures, real and mythological: two goddesses are named (Syn and Ilmr), and two valkyries, one twice (Hlǫkk, 2x, and Hildr); the watching women who see carnage accumulating on the banks of the Thames are referred to in language usually used of battlefield goddesses and placed in proximity to the beasts of battle, the valkyries' well-fed pets.[35] The London garrison would have had to know at least the basics of Norse mythology to catch the speaker's cheerful drift.

Two later praise poems by Cnut's skalds, Þórarinn loftunga's *Tøgdrápa* and Sighvatr Þórðarson's *Knútsdrápa*, introduce a new metrical form, *tøglag* or "journey meter," apparently invented at the English court.[36] Both works do without mythological allusions and concentrate on the king's seamanship. Þórarinn's extant stanzas follow the itinerary of the fleet that Cnut led from England to Norway in 1028. Sighvatr, the first skald to use the name *dreki* "dragon" for a viking ship, seems more eager to talk about Cnut's closeness to God than about that king's Scandinavian roots.[37] In 1027, Cnut sent a letter to England from Rome listing the political benefits accruing to his subjects from his friendship with the emperor of Germany and from his having St. Peter, the key bearer of the celestial kingdom, on his side.[38] The skald neatly compresses Cnut's double message into four words (234.10), three of which, alliterating on "k" (Cnut's initial), are loans from the continent, and the fourth is a biblical name. Our king, says Sighvatr, is "kærr keisara / klúss Pétrúsi" (dear to the Emperor, close to Peter). The eight syllables, linked by rhyme and consonance, seem to recapitulate Cnut's successful networking with the two great political powers of Western Europe.

Sighvatr's nephew Óttarr svarti composed for Cnut and for at least two other rulers, Óláfr Skötkonung, the first Christian king of Sweden (995–1022), and the viking adventurer turned missionary king of Norway, Óláfr the Stout, later known as "the Saint" (1015–28).[39] The six half-stanzas of the skald's praise poem for the Swedish ruler are in high mythological style, employing the god names Óðinn, Freyr, and Baldr as base words in both warrior- and land-kennings; the king himself is a "Freyr of battle." In contrast, the twenty full and half-stanzas of Óttarr's poem for the Norwegian Óláfr contain valkyrie-names (Gunnr, Gǫndul) and Óðinn-names (Yggr, Þróttr) but only in battle- and sword-kennings: the king feeds "the seagull of the meeting of Óðinn" (= battle, whose gull is a carrion bird); he wields "the snake of the storms of Óðinn" (= battle, whose snake is a sword). Óttarr assures Óláfr that "God strengthens [him] with great victory." The same skald's eulogy for Cnut, eleven full and half-stanzas of which are extant, lacks even these mythological bowwows. The poet remains solidly nonsectarian, filling up his stanzas with carrion beasts and multiple apostrophes to Cnut, including the pointed "O friendly offerer of great gifts" (274, 9).

Yet Cnut attracted ancien régime iconography to the end, as evidenced by a panegyric composed late in his reign. The otherwise unknown skald Hallvarðr Háreksblesi peppers his eulogy for the king with figures and names from northern mythology—valkyries and giants, the world serpent, the world tree, a pair of sea kings, the gods Hǫðr, Ullr, Yngvi, and Freyr—while insisting, in both the poem and its refrain, on Cnut's closeness to God. This is skaldic verse at its richest and most allusive, a startling blend of Christian and pagan imagery. The one full and two half-stanzas cited below provide a glimpse into what was thought to constitute Cnut's strength, what gave him his mandate to rule England (293–94):

4
Grund liggr und bǫr bundin
breið holmfjǫturs leiðar
(heinlands hoddum grandar
Hǫðr) eitrsvǫlum naðri.

[The broad land, wrapped around by the deadly-cold serpent (sea), lies under the tree (man) of the island-fetter's (Midgard serpent's) path (gold); the hone-land's (sword's) Hǫðr (warrior) destroys hoards (is generous).]

6
Englandi ræðr Yngvi
einn (hefsk friðr at beinni)
bǫðrakkr bœnar nǫkkva
barkrjóðr ok Danmǫrku;
ok hefr (odda Leiknar)
jalm-Freyr und sik malma
(hjaldrǫrr haukum þverrir
hungr) Nóregi þrungit.

[The prince, the battle-bold reddener of the bark (byrnie or mailcoat) of the ship of prayers (breast), alone rules England and Denmark; peace becomes easier. The Freyr of the noise of weapons (warrior) has also cast under him Norway; the battle-server (warrior) diminishes the hunger of Leikn's (the valkyrie's) hawks (ravens).]

7
Esat und jarðar hǫslu,
orðbrjótr Dǫnum forðar
moldreks, munka valdi
mæringr an þú næri.

[There is not under the earth-tree (Yggdrasill 'Óðinn's horse') an illustrious prince closer to the Lord of monks (God) than you; the breaker (generous sharer) of the soil-ruler's (giant's) words (gold) protects Danes.]

The Norse-speaking members of Cnut's household must have been able and willing to enjoy the mythological and legendary allusions that lent splendor to the praise of their king, that unlocked a colorful tradition stretching back to the gods and heroes of ancient times. In stanza 4, the opening image of a broad land (feminine *grund*) lying, bound, under a (masculine) tree (of gold = Cnut) recalls earlier pagan eulogies in which the conquest of a territory is expressed as a forced marriage. The stanza centers, literally, on the riches of Cnut's sea-girdled island girl: the "Midgarth serpent's path" is gold (what the dragon slain by Sigurðr lay on) and a "tree of gold" is a generous man (= Cnut). The parenthetical sentence beginning in line 3 announces that Hǫðr (Óðinn's son) of the sword (= Cnut) destroys treasure (spends like crazy)—a skaldic way of saying that, under pressure, England richly rewarded her suitor's attentions.[40]

Stanza 6, which lists Cnut's three major land takes in strict chronological order, calls the king by the names of the fertility gods Freyr and Yngvi, and speaks of peace and prosperity. Yet the poet's kenning for an English "mail-coat"—"bark [covering] of the ship of prayers [breast]"—colors this breast conspicuously Christian, perhaps a jibe at King Æthelred's recourse to a program of public penitence as a response to the invading armies.[41]

Hallvarðr in stanza 7 observes with typical skaldic hyperbole that no prince is closer to the "lord of monks" than Cnut. (The presentation miniature in the New Minster *Liber Vitae* depicts, in a circle beneath Cnut, the monks of the house in prayer.)[42] New land and old treasure will grace the seaman who is "like this" with heaven's king. But his praise of Cnut's godliness keeps strange company, surrounded as it is by old-lore allusions to the "earth-tree" and to a "soil-ruler [giant]" whose word is "gold." Perhaps some retainers in the royal hall found this evocative mixture of Christian rule and ancestral tradition comforting; perhaps others were put off by its Danish-modern design. But no one's beliefs were in danger of being shattered by the skald's juxtaposition of "Óðinn's steed" and "lord of monks" any more than our equilibrium is when faced with contradictory proverbs such as "many hands make light work" and "too many cooks spoil the broth." We trust each to be true in its own context.

※

The fragments of poetry examined in this talk survive only as quotations in much later Icelandic prose works, for the most part in sagas that treat pagan and Christian as opposite charges, as foes in a battle won long ago. But to a skald at the coal face of things, the directions of the winds above were not always so clear. The peripatetic Óttarr svarti resembles, at a certain distance, a chameleon slithering over a chessboard, no two squares of which were colored exactly alike. There were many paganisms and many Christianities in his North, many people knowing for certain in different ways. If a royal patron were Christian, what poet would remain a nonbeliever? Æthelstan's cosmopolitan court nourished at least two future reformers of the English Church, alongside a Norwegian prince whose funeral ode placed him in Valhalla, and an Icelandic skald on good terms with Óðinn. Perhaps the retainers around Eiríkr of York resembled the seventeenth-century immigrant Iroquois of Kahnawake near Montreal, who managed for a long time to keep old customs and new Jesuit ways chugging along in parallel tracks.[43] Still other Anglo-Scandinavian converts may have been like the Urapmin, a geographically isolated tribe in Papua New Guinea that, renouncing the past, has embraced a particularly austere form of Christianity.[44] The skald scurrying from court to court in strange lands had to respond to wrinkles in society we know little or nothing about.

Sociologists and epidemiologists, not to mention conference speakers, tend to describe the dynamics of conversion in terms of fission and fusion, contagion and antibodies, counterflows, mutations, cross-fertilizations, mutual assimilations, minglings, convergences, acculturations, infiltrations, interpenetrations, intertwinings, seesawing, feedback loops, and other vertiginous to-ings and fro-ings. Sifting Óðinn's mead for its swirling mythological precipitates, as I've tried to do in this paper, is like drinking wine for its calcium content—possible, even nourishing, but not necessarily the most interesting thing about it. For the goal of this verse was inebriation, a transformation of daily existence into something rich and rare. The Norse poet was a manipulator of the deep structure of language, a specialist in loving and hating. And he could be as playful and subversive, as obsessed with the vernacular and with intoxicating others as our own lively capitalists, advertising executives, and savvy marketers. His art had to be learned by studying the work of predecessors. Around 1030, one Icelandic skald paid tribute to the distinguished mentor who had taught him verse making: "The kind man led me often to the hallowed beaker of the raven-god [=Óðinn's mead]" (295.2). Scholarship is imbibed in much the same way. Those of us who were privileged to be Morton Bloomfield's students know what such a model can be worth.

Notes

This Morton W. Bloomfield Memorial Lecture, the eleventh overall, was delivered as a plenary talk at the conclusion of a conference on "Conversion" held in his memory at Harvard University, 23–25 September 2005. I am deeply grateful to the organizers, Daniel Donoghue, James Simpson, and Nicholas Watson, for their invitation, warmth, and generosity, and to Caroline Bloomfield for gracing the gathering with her presence.

1. *The Story of Egil Skallagrimsson: Being an Icelandic Family History of the Ninth and Tenth Centuries,* trans. William Charles Green (London: Stock, 1893), 132.

2. See Bjarne Fidjestøl, "'Har du høyrt eit dyrare kvæde?' Litt um økonomien bak den eldste fyrstediktninga," in *Festskrift til Ludvig Holm-Olsen,* ed. Bjarne Fidjestøl et al. (Øvre Ervik: Alvheim & Eide, 1984), 61–73; "'Have you heard a poem worth more? A note on the economic background of early skaldic praise-poetry,"

trans. Peter Foote, in *Bjarne Fidjestøl, Selected Papers*, ed. Odd Einar Haugen and Else Mundal, The Viking Collection 9 (Odense: Odense University Press, 1977), 117–32.

3. This incident is related by Donald R. Howard "The Philosophies in Chaucer's *Troilus*," in *The Wisdom of Poetry: Essays in Early English Literature in Honor of Morton W. Bloomfield*, ed. Larry D. Benson and Siegfried Wenzel (Kalamazoo, MI: Medieval Institute Publications, 1982), 151–75 and 288–90, at 151–52.

4. On the primary root meaning of this Arabic rhetorical term, see Ibn Gabirol, *Selected Poems of Solomon Ibn Gabirol*, trans. Peter Cole (Princeton: Princeton University Press, 2001), 13.

5. On the skald's self-referential asides, see Carol Clover, "Skaldic Sensibility," *Arkiv för nordisk filologi* 93 (1978): 68–81; also Anthony Faulkes, *What Was Viking Poetry For?* Inaugural Lecture, The University of Birmingham (Birmingham: University of Birmingham Press, 1993). For general introductions to this poetry, see E. O. G. Turville-Petre, *Scaldic Poetry* (Oxford: Clarendon Press, 1976); Roberta Frank, *Old Norse Court Poetry: The "Dróttkvætt" Stanza*, Islandica 42 (Ithaca: Cornell University Press, 1978); Roberta Frank, "Skaldic Poetry," in *Old Norse-Icelandic Literature: A Critical Guide*, ed. Carol Clover and John Lindow, Islandica 45 (Ithaca: Cornell University Press, 1985), 157–96; repr. with a new preface by Theodore Andersson, Medieval Academy Reprints for Teaching 42 (Toronto: University of Toronto Press, 2005); and Margaret Clunies Ross, *A History of Old Norse Poetry and Poetics* (Cambridge: D.S. Brewer, 2005).

6. The Icelandic poet, historian, and politician Snorri Sturluson (1179–1241) tells the story of the poetic mead in that part of his Edda dealing with skaldic diction. See Snorri Sturluson, *Edda, Skáldskaparmál*, vol. 1, *Introduction, Texts and Notes*, vol. 2, *Glossary and Index of Names*, ed. Anthony Faulkes (University College London: Viking Society for Northern Research, 1998), vol. 1, pp. 3–5; Margaret Clunies Ross, *Prolonged Echoes: Old Norse Myths in Medieval Northern Society*, vol. 1, *The Myths*, The Viking Collection 7 (Odense: Odense University Press, 1994), 128–31, 151–52, 216–18. On Snorri's inventiveness, see Roberta Frank, "Snorri and the Mead of Poetry," in *Speculum Norrœnum: Norse Studies in Memory of Gabriel Turville-Petre*, ed. Ursula Dronke et al. (Odense: Odense University Press, 1981), 155–70.

7. See *Skáldskaparmál*, 1:6–14. These and other poetry-kennings are discussed by Gert Kreutzer, *Die Dichtungslehre der Skalden: Poetologische Terminologie und Autorenkommentare als Grundlage einer Gattungspoetik* (Kronberg Taunus: Scriptor, 1974; 2nd rev. ed. Meisenheim am Glan: Hain, 1977), 94–111. See also Rudolf Meissner, *Die Kenningar der Skalden: Ein Beitrag zur skaldischen Poetik*, Rheinische Beiträge und Hülfsbücher zur germanischen Philologie und Volkskunde 1 (Bonn and Leipzig: Kurt Schroeder, 1921), 427–30. Unless otherwise noted, all quotations from skaldic poetry in this paper are from volume B1 of *Den norsk-islandske skjaldedigtning*, ed. Finnur Jónsson, 4 vols. (Copenhagen: Gyldendal, 1912–15; rpt. Copenhagen: Rosenkilde og Bagger, 1967, vols. A1–2; 1973, vols. B1–2).

8. This reading follows that of Russell Poole, "Skaldic Verse and Anglo-Saxon History: Some Aspects of the Period 1009–1016," *Speculum* 62 (1987): 265–98, at 270–71.

9. On Winchester, see Matthew Townend, "Contextualizing the *Knútsdrápur*: Skaldic Praise-Poetry at the Court of Cnut," *Anglo-Saxon England* 30 (2001): 145–79. On Cnut and his skalds, see Russell Poole, *Viking Poems on War and Peace: A Study in Skaldic Narrative* (Toronto: University of Toronto Press, 1991), 86–115 (*Liðsmannaflokkr*); Roberta Frank, "King Cnut in the Verse of his Skalds," in *The Reign of Cnut, King of England, Denmark and Norway*, ed. Alexander Rumble (London: Leicester University Press, 1994), 106–24; Roberta Frank, "When Poets Address Princes," in *Sagnaþing helgað Jónasi Kristjánsyni*, ed. Gísli Sigurðsson, Guðrún Kvaran, and Sigurgeir Steingrímsson, 2 vols. (Reykjavík: Hið íslenska bókmenntafélag, 1994), 1:189–95; Judith Jesch, "Knútr in Poetry and History," in *International Scandinavian and Medieval Studies in Memory of Gerd Wolfgang Weber*, ed. Michael Dallapiazza, O. Hansen, P. Meulengracht Sørensen, and Y. S. Bonnetain (Trieste: Parnaso, 2000), 243–56. Recent work on pre-Cnut skaldic verse in England includes: R. Poole, "Variants and Variability in the Text of Egill's *Hǫfuðlausn*," in *The Politics of Editing Medieval Texts*, ed. Roberta Frank (New York: AMS Press, 1993), 65–105; John Hines, "Egill's *Hǫfuðlausn* in Time and Place," *Saga-Book of the Viking Society* 24 (1994–97): 83–104; M. Townend, "Pre-Cnut Praise-Poetry in Viking Age England," *The Review of English Studies* 51 (2000): 349–70; and J. Jesch, "Skaldic Verse in Scandinavian England," in *Vikings and the Danelaw: Selected Papers from the Proceedings of the Thirteenth Viking Congress*, ed. James Graham-Campbell, Richard Hall, Judith Jesch, and David N. Parsons (Oxford: Oxbow, 2001), 313–25. On the late and dubious identification of the recipient of *Hǫfuðlausn*, Eiríkr of York, with Eiríkr Bloodaxe, see now Clare Downham, "Eric Bloodaxe —Axed? The Mystery of the Last Scandinavian King of York," *Mediaeval Scandinavia* 14 (2004): 51–77.

10. See, most recently, Judith Jesch, "Scandinavians and 'Cultural Paganism' in Late Anglo-Saxon England," in *The Christian Tradition in Anglo-Saxon England: Approaches to Current Scholarship and Teaching*, ed. Paul Cavill (Cambridge: D. S. Brewer, 2004), 55–68. On the much-abused word "pagan," see James J. O'Donnell, "Paganus," *Classical Folia* 31 (1977): 163–69. For the little known about the conversion of the Scandinavians settled in England, see Lesley Abrams, "Conversion and Assimilation," in *Cultures in Contact: Scandinavian Settlement in England in the Ninth and Tenth Centuries*, ed. Dawn M. Hadley and Julian D. Richards, Studies in the Early Middle Ages 2 (Turnhout: Brepols, 2000), 135–53; also Lesley Abrams, "Conversion of the Danelaw," in *Vikings and the Danelaw*, 31–44.

11. See Alan Cameron, "Wandering Poets: A Literary Movement in Byzantine Egypt," *Historia: Zeitschrift für alte Geschichte* 14 (1965): 470–509; also A. Cameron, "The Empress and the Poet: Paganism and Politics at the Court of Theodosius II," in *Later Greek Literature*, ed. John J. Winkler and Gordon Williams, Yale Classical Studies 27 (Cambridge: Cambridge University Press, 1982), 217–89.

12. See Glen W. Bowersock, "Nonnus Rising," *Topoi* 4 (1994): 385–99; repr. in *Selected Papers on Late Antiquity* (Bari: Edipuglia, 2000), 93–108.

13. Philostratus and Eunapius, *Lives of the Sophists*, trans. W. C. Wright (Cambridge, MA: Harvard University Press, 1968), 493.

14. Theodoricus in the preface to *Historia de antiquitate regum Norwagiensium* (ca. 1180) declares that much of his historical data came from Icelanders who "preserve them as much celebrated themes in their ancient poems." See *Theodoricus Monachus: An Account of the Ancient History of the Norwegian Kings*, trans. David and Ian McDougall, Viking Society for Northern Research Text Series 11 (University College London: Viking Society for Northern Research, 1998), 1. For Saxo's gratitude to "the diligence of the men of Iceland," see *Saxonis Gesta Danorum*, ed. Jørgen Olrik and Hans Ræder, vol. 1 (Copenhagen: Levin & Munksgaard, 1931), 5; English trans. of books 1–9 by Peter Fisher, *Saxo Grammaticus, History of the Danes*, vol. 1 (Cambridge: D.S. Brewer, 1979), 5.

15. On religious belief or lack of it in the kennings of court skalds, see Bjarne Fidjestøl, "Pagan Beliefs and Christian Impact: The Contribution of Scaldic Studies," in *Viking Revaluations: Viking Society Centenary Symposium 14–15 May 1992*, ed. Anthony Faulkes and Richard Perkins (University College London: Viking Society for Northern Research, 1993), 100–120, in which he responds to Jan de Vries's *De skaldenkenningen met mythologischen inhoud*, Nederlandsche bijdragen op het gebied van germaansche philologie en linguistiek 4 (Haarlem: Tjeenk, Willink & Zoon, 1934). Also Bjarne Fidjestøl, *The Dating of Eddic Poetry: A Historical Survey and Methodological Investigation*, ed. Odd Einar Haugen, Bibliotheca Arnamagnæana 41 (Copenhagen: Reitzel, 1999), 270–93. On late tenth-century new heathenism in Norway, see Bjarne Fidjestøl, "Skaldediktinga og trusskiftet. Med tankar om litterær form som historisk kjelde," in *Nordisk hedendom. Et symposium*, ed. Gro Steinsland et al. (Odense: Odense University Press, 1991), 113–31; translated as "Skaldic Poetry and the Conversion" in *Selected Papers*, 133–50.

16. On written sources, see Jenny Jochens, "Late and Peaceful: Iceland's Conversion through Arbitration in 1000," *Speculum* 74 (1999): 621–25. Orri Vésteinsson explores the slow and gradual development of institutional Christianity in *The Christianization of Iceland: Priests, Power, and Social Change 1000–1300* (Oxford: Oxford University Press, 2000). On the period of transition that followed the "conversion," see Peter Foote, "Historical Studies: Conversion Moment and Conversion Period," in *Viking Revaluations*, 137–144.

17. Moses Ibn Ezra's anecdote is cited by Ross Brann, *The Compunctious Poet: Cultural Ambiguity and Hebrew Poetry in Muslim Spain* (Baltimore: John Hopkins University Press, 1991), 76.

18. See Michael Lapidge, "Some Latin Poems as Evidence for the Reign of Athelstan," *Anglo-Saxon England* 9 (1981): 61–98, at 72–73.

19. On the ascription to a *Hákonardrápa* of Hallfreðr's stanzas describing the marriage of a ruler to his land, see Bjarne Fidjestøl, *Det norrøne fyrstediktet*, Univer-

sitetet i Bergen, Nordisk institutts skriftserie 11 (Øvre Ervik: Alvheim & Eide, 1982), 102-3.

20. My reading follows Ernst Albin Kock, *Notationes norrœnæ: Anteckningar till Edda och skaldediktning*, Lunds Universitets årsskrift, n. s., sec. 1 (Lund: Gleerup, 1923-44), §717. On the baptism of Óláfr Skötkonung in the 990s and his portrayal on coins as a Christian king, see Brita Malmer, "Sigtunamyntningen som källa till Sveriges kristnande," in *Kristnandet i Sverige: gamla källor och nya perspecktiv*, ed. Bertil Nilsson (Uppsala: Lunneböcker, 1996), 85-113.

21. On Ella/Ælle as the most frequently named Anglo-Saxon in skaldic court poetry, see Matthew Townend, "Ella: An Old English Name in Old Norse poetry," *Nomina* 20 (1997): 23-35. For a reading of Egill's allusion to Ella from both English and Norse perspectives, see Susanne Kries, "'Westward I came across the Sea': Anglo-Scandinavian History through Scandinavian Eyes," *Leeds Studies in English* 34 (2003): 47-76.

22. Sir Walter Scott, *Harold the Dauntless: A Poem, in Six Cantos* (Edinburgh: James Ballantyne, 1817), 14 (canto 1.5).

23. See Eric Christiansen, *The Norsemen in the Viking Age* (Oxford: Blackwell, 2002), esp. 155-57. On the "apostasy" of Hákon, king of Norway ca. 935-ca. 961, see Gareth Williams, "Hákon *Aðalsteins fóstri*: Aspects of Anglo-Saxon Kingship in Tenth-Century Norway," in *The North Sea World in the Middle Ages: Studies in the Cultural History of North-Western Europe*, ed. Thomas R. Liszka and Lorna E. M. Walker (Dublin: Four Courts Press, 2001), 108-26.

24. On the date of Eiríkr's death, see Peter Sawyer, "The Last Scandinavian Kings of York," *Northern History* 31 (1995): 39-44.

25. Suetonius, *De vita Caesarum libri viii*, ed. M. Ihm (Leipzig: Teubner, 1908), Tib.70.3: "quae mater Hecubae, quod Achilli nomen inter uirgines fuisset, quid Sirenes cantare sint solitae"; *Lives of the Caesars*, trans. Catharine Edwards (Oxford: Oxford University Press, 2000), 132.

26. Brann, *Compunctious Poet*, 41.

27. On the probable location of the Anglo-Saxon Cathedral, see Christopher Norton, "York Minster in the Time of *Wulfstan*," in *Wulfstan, Archbishop of York: The Proceedings of the Second Alcuin Conference*, ed. Matthew Townend (Turnhout: Brepols, 2004), 207-34 (map, p. 221); also Christopher Norton, "The Anglo-Saxon Cathedral at York and the Topography of the Anglian City," *Journal of the British Archeological Association* 151 (1998): 1-42. See, too, the plan of Anglo-Scandinavian York in Simon Keynes, "The Vikings in England, c. 790-1016," in *The Oxford Illustrated History of the Vikings*, ed. Peter Sawyer (Oxford: Oxford University Press, 1997), 66. Excavations beneath and outside the south transept of the present York Minster have revealed, in a tenth-century graveyard, one Christian gravestone with scenes from a Sigurd legend, along with a cross-headed stone bearing an image of Weland the Smith. See James T. Lang, *Corpus of Anglo-Saxon Stone Sculpture*, vol. 3, *York and Eastern Yorkshire* (Oxford: Oxford University Press, 1991), 58-59, 71-72.

28. See Keynes, "Vikings in England," 77–78.

29. *De laudibus Constantini* 3.5, in H. A. Drake, *"In Praise of Constantine": A Historical Study and New Translation of Eusebius' Tricennial Orations* (Berkeley: University of California Press, 1976), 87.

30. *Encomium Emmae Reginae*, ed. Alistair Campbell, Camden Society, 3rd series, 72 (London: Royal Historical Society, 1949), 36 (2.19); repr. with a supplementary introduction by Simon Keynes (Cambridge: Cambridge University Press, 1998).

31. BL, Stowe 944, fol. 6r is reproduced in Elzbieta Temple, *Anglo-Saxon Manuscripts 900–1066* (London: Harvey Miller, 1976), no. 78 and pl. 244; in C. R. Dodwell, *Anglo-Saxon Art: A New Perspective* (Manchester: Manchester University Press, 1982), 201 and pl. 46; and in *The Anglo-Saxons*, ed. James Campbell (London: Phaidon, 1982), 208 and pl. 182.

32. The frontispiece is that of a psalter in the Marciana Library in Venice (MS Marc. gr. Z.17). See Anthony Cutler, *The Aristocratic Psalters in Byzantium*, Bibliothèque des cahiers archéologiques 13 (Paris: Picard, 1984), cat. no. 58, figs. 412–13. For the verses, Ihor Sevchenko, "The Illuminators of the Menologium of Basil II," *Dumbarton Oaks Papers* 16 (1962): 272.

33. George Lakoff, *Moral Politics: What Conservatives Know that Liberals Don't* (Chicago: University of Chicago Press, 1996).

34. On the two names for the same poem (202–6), see Fidjestøl, *Fyrstediktet*, 115–16. Citations of *Liðsmannaflokkr* are to the edition of the poem in Poole, *Viking Poems*, 86–99.

35. See Jesch, "Scandinavians and 'Cultural Paganism,'" 61–62.

36. See Dietrich Hofmann, *Nordisch-englische Lehnbeziehungen der Wikingerzeit*, Bibliotheca Arnamagnæana 14 (Copenhagen: Munksgaard, 1955), §§98–100; Hans Kuhn, *Das Dróttkvætt* (Heidelberg: Winter, 1983), 300–304, 333.

37. On Norse ship terminology, see Rudolf Simek, *Die Schiffsnamen, Schiffsbezeichnungen und Schiffskenningar im Altnordischen*, Wiener Arbeiten zur germanischen Altertumskunde und Philologie 14 (Vienna: Halosar, 1982); on the illusory "dragon ship" of the vikings, see Judith Jesch, *Ships and Men in the Late Viking Age: The Vocabulary of Runic Inscriptions and Skaldic Verse* (Woodbridge: Boydell Press, 2001), 127–28.

38. *English Historical Documents*, vol. 1, *c. 500–1042*, ed. and trans. Dorothy Whitelock (London: 1955; 2nd ed. London: Eyre & Spottiswoode, 1979), 53 (p. 49 in 1st ed.); *Die Gesetze der Angelsachsen*, ed. Felix Liebermann, 3 vols. (Halle: Niemeyer, 1903–16), 1, 276–77.

39. For these three poems see, respectively, *Skjaldedigtning*, ed. Finnur Jónsson, 272–75, 267, and 268–72.

40. See M. K. Lawson, "The Collection of Danegeld and Heregeld in the Reigns of Æthelred II and Cnut," *English Historical Review* 99 (1984): 721–38; Peter Sawyer, *Da Danmark blev Danmark: Fra ca. år 700 til ca. 1050*, Danmarkshistorie 3, ed. Olaf Olsen (Copenhagen: Gyldendal & Politikens Forlag, 1988), 267.

41. Simon Keynes, *The Diplomas of King Æthelred "the Unready" 978–1016: A Study in their Use as Historical Evidence* (Cambridge: Cambridge University Press, 1980), 219.

42. See above, n. 31.

43. Allan Greer, "Conversion and Identity: Iroquois Christianity in Seventeenth-Century New France," in *Conversion: Old Worlds and New*, ed. Kenneth Mills and Anthony Grafton (Rochester: University of Rochester Press, 2003), 175–98.

44. See Joel Robbins, *Becoming Sinners: Christianity and Moral Torment in a Papua New Guinea Society* (Berkeley: University of California Press, 2003).

BIBLIOGRAPHY OF MORTON W. BLOOMFIELD'S PUBLICATIONS FOR THE YEARS 1981–1993

DANIEL DONOGHUE

The items below supplement "The Publications of Morton W. Bloomfield: 1939–May, 1981," compiled by George Hardin Brown in *The Wisdom of Poetry: Essays in Early English in Honor of Morton W. Bloomfield* (Kalamazoo, MI: Medieval Institute Publications, 1982), 241–58. Brown's list contains 203 items; hence the numbering below begins with 204. The nineteen new titles below (not to mention the 1993 collection of essays) show at a glance how wide-ranging and productive Morton Bloomfield's scholarship continued to be up to his last days. While I have tried to make this list comprehensive for the years following Brown's bibliography, some omissions, however regrettable, are possible.

204. Ed., *Allegory, Myth, and Symbol.* Cambridge, MA: Harvard University Press, 1981.

205. Review of *The Condition of Creatures: Suffering and Action in Chaucer and Spenser* by Georgia Ronan Crampton. *Revue belge de philologie et d'histoire* 59 (1981): 740–41.

206. "The Allegories of Dobest (Piers Plowman B XIX–XX)." *Medium Ævum* 50.1 (1981): 30–39.

207. "Chaucer's Squire's Tale and the Renaissance." *Poetica (Tokyo): An International Journal of Linguistic-Literary Studies* 12 for 1979 (1981): 28–35.

208. Review of *Irony in the Medieval Romance* by D. H. Green. *Speculum* 57.2 (1982): 377–78.

209. "The Franklin's Tale: A Story of Unanswered Questions." In *Acts of Interpretation: The Text and Its Contexts, 700-1600; Essays on Medieval and Renaissance Literature in Honor of E. Talbot Donaldson,* edited by Mary J. Carruthers, 189–98. Norman, OK: Pilgrim Books, 1982.

210. "The Friar's Tale as a Liminal Tale." *Chaucer Review* 17.3 (1983): 286–91.

211. "'The Canterbury Tales' as Framed Narratives." *Leeds Studies in English* 14 (1983): 44–56.

212. Review of Donaldson, E. Talbot, *The Swan at the Well: Shakespeare Reading Chaucer. Studies in the Age of Chaucer* 8 (1986): 177–79.

213. "The Elegy and the Elegiac Mode: Praise and Alienation." In *Renaissance Genres: Essays on Theory, History, and Interpretation*, edited by Barbara Kiefer Lewalski, 147–57. Cambridge, MA; London: Harvard University Press, 1986.

214. "'Interlace' as a Medieval Narrative Technique with Special Reference to Beowulf." In *Magister Regis: Studies in Honor of Robert Earl Kaske*, edited by Arthur Groos et al., 49–59. New York: Fordham University Press, 1986.

215. "Deor revisited." In *Modes of Interpretation in Old English Literature: Essays in Honour of Stanley B. Greenfield*, edited by Phyllis Rugg Brown, Georgia Ronan Crampton, and Fred C. Robinson, 273–82. Toronto: University of Toronto Press, 1986.

216. "Chaucerian Realism." In *The Cambridge Chaucer Companion*, edited by Piero Boitani and Jill Mann, 179–93. Cambridge: Cambridge University Press, 1986.

217. "Poetry in Early Societies." *Proceedings of the American Philosophical Society* 130.2 (Jun. 1986): 247–50.

218. With Shuli Barzilai. "New Criticism and Deconstructive Criticism, or What's New?" *New Literary History* 18.1, Studies in Historical Change (Autumn, 1986): 151–69.

219. "Varieties of Allegory and Interpretation." *Revue internationale de philosophie* 41.162/3 (1987): 329–46.

220. "History and Literature in the Vernacular in the Middle Ages?" In *Medieval English Studies Presented to George Kane*, edited by Edward Donald Kennedy, Ronald Waldron, and Joseph S. Wittig, 309–15. Woodbridge, NJ; Wolfeboro, NH: Boydell & Brewer, 1988.

221. "Reflections of a Medievalist: America, Medievalism, and the Middle Ages." In *Medievalism in American Culture; Papers of the Eighteenth Annual Conference of the Center for Medieval and Early Renaissance Studies*, edited by Bernard Rosenthal and Paul E. Szarmach, 13–29. Binghamton, NY: Medieval and Renaissance Texts and Studies, 1989.

222. With Charles W. Dunn. *The Role of the Poet in Early Societies*. Cambridge: Brewer, 1989.

223. *Light of Learning: Selected Essays of Morton W. Bloomfield, 1970–1986*. Edited by Elizabeth Walsh and Susie M. Barrett. New York: P. Lang, 1993.

Notes on Contributors

Larry D. Benson is Francis Lee Higginson Professor of English Literature, Emeritus, Harvard University.

Giles Constable is professor emeritus in the School of Historical Studies at the Institute for Advanced Study in Princeton.

Richard K. Emmerson is Dean of the School of Arts at Manhattan College and former Executive Director of the Medieval Academy.

Richard Firth Green is Director of the Center for Medieval and Renaissance Studies at the Ohio State University.

Roberta Frank is Douglas Tracy Smith Professor of English at Yale University.

†George Kane, before his death in 2008, was William Rand Kenan, Jr., Professor of English, Emeritus, University of North Carolina at Chapel Hill.

Kathryn Kerby-Fulton holds a chair as The Notre Dame Professor of English at University of Notre Dame.

Jill Mann is Emeritus Professor of English in the University of Notre Dame and a Life Fellow of Girton College, Cambridge.

Bernard McGinn is Naomi Shenstone Donnelley Professor, Emeritus, at the University of Chicago.

Anne Middleton is professor emerita in the English Department of the University of California, Berkeley.

Derek Pearsall is Gurney Professor of English, Emeritus, at Harvard University.

Fred C. Robinson is Douglas Tracy Smith Professor of English, Emeritus, at Yale University.

Siegfried Wenzel is professor emeritus at the University of Pennsylvania.

Typeset in 10/13 ITC New Baskerville
Designed and composed by Linda K. Judy
Manufactured by Sheridan Books, Inc.

Medieval Institute Publications
College of Arts and Sciences
Western Michigan University
1903 W. Michigan Avenue
Kalamazoo, MI 49008-5432
http://www.wmich.edu/medieval/mip

WESTERN MICHIGAN UNIVERSITY